This is the first comprehensive study of the system of literary patronage in early modern England; and it demonstrates that far from declining by 1750 – as many commentators have suggested – the system persisted, though in altered forms, throughout the eighteenth century. Combining the perspectives of literary, social, and political history, Dustin Griffin lays out the workings of the patronage system and shows how authors wrote within that system, manipulating it to their advantage or resisting the claims of patrons by advancing counter-claims of their own. Professor Griffin describes the cultural economics of patronage and argues that literary patronage was in effect always "political." Chapters on individual authors, including Dryden, Swift, Pope, and Johnson, as well as Edward Young, Richard Savage, Mary Leapor, and Charlotte Lennox, focus attention on the author's role in the system, the rhetoric of dedications, and the larger poetics of patronage.

LITERARY PATRONAGE IN ENGLAND, 1650–1800

E. M. Ward, *Doctor Johnson in the Ante-Room of Lord Chesterfield, waiting for an Audience, 1748*, a reconstruction (1845). The Tate Gallery, London

LITERARY PATRONAGE
IN ENGLAND, 1650–1800

DUSTIN GRIFFIN

CAMBRIDGE
UNIVERSITY PRESS

PR
448
A87
G75
1996

Published by the Press Syndicate of the University of Cambridge
The Pitt Building, Trumpington Street, Cambridge CB2 1RP
40 West 20th Street, New York, NY 10011–4211, USA
10 Stamford Road, Oakleigh, Melbourne, 3166, Australia

First published 1996

Printed in Great Britain at the University Press, Cambridge

A catalogue record for this book is available from the British Library

Library of Congress cataloguing in publication data

Griffin, Dustin H.
Literary patronage in England, 1650–1800 / Dustin Griffin.
p.   cm.
Includes bibliographical references and index.
ISBN 0 521 56085 3 (hardback)
1. English literature – 18th century – History and criticism.
2. English literature – Early modern, 1500–1700 – History and criticism.
3. Authors and patrons – England – History – 18th century.
4. Authors and patrons – England – History – 17th century.
5. Politics and literature – England – History.
6. Literature and society – England – History.
I. Title.
PR448.A87G75 1996
306.4'7–dc20   95–37985 CIP

ISBN 0 521 56085 3 hardback

Publication of this book has been aided by a grant from the Abraham and Rebecca Stein
Faculty Publication Fund of New York University, Department of English.

CE

To Jenny and Colin
and
in memory of Daisy
(1980–1995)

Contents

Acknowledgments

Part of chapter 5 appeared as "Swift and Patronage" in *Studies in Eighteenth-Century Culture*, 21 (1991), 297–305. An earlier version of chapter 9 first appeared as "Johnson's *Lives of the Poets* and the Patronage System" in *The Age of Johnson*, 5 (1992), 1–33. I thank the editors for permission to reprint.

I owe thanks to the staff of several libraries where most of my research was conducted: the British Library, the Public Records Office (London), the New York Public Library, the Butler Library at Columbia University, and Bobst Library at New York University.

Much of the writing of this book was done during two sabbatical leaves (in Fall 1990 and Spring 1994), during which I was relieved of teaching responsibilities at New York University. For such leaves, and for travel funds to support my work, I thank C. Duncan Rice, Dean of the Faculty of Arts and Science.

CHAPTER I

Introduction

My goal in this study of literary patronage is to shed new light on literary texts and to understand how those texts functioned within the literary, political, and economic culture in which they were written. Underlying my argument is the assumption that to consider literary texts and writers apart from the complex system of sponsorship, financing, production, and distribution, is arbitrarily and myopically to abstract literature from its living cultural context, and to misconceive its full *meaning* for its original audiences.

Literary patronage has long been a familiar – if neglected – topic in the literary history of early modern England, though it has not been systematically examined since the two books published by A. S. Collins in 1929, *Authorship in the Days of Johnson*, and *The Profession of Letters*,[1] or even since the older book (which had served as Collins' guide), Alexandre Beljame's *Men of Letters and the English Public in the Eighteenth Century*, first published in 1881.[2] But in my view, neither Collins nor Beljame, despite their knowledge of the period, took sufficient account of the historical context, and neither was sufficiently alert to the nuances in the voices of writers they celebrated. Indeed, their very celebration of their literary heroes as independent "men of letters" limited their ability to understand the system they were describing. For to both Collins and Beljame, and indeed to most writers on the subject, the patronage system was by definition oppressive and demeaning. For them the only *proper* relationship between a writer and society is proud independence. Their moral –

---

[1] The first and better known book is subtitled *A Study of the Relation between Author, Patron, Publisher and Public, 1726–1780*. The second is offered as a continuation of "the history of the profession of letters" up to 1832.

[2] First published as *Le Public et les Hommes de Lettres en Angleterre au 18e Siècle* (but not widely read in England until it appeared in an English translation by E. O. Lorimer in 1948). Beljame's story, as Collins pointed out (making room for his own work), ends "about 1726." It is subtitled *1660–1744, Dryden, Addison, Pope*.

and implicitly political – stance blinded them, so I argue, to the ways in which the system of literary patronage in fact functioned.

Collins and Beljame inherited their disapprobation of the patronage system from even earlier writers. Boswell and other early commentators on Johnson commonly took note of his manly independence from servility – Johnson's famous letter to Chesterfield was celebrated even in his own day[3] – and Johnson himself deplored the obsequiousness of Dryden's dedications. Isaac D'Israeli's many volumes of literary anecdotes and "curiosities," published from about 1790 to 1840, maintained the bias: he typically treated dedicators and patrons under the general rubric of "the calamities of authors." The nineteenth century retained some critical interest in the dedication as a literary genre: Johnson's many dedications (written on behalf of other authors) were gathered and presented as a separate group in volume III of the 1810 edition of his *Works*. In the wake of Beljame's book Henry Wheatley published *The Dedication of Books to Patrons and Friends* (1887). An antiquarian with very little critical sense except for a strong animus against literary "prostitution," Wheatley predictably deplored Dryden's dedications as fulsome, florid, and extravagant, and approved Johnson's as "the perfection of courtly compliment without adulation" (p. 176).[4]

More recent studies of the financial conditions under which literature was produced in the eighteenth century, whether they focus on the rise of the "professional" writer (as James Saunders does in his 1964 book on *The Profession of English Letters*), on the aristocratic patrons of the eighteenth century (as does Michael Foss in *The Age of Patronage: The Arts in England, 1660–1750* in 1972), or on the booksellers, the copyright debate, or the "commercialization of leisure,"[5] all

---

3   Although not published until Boswell printed what he called a "perfect transcript" in the 1791 *Life of Johnson*.

4   For another compiler's anthology, see *Dedications: An Anthology*, by Mary Elizabeth Brown. Brown includes a bibliography of primarily nineteenth-century discussions of the dedication as a form (pp. 449–51). For a recent survey of eighteenth-century dedications, see Pat Rogers, "Book Dedications in Britain 1700–1799," 213–33.

5   On copyright and the book trade, see especially John Feather, "The Book Trade in Politics," 19–44; "The English Book Trade and the Law, 1695–1799," 51–75; and "The Commerce of Letters," 405–24; Terry Belanger, "From Bookseller to Publisher," 7–16; and "Publishers and Writers in Eighteenth-Century England," 5–25; and Mark Rose, *Authors and Owners*.
    On the "commercialization of leisure," see J. H. Plumb, "The Commercialization of Leisure in Eighteenth-Century England," 265–85; Deborah Rogers, "The Commercialization of 18th-Century English Literature," 171–78.

broadly share the view that patronage was an old and dying cultural form that never provided adequate support to authors and fortunately gave way, in the eighteenth century, to a superior system in which authors were at last properly recognized as independent owners and professionals.

One salutary exception to this trend is Paul Korshin, who in a pioneering article in 1974 called for a reconsideration of the topic of literary patronage on a sounder historical (and even statistical) base. In a brief survey he distinguished among many different forms of patronage, and suggested that fuller study would show that, although it "benefited relatively few writers" and provided rather small amounts of support, the system of literary patronage in the eighteenth century was in fact "surprisingly workable," and that it "survived because it was necessary."[6] Since 1974 we have learned a good deal more about the various forms of patronage, about the economic careers of individual writers, and about the network of patronage and dependency that sustained eighteenth-century society. This book takes up the sustained reconsideration of patronage that Korshin implicitly calls for, and although it does not proceed along the lines he proposes, tries (as he does) to shed the prejudice that the patronage system was inevitably demeaning to writers and a cultural practice that had well outlasted whatever usefulness it once had.[7]

But in attempting a responsibly contextualist study of literary patronage in the eighteenth century, it is well to begin by acknowledging the late-twentieth century context, in which we (not only as descendants of the proudly alienated Romantics, but also as marginalized intellectuals) prefer to see great writers of the past as proud, independent, and adversarial (even subversive) in relation to the culture of their day, or at least to the hegemonic authority that they covertly or overtly resist. We prefer to think of the *Aeneid* as a profoundly troubled vision of the sacrifices, both personal and political, required by the founding of imperial Rome, than to think of Virgil as a celebrator of Augustus, would rather see Horace as a sly skeptic than as a "court slave," would rather find in the great writers of the "American Renaissance" a tradition of doubt and dissent than national self-discovery and affirmation. Such preferences

---

[6]   "Types of Eighteenth-Century Literary Patronage," 473.
[7]   Even Korshin, however, sees "dependence" as offensive. For more on this, see below, pp. 254–55.

reflect the academy's sense of itself and of its present relation – which it thinks of as independent and even adversarial – to the larger culture. Acknowledging the preferences myself, I would admit and even argue that both the academy and high culture generally continue in our own time to be dependent on, and the beneficiaries of, a system of patronage, disguised though it may be in the form of foundation grants, tax policies, fellowships, academic appointments, art collectors, theatre subscribers, and private contributors. To recognize the surviving forms of patronage, along with the imbeddedness of the academy in a predominantly commercial culture, may help us to understand more completely literature's *dependent* status in early modern England. Second, any present-day discussion of literary patronage in the eighteenth century takes place (or should take place) in the context of the current historiographical debate between the descendants of the old "Whig" interpretation of early modern English history – focusing on progress toward modernity, the growth of a commercial middle class, and the rise of parliamentary democracy – and a "neo-Tory" school of historians which since about 1980 has been increasingly emphasizing that the eighteenth century is not so much the age of the rising bourgeoisie as it is an "aristocratic century," more remarkable for the persistence and even strengthening of an "*ancien régime*" than for the arrival of "revolution" or even "reform."[8] My sense is not only that most literary critics are – perhaps without knowing it – in the "Whig" camp, but that they are inadequately familiar with the "neo-Tory" account of the eighteenth century. My discussion of literary patronage will suggest that John Cannon and Jonathan Clark, while they have not completely won the day, have successfully challenged the older view.[9]

It was once assumed that the "historical context" of a literary topic such as eighteenth-century patronage was simply *there*, and available for any student of history or literature to retrieve. But renewed historiographical debates, along with arguments by Hayden White and others that history-writing itself is always a form of literature, if only because it *decides* what constitutes a piece of "evidence" and *selects* from the available materials, have made us

[8]   John Cannon, *Aristocratic Century*; J. C. D. Clark, *English Society, 1688–1832*. See also Linda Colley, *Britons*. For an earlier study relatively innocent of historiographical consciousness, see James Lees-Milne, *Earls of Creation*.

[9]   Cannon and Clark have both recently written books on Samuel Johnson, in which they comment briefly on patronage and pensions. See Cannon, *Samuel Johnson and the Politics of Hanoverian England*, 173–82; and Clark, *Samuel Johnson*, 193–97.

properly wary of the old positivist view of history. We cannot simply suppose that we all look at the same eighteenth century, or that we can with confidence assume that what we see are the "facts." Reconstruction of an eighteenth-century historical context will inevitably reflect one's own late-twentieth-century assumptions and limitations. My own limitations are those of a literary historian and critic working on a topic that requires considerable knowledge of political, social, and economic history. But establishing a context in which to consider texts is not simply a matter of accumulating enough knowledge. Choices have to be made about which parts of the various world of the eighteenth century are to be defined as relevant context. We use the literary texts under scrutiny to establish the "context" and then use the context to illuminate the texts. There is a constant moving back and forth from text to context, and a circularity that, if it cannot be avoided, can at least be kept constantly in mind.[10] The proof will be in the pudding: do the interpretations I provide of literary careers and literary texts adequately take account of what seem to be the pertinent phenomena?

I take the view that, especially with a matter like literary patronage, the relation of text – whether dedication, preface, or poem – to context is not that of "figure" and "background" but of fish to sea: context is the vital element from which text derives its nutrients, and through which it swims its particular path. To examine text within context is to gain a sense of the circumambient medium which sustains it, and the currents and pressures with which and against which it moves and to which it responds. Context does not determine meaning, but it alerts us to a wider range of possibilities, and proposes a world of diverse interests and controversies in which original writers and readers operated.

In the chapters that follow I propose that the patronage system is a pervasive feature of eighteenth-century English culture, and that the relevant context is therefore a broad one. Previous studies of patronage have focused too narrowly on the growth of a literary marketplace which apparently made patronage outmoded. I argue that the patronage system was a complex institution, and that literary patronage took many forms, and try to bear in mind a number of features – most of them well substantiated in recent historical work on early modern Britain – of the socio-political

---

[10] For a good discussion of the theoretical implications of contextualizing, see Robert Hume, "Texts Within Contexts," 69–100.

landscape. Except where I think a point has received inadequate attention, I here offer concise summaries of these features as a way of setting the stage.

(1) *The consolidation of a central governmental apparatus in the 1690s.* In order to fight foreign wars William III had to organize a system of public credit – the Bank of England, deficit financing, and a strong administrative state to implement it– so that the burden of taxation would not be intolerable. The so-called "financial revolution" and "administrative revolution" concentrated greater power and resources in the hands of the crown and the ministers, and both required and enabled them to use the resources of the crown (pensions and places) to reward their friends and promote their political programs in the emerging periodical press. Hence followed, through the Civil List and through Secret Service funds, a program of state support of friendly or useful writers that was to remain in place throughout the eighteenth century. It is probably not mere coincidence that among those officials accused of the misappropriation of state funds were two of the major patrons of the day, Halifax and Walpole,[11] and that another of the most generous patrons, the Duke of Chandos, made his fortune as Paymaster of the Forces under Marlborough. Although attacked throughout the century, the system of rewards had its defenders (including Burke), who argued that effective government required its use.

(2) *The rise of "Country Party" ideology and rhetoric.* As the central state grew stronger, country gentlemen feared the loss of their own power and authority and the increase of the land tax to pay the increasing costs of government. In response to the perceived threat, they constructed an ideology of the independent citizen-soldier-landowner, the bulwark of traditional English liberties, and warned against the dangers of court influence as extended through pensions and places. Pope's vaunted "independence" from patronage cannot be divorced from his political affiliations with Country Party ideologues. Descendants of the Country Party continued to complain about the abuse of pensions and places in the 1760s.

(3) *The well-developed system in which political "patrons" controlled the electoral process,* insuring that their hand-picked (and beholden) candidates were nominated, stood without opposition, or received enough votes to be elected.[12] One historian has estimated that more than

---

[11] See H. T. Dickinson, *Liberty and Property*, 109.
[12] Sir Lewis Namier long ago described and analyzed the power of government and some

half of the seats in the House of Commons were "under the control of private patrons or Government departments," and that private patrons "gained rather than lost influence as the century continued."[13] Modern commentators on the system of political patronage commonly see it as a "network" or a "web." Cobbett in the 1820s still saw it as a "chain of dependence running through the whole nation" (quoted in Cannon, *Aristocratic Century*, p. 169). This system often drew in "literary" men, including Young, Addison, and Soame Jenyns (who stood for parliament), and Congreve, who was granted a freehold so that, as an elector, he would cast his vote for his patron's candidate.

(4) *An equally powerful – and controversial – system of church patronage, in which appointments to "livings" were in the gift of the local landowner, whether peer or squire.* The Duke of Chandos, for example, not only had his own chaplain but also controlled eight ecclesiastical livings.[14] The traditional system – still alive in the Mansfield Park of Jane Austen's day – came under continued fire (particularly in Scotland) from proponents of the "popular election" of ministers, and was sustained by equally vocal defenders, as witnessed by a stream of pamphlets, from *A Discourse of Patronage* (1675), by "Z. C.," to *The Nature of Patronage* (1735), by "Generosus," and a flood of tracts published in Scotland from *The Right of Patronages Considered, and Some of the Antient and Modern Arguments for the Exercise of that Right in Presenting to Churches, Surveyed* (Edinburgh, 1731) to *Patronage Anatomized and Detected* (Glasgow, 1782).[15] The issue was (so to speak) not merely a parochial one: Johnson and Boswell discussed the "much agitated" question of the rights of church patrons in 1772 and 1773.[16]

(5) *The intricate interweaving of the systems of literary, political, and church patronage.* Not surprisingly, since a single landowner/patron might control several church livings and several seats in Parliament, and

---

private patrons: some had "absolute authority" of "nomination," others such "influence" that electors would adopt their candidate. See *The Structure of Politics at the Accession of George III.*

[13] J. B. Owen, "Political Patronage," 377–78. See also Owen, *The Rise of the Pelhams*, 62; J. H. Plumb, *The Growth of Political Stability in England, 1675–1725*, 188–89; Cannon, *Aristocratic Century*, esp. 112–15.

[14] *Ibid.*, 70.

[15] Other titles of rare pamphlets in the ESTC include *Considerations on the Right of Patronage*, *The Cause Between Patronage and Popular Election*, and *The Case of Patronage Stated*, among many more.

[16] Johnson even dictated a formal "opinion" on the matter. See Boswell, *Life of Johnson*, II, 149, 242–46.

might have both political and literary interests, a client too might operate in several arenas at once. Two brief examples might make the point. In the late 1750s William Warburton, author of *The Divine Legation of Moses* (1738–41) and Pope's literary executor, was married to the niece of Ralph Allen, of Prior Park, near Bath, best known now as friend and benefactor of Pope and Fielding. Allen was a substantial landowner and an important political power in Bath. In the 1750s he often corresponded with William Pitt, Prime Minister and MP for Bath. In October 1759, for example, he wrote to Pitt asking that Warburton be appointed Bishop of Gloucester, and two months later wrote to thank Pitt for arranging it.[17] The next week Warburton wrote to Pitt with his thanks, and enclosed a copy of an address (previously approved by Allen) to Pitt from the electors of Bath.[18] The correspondence from Allen to Pitt continues, Allen reporting in October 1760 that the members of the Bath corporation want Pitt to represent the constituency again, and in March 1761 that Pitt has been unanimously elected. As the Pitt–Allen–Warburton nexus suggests, literary, church, and political patronage are all interrelated parts of what one should perhaps call not the chain but the interwoven braid of dependency.

That the interweavings were much on the mind of eighteenth-century observers of patronage is suggested by a manuscript commonplace book in the British Library entitled "The Patron or a Portraiture of Patronage and Dependency."[19] The unknown author gathers anecdotes from the lives of Spenser, Cowley, Otway, Oldham, and other writers, as well as English history generally, to illustrate the perils of dependency, and addresses them "to a Gentleman who upon the Loss of Friends was about to settle in a Great Family" – presumably as a chaplain or a private secretary.[20] Many of

---

17 Chatham Papers, PRO 30/8 vol. 17.
18 Chatham Papers, PRO 30/8, vol. 66, fos. 148–53.
19 Add. MS 12523, catalogued as William Oldys, "Patronage and Dependency," in a "Common-Place Book," 1718. But the attribution is doubtful and the title and date are clearly wrong. The commonplace book, dated on its title page "1730," includes passages copied from the *Dunciad*, 1727, and from John Kelly's comedy, *The Levee*, 1741 (fos. 43, 76). The book may be attributed to Oldys because it includes two epigrams from Plautus with translations attributed to "Oldys." Oldys was himself a dependent of Edward Harley, second Earl of Oxford, whom he served as librarian and literary secretary (*Dictionary of National Biography*).
20 The author cites Oldham's "Fable of the Two Dogs" and "Of Chaplains," references apparently to his "Satyr. Address'd to a Friend, that is about to leave the University, and come abroad in the World" – which warns against the servility that awaits the private chaplain, and concludes with a "tale" of a dog and a wolf.

his anecdotes are from literary history – he is familiar with the tradition of distressed poets from Spenser to Cowley and Oldham – but, with a cue from Lucian, he broadens his focus to include "Followers or Domestic Dependants or those who enlist themselves in great Families and submit to the Commands of Rich Men for an Annual Stipend Sallary or Wages" (fol. 67).[21] The topic of "Patronage" for him embraces the 1675 *Discourse of Patronage* (on church patronage) – which he cites by title[22] – as well as a letter from Francis Osborn in his *Miscellaneous Works* (1722) on those who attend "Honourable Persons ... in any near Relation" (fol. 43). Dependent writers are clearly for him a species of the genus "Domestic Dependents."

The two examples will perhaps serve to suggest the pervasiveness of patronage in eighteenth-century England, woven as it was into the very fabric of a hierarchically organized culture. And it may suggest how patronage might take one or more of many forms, from gifts (which have been given undue attention in studies of patronage) to pensions and places at court, to appointments in the church or universities.

(6) *The commercialization of culture.* In the course of the century high culture became increasingly accessible to (and paid for by) large numbers of people, though in new cultural forms – subscription concerts, public exhibitions of painting, landscaped pleasure grounds.[23] But it is important not to overestimate the cultural shift from aristocratic to middle-class sponsorship. Many of the arts in eighteenth-century England still depended heavily on the patronage of the aristocracy and the gentry. Painting and music required the support of those wealthy enough to commission portraits or collect paintings, and the space required even to house a chamber ensemble. Opera, architecture, and landscape gardening all required large sums from private sources to sustain. Even porcelain-makers, furniture-makers, and dressmakers relied on wealthy patronage to set the fashion. The landed gentleman retained considerable authority in matters of culture as well as politics.[24]

---

[21]   "On Salaried Posts in Great Houses," cast in the form of advice to a young man against taking up such a post (*Lucian*, III, 411–81). Lucian's work is clearly Oldham's model.

[22]   "Disc. of Patronage 4°," by "Z. C."

[23]   See J. H. Plumb, *The Commercialization of Leisure in 18th-Century England*; Neil McKendrick, John Brewer, and J. H. Plumb, *The Birth of a Consumer Society*; and Roy Porter, *English Society in the Eighteenth Century*, esp. chs. 5–6.

[24]   See John Barrell, *English Literature in History, 1730–1780*, esp. "Introduction: Artificers and Gentlemen," 17–49.

It is within such a context that I want to situate my argument about literary patronage, an argument that I lay out baldly here in the form of a series of propositions.

(1) The patronage system, as inherited from the Renaissance and strengthened during the first part of the eighteenth century, operated in such a way as to sustain the cultural authority of the traditional patron class – peers and country gentlemen.

(2) Despite the conventional view, there was no rapid or complete changeover during the century from an aristocratic culture to a commercial culture, no sudden change from a patronage economy to a literary marketplace.

(3) The "golden age" of literary patronage, in which all the best English poets enjoyed handsome pensions from the court or from aristocrats with literary tastes, is a myth fostered by disappointed writers in later years who assumed that things *must* have been better in the past, and that England *must* have once been as enlightened in this respect as Louis XIV's France.

(4) The system of patronage was never simply a form of *noblesse oblige* or disinterested generosity. It was in effect an "economic" arrangement that provided benefits to both parties.

(5) The system of patronage was *always* political. Walpole, usually branded as the villain who politicized literature and patronage, was simply making effective use of well-established principles, and his practice does not significantly differ from that of the ministries that preceded or followed him.

(6) During the course of the century booksellers gained both economic power and cultural authority, but did not supplant the traditional patrons: the period is characterized by overlapping "economies" of patronage *and* marketplace.

(7) Patronage in the later eighteenth century depended relatively less than previously on wealthy peers like Dorset and Halifax, and relatively more on other forms of support such as subscription and employment in church or civil service, but in many respects the patronage system of 1800 was similar to that of 1700: it never involved an exclusive and dyadic arrangement between a patron and a loyal client; it always involved job-related patronage and relatively small grants; it almost always provided not primary but supplementary income.

(8) Although the system sustained patronal authority, it was roomy enough to allow for resistance and manipulation on the part of the

writers who worked within it. Indeed, what is most striking about the system in operation is that it was always a site of contestation, as authors and patrons, later joined by booksellers and critical reviewers, jockeyed for position and for authority.

(9) That contestation can be observed in the language of dedications, prefaces, letters, novels, and poems, in which authors, whether explicitly or obliquely, engage the topics of obligation, debt, gratitude, benefit, dependence, and independence.

Finally, a few words about the scope of my discussion. I do not propose an archival study of the sort called for by Korshin, in which the names of all active patrons are established, together with their recipients, the kinds of patronage, and the amounts and the kind of support.[25] I propose instead to offer several complementary perspectives on the topic. In some plenary chapters I will argue that the system of patronage needs to be understood in economic and political terms, and that as a system it persisted well past 1755 at least to the end of the century. But the bulk of the argument and the heart of the project will be focused on the ways in which individual writers consciously worked within the patronage system. I am concerned not only to track writers through their literary careers, but to demonstrate that a preoccupation with patronage, and a determination to manipulate or resist the system, can be seen in their writing. Reading their verse, essays, narrative, or dedicatory prose in effect requires that we think about the rhetoric of patronage, the poetics of dedication. I have chosen some canonical writers (Dryden, Swift, Pope, and Johnson) as well as some less central figures, some of them always marginal (Richard Savage, and the newly rediscovered Mary Leapor), some of them well regarded and popular in their own day but no longer canonical (Edward Young, Charlotte Lennox). Most are men, if only because most of the writers who attracted patronage were men. Most are poets, if only because the drama (as a performing art) was sustained by a different economy and the novel was by and large not yet accepted as a genre that deserved to have patronal authority conferred on it.

In the chapters on individual writers I am often concerned to

---

[25] The Book Subscription List Project at Newcastle has in a series of publications been building a substantial catalogue of all the books published by subscription in the period 1700–99. There is as yet no list of *all* eighteenth-century books published with dedications. Rogers estimates that the 933 dedications in his survey represent between one-third and two-thirds of the total ("Book Dedications," 217). For the earlier period, see Franklin B. Williams, Jr., *Index of Dedications and Commendatory Verses*.

challenge and revise received opinion, to argue for example that
Dryden in his dedications was not merely a flatterer, that Pope was
an active participant in the patronage system, that Young and
Savage were more successful in obtaining patronage than they liked
their readers to think, and that Johnson was not hostile to the system.

CHAPTER 2

The cultural economics of literary patronage

My thesis in this chapter is that literary patronage is a systematic economic arrangement, a complex exchange of benefit to both patron and client. I use the term "economics" to emphasize that significant goods and services are exchanged. "*Cultural* economics" tries to suggest that patronage is not simply money and housing in exchange for printed dedications; that economics in eighteenth-century society, still based on rank and honor, needs to be understood broadly; and that what is ultimately at stake is the control of high literary culture.

We have neither an adequate history nor a comprehensive and coherent *theory* of literary patronage. Most studies of literary patronage have been biographical in their focus, descriptive rather than analytic, and relatively innocent of theoretical method. Such scattered theoretical remarks as we have imply that cultural patronage is not economic behavior. Dedicating authors sometimes claim that their patrons act from the simple "pleasure" of doing good."[1] Such claims may seem to us to be little more than credulous compliments. But before we dismiss them, we should consider that they reflect cultural habits no longer familiar to us – an eighteenth-century preoccupation with the various forms of "pleasure," and the traditionally aristocratic practice of publicly displayed generosity. To understand, for example, what lies behind Fielding's claim that "the communication of benefits to others" is "accompanied with a very delicious relish upon the mind of him that practices it"[2] requires some reconstruction of the relationship between the giver and receiver of "benefits."

[1] See John Gay's "Epistle to Paul Methuen, Esq.," on the disinterested generosity of the Duke of Chandos, and John Dennis' flattery of Granville: "You aim at nothing by doing daily good, but the God-like Pleasure which results from your Actions" (*Critical Works*, II, I).

[2] *Covent Garden Journal*, 29 (April 11, 1752). Fielding is in fact quoting Isaac Barrow's *Sermon XXXI* (1671).

Patronage of painting has been more thoroughly studied from the point of view of the relationship between art and society, but the focus has remained – in Francis Haskell's terms – on the "mechanics" of patronage, on contacts, commissions, visits to studios, exhibitions.[3] For theoretical work it is necessary to turn to political scientists and social anthropologists who see patronage, whether in modern or feudal societies, as a personal relationship between two parties unequal in status and resources, designed for mutual benefit of the two parties, and ultimately as a means of socio-political organization.[4] Political patronage in twentieth-century Sicily or Chicago may seem a long way from literary patronage at the English court, and it may be easier to see common underlying principles in traditional societies, where there is a "nearly universal sense" that the wealthy and powerful have an "obligation" to support those in need. This obligation is "not only a precept of religion, but a moral imperative."[5] The patrons also derive some political benefit from their support: "it is largely by virtue of some contribution of the powerful to the welfare of the group that their power is legitimated and becomes authority" (Scott, "Patronage or Exploitation?", p. 28). In both traditional agrarian societies and in modern political bureaucracies, gift-giving, gift-exchange, and clientage constitute a ritualized means of consolidating community. But most social scientists see such contributions as "uneconomic behavior" – that is, governed by other than economic considerations.

Some of this theoretical work has been applied to courts of seventeenth-century England and France, where gift-giving served as a means to construct political alliances.[6] And a moral foundation for such ritualized gift-giving has been recovered from classical anti-

---

[3] Francis Haskell, *Patrons and Painters: A Study in the Relations between Italian Art and Society in the Age of the Baroque*. See also G. F. Lytle and S. Orgel, eds., *Patronage in the Renaissance*.

[4] I have consulted Verena Burkolter, *The Patronage System*; Ernest Gellner and John Waterbury, eds., *Patrons and Clients in Mediterranean Societies*; S. N. Eisenstadt and L. Roniger, "Patron-Client Relations as Model of Structuring Social Exchange," 42–77; and Eisenstadt and Roniger, eds., *Patrons, Clients, and Friends*. The classic work on gift exchange is Marcel Mauss, *Essai sur le Don* (1924). For a more recent work in this tradition, applying the idea of gift exchange to the world of art, see Lewis Hyde, *The Gift*.

[5] James Scott, quoting Pitt-Rivers, in "Patronage or Exploitation?", in Ernest Gellner and John Waterbury, *Patrons and Clients in Mediterranean Societies*, 27.

[6] See Linda Levy Peck, *Court Patronage and Corruption*, 1–29, and Sharon Kettering, *Patrons, Brokers, and Clients in Seventeenth-Century France* (New York: Oxford, 1986). For other recent discussions of seventeenth-century patronage, see *Patronage, Politics, and Literary Traditions in England, 1558–1658*, ed. Cedric Brown, 21–174, and Robert C. Evans, *Ben Jonson and the Poetics of Patronage*.

quity, and in particular in the seven books of Seneca's *De Beneficiis*.[7]
In this tradition *beneficiae* or "benefits" are favors freely granted
through generosity, and freely received in gratitude. But the free gift
in fact confers an obligation which "binds two persons together,"
and giving benefits thus "constitutes the chief bond of society."[8]
Seneca's work was translated into English by both Arthur Golding in
1578 and Thomas Lodge in 1614. Shakespeare uses the word
"benefit" in its Senecan sense,[9] and James I deploys the Senecan
language of benefits in his *Trew Law of Free Monarchies*. L'Estrange's
redaction of *Seneca's Morals by way of Abstract* (1678) went through ten
editions by 1699. But its survival into the eighteenth century is almost
unnoticed because it has been assumed that the tradition of freely
given *beneficiae* was supplanted by a Hobbesian world in which
benefactions might be received with resentment rather than gratitude
(precisely because they conferred an obligation), and in which social
relations were based on an implicit contract (a quid pro quo).[10] The
word "benefit" in Hobbes tends in fact to mean simply something of
value, of advantage. To the casual reader today the word "benefits"
has now lost its special sense, and seems a colorless general term.[11]
But it is the word Fielding used in discussing "the delight ... of doing
good," and it occurs regularly in discussions of generosity and
gratitude in the eighteenth century,[12] and is very common in
Johnson's references to patronage.[13]

One problem with these accounts of "uneconomic" conduct is
that while they may explain gift-giving in an archaic economy or in

[7] The first scholar I know of to notice the importance of *beneficiae* in seventeenth-century
English culture is John Wallace, in "John Dryden's Plays and the Conception of a Heroic
Society," 113–34. Peck (*Court Patronage and Corruption*, 12–29) discusses the "Senecan
language of benefits."

[8] *De Beneficiis*, I, iv, VI, xl, in *Seneca, Moral Essays*, III, 19, 449.

[9] *As You Like It*, II, 7, lines 184–86 (on "benefits forgot"); *King Lear*, IV, 2, line 45.

[10] Wallace, "John Dryden's Plays and the Conception of a Heroic Society," 128. Hobbes on
"benefits" is discussed by John Dussinger in "Dr. Johnson's Solemn Responses to
Beneficence," 67–69.

[11] Locke knows the Senecan sense: "Birth may subject some, and alliance or benefits others,
to pay an observance to those whom Nature, gratitude, or other respects, may have made
it due." See *Essay concerning Civil Government (Second Treatise)*, chapter 6 ("Of Paternal
Power"), in *Second Treatise of Government*, ed. Thomas Peardon (Indianapolis, Bobbs-Merrill,
1952), 31.

[12] Richard Savage declares to his patron Tyrconnel that "to forgive Injuries, and confer
Benefits, is your Delight" (*Poetical Works*, 96). Lady Mary Wortley Montagu sneers at Pope
that "even Benefits can't rein thy Hand" ("Verses Address'd to the Imitator of the First
Satire of the Second Book of Horace," line 41).

[13] See for example *Rambler* 136, the "Life of William King" (*Lives of the Poets*, III, 30), the "Life
of Watts" (*ibid.*, III, 305), and the *Life of Savage*.

classical Rome, they cannot explain how literary patronage could have remained strong – and perhaps become an even more entrenched system – in the early eighteenth century, when England was slowly beginning to evolve from a traditional society based on hierarchy and natural obligation to a commercial society based on contract. To try to think in economic terms might help explain why the system of literary patronage in England survived for another hundred years beyond the reign of Queen Anne.

In what sense might patronage be described as "economic" behavior? Pierre Bourdieu has in effect argued for an "economic" interpretation of traditional gift-giving. In his view an "archaic economy" is still very much an economy. "Practice" in such an economy "never ceases to conform to economic calculation even when it gives every appearance of disinterestedness by departing from the logic of interested calculation (in the narrow sense) and playing for stakes that are non-material and not easily quantified." Such non-material goods as legitimacy and authority, he argues, have genuine "economic" value.[14]

Bourdieu also helps us make the move from traditional or archaic societies to modern commercial societies in which patrons direct some part of their wealth to the support of culture. He suggests that the "cultural sphere" of commercial societies corresponds to the "economic sphere" of an archaic economy. Dominant groups may secure symbolic "credit" by making gifts to poets, painters, and musicians. As collectors of luxury goods such as works of art, they not only possess valuable objects but also accumulate "symbolic capital," for the objects attest to the "taste and distinction of their owners." Their "symbolic capital" is furthermore convertible, in a society organized around rank, into economic capital and material goods. (In the eighteenth century, office holders – typically men of rank – commonly enjoyed not only salaries but fees.[15]) In the "domain of art and culture," Bourdieu concludes, patrons and collectors are engaged in accumulating and exercising power.

But benefits do not flow only to the patron. In the terms of sociological studies, twentieth-century patronage (in societies still organized traditionally) is properly understood as an "exchange" of

14 *Outline of a Theory of Practice*, 177.
15 Cf. E. P. Thompson's remark that "use-rights, privileges, liberties, services – all could be translated into an equivalent in money" ("Eighteenth-Century English Society," 138).

"resources," in which the patron grants "favours, protection, and help" and the client offers "material assistance, services, loyalty, and political allegiance."[16] To argue that eighteenth-century literary patronage is likewise an economic "exchange" is not to impose an anachronism.[17] Even in the old Senecan tradition of *beneficiae* there was always a strong presumption that the patron would receive some kind of "return." At the very least, "If a benefit is acknowledged, it is returned ... He who receives a benefit gladly has already returned it" (Seneca, *De Beneficiis*, vol. III, pp. 5, 113). While Seneca is anxious to distinguish between a freely granted benefit (for which nothing is actually looked for "in exchange") and other transactions (loans, investments, merchandise, barter, bargaining[18]), his very language in fact suggests a latent economism: a benefactor gains "some *advantage* [*aliquod commodum*] from having a person grateful" (p. 117); "He who receives a benefit with gratitude *repays* the first instalment on his *debt*" [*primam eius pensionem solvit*](p. 97). And the pressure from his interlocutor – who keeps asking about the "return," "advantages," and *utilitas* of benefactions[19] – suggests that even in Seneca's day the benefit was understood as a two-way street. Indeed, "although we say that he who receives a benefit gladly has repaid it, we nevertheless also bid him return some gift similar to the one he received" (p. 121).

Other evidence that patronage involved a kind of exchange is found in the very language of eighteenth-century dedications. These dedications must of course be read very cautiously: the client presumably says only what he knows the patron wants to hear, or credits the patron with virtues and motives currently fashionable.[20] Paradoxically, however, although written dedications may not account for motives in individual cases, their generic nature provides some insight into the *system* of patronage and the function it is expected to perform. One significant element is reciprocity. Dedicating poets speak of the poet's "right" to receive the support of the great, and of the sole "right" of the great to provide such support.

16 Burkolter, *The Patronage System*, 1.
17 Peck views political patronage at the early Stuart court as "a form of general exchange" (*Court Patronage and Corruption*, 12–29).
18 Seneca, *Moral Essays*, 65 (*fenerare*), 113 (*negotiatio*), 152 (*merx*), 209 (*fenus*).
19 See *ibid.*, 153, 244, 251.
20 "Modern Dedications," says *The True Briton* in 1723, "do not give us the least Insight into the *Virtues* of the Person they are ascribed to, yet acquaint us with what [virtues] are in *Vogue*" (vol. I, p. 258). See also Pope's *Guardian* No. 4, "On Dedications," and Thomas Gordon's *Dedication to a Great Man Concerning Dedications*.

Tatler 177 (1710) describes ancient patronage – and ideal patronage –
as "a memorable Honour to both Parties, and a very agreeable
Record of their Commerce with each other"[21] – where "commerce"
clearly suggests the implicit economism. Congreve wrote to a patron
that between "Poetry" and "the Good and Great" the "relation ...
is reciprocal." The "commerce" between the two parties, in other
words, had a quasi-legal status, and though it did not amount to a
contract, it involved a complex exchange of "benefits."

Those "benefits" are often difficult to measure; indeed, they are
often immaterial. And the evidence to substantiate them is limited.
Authors' names sometimes appear in treasury ledger books, and
details are occasionally supplied in correspondence and other
written records. But even if most acts of patronage went unrecorded
in any formal way, they are usually acknowledged, both in letters
and in written dedications. Although highly conventional and even
courtly, the vocabulary of dedications can still be deciphered.
Literary historians have too readily assumed that, because it is
conventional, such language is mere form, and that when authors
thank their patrons for their "favor" or "protection" they are
merely spooning out unctuousness.[22] But by reconstructing the
context of patronage, it is possible to assign a more precise meaning
to such terms, and also to see how the patron's "honour" and
"fame" represented values almost tangible, and convertible into
substantial form.

WHAT PATRONS PROVIDE

Money from their own pockets – a one-time gift in response to a
dedication,[23] an annual pension, a letter of credit to cover expenses,
a direct subsidy to a bookseller – is only one of the resources that
patrons provided their clients, and it has received a disproportionate
amount of attention in studies of patronage.[24] Hospitality of one

---

21 *The Tatler*, II, 464–65.
22 See for example David Roberts, who in *The Ladies* claims that while dramatists regularly
    thank patrons for "favour" and "protection" there are only "a few instances" of "practical
    assistance," and very little is said about "what favour and what protection were actually
    bestowed" (p. 99).
23 The going rate in the mid-eighteenth century was between £10 (Korshin, "Types of
    Eighteenth-Century Literary Patronage," p. 467) and twenty guineas (Pope, *Correspondence*,
    II, 473).
24 Deborah Payne has recently surveyed the "material benefits" of patronage in "'And Poets
    Shall by Patron-Princes Live'," 107–110.

form or other – an invitation to dinner, a weekend houseparty,[25] a summer in the country, quarters in a patron's town house (Pope stayed six weeks in Charles Jervas' London house in 1713, Gay lodged with Burlington and Queensberry, and Handel with Burlington and Chandos), an extended stay (Watts lived with Sir Thomas Abney for thirty-five years) – has likewise received adequate attention.[26] "Hospitality," however, should not be thought of narrowly as food and lodging. Equally important is something less tangible, what Johnson and others called "familiarity," whereby persons of talent are permitted to cross a line, under controlled conditions, that normally separates the ranks of a hierarchical society. To be admitted to a lord's "conversation" does not simply bring the opportunity to hear well-bred remarks (and to store them up for later imitation). It implies a rise in status,[27] which in turn carried economic value at a time when income and access to economic resources were closely correlated with rank.

"Familiarity" is only one of the intangibles for which authors thank their patrons. Other such gifts are "encouragement," "protection," "favour," and "authority." As one of the meanings of "encouragement" Johnson gives "favour; countenance; support." Patronly encouragement began with kind words and assurances of interest. In a culture officially based on elaborate courtesies, formal and even ceremonial rhetorical exchanges, verbal "encouragement" implied a sense of obligation, and to the hopeful even a promise of further support. In practice, encouragement often never went further than words. Johnson reminds Chesterfield that he visited him after receiving "some slight encouragement." He subsequently found his attendance "so little encouraged that neither pride nor modesty would suffer me to continue it," and completed his work without "one word of encouragement." Dryden wittily laments that he was "encourag'd only with fair Words, by King *Charles* II, my little Sallary ill paid, and no prospect of a future Subsistance, I was then

25 "I am to pass three or four days in high luxury, with some company at my Lord Burlington's; we are to walk, ride, ramble, dine, drink, & lye together." Pope to Martha Blount in 1716, in Pope, *Correspondence*, I, 338.

26 G. B. Hill notes that among other writers who enjoyed a "refuge ... in the houses of the opulent" were Prior, Fenton, Akenside, and Johnson (Johnson, *Lives of the Poets*, III, 305n).

27 Cf. Congreve's dedication of *The Way of the World*, thanking his patron for "the Honour of Your Lordship's Conversation" (*Complete Plays*, 390). "Honour" suggests the gain in status – and Congreve was sensitive to such matters: he wanted to be thought of as a "gentleman" (see below, pp. 138–39).

Discourag'd ..."[28] But luckier writers would have found that a patron's verbal encouragement was followed by a more material reward. "Encouragement" might also take the form of public notice or praise – of the sort that Chesterfield delayed until Johnson professed himself "indifferent" – that would help improve the public sale. "Encouragement," in other words, was convertible into financial gain. By the 1720s the term was quantifiable in cash. Mallet writes in 1723 of a tutorship for which "My encouragement is £30." In 1725 Pope was granted £200 "as his Matys Encouragement" of his translation of the *Odyssey*.[29]

"Protection" in the rough-and-tumble world of the Restoration might literally mean protection from physical beating of the sort Dryden received in Rose Alley[30] or from political reprisal. Rochester and Sedley were said to have interceded on behalf of Wycherley with the Duke of Buckingham, who was angry that Wycherley had become "a rival for the affections of the Duchess of Cleveland."[31] It more commonly meant protection from the verbal attacks of critics or rivals, and required little more than that the patron pronounce favorable opinion of his protégé.[32] Dryden thus thanks Rochester for coming to his defense: "You have been often pleas'd not onely to excuse my imperfections, but to vindicate what was tolerable in my Writings" from the "censures" of critics.[33] It is plausible to suspect, as Winn does, that Dryden's royal patronage gave him some protection against verbal attack, perhaps leading some to blunt the edge of criticism that might otherwise have been sharper.[34] Dennis thanked Mulgrave for "the Protection and Patronage" of Dryden when he was "oppress'd, by a very formidable Party in the Court of King *Charles* II. a Faction that wanted neither Power nor Authority to crush him."[35] After the Revolution Dryden's dedications to Protestant patrons and to Williamite Whigs probably helped to protect him

---

28   *Works*, IV, 23. Cf. James Moore, "paid with kind words, which, as is common, raised great hopes, that at last were disappointed" (Johnson, "Life of Lyttelton," in *Lives of the Poets*, III, 448).

29   Johnson, *ibid.*, 400; Pope, *Correspondence*, II, 160n.

30   Ironically, it may have been the satire in his patron Mulgrave's *Essay upon Satyr* (thought at the time to be by Dryden) which led to the beating. See the notes in the California Dryden, *Works*, II, 279.

31   Quoted from Greene, *Lord Rochester's Monkey*, 178.

32   Etymologically, "one who is protected."

33   Dedication to *Marriage A-la-Mode*.

34   See James Winn, "The Laureateship," 320. But his office as Poet Laureate did not in fact protect Dryden in the famous Rose Alley incident.

35   Dedication to *The Advancement and Reformation of Modern Poetry* (1701), in *Critical Works*, I, 198.

from reprisals that might otherwise have fallen on a Catholic and a Jacobite.[36]

In the more polite world of the eighteenth century a poet had less need of physical "protection," but "the life of a Wit," as Pope (who sometimes even wore a sword) observed, could still be "warfare upon earth."[37] In such a climate some protection would have been welcome, but there is little evidence that Pope's enemies were deterred from their verbal attacks by the knowledge that he had been befriended by ministers and magnates. Nonetheless, the belief that one's patron might provide some kind of defensive shield seems to have persisted. Pope repeatedly makes a point about his "friends" in high places, not only to boast of his "splendid acquaintance" (as Johnson said) but to suggest that he had defenders at the ready.[38] By 1748 Thomson looked to patrons for a new kind of "protection": "Is there no patron to protect the Muse,/ And fence for her Parnassus' barren soil?" (*The Castle of Indolence*, Canto II, stanza ii, lines 1–2). Thomson's editor suggests that he is probably asking for help in securing the property rights of authors against the claims of booksellers.[39] As late as 1755 Johnson was able to define patron as "advocate; defender; vindicator." The writer, so Johnson suggests, is assumed to stand among enemies, rivals, critics, or accusers, and to need defense of the sort that patrons could provide.

"Protection" also had a specifically economic dimension. Just as the theory of economic "protectionism" safeguarded domestic manufacturers against competition from foreign interlopers, so too a patron's "protection" guarded an author against the competition of other authors – especially those not educated as gentlemen – thrusting up from below. (Some aristocratic patrons liked to think of the authors they supported as gentlemen of good birth but little means – and thus acceptable in one's drawing room).[40] In theory the patronage system functioned to direct support to a limited

---

[36] See below, pp. 50–51, 73, 75.

[37] Preface to the 1717 *Works*, in Ault, ed., *Prose Works*.

[38] *Lives of the Poets*, III, 90. See Pope's *Letter to a Noble Lord*, where he speaks ironically of "THOSE [i.e., the queen and Walpole] under whose *Protection* I live." I discuss Pope more fully below, pp. 147–52.

[39] James Thomson, *Liberty, The Castle of Indolence, and Other Poems*, 390. Later in the poem Thomson laments that "we live too late in Time" for the support and protection of patrons, but "still remains / Th' Eternal Patron, LIBERTY; whose Flame,/ While she protects, inspires the noblest Strains" (II, xxiii, 199, 204–06).

[40] See below, pp. 171, 206.

number of writers, and in effect to preserve their status as a kind of
guild. "It is only by the Countenance of your Lordship, and the *Few*
so qualified," says Congreve to his patron, "that such who write
with Care and Pains can hope to be distinguish'd: For the
Prostituted Name of *Poet* promiscuously levels all that bear it."[41]
Despite Congreve's disavowal of economic motive – it is *other* pens
who are prostitutes – to be "distinguished" was not only a matter of
reputation: it also had an economic dimension, particularly in the
theatre, where the number of theatres (and the number of plays a
theatre could mount in a season) was sharply limited. Access to
theatre managers like Cibber was difficult, and an influential patron
could help. But there was no such limit – after 1697 anyway, when
the Licensing Act lapsed – on the number of printers and booksellers. So many writers complained of competition from below that
by 1704 Swift could both laugh at and share their sentiments in the
"Preface" to *A Tale of a Tub*.[42] Even access to a patron did not
elevate a writer above the rabble and protect him from degrading
competition.

In theory the great patrons of the early eighteenth century were
discriminating men of taste, but in practice they were not always
very discriminating in distributing their bounty. Johnson called
Dorset and Halifax "universal patrons." It was said that no one who
applied to Halifax went unrewarded. Nor did a patron always
"protect" a writer from a rival poet. Dorset supported Shadwell and
Dryden at the same time. Chandos subscribed to Pope's Homer but
also to the Shakespeare of Pope's great rival, Theobald, and to the
works of many other undistinguished writers as well.[43] Halifax did
not "protect" Pope against the rival Tickell translation. He subscribed to Pope's version and accepted a dedication from Tickell.
Pope's good friend Orrery was one of the leading patrons of
Theobald's Shakespeare.[44] And the Earl of Hardwicke befriended
both Warburton and Thomas Edwards at a time when they were
adversaries.[45]

---

[41] Dedication to *The Way of the World*, in *Complete Plays*, 391.
[42] He cites "Examples" from modern prefaces: "For a Man to set up for a Writer, when the
      Press swarms with, &c … When every little Would-be-wit takes Pen in hand, 'tis in Vain
      to enter the Lists, &c."
[43] C. H. C. Baker and M. I. Baker, *The Life and Circumstances of James Brydges, First Duke of
      Chandos*, 68–69.
[44] Peter Seary, *Lewis Theobald and the Editing of Shakespeare*, 201.
[45] See Philip C. Yorke, *Life and Correspondence of Philip Yorke*.

AUTHORITY

Perhaps even more important to a writer than "protection" against a variety of perils is the "authority" by which he speaks. And this too is – ideally – provided by the patronage system. The patron, equipped in theory by birth, education, taste, and leisure is better qualified than his inferiors or even nascent professionals to serve as the judge of literary merit. Thus Chesterfield, because of his rank and his publicly expressed concern for usage, is acknowledged to possess "authority in our language."[46] Thus Dryden tells Dorset, "the greatest Genius, the truest Judge, and the best Patron," that as "the King of Poets" he possesses a symbolically regal "Authority."

I mean not the Authority, which is annex'd to your Office [as Lord Chamberlain]: I speak of that only which is inborn and inherent to your Person: What is produced in you by an excellent Wit, a Masterly and Commanding Genius over all Writers: Whereby you are impower'd, when you please, to give the final decision of Wit; to put your Stamp on all that ought to pass for current, and set a Brand of Reprobation on Clipt Poetry, and false Coyn. (Dryden, *Works*, vol. IV, p. 5, lines 9–10)

It is implicitly only because Dorset "will not" write, or chooses to write so little, that Dryden can speak *in his name*.

The patron is not only the guarantor of wit, reassuring the hesitating bookseller or bookbuyer, but is himself the source of it. It is only by acknowledging that authority, and in effect drawing on its power, that the client-writer may speak. In the dedication to Mulgrave of *The Advancement and Reformation of Modern Poetry* Dennis takes the "Opportunity, of confirming, by your Lordship's Authority, the Assertion which is the Foundation of the following Treatise."[47] Dennis casts himself as lawyer and Mulgrave as "his Awful Judge" with a "perfect Knowledge of his Cause, and a Sovereign Authority to decide it" (vol. I, p. 200). It was, says Dennis elsewhere, the "Zeal," the "Capacity," and the "Authority" of Mulgrave and other Restoration court wits – Buckingham, Rochester, Dorset, and others – that shaped the reception of a new play: "When these or the Majority of them Declard themselves upon any new Dramatick performance, the Town fell Immediately in with them." When

---

[46] Johnson, *Plan of a Dictionary*, 31. See J. H. Neumann, "Chesterfield and the Standard of Usage," 463–75.

[47] *Critical Works*, I, 198. Mulgrave's authority is for Dennis based primarily on his "perfect Knowledge in Criticism," his achievement as both critic and poet.

Wycherley's *Plain Dealer* was first presented, "the Town ... appeard Doubtfull what Judgment to Form of it; the aforemention'd gentlemen by their loud aprobation of it, gave it both a sudden and a lasting reputation."[48] Even as late as the 1740s no less a writer than Johnson writes to Chesterfield that he hopes to gain "authority" and "power" as Chesterfield's "delegate," in legal terms "exercising a kind of vicarious jurisdiction" (*Plan of the Dictionary*). And Chesterfield responds by assuring the world that he has indeed assigned his authority to Johnson. Declaring that "good order and authority" are now necessary to regulate the language, he casts his "vote" for Johnson to "fill that great and arduous post" of "dictator."[49]

The "authority" of the patron, when delegated to the author, is also convertible into material assets. If a work comes complete with a dedication to a noble lord who has in some sense authorized it or given his stamp of approval, it will tend to sell better. As Fielding noted in the Preface to *The Historical Register*, the booksellers think of a patron as "a kind of godfather to a book," for he in effect gives the book its "name" (with a pun on *name* as reputation): "What ... does more service to a book, or raises curiosity in the reader, equal with 'Dedicated to his Grace the Duke of – ' or 'for the Right Honourable the Earl of – ', in an advertisement?"[50] The bookseller assumes less risk in buying the property, and is thus more likely to buy, or to offer a good price for the copyright. It is thus in the bookseller's interest, as well as the author's, for the patron to lend his authority. This point was not lost on Jacob Tonson, founder and chief organizer of the Kit-cat Club, which brought together Whiggish patrons and Whiggish authors. Nor was it lost on Robert Dodsley, who contracted to publish Johnson's *Dictionary*. After reviewing Johnson's initial proposal, Dodsley encouraged Johnson to call on Chesterfield in hopes that the earl might agree to accept a dedication. He even appears to have helped set up a meeting. When the *Plan*, addressed to Chesterfield, was published in 1747, it was hailed in *The Museum*, a periodical Dodsley controlled, in language that suggests that Dodsley well understood the economic value of Chesterfield's endorsement:

---

[48]   *Ibid.*, II, 277. By the same token, influential courtiers could damn a play. The Maids of Honor caballed to denounce Wycherley's *Country Wife*. For details, see Roberts, *The Ladies*, 107–09.

[49]   *The World*, No. 100 (November 28, 1754).

[50]   Preface to the Dedication of *The Historical Register for the Year 1736*, in *Complete Works*, XI, 231. Cf. Richard Hurd: "A noble name in the front of a new work does the office of a fair sign. It catches the eye of passengers, and invites custom" (*Moral and Political Dialogues*, xii).

"The great Importance and general Usefulness of such a Body of Language appeared so clearly to the noble Person to whom this Plan is addressed, that he signified a Willingness of becoming its Patron." Chesterfield, he assures the prospective reader in what sounds almost like a blurb on a modern dust jacket, "is incapable of giving Countenance to any thing but Merit."[51] When Chesterfield in 1754 finally published his essays complimenting the forthcoming *Dictionary*, they appeared in *The World*, another of Dodsley's magazines.[52] And even though Johnson responded to Chesterfield's compliments with the famous private letter, Dodsley republished the 1746 *Plan* (with its address to Chesterfield) when he printed the *Dictionary* in 1755. He regretted Johnson's letter, he said, because he had a "property" in the book. Had the *Dictionary* itself been dedicated to Chesterfield, as Dodsley clearly hoped, he would have expected even better sales. But by 1755 Johnson no longer wanted the use of Chesterfield's "authority."

For the patron too there is a quasi-economic gain to be derived from the delegation of authority. In financial terms the patron "invests" symbolic capital in a poem or play with the hope that its success will reflect well on him as an arbiter of taste. Rochester gained a kind of power at the court of Charles II in part by identifying and promoting literary talent. (Lyttelton was a similar talent-spotter for the Prince of Wales in the 1730s.) In the 1670s Rochester accepted dedications from Shadwell, Dryden, John Crowne, Sir Francis Fane, Otway, and Lee, and drew royal attention to their work. This is of course not risk-free for the patron; he does not want to declare approval in public for plays or poems that come to be thought bad, or else his reputation for taste and judgment will suffer. As Bubb Dodington (himself a patron) later wrote in his "Epistle to Sir Robert Walpole," rewarding "true merit" will enable a patron to "gain the good" (the verb carries strong suggestions of gaining a profit): "When princes to bad ore their image join, / They more debase the stamp, than raise the coin."[53]

INTRODUCTIONS

"Protection" and the delegation of "authority" were valuable resources, more valuable in some respects than grants of money,

---

[51] *The Museum*, 36 (1747), 385, 389.   [52] Nos. 100, 101.
[53] In the *Poetical Works of Edward Young*, II, 328.

because as symbolic "capital" they could be used to procure material return. "Introductions" had a similar value: they could lead to other favors. In economic terms introductions provided clients with access to other resources. Young is reported to have said that "a dinner with his lordship, has procured him invitations for the whole week following: that an airing in his patron's chariot has supplied him with a citizen's chariot on every future occasion."[54] More formal introductions were also invaluable, whether of the poet or his work. Dorset presented Charles Montagu (later Earl of Halifax) to King William – who gave him a pension on the spot. Lyttelton commended Fielding to the Duke of Bedford, who arranged to have him named a Justice of the Peace for Westminster. Restoration dramatists thank their patrons for placing copies of their plays before the eyes of the royal family. Thirty years later Walpole himself, in effect acting as Pope's patron, presented a copy of the *Dunciad* at court to the very "ear of Kings."[55] By contrast, Richard Savage lacked "a friend either to get him introduced, or his poems presented at Court."[56] Such official notice of a poem could still as late as Johnson's day enhance the writer's and the poem's status. That Johnson was not formally "introduced" to the king in the famous scene in the King's Library is a mark of Johnson's eminence. As a famous author and a royal pensioner he perhaps needed no "introduction." But the king's formal notice of him clearly enhanced Johnson's status, as Boswell realized immediately.

Patrons were in other ways able and sometimes willing to intercede on a writer's behalf and to provide access to other resources. This was common in the Restoration where, as Dennis later noted, the management of the theatres was "in the Hands of Gentlemen."[57] In the first five seasons after Charles' return fifteen of the nineteen new plays performed by the King's Men were written by the relatives of the patent-holder, Sir Thomas Killigrew, or by other "friends" and

---

[54] In Goldsmith, *Enquiry into the State of Polite Learning*, ch. 10, in *Collected Works*, I, 311.

[55] The *Dunciad Variorum* was officially presented to George II on March 12, 1729. Walpole was apparently not bringing dangerous satire to the king's attention, but doing a "favor" (as Mack calls it, *Alexander Pope*, 501) to a writer he had been entertaining at dinner for some years.

[56] From a letter by Thomas Birch, introducing "The Volunteer Laureate" to readers of the *Gentleman's Magazine* in 1738 (quoted in Savage, *Poetical Works*, 170). Johnson also noted that Savage had no "friend" to "present" his poem "Of Publick Spirit, with Regard to Publick Works" to the Prince of Wales (*Lives of the Poets*, II, 397).

[57] *Critical Works*, II, 278.

"insiders."[58] Rochester helped arrange a performance at court in 1671 of Settle's *Empress of Morocco*. He later "seemed almost to make it his business" to establish Otway's *Alcibiades* "in the good opinion of the King and his Royal Highness [i.e., the Duke of York]."[59] The Duchess of Ormonde arranged for a rehearsal of Durfey's *Don Quixote* (1694) before "Nobility and Gentry." This led, so Durfey thanked her, a "dazzling and numerous ... Constellation" of ladies to attend the poet's third day performance.[60] When Queen Mary disapproved of Dryden's *Cleomenes* (1692), Lawrence Hyde, Earl of Rochester, spoke with the queen and his daughter-in-law pleaded with the Lord Chamberlain (who had the authority to ban the play's performance).[61] Ministerial intercession continued to have a similar impact in the next century. In 1728 a word from the court could induce Cibber and Wilkes (the theatre patent holders) to look with favor on a new play.[62] As late as 1758 Bute exercised influence on Garrick to the same end.[63] Patrons might also recommend an author to a bookseller, as Walsh introduced Pope to Jacob Tonson, Shenstone arranged to have the poems of James Woodhouse, the "Poetical Shoemaker", published by Robert Dodsley, and Hannah More sponsored the subscription edition of Ann Yearsley's poems in 1785.[64]

More generally, some nobles, because of their social standing, and sometimes because of their political position at court, had the power to direct or deflect the "flow" or to block the "rays" of favor.[65] Thus Otway thanks the Duchess of Portsmouth for rescuing him from the malice of his enemies at court who "kept back and shaded me from

---

58 Robert Hume, "Securing a Repertory," 167.

59 Preface to *Don Carlos*.

60 The Duchess of Portsmouth provided similar assistance to Lee for *Sophonisba* (1675). Cf. also Dryden's dedication of *Amphitryon* (1690) to Sir William Levenson-Gower.

61 See Dryden's dedication to Hyde.

62 See Battestin, *Henry Fielding*, 59. Boswell suspects that Johnson's *Irene* was not accepted by the patentee of Drury Lane in 1737 "probably because it was not patronized by some man of high rank" (*Life of Johnson*, II, III).

63 See below, p. 61.

64 See Betty Rizzo, "The Patron as Poet Maker," 255. For Yearsley's relations with her patron, see Moira Ferguson, "Resistance and Power in the Life and Writings of Ann Yearsley," 247–68.

65 The metaphors of life-giving fountain and sun persist into the eighteenth century, when Cibber reminds Savage that the king is the sole fount of all honor – and ultimately of all patronage (and that no man can appoint himself "Volunteer Laureate"). Cf. also Lyttelton's 1733 manuscript "Observations on the Reign and Character of Queen Elizabeth," on "the warm beams of Royal Favour," quoted in Christine Gerrard, *The Patriot Opposition to Walpole*, 166.

those royal beams, whose warmth is all I have, or hope to live by."
The duchess has "placed me in the sun, and I have felt its comfort."[66]
Halifax's memoirist recalls in 1715 how, during the reign of James II,
the King's Catholic advisors "had wholly engross'd the King's Ear,
and intercepted the Rays of his Majesty's Favour, from shining upon
any other than themselves and their Creatures."[67] Dryden appeals to
Rochester's ability to influence the prompt payment of his salary,
often "stopped" in the hands of the king's ministers, "who have the
liberality of Kings in their disposing; and who dishonouring the
Bounty of their Master, suffer such to be in necessity, who endeavour
at least to please him: and for whose entertainment He has generously provided, if the Fruits of His Royal favour were not often
stopp'd in other hands."[68] And he thanks his patron Thomas
Clifford, Lord Treasurer, who acted as the dispenser of the king's
gifts: "You Distributed your Masters Favour with so equal hands,
that *Justice* her self could not have held the Scales more even ... By
your own Integrity ... the King gave all that He intended."[69]

At the end of the eighteenth century Johnson still clearly understood that the advisors to a king or prince were in a position to
dispense patronage on his behalf. Thus he notes that although King
William paid little attention to poetry, his ministers (eager to
promote their own reputations as patrons) saw to it that the royal
bounty flowed into literary hands and that the king (as well as his
ministers) received tribute in response.[70] As advisor to the Prince of
Wales, Lyttleton encouraged him to build his "popularity" by
patronizing a set of writers whom Lyttelton brought to his attention.
After he joined the Pelham ministry he pressed the Prime Minister to
provide his old client Thomson with a pension.[71]

PLACES AND LIVINGS

Royal pensions, and appointment to the posts of Poet Laureate or
Historiographer Royal, were almost always awarded upon the

---

[66] "Epistle Dedicatory to Her Grace the Duchess of Portsmouth," *Venice Preserv'd* (1682).

[67] Halifax, *Poetical Works*, 9.

[68] Dedication to *Marriage A-la-Mode*, in *Works*, XI, 223.

[69] Dedication of *Amboyna*, in *Works*, XII, 4. Perhaps, however, Dryden implies some regret
that the patron is only a conduit for a king who "gave all that he *intended*" – but less than
Dryden hoped for – and provided support to several writers with "equal hands" – but did
not single out Dryden for special favor.

[70] *Lives of the Poets*, II, 85, 298.

[71] *Ibid.*, III, 448. Chesterfield, *Letters*, III, 1119.

recommendation of a highly placed intermediary. Even though the number of writers who received such pensions and appointments was very small, these two positions (which both Dryden and Johnson held) have diverted the attention of literary historians from two forms of patronage that were much more common: appointments to "places" in the substantial administrative bureaucracy (made upon the recommendation of a politically connected "friend") and appointments to livings in the established church (made upon the "presentation" of the living by the patron, typically the largest landowner in the neighborhood, and the leading political force). Many of the writers who enjoyed state patronage, from the days of Queen Anne through the days of George III, in fact held salaried appointments, some of them substantial positions (like Addison's secretaryship, or Prior's diplomatic post), some sinecures, and some whose duties could easily be delegated to a deputy (like Thomson's post as Surveyor-General of the Leeward Islands). Such positions were not always earmarked for authors; nor did they require special training, or even a reputation for learning.[72] Appointments in the church, by contrast, typically required that the candidate have a university degree, and take holy orders. By one contemporary estimate peers had the gift of about 1200 of the nearly 10,000 church livings,[73] and many patrons controlled multiple livings.[74] Among the poets in the period whose primary form of patronage was church livings were Young, Dyer, and Crabbe.

WHAT THE AUTHOR PROVIDES

When a patron receives the poem or play as a gift, it becomes his property: "It is dedicated to you," says Erasmus to More of his *Praise of Folly*, "so henceforth it is yours, not mine."[75] Dryden's *Secret Love* was such a favorite of Charles II – he saw it five times in

---

[72] Even after the Civil List was reformed and the Board of Trade abolished in 1782, and despite successful efforts to make civil administration efficient and professional, there remained numerous sinecures suitable for writers and other political placemen, especially in the Exchequer and the Customs. See John Brewer, *The Sinews of Power*, 70–85.

[73] See Browne Willis, *A Survey of the Cathedrals of England*, 3 vols. (1727–30), quoted in Cannon, *Aristocratic Century*, 63. The total number of church livings in the gift of private patrons *increased* over the course of the century. In 1831 peers presented to 1,400 livings (see Samuel Lewis, *Topographical Dictionary* [1831]).

[74] In 1831 sixty-four peers controlled eight or more livings each. See *Patroni Ecclesiarum* (1831), quoted in Cannon, *Aristocratic Century*, 67.

[75] Erasmus Desiderius, *Praise of Folly*, tr. Betty Radice (Harmondsworth: Penguin, 1971), 56.

1667 and 1668 — that the king "grac'd it with the Title of His Play."[76] He "owns" it not only by acknowledging his approval, but by symbolically taking title. And by taking title, the patron in fact improves the work, adds value: "Whatever Value may be wanting to this Play [*The Way of the World*]," says Congreve to the Earl of Montague, "will be sufficiently made up to it, when it is once become your Lordship's."[77] Stephen Duck writes to the queen that she has the same "Right" to his poems "as you have to the Fruits of a Tree, which you have transplanted out of a barren soil into a fertile and beautiful garden."[78] It is not simply that the writer makes a "gift" of his work by laying it at the patron's feet. In some sense the work was always his — the poet simply restores it to its rightful parent or owner.[79]

At a time when the concept of intellectual property and of an author's (as opposed to a bookseller's) copyright was not yet fully established, the idea that a patron (and later a bookseller) might hold the "property" should not be dismissed as merely figurative. Our post-Romantic sense of the writer as the creative or "original" genius partially blinds us to the older distinction between labor of the head and labor of the hand,[80] and to the implication of the even older idea that the artist is only a craftsman: the true author and only begetter of a work is a patron. The artisan or artificer merely executes the patron's design, reduces the "idea" of the work into writing.[81] The provider of the design, the originator of the idea, the source of the inspiration, or even the model for the virtues celebrated in the work is the true *auctor* who possesses both property and authority.[82]

---

[76] *Works*, IX, 115, 331.
[77] *Complete Plays*, 390.
[78] *Poems on Several Occasions*, 2nd ed. (London, 1737), pp. iii–iv.
[79] Thomas Percy, dedicating his *Reliques of English Poetry* to the Countess of Northumberland in 1765, told her that "those songs which the bounty of your ancestors rewarded, now return to your Ladyship by a kind of hereditary right."
[80] This distinction, deployed in fact by Italian humanists like Vasari to raise the prestige of the painter from mere artisan to inventor, survives in Young's contrast between "one who thinks and composes" — i.e., "an author," who thereby holds "the sole property" in his works — and those who "only read and write" — i.e., mere hacks, "invaders of the press" (*Conjectures on Original Composition*, 1759, facs. ed., 1966, 57). It survives too in eighteenth-century theories of genius and legal debates about copyright. See below, pp. 281, 282.
[81] As late as 1794 Uvedale Price distinguished between a "painter" – i.e., "any man of a liberal mind, with a strong feeling for nature as well as art, who has been in the habit of comparing both together" – and "merely a professor [of that art]." *Essays on the Picturesque*, I, 9n.
[82] For the distinction between *auctor* and *artificer*, see Hannah Arendt, who traces both

By the same token, the patron metaphorically takes title to the poet. "I am yours" is not simply a shortened form of the closing formula declaring that the writer is "your lordship's obedient and humble servant." It suggests not only that I am "your creature" (as Shadwell says to the Duke of Newcastle)[83] but also that "I belong to you" – as a wife or servant was still considered part of a man's "property."

In exchange for his protection, encouragement, and use of his authority, and as a kind of freeholder, the patron could expect a variety of services. Simplest of these might perhaps misleadingly be called "entertainment." To have a witty poet at the table could enliven the evening and enhance the pleasures of the feast. Such service has sometimes been thought demeaning, as if the poet were little more than a trained monkey, or at best a domestic servant expected to be ingratiating and clever, though not so clever as to upstage the host. Swift paints a dark picture of the writer as a kind of "pimp" in his patron's service, pandering to his "vicious mind" by providing topics on which the patron can exercise his debased wit.[84]

But Swift was not a disinterested observer, and we need not conclude that the meeting of lord and wit could never be an occasion for a Popean feast of reason and flow of soul. When Johnson notes that Robert Harley, Earl of Oxford, liked to unwind with the Scriblerians (Swift, Gay, Pope, Arbuthnot, and Parnell), he finds nothing offensive or demeaning about the inequality of the situation. What he censures is that Harley did not fulfill his part of the bargain: he admitted Parnell "as a favourite companion of his convivial hours, but, as it seems often to have happened in those times to the favourites of the great, without attention to his fortune."[85] When Pope satirizes the scene at a lord's table –

> Is there a Lord, who knows a cheerful noon
> Without a Fiddler, Flatt'rer, or Buffoon?
> Whose table, Wit, or modest Merit share,
> Un-elbow'd by a Gamester, Pimp, or Play'r?[86]

– he ridicules not the institution but its perversion. It is not that lords

"author" and "authority" back through *auctoritas* in "What is Authority?", *Between Past and Future*, 122–23.

83 Dedication of *The Virtuoso*.
84 See his "Libel on the Reverend Dr. Delany" (1730), lines 21–26, discussed below, pp. 119–20.
85 *Lives of the Poets*, II, 50–51.
86 "Epistle to Bathurst," lines 239–42.

should not invite their social inferiors, but that they should be more careful about the *other* guests. Men of "Wit, or modest Merit" shouldn't have to share the space at the table with mere musicians, obsequious lickspittles, and crude jesters, to say nothing of *their* inferiors, the pushy "Gamester, Pimp, or Play'r." This point is made clear when Pope continues, by turning to address Bathurst himself, an example of a lord who knows the "true use of riches":

> Who copies Your's, or OXFORD's better part,
> To ease th'oppress'd, and raise the sinking heart?
> Where-e'er he shines, oh Fortune, gild the scene,
> And Angels guard him in the golden Mean!
> There, English Bounty yet a-while may stand,
> And Honour linger ere it leaves the land.   (lines 243–48)

Plainly Pope idealizes his wealthy friends. But at the same time the ideal of "English Bounty" that he holds up is not a mere fiction, but – from his point of view – an honorable tradition exemplified in the best of patrons, who dispense their largesse not only to ease the oppressed but also to share a lordly table with writers of "modest Merit" – they don't need to elbow their way in because their "Merit" is simply acknowledged. From the patron's point of view, the idea that a poet might grace one's table survives at least until the 1780s, when (according to Crabbe's son) the Duke of Rutland thought that a young writer of genius "would be a valuable acquisition to the society of his mansion, where, like a genuine English peer of the old school, he spent the greater portion of his time in the exercise of boundless hospitality and benevolence."[87]

Another kind of benefit a patron might derive is personal "literary services." The writer is invited to the patron's circle or household and asked to lend what we might now call his professional expertise. Buckingham is said to have received assistance from Samuel Butler in the writing of *The Rehearsal*. Dryden "corrected" Mulgrave's *Essay upon Satyr*. Half a century later it was the practice of the Countess of Hertford, as Johnson says, "to invite every summer some poet into the country to hear her verses and assist her studies."[88] Several of them expressed their gratitude by writing poems in praise of her seat, Percy Lodge.[89] Fielding defended Lyttelton in print against an

---

[87] *The Life of George Crabbe*, 98.
[88] *Lives of the Poets*, III, 287.
[89] Among them Thomson, Shenstone, and Isaac Watts. See David Hill Radcliffe, "Genre and Social Order," 445–65.

"impudent Libeller."[90] And the old Dowager Duchess of Marlborough, although she had no taste for literature herself, was determined to defend her besmirched honor, and in effect hired Nathaniel Hooke, a minor writer of Pope's acquaintance, to write *An Account of the Conduct of the Dowager Duchess of Marlborough* (1742), for which he reportedly received £5,000.[91] She attempted as well to secure literary services in defense of her late husband, and left the duke's papers and legacies of £500 each to Mallet and Glover, on condition that they write his life. In addition to such personal literary services, authors were of course also engaged to write pamphlets or edit journals articulating a patron's political views, attacking his enemies, or defending the patron, but I defer further discussion of such services until I take up the subject of patronage and party politics in the next chapter.

But "politics" in eighteenth-century England was not only a matter of Whig and Tory, "Court" and "Country." In a country still governed by a king, politics was also a matter of access to the court, maintaining one's place (and many of the great went in and out of favor regularly), and pleasing one's superiors. In such a world, where "politics" was personal, it could be very useful to have writers on one's side to circulate manuscript satires attacking one's enemies or panegyrics praising one's conduct, family, or country seat. Dryden's political service to the Stuarts is well known, but his praise of Mulgrave was probably of "political" value too. After Dryden was dropped by Rochester, he turned to Rochester's rival court wit, the Earl of Mulgrave, dedicating *Aureng-Zebe* to him in 1676. In the following year Dryden alluded rather openly, in the preface to *All for Love* (dedicated to Danby) to Rochester's feeble pretensions to wit. Dryden's allusions serve his own purposes,[92] but they also serve Mulgrave's. The satiric reflections on Rochester could only improve Mulgrave's standing as a fashionable court wit in relation to his rival. It is noteworthy that "sharp judging *Adriel*," as Dryden later called his new patron, advanced in the royal counsels in the late 1670s, succeeding to three of Monmouth's offices.

In the mid-eighteenth century, politics, as Namier and his fol-

---

90 In the *Jacobite's Journal*, 18 (1748), *The Jacobite's Journal and Related Writings*, 217–20.
91 She later gave him a pension. See Pope, *Correspondence*, IV, 383, 386. Fielding defended the *Account* (and the duchess) against subsequent attacks, and while Battestin suspects he was paid for it, he can find no hard evidence (*Henry Fielding*, 345).
92 See below, pp. 81–83.

lowers have emphasized, was often a matter of promoting the interest of one's family and immediate friends. Philip Yorke, the first Earl of Hardwicke, who rose to be Lord Chancellor, was like many powerful magnates ambitious on behalf of his sons. With the help of Hard-wicke money and influence, his first son, Philip, was elected to represent Cambridgeshire.[93] His second son, Charles, followed his father up through the legal ranks and eventually became Lord Chancellor too. Patronage of friendly writers was one means of promoting the family's interests. Soame Jenyns, who held the other seat in the Commons for Cambridgeshire, produced verse tributes in honor of several members of Hardwicke's family. Horace Walpole called him "the poet laureate of the Yorkes."[94]

FAME

In a culture still imbued with notions of family honor and reputation, patrons would be prepared to offer their support not only for political services but for the kind of "fame" that could be conferred on them by a poet. "Rank may be conferred by princes," says Johnson's Rambler, "and wealth bequeathed by misers or by robbers; but the honours of a lasting name and the veneration of distant ages only the sons of learning have the power of be-stowing."[95] As if to illustrate the point, the *Gentleman's Magazine*, defending Bute's patronage of Johnson, observed that "as *Maecenas*, will be esteemed wherever the works of *Horace* or *Virgil* are known, so will the name of *Bute* be co-eval with that of *Johnson*."[96]

Johnson's essay suggests that patrons are primarily concerned for immortal fame, but in his day to enjoy fame in the eyes of contemporaries had a strong and perhaps increasing allure. And to be praised in print was increasingly the chief means by which one might attain fame in one's lifetime.[97] Johnson's *Lives of the Poets* in effect concedes that Somers, Dorset, Halifax, Granville, Lyttelton, and Dodington – each of whom had his own literary pretensions – all

---

[93]　See Owen, "Political Patronage," 375.
[94]　*Memoirs of the Reign of King George II*, II, 140.
[95]　*Rambler* 136, in *Works*, IV, 354–55.
[96]　*GM*, 33 (1763), 402. The writer goes on to worry whether "the name or glory of George the Third will be known a few generations hence, if his reign is altogether destitute of men of letters."
[97]　Leo Braudy has suggested that by 1700 "the book was defining itself as a prime new place of fame" (*The Frenzy of Renown*, 361).

probably owed what fame they enjoyed not to their own writings but to the writers who memorably praised them – Dryden, Pope, Swift, Thomson, Young, and Fielding. And the praise of an eminent poet counted far more than the praise of a mere hack. Or so Pope liked to claim: he dismissed the value of the ephemeral "Gazeteers" (writers for the pro-ministry *Gazette*) and noted that his own praise of Walpole did him more "credit" (both a moral and an economic term) than the forgotten "Panegyrics" of his paid flatterers.[98] To judge by Walpole's reputation – from Smollett's day to the present – Pope's implicit claim about the poet's power over reputation does not seem inflated. Ironically, however, what literary students remember of Walpole is his infamy, not Pope's praise of a genial host but his more potent satirical image of Walpole as corrupt politician and cynical manipulator of the press.

MAGNIFICENCE

The idea that winning and displaying "glory" might vindicate one's favored place in society is as old as Homer and as new as Pope's translation of the "Episode of Sarpedon." While the great men of Pope's day were not all expected to perform as military heroes, they were still respected – according to an equally old idea – for displaying what Pope called "Magnificence." His "Epistle to Bathurst" on the proper use of riches urges the addressee to teach by his example how "To balance Fortune by a just expence,/ Join with Oeconomy, Magnificence" (lines 223–24). The word "Magnificence" has for us degenerated into a general term denoting sumptuousness and grandeur in material things, but denoting little or nothing about the owner. By contrast, Pope and his contemporaries were inheritors of a long and still living tradition that regarded magnificent display as a sign of aristocratic virtue and power. By celebrating the "Magnificence" of his friends and patrons Bathurst and Burlington, Pope is bestowing on them the title and reputation that shows them to deserve the positions they hold as wealthy landed magnates.[99]

In his argument to the "Epistle to Burlington" Pope points to

---

[98] Pope's note to *Dunciad* (1743), II, line 314.
[99] Korshin notes a tendency in modern discussions of patronage to regard it as a "dwindling leftover of Renaissance magnificence in an age of increasing democracy" ("Types of Eighteenth-Century Literary Patronage," 454). But the evidence of Pope's poems suggests that the idea of magnificence was still very much alive in the eighteenth century.

Timon's villa as illustrating the principles of "the false Taste of
Magnificence," and discovers in Burlington himself "the proper
Objects of Magnificence." As scholars have shown, the term derives
ultimately from Aristotle.[100] What has not received enough emphasis
is that the term had a long and continuous history in Western
culture, and still had some resonance for writers and readers in
Pope's day as an attribute of the ideal patron, and as an implicit
explanation of what a patron acquired with the proper "use of
riches."

In the *Nicomachean Ethics* (bk. iv, ch. 2) magnificence is a central
virtue, denoting "fitting expenditure involving largeness of scale,"
fitting with respect both to the agent and the object. The magnificent
man spends large sums of money "tastefully," not "to show off his
wealth" but "for honour's sake." And yet by spending he also gains
in "greatness and prestige." Magnificence is rather a public than a
private virtue. It involves spending publicly, on "public objects," of
interest to "the whole city or the people of position in it." This may
include one's own private house, "for even a house is a sort of public
ornament," and will preferably include "those works that are
lasting."

For Ercole I, Duke of Ferrara in the fifteenth century, ruling a city
state required maintaining what Werner Gundersheimer called the
appropriate "public style" – manifested in the way he decorated the
city and the palace and the brilliant court he assembled, adorned
with scholars and artists. In such a world patronage of the arts had a
clear political value, enabling Ercole to cultivate "the image of
Augustan majesty" (p. 212), consolidating his own power and rivaling
the power of other city states.[101] From the vantage of another city
state, and only a generation later, Machiavelli's *The Prince*, addressed
to Lorenzo the "Magnificent," acknowledges that conventional
wisdom dictates that one can only "reach the highest positions
through being liberal or being thought so" – he tends to blur
Aristotle's distinction between "liberality" and "magnificence." To
"obtain the reputation of liberality among men," a prince "must not
omit every kind of sumptuous display." But this is a risky policy, for
it involves great expense and can lead to financial ruin. "It is
certainly necessary to be considered liberal" – but it is best to be

---

[100] Earl Wasserman, *Pope's Epistle to Bathurst*, 37–38; Miriam Leranbaum, *Alexander Pope's Opus Magnum*, 111–21.
[101] For an account of the "magnificence" of Ercole I, see Gundersheimer's *Ferrara*.

liberal with other people's money. Still, a prince must show himself to be a lover of merit, and can gain reputation through rewarding talent. He should "give preferment to the able, and honour to those who excel in every art" (ch. 21). In Machiavelli's hands magnificence becomes even more clearly a political virtue, a means whereby a great man can enhance his power.

But the ideal had not become a mere shell, and the tradition's origin in Aristotle was not forgotten. Spenser's *Faerie Queene*, dedicated pointedly to "the Most High, Mightie and *Magnificent* Empresse Renowned for Pietie, Vertue, and All Gratious Government," celebrates the virtues that become a gentleman, and above all magnificence: "in the person of Prince Arthure I sette forth magnificence in particular, which vertue for that (according to Aristotle and the rest) it is the perfection of all the rest, and conteineth in it them all" (*Letter to Raleigh*). And at the end of the seventeenth century Louis XIV put the principle into practice not only in his building projects at Versailles but also in his munificent patronage of painters, poets, and musicians. Dryden speaks of his "Magnificence and Encouragment ... in supporting painting and sculpture." His "magnificence envers les arts," says Voltaire, insures Louis' "immortalité."[102]

Even if English monarchs lacked the treasury to support a reputation for magnificence, the tradition was alive across the Channel, but more likely to be carried on by the great Whig magnates of the early eighteenth century who built and collected on a grand scale at Cannons, Stowe, Castle Howard, Houghton, and the other showplaces of the day. When Pope urges Bathurst to "Join with Oeconomy, Magnificence," he remembers Aristotelian moderation: "Oh teach us, BATHURST! yet unspoil'd by wealth! / That secret rare, between th'extremes to move / Of mad Good-nature, and of mean Self-love" ("To Bathurst," lines 226–28). "Mad Good-nature" manifests itself perhaps in lavish and senseless expenditure, "mean Self-love" in niggardliness, the excess and defect of magnificence that Pope had just identified in old Cotta and his son.[103] Burlington too is a hero of magnificence, and a reproach to the tasteless extravagance of "wealthy fools" like Virro and Sir Visto, who prove "That never

[102] From *Lettres sur les Anglais* (Cambridge: Cambridge University Press, 1931), 98. In his English version Voltaire translates "magnificence" as "Munificence" (*Letters concerning the English Nation*, 112).
[103] *Nicomachean Ethics*, IV, 2, on vulgarity and niggardliness.

Coxcomb reach'd Magnificence" ("To Burlington," line 22), or Timon, a clear instance of Aristotelian vulgarity (Pope calls it "the false Taste of Magnificence"). At the close of the epistle Pope turns from Burlington's own houses to his wider concern for establishing Palladian models and for the state of England's highways and bridges. His note (to line 195) indicates that "The poet after having touched upon the proper objects of Magnificence and Expence, in the private works of great men, comes to those great and public works which become a Prince." Just as Aristotle had emphasized that magnificence is most truly displayed in "public objects," so Pope turns from private to public in a passage of pointed political significance.

> You too proceed! make falling Arts your care,
> Erect new wonders, and the old repair,
> Jones and Palladio to themselves restore,
> And be whate'er Vitrivius was before:
> Till Kings call forth th'Ideas of your mind,
> Proud to accomplish what such hands design'd,
> Bid Harbors open, public Ways extend,
> Bid Temples, worthier of the God, ascend ...
> These Honours, Peace to happy Britain brings,
> These are Imperial Works, and worthy Kings.
>
> ("To Burlington," lines 191–204)

Pope's imperatives (the repeated "Bid") float ambiguously between Burlington and the king, hinting that Burlington could if he chose play a royal part. Just as such "Imperial Works" are "worthy" of kings, so perhaps Burlington himself is more "worthy" to be king than the reigning monarch through whose neglect, Pope's footnote implies, churches had been allowed to fall. But it is ultimately Pope who "bids" Burlington as patron to embrace the imperial responsibilities of magnificence.

Pope is perhaps the last writer in the century to articulate clearly the old idea that magnificence is both the great patron's responsibility and reward.[104] The fact that a vast house like Walpole's Houghton was given ironic praise for the "Magnificence of the *House, Gardens* and *Stables*," and (in ludicrous parody) for a "huge and most sumptuous LANTHORN," suggests that the ideal of magnifi-

---

[104] Or to couch his praise of writers in such terms. Homer, Pope says, "scatters with a generous Profusion, *Virgil* bestows with a careful Magnificence" (Preface to the *Iliad*, in *Prose Works*, ed. Ault, 237). "Generous," "bestows," and "Magnificence" all suggest that Pope implicitly thinks of the great writer as a kind of patron. For more, see below, ch. 6.

cence was being perverted by patrons without taste.[105] Although
the term for some became associated with vulgar display,[106] and for
others became a general term for grandeur of appearance,[107] some
uses show that its older and more precise meaning persisted.
Horace Walpole thought Castle Howard "the grandest scene of real
magnificence I ever saw."[108] Writing to Algarotti, who was then
Chamberlain to Frederick the Great, Gray commended his efforts
to reunite the several arts, which, if "regulated by Taste, &
supported by magnificence & power, might form the noblest scene,
and bestow the sublimest pleasure, that the imagination can
conceive."[109] Johnson once wrote that "Magnificence cannot be
cheap, for what is cheap cannot be magnificent."[110] He later
recalled that Dryden, upon dedicating his *Fables* to the Duke of
Ormonde, received £500 from the Duchess, "a present," says
Johnson, "not unsuitable to the magnificence of that splendid
family."[111]

THE CONTROL OF CULTURE

In the patronage economy giving is itself often a means of getting, or
of affirming one's rightful privileges and possessions. For an aristocratic patron to give his opinion in favor of a play – especially if the
Town follows suit – is to confirm aristocratic authority over "the

[105] See Fielding's "The Norfolk Lantern," first printed in the Opposition journal *The Craftsman* in 1728 and repr. in *New Essays by Henry Fielding*, ed. Martin Battestin, 510–11. The Earl of Oxford thought Houghton "neither magnificent nor beautiful, there is a very great expense without either judgment or taste." Quoted in Lees-Milne, *Earls of Creation*, 192.

[106] See Thomas Warton, "tasteless splendour and magnificence" ("The Pleasures of Melancholy" [1747], line 95). Cf. Richard Savage, "Of Public Spirit," contrasting an artificial cascade at a nobleman's park with the useful work of draining fens: "Let those [works] of Luxury, with These to vie,/ Magnificently useless strike the Eye" (*Poetical Works*, 224). But Aaron Hill, commenting on Savage's poem, noted the public's interest in "those ideas of *public spirit*, and *magnificent purposes*" (*ibid.*, 219, quoting from Hill's *Works*, I, 324).

[107] Pope seems to use "splendour" as a near-synonym of magnificence. See *Moral Essays*, III, line 225, IV, line 180. Thomson in the 1726 Preface to "Winter" speaks of the "magnificence" of the works of nature, and Mary Wollstonecraft in *Mary: A Fiction* (1788) of the "magnificent objects of nature." Johnson defines "magnificence" as "grandeur of appearance; splendour," suggesting that the old meaning was disappearing.

[108] L. Whistler, *Sir John Vanbrugh, Architect and Dramatist*, 57. Bubb Dodington is described in Walpole's *Catalogue of Royal and Noble Authors* as "generous, magnificent, and convivial" (IV, 250).

[109] Gray, *Correspondence*, II, 810.

[110] Preface to John Gwynn, *Thoughts on the Coronation* (1761), attributed to Johnson by Arthur Sherbo in "Some Observations on Johnson's Prefaces and Dedications," 128.

[111] *Lives of the Poets*, I, 408.

taste of the Town."[112] By granting "protection" to poetry, says
Congreve, patrons remind the world that it is their "Prerogative
alone to give it Protection."[113] To exercise authority is a way of
claiming it as one's own. For Chesterfield to delegate authority, by
the same token, affirms his power to do just that. In the act of
offering his "vote" to Johnson, he asserts his own "rights and
privileges":

I hereby declare, that I make a total surrender of all my rights and
privileges in the English language as a free-born British subject, to the said
Mr. Johnson, during the term of his dictatorship.

Readers of *The World* in 1754 no doubt found it amusing to see an
earl pretend to surrender all his "rights and privileges" to an
unknown author named "Mr. Johnson," but probably did not fail to
notice that, in this imagined electoral scene, Chesterfield is the only
elector, and that Johnson's "dictatorship" is for a limited "term."
Chesterfield himself seems to underline that point by declaring that
he will consider Johnson to be as "infallible" as a Roman pope
"while in the chair" – but no longer.

By dispensing favors the patronage class also fulfilled its traditional
responsibility for promoting the honor of the nation by promoting
culture. This is Dennis' point in his dedication of *The Advancement and
Reformation of Modern Poetry* (1701) to the Earl of Mulgrave: "you are an
Encourager of Arts, and a great Statesman, who knows, that the bare
Endeavour to advance an Art among us, is an Effort to augment the
Learning, and consequently the Reputation, and consequently the
Power, of a great People."[114] It is "the Duty of the *Great*, to draw up
Merit, out of Obscurity," Aaron Hill wrote in 1724, and it is also in
"a State's true Interest," because it will "do Honour to our
Nation."[115] Such claims from supplicating writers are obviously self-
serving, but they echo traditional commonplaces and perhaps found
a more receptive ear because of an increasing official self-conscious-
ness about the importance of building a distinctively British culture,
inheritor of ancient traditions but independent of the Continent (and
especially of France).[116] Shaftesbury spoke for many in hoping that

---

[112] Dennis, *Critical Works*, II, 277.
[113] *Complete Plays*, 392.
[114] *Critical Works*, I, 207. From his *Reflections on an Essay on Criticism*, cf. "Whenever we have a
Prince and Ministers, who truly understand either their own Interest, or that of the
Publick, Arts and Learning will be then encourag'd" (I, 412).
[115] *The Plain Dealer*, No. 16 (May 15, 1724).
[116] On this theme, see Howard Weinbrot's *Britannia's Issue*.

Britain (then at war to challenge France's military and commercial power) might become "the Principal Seat of Arts."[117] Aaron Hill urged the "Great Spirits of Great Britain" to look upon patronage as a "noble (and indeed a *National*) Part, of your Discharge of the Publick Trust."[118] Johnson offered his *Dictionary*, he says in the Preface, to "enhance the honour of my country, that we may no longer yield the palm of philology without a contest, to the nations of the continent."[119] When James Ralph, Johnson, and Isaac D'Israeli all claimed that the nation's "glory" depends largely on its authors, they were endorsing a political-cultural commonplace (with considerable durability) that implicitly imposed a responsibility on those in power, and created an opportunity for the powerful to bask in reflected glory.[120]

It often appears, however, that supplicating poets had to remind patrons of their national responsibility. This is frequently the subtext of Dryden's dedications and critical prefaces.[121] To sharpen the sense of obligation Dryden unfavorably compares support for the arts in England with the situation in France, where Louis is "the Patron of all Arts" who distributes his "Bounty" to "Men of Learning and Wit."[122] (Louis' beneficence and the niggardliness or mis-spending of English monarchs is something of a cliché).[123] Crabbe attempted without initial success to remind Lord Thurlow that the encouragement of literature had once been considered part of the Lord Chancellor's duty.[124] But Thurlow eventually responded with a small gift. Some patrons apparently sensed that they were playing a public role, or felt it appropriate to say so. Johnson reported that "the nation" – by which he meant those relatively few powerful men who constituted the *political nation* – "considered its honour as interested in [the publication of Dryden's Virgil.]"[125] And

---

[117] "Letter Concerning Design" (1712), in *Characteristicks*, III, 271.
[118] *Advice to the Poets. A Poem* (1731), "Epistle Dedicatory," ix.
[119] Cf. also a 1761 letter on behalf of Johnson to Bute. See below, p. 66.
[120] "If Heroes and Patriots constitute the first Column of national Glory, Authors of Genius constitute the second" (Ralph, *Case of Authors*, 3); "the chief glory of every people arises from its authours" (Johnson, *Dictionary*, I, xii); "It is a glorious succession of AUTHORS ... which has enabled our nation to arbitrate among the nations of Europe" (D'Israeli, *An Essay on the Manner and Genius of the Literary Character*, II, 280).
[121] See ch. 4, below.
[122] *Works*, IV, 12–13.
[123] Pope invokes it in 1743 (*Dunciad* II, 314n) as does Goldsmith in 1759 (*Enquiry*, ch. 8). But Dennis dissents (*Critical Works*, I, 412).
[124] In a poem now lost. See George Crabbe, *The Complete Poetical Works*, I, 673.
[125] *Lives*, I, 448.

the Duke of Wharton offered Young an annuity of £100 in recognition, he said, that "the public good is advanced by the encouragement of learning and the polite arts."[126]

Supporting the arts enabled the patronage class to say that it was advancing the nation's interests. It also enabled the members of the class to advance their own narrower interests. By dispensing bounty the patron (at least in theory) preserved his *own* "honour."[127] And "honour" is after all one of the key distinctions between a peer and a commoner.[128] Louis XIV gains "honour" by granting "annual Pensions to learned men all over Europe."[129] In addressing the *Plan* of the *Dictionary* to Chesterfield in 1747 Johnson notes that once "princes and statesmen thought it part of their honour to promote the improvement of their native tongues." He clearly hopes that Chesterfield – as an earl and as Secretary of State – will continue to think it part of *his* honor to promote the *Dictionary*. Conferring gifts not only maintains and confirms the status of a noble patron; it is also a way for newly created peers to create status distinctions and thus validate their new rank. This may help account for the prominent display of patronal activity by such new peers as Somers, Oxford, Halifax, Chandos, Dodington, and Thurlow.

But "honour" is only part of the patron's concern. Dispensing favors also confirms the patron's almost proprietary interest in culture. Distributions to dramatists, musicians, and painters resulted of course in private performances and in collections of pictures, books, and manuscripts. But more generally they also tended to confirm the control of culture – what gets supported, what even counts as "culture" – by a class of hereditary aristocrats. Restoration heroic plays, Italian opera, Palladian architecture, and landscape gardening – each of them quite expensive undertakings – became part of English high culture in the minds of contemporaries and of later scholars largely because they were promoted by avid patrons. The world of "popular culture," which Pat Rogers, Ronald Paulson, and others have begun to document and reconstruct, remained largely beneath official notice. Control of high

---

[126] Harold Forster, *Edward Young*, 61.

[127] Aaron Hill claims that a patron's act of bounty "draws that Honour on his own Name, which he wou'd bestow upon another's; and becomes *Himself*, the Reader's idol, while he is pointing him where to Worship!" (*The Plain Dealer*, No. 16, May 15, 1724).

[128] To be "honourable" means to be "of distinguished rank" (*OED*, 2). Cf. the honorific prefix, "The Right Honorable ..."

[129] Pope's footnote to *Dunciad* II, 314.

culture is publicly declared in the published dedications and the printed subscription lists, common features of major eighteenth-century bookselling ventures. It is manifested in the court's much-observed attendance at the Restoration playhouse, and in the custom – lasting until 1762 – whereby noblemen were permitted to sit on the stage during the performance of plays.[130] It is announced by the patron's very country seat, to which authors are invited, where concerts are performed, and pictures displayed. (The reading public, while largely excluded, except as tourists, could still gaze on engraved drawings of houses like Cannons and Stowe.) An architectural historian calls these country houses – some 150 were built during the period 1710–40 – "a visible witness of surplus, and thus of influence."[131]

Control of culture has an analogue in the control of a society's wealth. Strategic distributions of small portions of their symbolic and material capital to good works of various kinds – like Mrs. Montagu's famous annual dinner for chimney sweeps – would tend to justify the inequities of wealth, rank, and power. Patronage of working-class poets in the mid-eighteenth century, so it has recently been argued, by providing "certain ameliorations and amenities," served to reconcile the poets to their "'rightful place'."[132] Or just keep them in their place. After Mrs. Montagu made James Woodhouse her bailiff and steward, he was no longer invited to dine at her table, but had to stand in attendance.[133] Johnson thought that such patrons looked on their protégés as "mirrours of their own superiority" (*Life of Johnson*, vol. II, p. 127), but conceded that inequities in matters of wealth and status were both inevitable and proper: those who sought to improve their condition by accepting "favour" implicitly acknowledged the benefactor's "superiority." Such beneficence in effect served the interests of the benefactor. As Swift once observed, "if the Poor found the Rich disposed to supply their Wants ... or if the Weak might always find Protection from the Mighty, they could

---

[130] The custom ceased only when legislation forbidding it was passed and Garrick enlarged the seating capacity of the pit. See G. W. Stone, *The London Stage, 1747–1776*, xxxi–xxxii.

[131] Sir John Summerson, "The Classical Country House in 18th-Century England," 544. Cf. Carole Fabricant's argument that permitting eighteenth-century tourists to view the great houses during specified hours "reinforced" the "hegemony" of "the ruling classes ... by enlisting the complicity of the ruled in the fiction of their *in*clusion in an increasingly *ex*clusionary society" ("The Literature of Domestic Tourism," 257).

[132] Donna Landry, "The Resignation of Mary Collier," 101. See also Betty Rizzo, "The Patron as Poet-Maker," 241–66.

[133] See Katherine Hornbeck, "New Light on Mrs. Montagu," 355.

none of them with the least Pretence of Justice lament their own Condition."[134]

But if some working-class poets like Mary Collier were resigned to their lot, and willing to defer to the superiority of their patrons, there were many other writers – from Dryden to Johnson to James Woodhouse – living and writing under the system of patronage who were not content with their "condition of subservience." The "economy" I have been describing, in which both parties stood to gain, was never the static system that I have for the moment assumed. It was constantly in flux, as authors resisted or challenged the claims of patrons, and patrons reaffirmed their traditional privileges. But before I turn to discussions of the ways in which individual writers worked within the system, accepting patronage but also resisting its claims, I take up a topic closely associated with the cultural economics of patronage, its role in the theatre of partisan politics.

[134] Johnson, *Rambler* 104; Swift, *Prose Works*, IX, 147.

CHAPTER 3

The politics of patronage

Pope and Swift regularly complained that Walpole disregarded the best authors of the day, and apparently cared little or nothing for poetry: he only paid for what Swift ironically called "solid Work" – i.e., for writing that advanced his political program.[1] Walpole had, so they claimed, corrupted the process of patronage by politicizing it. Similar complaints were made against Bute by the anti-ministerial writers in the 1760s at a time of equally intense partisan feeling. Authorial complaints were in turn taken up by sympathetic nineteenth-century biographers like Forster, who lamented that fine writers like Goldsmith were ignored while shameless but serviceable hacks were rewarded, and by literary historians like Collins who distinguished between the "less honourable" pensions paid to purely "political" writers, and the "honourable" pension awarded to Johnson.[2] Pope's mid-twentieth century critics and biographers have likewise tended to adopt rather uncritically his view of Walpole's "stable" of "hacks," "hirelings" and "creatures."

But why should we assume that Pope was right, when his views are clearly not those of a disinterested observer? It is not mere coincidence that complaints about the abuse of patronage by government ministers tend to come from the political opposition. Reconstructing the context of the 1760s confirms that Bute's practice was in fact not significantly different from that of Walpole. Indeed, Walpole was not the exception but the rule. He differed from those ministers who preceded and followed him primarily in that he made more efficient use of techniques that they too practiced. Literary patronage throughout the eighteenth century, I would argue, was *always* political.

Furthermore, to look closely at the major patrons of the period is

---

[1]   "A Libel on Dr. Delany and a Certain Great Lord," (1730), line 90 (*Poems*).
[2]   *Authorship in the Days of Johnson*, 199, 202.

to discover that virtually all of them had powerful political interests, and that it is very difficult for us to separate their "political" activities from their work as "patrons" of literature, just as they too would have found it difficult to separate "politics" from "literature." By the same token, the easy distinction we once made between "real" writers and merely "political" writers seems increasingly untenable. Most of the canonical writers of the century – Dryden, Swift, Defoe, Pope, Thomson, Fielding, Johnson, Smollett, Gibbon – at some point wrote for political paymasters, or at least in direct support of partisan political causes. Other writers who occupy a lower rank in the canon – Churchill, Wilkes, "Junius" – were in their own day known primarily for their partisan political writing. And a number of other writers whom we once dismissed as "hacks" – James Ralph, Arthur Murphy, Thomas Birch, David Mallet, John Shebbeare – were regarded by their contemporaries (setting aside their polemical adversaries) as men of literary ability, and were not so easily dismissed from the republic of letters. In such circumstances, it is unhistorical, and somewhat quixotic, for us to try to determine that a pension from the government was or was not granted for "political" reasons.

The great age of patronage in England, so it has been suggested since the days of Goldsmith, was the period from the Revolution in 1688 until the death of Queen Anne in 1714. Those were the days, wrote Goldsmith, "when the great Somers was at the helm,"[3] and distributed largesse to Addison, Steele, Garth, and Swift – among many others. He was not the only great patron active in those years. The Earl of Dorset and Charles Montagu, Baron Halifax (and later Earl Halifax) were equally eminent; their reputations as patrons lasted throughout the century.[4] It is in this period too that Robert Harley cultivated Defoe, Swift, Pope, and the Scriblerians. There is no reason to doubt that each of these famous patrons had a genuine interest in literature. Somers, Dorset, and Halifax were themselves writers.[5] Somers also had a large book collection, and Harley laid

---

[3] *Enquiry into Polite Learning*, in *Collected Works*, I, 310–11. John Somers, later Baron Somers, rose to be Lord Chancellor under William, and attracted a reputation as a great patron of literature in the 1690s. In 1752 Orrery, in his *Life of Swift*, called Somers "the general patron of the literati" (p. 93).

[4] Johnson called Dorset "the universal patron ... celebrated for his patronage of genius" (*Lives of the Poets*, II, 181), and Halifax "the general patron," who scattered his bounty on "almost all" the poets of the day (*ibid.*, 47).

[5] Although Somers no longer has a literary reputation, he was still considered as a writer in James Ralph's 1758 *Case of Authors*. He had translated Ovid, Plutarch, and Demosthenes for

the foundation for what would be the great Harley Library. It has often been implied that, compared to later patrons, their motives in supporting contemporary writers were somehow purer. But a careful consideration suggests that their patronage of letters was undertaken for political reasons, with the expectation of political benefits.

It is surely not coincidental that the great patrons in Somers' day were well-connected court Whigs, and that they were connected to each other in a political as well as a patronage network. Because Somers was at the head of the government, he was the leading patron; it appears that most of the patronage he dispensed was in fact royal bounty. The elderly Dorset, Dryden's patron, was a senior statesman, serving as Lord Chamberlain (in which capacity he "had it in his Power to recommend Men of Desert to the Royal Favour"[6]), and as a member of the regency commission in 1698. Halifax, who began his career as a client of Dorset, rose rapidly to become a member of the governing Junto, and in 1697 became First Commissioner of the Treasury and Chancellor of the Exchequer. The famous Kit-cat Club, in which writers mixed freely with the leading Whigs of the day, was (whatever its beginnings in "free and chearful Conversation"[7]) not simply a literary club in which political interests were left at the door. Somers' biographer calls the Club "the Whig Party in its social aspect."[8] Besides Somers, its members included four men who later led Whig ministries (Stanhope, Walpole, Pulteney, and Pelham). Tonson, the organizer, was a key figure not simply in his role as leading bookseller, but as the holder of important government printing contracts. He was in a good position to identify talent both for his own use and for that of the ministers, and to match Whig patrons and suitable clients.[9]

several of Tonson's collections. For details, see Robert M. Adams, "In Search of Baron Somers," 195.

[6] Halifax, *Poetical Works*, 17.

[7] Oldmixon claimed that the Club began before 1688 when Tonson and Somers used to meet at a tavern to "unbend themselves after Business, and have a little free and cheerful Conversation in those dangerous Times." *History of England*, 479. Foss (*Age of Patronage*, 152) notes of the various clubs of the day that "their patronage was never disinterested, for no one could forget their political bias."

[8] William Sachse, *Lord Somers*, 190. A fuller treatment of Somers as patron is found in Adams, "In Search of Baron Somers."

[9] Cf. the pro-ministry "Society," organized by Bolingbroke in 1711, ostensibly, as Swift claimed, "to advance conversation and friendship, and to reward deserving persons with our interest and recommendation" (*Journal to Stella*, 294), but whose real purpose, as Ehrenpreis notes (*Swift*, II, 503), was "to direct patronage toward writers who had served their cause." Swift, Arbuthnot, and Prior were members, along with a number of Tory ministers and lords.

The writers who received the support of Somers, Dorset, and Halifax were not simply men of merit, but men who were able and willing to support the Whig cause.[10] One of Addison's first poems was addressed "to his Majesty" and contained an extended compliment to Somers. In 1697 he addressed a poem in praise of the Peace of Ryswick to Halifax. And in 1699 Addison, having demonstrated his literary and political credentials, was given £200 of government money to go on a sort of extended travelling fellowship. (Out of it came, among other things, his *Remarks on Several Parts of Italy*, dedicated to Somers.) Addison repaid the investment. After his return to England he celebrated the victorious *Campaign* of the Whig hero Marlborough (1705). He was subsequently made an under-secretary of state in 1706, and later, as author of *The Free-Holder* (1715–16), became a valuable defender of government policy at the time of the Jacobite rebellion, rising through several offices ultimately to be Secretary of State in 1717.[11] When he resigned the office he was pensioned with £1500 a year. It was clear to eighteenth-century observers that Addison's was a political appointment. James Ralph, looking back in 1758, noted that Addison's "party-Services contributed more to [his advancement] than all his laudable Efforts to refine our Manners and perfect our Taste."[12] Steele, with his own political ambitions, made the same point more delicately. In dedicating volume IV of *The Tatler* to Halifax, he praised his patron's eye for "Business": "It is to you we owe, that the Man of Wit has turned himself to be a Man of Business ... Experience has shown, that Men of Letters are not only qualify'd with a greater Capacity, but also a greater Integrity in the Dispatch of Business."[13] Steele was offering a double compliment. Halifax himself, who first entered public life as a wit, went on to prove his usefulness as a "Man of Business." His ridicule of Dryden's pro-Catholic *Hind and the Panther* got him presented to King William.[14] He went into Parliament, so reports his memoirist, and soon

[10] Even Beljame concedes that patronage in Queen Anne's days was not disinterested. Writers, he said, "owed their new position in society solely to their political activity" (*Men of Letters*, 330).

[11] Johnson reports that (ironically enough) Addison in the House of Commons "could not speak and was therefore useless to the defence of the government" (*Lives of the Poets*, II, 111).

[12] *Case of Authors*, 34. For Ralph, Addison is an example of an author who wrote "for a Faction" (pp. 29–31).

[13] *The Tatler*, I, 13.

[14] For the famous story, see Johnson's "Life of Halifax." The story had earlier appeared in the *Memoirs of Halifax* (1715), 17.

revealed "such an Address in the Arts of Speaking, and Perspicuity of Judgment" as to compel even his opponents to admire his abilities.[15]

Since this testimony about the political usefulness of writers comes not from enemies but from friends, we should assign it greater weight. It is understood by Steele and Ralph that patronage goes not simply as a reward for "merit," but in order to encourage an alliance between "Wit" and "Business." Swift's defense of the impeached Whig lords – including Somers and Halifax – in his *Contests and Dissensions* (1701) brought him hopes and promises of preferment. To be sure, Somers probably admired Swift's wit. But he always kept political considerations in mind, as he did when he granted Congreve a freehold property: the property lay in a borough that Somers sought to control, and as freeholder Congreve was an elector on whom the Chancellor could count in an upcoming election.[16]

There are a few apparent exceptions to the rule that patronage, even in the glory days of Somers, was politically oriented and motivated, but in most cases they too can be shown to have a political connection. Somers and Halifax both took a keen interest in Tonson's lavish 1688 folio edition of Milton's *Paradise Lost*, in large part because they probably sensed that Milton might be claimed as a kind of "Whig poet" – and indeed he was commonly regarded in the eighteenth century as a poet who (had he lived on) would have endorsed the Revolution.[17] Tonson himself noted that it was Somers' "Opinion and Encouragement" which "occasion'd the first appearing of [*Paradise Lost*] in the *Folio* Edition."[18] Somers' support of works of British history also had a political dimension, because of Whig interest in fostering the idea of the "ancient constitution."[19] He encouraged the historian Thomas Madox, whose *Formulare Anglicanum, or a Collection of Ancient Charters and Instruments* appeared in

---

[15] *Ibid.*, 28.

[16] "Several of his Lordship's Friends in Town, became Freeholders in his Manor, as Mr. Congreve, Mr. Tonson, and others to strengthen that Interest against the Riotous Expenses, and Factious Cabals of his numberous Opponents" (Sachse, *Lord Somers*, 138, quoting the *Memoirs of Somers*). Somers' candidate, Stephen Harvey, was himself a minor poet (R. M. Adams, "In Search of Baron Somers," 174).

[17] See for example Newton's 1748 edition of *Paradise Lost*. For a discussion of Milton as Whiggish political hero, see Griffin, *Regaining Paradise*, 11–21.

[18] From Tonson's dedication to his 1711 pocket edition of *Paradise Lost*.

[19] Steele notes Somers' "most exact Knowledge of our Constitution" (dedication of volume 1 of the collected *Spectator* papers in 1712).

1702,[20] and (with Halifax) the collection of British "leagues, treaties, alliances, capitulations, and confederacies" published by Rymer under the title of *Foedera* (1704). Both Rymer and Madox served Whig governments as Historiographer Royal.[21] In other instances it was writers with Whiggish sympathies who dedicated their works to Somers – the young Swift's *Tale of a Tub* in 1704,[22] John Philips' *Vision of ... Ramillies* (1706), Shaftesbury's *Characteristics* (1711), Addison's and Steele's collected *Spectator*, volume 1 (1712), and John Hughes' 1715 edition of the *Works of Spenser*.[23] Garth's *Dispensary* (1699) closed with a celebratory address to Somers under the transparent name of "matchless *Atticus*" – "Arts he supports, and Learning is his Care."[24]

In one case of patronage Somers seems to have ignored politics. He offered financial support to Pierre Bayle for his *Dictionnaire Historique et Critique* (1697), but Bayle declined since Somers' master, King William, had (in his capacity as Statholder in Holland) some years earlier deprived Bayle of his chair at the University of Rotterdam and his pension.[25] Sachse sees here "generosity without regard for political implications or consequences" (*Lord Somers*, p. 201), but it seems likely that Somers would have cleared the offer with William, who may have seen an opportunity to establish a connection with an anti-absolutist French writer at a time when he could not officially support him. Something similar may have gone on in 1688, when the Catholic and Jacobite Dryden lost his position as Poet Laureate and Historiographer Royal. Dorset, his old patron, then Lord Chamberlain (and responsible for replacing Dryden with the pro-Whig Shadwell), is said to have provided Dryden with an allowance equal to his former salary.[26] Although this piece of patronage is often cited as generous and disinterested support of

---

20 Dedicated to Somers, as a "great Lover of Ancient Monuments," and whose "Approbation was the Principal Encouragement I had in the Beginning and Progress of this Undertaking" (Sachse, *Lord Somers*, 202). Other works on British history dedicated to Somers include Edmund Gibson's edition of Camden's *Britannia* (1695), John Cary's *Vindication of the Parliament of England* (1698), and Guy Miège's *New State of England* (3rd ed., 1679).

21 Rymer was appointed in 1693 and Madox in 1714.

22 See below, pp. 101–02.

23 Philips had also celebrated the Whig victory at Blenheim (1706). Hughes had earlier praised William in *The Triumph of Peace* (1698) and *The House of Nassau* (1702).

24 *The Dispensary*, 6th ed. (London, 1706), 117–18.

25 For the story, see the *Memoirs of the Life of John Lord Somers*, 48, and *Biographia Britannica* (London, 1763), VI: 1, 3749.

26 The story, which appears in Johnson's "Life of Dryden", originated with Prior in 1709. Dryden's recent biographers, Ward and Winn, find no other corroborative evidence.

literature,[27] it again seems likely that William must have known and approved the arrangement, and that Dorset was not acting as a "nonpartisan patron."[28] It would have been politically useful to the king and ministry to have the country's greatest poet beholden to the Lord Chamberlain. In the 1690s Dryden's Jacobitism – emphasized by many recent commentators – was kept fairly covert; it may have provided some gratification to his fellow sufferers, but it would not have been perceived as a political threat. Dryden remained in contact with Dorset, still hoping as late as 1699 that he might get a pension, indicating that he was prepared to "forbear Satire [on] the present Government."[29]

WALPOLE AS PATRON

Under the first two Georges, so the received account goes, literary patronage was completely subordinated to the political aims of Walpole's ministries. It used to be said that the Hanoverian court had no interest in literature or the arts, though that notion (ultimately derived from their political opponents) has been challenged.[30] Walpole himself is said to have had only a pragmatic or instrumental interest. How could a writer help him? "He looked upon writing to be a mechanical kind of business, and he took up the first pen that he could find in public offices, or whom he could oblige by public liberality ... He looked upon political writing as a kind of currency that would pass by its nominal value [i.e., its paraphrasable content], let its intrinsic worth be ever so inconsiderable."[31] It is not necessary to belabor the point that Walpole used the Civil List and his Secret Service funds to support writers who would support him most publicly and effectively. Large sums of money went to political journalists, including most spectacularly William Arnall, said to have

---

27 Dryden himself thanked Dorset for "laying aside all the Considerations of Factions and Parties, to do an Action of pure disinteress'd Charity" (*Works*, IV, 23).

28 Winn's term (*John Dryden*, 435).

29 Charles Ward, *Letters of John Dryden* (Durham, NC: Duke University Press, 1942), 123.

30 George II, says Chesterfield (not a disinterested witness) had "a contempt for the *belles lettres*, which he called trifling." The Hanoverians' interest in Handel's music and painting is well established. (Korshin calls George II "a most astute collector of paintings," "Types," 104). But they also showed some interest in literature. Queen Caroline offered patronage to men of learning and to poets (including Richard Savage, see below). George II "had a library large enough to form the nucleus of the British Museum" (Paul Korshin, in a review of Foss in *Eighteenth-Century Studies*, 7 [1973], 104).

31 Matthew Tindal, in Chesterfield's *Characters*, 35.

received £11,000 over three years, William Guthrie, and Matthew Concanen.[32] It is less often remembered that Walpole threw his support to writers who still have a literary reputation. Young got a pension of £200 a year in 1726, and Pope received a present of £200 for his *Odyssey* in 1725. Walpole funneled money to Thomson, Savage, Fielding, and Voltaire.[33] Young, Fielding, and Thomson provided public praise, and Walpole dined with Pope, probably in part because he found it useful to keep the country's greatest poet from listening only to his Tory friends.

Pope's compliment about Walpole "in his happier hour/ Of Social Pleasure" ("Epilogue to the Satires," Dial. 1, lines 29–30) suggests a side of the Lord Treasurer that does not often receive attention, and hints that his attitude toward poetry may not have simply been pragmatic, not to say utilitarian. One of the poets whom Walpole patronized can have done him little good in the political realm. Joseph Mitchell was a very minor poet who joined the ranks of those in the 1720s (including Young and Thomson) who hoped that the ministry might smile. Mitchell apparently resolved not to make the conventional approach – via high compliment – but to appeal to Walpole's sense of humor. His 1725 poem, frankly entitled *The Sinecure*, recalls that in the days of Charles II, the Chevalier de St. Evremond was made Governor of Duck Island, in St. James's Park, and given a pension. Mitchell's poem is designed as, and subtitled, "A Poetical Petition to the Right Honourable Robert Walpole, Esq; for the Government of Duck-Island, in St. James's Park."

> I, not for Lordly Post, or Pension, plead –
> (Sure, Heav'n will my reduc'd Desires succeed!)
> St. James's *Wilderness*, the *Park*'s fair *Isle*,
> Would crown my Wish, and Care's long hand beguile.
> On that delightful, and sequester'd, Spot,
> Fitted for me, as *Zoar* was for LOT!
> I'd full Content and Satisfaction find,
> And cultivate the Garden of my Mind.
> Like good St. EVREMONT, I'd grow a *Sage*,
> And War with Nonsense, Vice, and Folly, wage.   (p. 4)

---

[32] Support also went to James Pitt, James Ralph, Ralph Freeman (a.k.a. Ralph Courteville). See Laurence Hanson, *Government and the Press, 1695–1763*, 112–20.

[33] As an anonymous correspondent to the *Grub Street Journal*, No. 248 (September 26, 1734) pointed out, Walpole may have smiled on "Concanen, Cibber, Mitchell, Ralph," but also poured his "friendly care" on "Pope, Young, Welsted, Thompson, Fielding, [Philip] Frowde." Walpole's name appears on sixty-four subscription lists during the period 1700–50 (W. A. Speck, "Politicians, Peers, and Publication by Subscription 1700–1750," 52).

Mitchell not only facetiously renews St. Evremond's appeal, but plays wittily with the familiar poetical petitions of the day (like Pomfret's very popular "The Choice") for a "retreat" to a simple life of contented retirement. Mitchell went on to beg a similar boon in *The Equivalent: A Second Poetical Petition to the Right Honourable Robert Walpole Esq; for the Dignity of Poet-Laureat, in Scotland* (1725) – similar because in the days before Ramsay and Burns dour Scotland was by no means associated with the graces of poetry (Mitchell was himself a Scot, though not a dour one). In the following year appeared *The Promotion, and the Alternative,* in which Mitchell asks first for "the Office and Importance of Secretary of State for Scotland," and next for "the Power and Glory of a Royal COMMISSION, to superintend the next Publick LOTTERY, or the next General Assembly of the KIRK." The subtitles were enough to let Walpole know that the poems were facetious (*The Alternative* is "An Anacreontic Petition," suggesting that the tone is light and the context bibulous). It is as if Mitchell set out to do little more than make Walpole laugh. It would appear that he succeeded, for Mitchell continued annually addressing his patron until as late as 1735, when he produced *A Familiar Epistle to the Right Honourable Sir Robert Walpole; Concerning Poets, Poverty, Promises, Places, &c.*:

> But you, SIR, have been sung by me
> From Seventeen Hundred Twenty Three,
> Down to this Day, in various Strain,
> At great Expence of Time and Brain.
> Yet, tho' at sundry Times befriended,
> No Steps of Honour I've ascended;
> Nor find my Circumstances mended! (p. 7)

Mitchell had apparently received some £500 over the years – perhaps doled out in annual presents of £50 – and now presumed (facetiously) to ask for a place. Walpole's patronage of Mitchell, which brought him no honor, almost suggests that he looked on "his poet" (so Mitchell described himself) as the sort of licensed fool that once attended a Renaissance court. For other kinds of literary services, including a published defense of his use of places and pensions, Walpole looked elsewhere.[34]

---

[34] See Thomas Horne, "Politics in a Corrupt Society," 601–14. Arnall argued that the ministry needed to use places and pensions – for which it was roundly criticized by the Country gentlemen – to redress the imbalance of power (power that tended to follow land, and thus to make the Commons over-strong).

Walpole's political allies also looked on literary patronage as a means of advancing the cause of the court party. Lady Mary Wortley Montagu was a political friend of Walpole's and a cousin of Henry Fielding, who looked to her for support for his first play, *Love in Several Masques* (1728). George Bubb Dodington, who followed Walpole for fifteen years before going into Opposition in the late 1730s, cultivated a stable of writers in the 1720s, including Young, Thomson, Fielding, James Hammond, Leonard Welsted, and James Ralph. His motives perhaps included the monstrous vanity with which Pope and others charged him, but he seems to have given some thought to the political uses of patronage, as evidenced by his poetical *Epistle to Sir Robert Walpole*. One of the returns of "bounty," he notes in the poem, is of course "gratitude." But there is an art to bestowing bounty, he suggests. The man who gives well "Knows when to stop with grace, and when advance,/ Nor gives through importunity or chance." Favors should be "bestow'd," not "extorted." The point is to "oblige" – i.e., create a sense of obligation in the recipient.[35]

> ... few there are, that can be truly kind,
> Or know to fix their favours on the mind;
> Hence, some, whene'er they would oblige, offend,
> And while they make the fortune, lose the friend;
> Still give, unthank'd; still squander, not bestow;
> For great men want not, what to give, but how.[36]

Dodington's deft epistle, drawing implicitly on the Senecan commonplaces about "benefits," serves both as political advice from a highly placed supporter – Dodington at the time was a Commissioner of the Treasury – about "how" to bestow the crown's "favours," and as a discreet appeal that Walpole continue to shine on *him*.

As his sympathetic biographer notes, Dodington "undoubtedly found the writers and artists whom he cultivated useful." James Ralph, for example, was "editor of a succession of journals advertising the views of Dodington and his friends."[37] His great house in Eastbury, where he invited writers and politicians to visit, functioned like the Kit-Cat Club of the previous generation, "one of the great forums" (so his biographer says) "where the commerce between

---

[35] OED III, 2, "To bind or make indebted by conferring a benefit or kindness."

[36] Printed in Young, *Poetical Works* II, 326, 327.

[37] John Carswell, in Dodington, *The Political Journals*, xiii. See also Carswell's life of Dodington, *The Old Cause*.

letters and politics, so vital an element in eighteenth-century Whig-gism, was carried on."[38] New to his wealth, Dodington was a commoner (born George Bubb) who took his benefactor's name and eventually won a peerage. Politically ambitious, his "reigning passion," so wrote Horace Walpole, "was to be well at court, and to this object he sacrificed every circumstance of his life."[39] A creature of patronage, he seems to have turned patron himself as a means of self-promotion, perhaps in imitation of his master Walpole, who was unsurpassed in his use of patronage to consolidate his political power.

The leaders of the opposition to Walpole, though they complained that royal and ministerial patronage was going to subservient hirelings, were no less active as patrons of literature – and for similar purposes. Many of the patrons and writers of the 1730s were connected by means of a kind of network of Opposition, with centers at Cobham's Stowe and (after he left Walpole) Dodington's East-bury, and elsewhere. Among the active patrons in this network were the Prince of Wales (then in opposition to his father),[40] Chesterfield, Lyttelton, and Cobham (Pope's friend). Others who were associated with the "Boy Patriots" or "Cobham's Cubs" include the Duke of Bedford, the old Duchess of Marlborough,[41] her grandson the third Duke, William Pitt, and Richard and George Grenville – the last three of whom were to become senior ministers after 1756. The writers they supported include Pope, Thomson, and Fielding (who intrigued both for and against Walpole), as well as a number of lesser figures: Richard Glover, David Mallet, Gilbert West, James Hammond, and James Ralph. Links were political, familial, and personal. Lyttelton, Fielding, and West were all at Eton together. West was Cobham's nephew. Fielding at one time or other sought support from Chesterfield (to whom he dedicated his *Dramatic Works*), Lyttelton (dedicatee of *Tom Jones*), and Dodington (dedicatee of *Jonathan Wild*). Thomson is indebted to the same nexus: his *Liberty* (1735) is inscribed to the Prince of Wales, his *Edwin and Eleonora* (1738) to the Princess; his "Winter" includes a digression added in 1744

---

38   *Ibid.*, 161.
39   Horace Walpole, *A Catalogue of the Royal and Noble Authors of England, Scotland, and Ireland*, IV, 250.
40   On Frederick as a patron, in myth and in fact, see Christine Gerrard, *The Patriot Opposition to Walpole*, 46–67.
41   Battestin notes that she used her "vast wealth at every turn to counter Walpole's bribery" (*Henry Fielding*, 344) – but it is not clear how her use of wealth was any different from his.

(lines 656–90) in praise of Chesterfield, and his "Summer" is addressed to Dodington. The masque of *Alfred*, featuring the politically charged "Rule, Britannia," was performed before the prince in 1740. Thomson has words of praise for the politically allied Lyttelton, Hammond, and Young, as does Fielding for Glover.[42] His "Epistle to Dodington, Of True Greatness" compliments not only its addressee but also Lyttelton and Chesterfield. Glover's *Leonidas* (1737), dedicated to Cobham, became a kind of covert party-piece, celebrating resistance to "tyranny."

An apparent exception to the rule of politically oriented literary patronage is the Earl of Burlington, the friend of Pope and the patron of Gay, Handel, and Palladianism. Modern accounts of his literary patronage suggest that his generous and wide patronage of the arts cannot be explained by politics.[43] But it is worth noting Burlington's impeccable Whig credentials and lineage.[44] Somers was his guardian and Shaftesbury a kind of mentor. He belonged to the Kit-cats. Like many other Whig lords he supported Walpole in the 1720s, served as a member of the Privy Council in 1729, and went into Opposition in 1733 (at the time of the Excise Bill crisis) for reasons that remain unclear.[45] Although he supported a wide range of writers and artists, and was passionately devoted to Palladian architecture, he seems to have taken care that his patronage did not conflict with his political loyalties. Thus he broke off support of his old client Gay when political reflections unmistakably hostile to Walpole appeared in Gay's *Polly* (1729). Pope's "Epistle to Burlington" (1731) casts him as a Palladian rather than a "Patriot" (he was still a Walpole Whig at that point), but in his later years he accepted the dedication of a play entitled *The Independent Patriot* (1737), which promoted Bolingbrokian (and thus anti-Walpolian) notions of being above party.[46] Politics thus seems to have played a role in his

---

[42] Thomson, "Spring," 906ff, "Winter," 555ff, "Autumn," 667; Fielding, *Champion* No. 13, in *Complete Works*, xv, 100.

[43] James Lees-Milne, *Earls of Creation*, 85–151, and Jacques Carré, "Burlington's Literary Patronage," 21–33. Lees-Milne thinks Burlington had "little more than perfunctory" interest in national affairs (*Earls of Creation*, 87).

[44] On the basis of weak circumstantial evidence, Jane Clark sees a "possibility" of Jacobite sympathies about 1715. See "The Mysterious Mr. Buck," 317–22.

[45] Perhaps because his protégé, William Kent, whose career he vigorously promoted, did not receive a royal commission? (See Vertue, *The Notebooks*, xii, 139. Because he himself did not receive a coveted office? (See Lees-Milne, *Earls of Creation*, 87), and Carré, "Burlington's Literary Patronage," 23). Or for reasons of political principle?

[46] Francis Lynch claimed that his central character was inspired by Burlington, "an Enemy to Corruption, and the False Taste of the Age ... Impartial in his Legislative Capacity,

thinking about patronage, but to account for his zeal it may also be necessary to appeal to traditional notions of "magnificence."[47]

The "Broad Bottom" coalition that succeeded Walpole's ministry included men who had been leaders of the Opposition and had (not coincidentally) been among the most prominent literary patrons: Dodington, Lyttelton, Chesterfield, Cobham, and Bedford. Once in power they continued to be active as patrons throughout the 1740s and 50s. Dodington, in office as Treasurer of the Navy or in attendance upon the Prince of Wales (who served as titular head of the Leicester House "Opposition"), lavishly decorated a villa at Hammersmith to serve as a political center. He sponsored a tendentious *History of England* (1744) by James Ralph, and co-authored with Ralph a treatise on *The Use and Abuse of Parliament* (1744). He is said to have had a "considerable share" in the writing of *The Wishes* by the minor dramatist Richard Bentley, and (while it was in rehearsal for a London production) had it acted in his garden at Hammersmith.[48] He even made an approach (unsuccessful, as it turned out) to Johnson, inviting "the Rambler" to his house "when he should be disposed to enlarge his acquaintance."[49]

Lyttelton joined the ministry in 1744 as a Lord of the Treasury and continued to plead the cause of his former clients, West and Thomson, once writers for the Opposition. Lyttelton was an "active intermediary between Henry Pelham and writers seeking governmental recognition for services rendered,"[50] and commended Fielding to the attention of the Duke of Bedford, made First Lord of the Admiralty at Walpole's fall, who in turn recommended him to Lord Chancellor Hardwicke, who approved his appointment as Justice of the Peace for Westminster.[51] The administration found it convenient to pension James Ralph and William Guthrie, who had provided literary services to Walpole, not for what they would write but for what they would agree not to write.[52]

Zealous in the genuine Interest of his Country, and a Despiser of the Covetous of all Party Denominations" (*The Independent Patriot* A2–A2v).

47 See above, pp. 35–39.
48 Horace Walpole, *Catalogue of Royal and Noble Authors*, IV, 250.
49 Nichols, *Literary Anecdotes*, V, 39–40. See also *Johnsonian Miscellanies*, ed. G. B. Hill, 2 vols. (Oxford: Clarendon, 1897), II, 104.
50 W. B. Coley, in Fielding, *The Jacobite's Journal*, lxii.
51 See the dedication to Lyttelton of *Tom Jones*. For a good sense of the interrelations of politics and literature during Fielding's career, see Battestin, *Henry Fielding*.
52 Hanson, *Government and the Press*, 119–20.

In the 1750s Pelham's brother the Duke of Newcastle continued to find it useful to pension a few writers. But the nexus between authors and the political elite in that decade is perhaps better illustrated by the patronage of Philip Yorke (1720–90), son of the Lord Chancellor, a teller in the Exchequer, Viscount Royston (from 1754), and later second Earl of Hardwicke (from 1764). Yorke was a member of one of the most prominent political families in the country at a time when family connections counted for a great deal. His father, Philip Yorke (1690–1764), the first Earl, rose to be Lord Chancellor, as did his brother Charles (1722–70). All three maintained extensive links with other members of the political elite, links which Lord Hardwicke (the first Earl) defended as Burkean "honourable connections," sustained not in the spirit of faction but as "necessary engagements in order to carry on and effectuate right and necessary measures."[53] They also maintained links with writers: Fielding's *Enquiry into the Causes of the Late Increase of Robbers* (1751) is dedicated to the Lord Chancellor. Interwoven with the political "connections" were numerous threads of literary correspondence. These letters were apparently important enough to be kept among the family papers (which eventually went to the British Library), letters addressed to the second Earl from an impressive roster of artists and men of letters: Boswell, Burke, Chesterfield, Gainsborough, Garrick, Gibbon, Goldsmith, Hume, Montesquieu, Percy, Reynolds, Robertson, Young, among many others.[54]

Philip Yorke himself had some literary pretensions. As a young man he and his brother published a collection of imaginary political correspondence entitled *Athenian Letters; or the Epistolary Correspondence of an Agent of the King of Persia, residing at Athens during the Peloponnesian War* (1741),[55] with the assistance of two older men of letters, Thomas Birch and Daniel Wray, who were in effect clients of the family.[56] Wray was to become Hardwicke's deputy at the Exchequer in 1745 (and remained in the office almost until his death). More important, both Wray and Birch served as Hardwicke's eyes

---

[53] In a letter to Newcastle in 1763, found in the massive Hardwicke Papers in the British Library (Add. MS 32948, fol. 276), quoted in Brewer, *Party Ideology*, 70.

[54] Hardwicke Papers, Add. MS 35350.

[55] 4 vols. (London, 1741). Hardwicke later edited genuine historical papers, the *Letters to and from Sir Dudley Carleton* (1757, 1775, 1780), a collection of *Miscellaneous State Papers from 1501 to 1726* (1778), and *Walpoliana* (1783).

[56] Birch (1705–66), a prolific historian and biographer, had secured several ecclesiastical preferments through the help of the first Earl. Wray (1701–83) was a Cambridge man who first met the second Earl in 1737.

and ears in the London political and literary worlds, and sent regular reports to their patron in the country.[57] Wray's weekly letters report news from the Exchequer, the latest political gossip "from the Great World,"[58] and comments on the latest books and plays. He sent packets of books – Johnson's *Life of Savage* in October 1754, Matthew Green's *The Spleen* in September 1755, "two new volumes of Swift" in 1762[59] – and "Intelligence from the Theatre," along with news of the latest "Exhibition of Paintings in the Strand."[60] As a Fellow of the Society of Antiquarians, Wray was also in a position to report on affairs in "the Antiquarian Republic." In one letter he sends, as an elegant compliment to Yorke as classicist and as patron, his own imitation of an epistle by Martial to his patron, Castricus, whom Wray describes as "a good Writer & a generous Patron; not that he is recorded any where to have made Martial his Deputy [as Yorke did Wray]; or to have procured Pontificates & Flamenates for other Good Men; much less to have offered LX *Millia Nummum* to a Friend in Distress." Wray closes with "I am … Dear Patron, ever your devoted D. Wray" (Add. MS 35401, fol. 160).

Wray notes that Yorke served as a patron for other "Good Men" too. One of those men was the poet and painter, John Dyer. With Wray acting as intermediary, Yorke made Dyer his wife's chaplain in 1750,[61] and recommended him to his father, the Lord Chancellor, as a deserving churchman who had begun work on an ambitious poem on England's wool trade, a matter of national interest and pride.[62] (It appears that one way of gaining access to the patronage of the Lord Chancellor was to appeal to his sons.[63]) Lord Hardwicke, who had the disposal of several church livings, gave two of them to Dyer in

---

57   British Library, Add. MSS 35396–35400 (Birch) and 35401 (Wray). Birch had served in the same capacity for the first Earl. See Add. MSS 4244, fol. 7; 4325, fos. 1–8.

58   On May 6, 1763 he reported on John Wilkes (Add. MS 35401, fol. 270).

59   Add. MS 35401, fos. 190, 203, 263. Yorke also asked Birch to send him books, including Rousseau's *Emile*, "the last Scotch Defense of Q. Mary," and "the 13th and 14th vol. of Swift" (Add. MS 35399, fos. 333, 335).

60   Add. MS 35401, fos. 154 (on Mason's *Elfrid*), 207 (gossip about Garrick), 269 (on the "Exhibition of Paintings"). Wray also arranged with Arthur Pond, an art dealer, to have picture frames cleaned – apparently at Yorke's London house (fol. 163). Pond was a friend of Dyer (Ralph Williams, *Poet, Painter, and Parson*, 35).

61   *Ibid.*, 127.

62   The editor of the *Memoirs of Wool* urges that his subject is "very particularly the Gentlemens Care and Study" and "of POLITICAL Consideration" (I, xiii).

63   The fourth of Young's *Night Thoughts* was dedicated in 1743 to young Philip Yorke (aged 23), perhaps with hopes of ecclesiastical preferment from the Lord Chancellor. See Forster, *Edward Young*, 194.

1751.[64] Six letters from Wray to Yorke from July 1750 to August 1752 send reassuring news of Dyer's slow progress on *The Fleece,* and assurances of Dyer's gratitude:

the part you generously take in Dyer and his Fleece encourages me to mention that I hear to day he has resumed that work, after a Fit of illness. (July 9, 1750)

Dyer, I trust, will not discredit the protection you grant him. However awkward he may appear in this Bad World he has two of the characters which qualify him for a place in Elysium, *Sacerdos Custos* and *Pius Vates.* (July 30, 1750)

After all your solid Benefits to poor Dyer, you are extremely gracious to pursue him with your good Wishes. (August 15, 1751)

Dyer has transported his Wife & Children & All to Coningsby [another living conferred with assistance from the Lord Chancellor]; he is full of spirits & gratitude to his Benefactors [presumably Yorke and Lord Hardwicke], and forgets not his Fleece. (September 26, 1751)

Dyer has sent us more than 600 Verses of his fourth book [i.e., *The Fleece,* Book IV]. (August 27, 1752)[65]

Yorke also arranged to get Dyer a Cambridge degree,[66] with support from Akenside (who was indebted to Yorke for earlier patronage)[67] and to have Akenside provide assistance to Dyer in revising his manuscript for publication.[68]

Although it cannot be shown that Dyer's *Fleece* was hoped to advance Yorke's political career or his political agenda, the example of his patronage demonstrates how intimately related were political and literary matters in the daily life and correspondence of the political elite. The same agent and the same network of friends and "connections" – Thomas Birch, Daniel Wray, Thomas Edwards, Arthur Pond – were employed in each arena.

---

[64] In a letter to John Duncombe in 1756, Dyer summarized his indebtedness to his patrons, including "the Lord Chancellor," who gave him Belchford (£75 a year) "through Mr. Wray's interest" and then Kirkby (£110 a year) "through the same interest ... without my solicitation." *Letters by Several Eminent Persons,* II, 107–17. See also the "Advertisement" to Dyer's posthumously-published *Poems,* iv–v.

[65] Add. MS 35401, fos. 130, 132, 150, 151, 163. See also fol. 134. Wray continued to write to Yorke about Dyer. See fos. 185, 196.

[66] Williams, *Poet, Painter, and Parson,* 123.

[67] "As you are the Doctors [i.e., Akenside's; Akenside was a member of the College of Physicians] Patron of old, and ever ready to promote the credit of the University ..." Add. MSS 35401, fol. 165.

[68] Williams, *Poet, Painter, and Parson* (128) suggests that Wray and Thomas Edwards were the intermediaries. See *Letters by Several Eminent Persons,* III, 59.

THE PATRONAGE OF LORD BUTE

Whatever his interest in arts and letters, Hardwicke's chief concern was politics. For patrons like the Earl of Bute, who were able to influence royal patronage, political considerations were even more important – whether he was promoting his own interests or those of his master. When Bute met the Prince of Wales in 1746 he was still an impoverished Scottish peer. But he rapidly gained Frederick's confidence, and became Lord of the Bedchamber and then (in 1755, after Frederick's death) tutor to his son George, the future George III, and thence Groom of the Stole to the young prince. Bute in effect took charge of George's political education, and used the prince's money to this end. He seems to have had literary tastes – he was himself an amateur actor – and appointed the Scots playwright John Home as his private secretary.[69] He took a lively interest in Home's plays, suggesting revisions, pressing Garrick to produce them at Covent Garden, and bringing them to the attention of the prince,[70] and thereby playing several of the traditional roles of aristocratic patron. But *Agis* and especially *Douglas* had the additional virtue, in Bute's eyes, of teaching patriotic "virtue" of the sort that Bute had been trying to inculcate in the prince.[71]

At the accession of George III in October 1760 Bute was appointed Privy Councillor, then Secretary of State for the Northern Department, and finally (in 1762) First Lord of the Treasury (or Prime Minister). He continued to act as dispenser of the royal bounty, and – as his enemies lost no time in charging – he consulted political ends. One goal was to make the king seem a generous supporter of the arts, and friendly contemporary journalists duly remarked, even before the accession, on the prospects for a "new Augustan age of Learning and the fine arts."[72] Another was to reassure those who

[69] He also got Home a pension of £100 a year from the prince.

[70] When Home's tragedy of *Agis* was performed in 1758 Bute was puffed in print for having "stamp[ed] the bullion with his seal of praise" and "procure[d] for Home "the favour of his prince." See *The Story of the Tragedy of Agis, with Observations on the Play, the Performances, and their Reception*. Home's *Dramatic Works* (1760) were dedicated to the prince. Bute also saw to it that members of the royal family attended a performance of Dodsley's *Cleone* in 1758.

[71] I follow here the argument of Richard Sher, in "The Favourite of the Favourite," 196–205. Sher cites praise of Bute as a new Maecenas by Alexander Carlyle, who went on to observe the desired political effect: "it can forbode nothing but good to Britain, that a play full of the high spirit of patriotism and heroic virtue, drew the attention of her princes, and received the most distinguishing marks of their approbation" (in the *Critical Review*, 5 [March 1758], 242).

[72] *Ibid.*

already held places. Boswell noted that Bute "advised the King to agree that Judges should hold their places for life, instead of losing them at the accession of a new King," and "thought to make the king popular by this concession."[73] (Johnson made the same observation about Lyttelton's advice to the king's father: dispensing patronage was a way of becoming "popular".) A third end was to reward his backers and political "friends." Among early recipients of royal pensions were a number of Bute's fellow Scotsmen, including Home, who received an additional pension of £300 a year, and a place worth another £300,[74] and David Mallet, who was made Keeper of the Books of the Port of London in 1763.[75] Bubb Dodington was made Lord Melcombe in April 1761 through Bute's offices, in recognition of his services to the new king while he was still Prince of Wales. One of Dodington's favorites, Edward Young, was given a sinecure (Clerk of the Closet to the Princess Dowager) worth £200 a year.[76] Thomas Sheridan was rewarded with £200 a year in 1763 not only (so Boswell suggests) because he was "a sufferer in the cause of government," but because, as author of *Lectures on the English Language and Publick Speaking*, he taught Scotsmen in London how to lose their accents.[77] In particular, he taught "pronunciation" to Alexander Wedderburne, an important member of Bute's circle.[78]

Bute seems at the same time to have sought to create the impression that the new king's policy was to reward merit wherever it might be found – in effect claiming that his patronage would not be politically motivated. This policy was a reflection, in the arena of patronage, of the non-partisan "patriotism" and "public spirit" which was repeatedly announced as the keynote of the new king's reign, and may have been the prime cause of expectations of a new "Augustan age" of letters.[79] A writer supporting the ministry picked

---

73 *Life of Johnson*, II, 353.
74 Home was given the increased pension in 1761 and made Conservator of Scots Privileges at Campvere in 1763.
75 Mallet's *Elvira* (1763) was dedicated to Bute, as was his *Truth in Rhyme: Address'd to a Certain Noble Lord*. For complaints about Bute's patronage of Scots writers, see Charles Churchill's *Prophecy of Famine*, lines 123–38 (*Poetical Works*).
76 His promoter – apart from Dodington – was apparently not Bute but Newcastle, prompted by the Duchess of Portland. See Forster, *Edward Young*, 333–34.
77 *Life of Johnson*, I, 386. His *Plan for a Pronouncing Dictionary* had been dedicated to Bute.
78 Boswell notes that Wedderburne's sister was married to an "intimate friend" of Bute (*Life of Johnson*, I, 386).
79 Writers flocked to Bute's door. A "Register of [Bute's] Correspondence" in the British Library includes letters soliciting favors or offering assistance from David Garrick, Arthur

up the theme. The new reign, wrote John Douglas in *Seasonable Hints From an Honest Man on the Present Important Crisis of a New Reign and a New Parliament* (1761) would see the end of corruption, "worn-out distinctions of party," "ministerial dictators," and "unnecessary pensions": "in the future disposal of court favors, when there are vacancies by deaths and not by removals, they [the Tories, no longer proscribed] will stand an equal chance of being taken notice of, with the rest of his majesty's good subjects" (p. 33). The same theme is heard in a remark of Wedderburne's to the effect that it was "the resolve of the ministry no longer to restrict the bounty of the crown by political considerations, provided there was 'distinction in the literary world, and the prospect of approaching distress'."[80] Boswell had evidently heard and believed, referring as he does to the "change in system which the British court had undergone upon the accession of his present Majesty."[81] – presumably the "system" whereby royal rewards are granted.

Bute himself is said to have declared that his principle in granting favors was "detur digniori" – let it be given to the more worthy.[82] He was accused by his political enemies of plotting to bring back the exiled Tories and ex-Jacobites, and it is possible (if far-fetched) to read announcements of ministerial impartiality as a cover for a Scottish–Tory–Jacobite plot. It is of course also simply good politics to declare that, as opposed to the previous administration, the current one will be non-political.[83] Ministerial professions that patronage will go only to merit should not be taken at face value. The real political payoff might well have been in such gratifying

Murphy, Bubb Dodington, the Earl of Chesterfield, James Ralph, Thomas Campbell, Allan Ramsay, David Mallet, and Richard Bentley – among many others. Add. MS 36796, fos. 117, 121, 135, 162, 163, 168. See also Add. MS 5720, fos. 88, 112, with requests from Lord Kames and Hawkesworth.

80 Forster, *Oliver Goldsmith*, II, 387. It is difficult to date Wedderburne's remarks, but they are associated with the granting of a pension to Johnson in 1762. But elsewhere Forster reports that the king's ministers made "writing in favour of the administration" to be "the condition of any favour granted by them to literary men" (II, 71n).

81 *Life of Johnson*, II. 112. Boswell applies to Bute the Latin *spes prima* – "a man of distinguished influence, our support, our refuge, our *praesidium*, as Horace calls Maecenas" (*Life of Johnson*, II, 23).

82 See Bute's February 2, 1764 letter to his brother (Lord Privy Seal for the Northern Department), in *Caldwell Papers* II, I, 232. See also I, 33.

83 Cf. Burke's account of the new policy: "Now was the time to unlock the sealed fountain of Royal bounty, which had been infamously monopolized and huckstered, and to let it flow at large upon the whole people" (*Thoughts on the Causes of the Present Discontents* [1770], in *Writings and Speeches of Edmund Burke* II, 266). Burke's sarcasm suggests that he claimed to see through the policy.

reports as that in the *Critical Review* (a pro-government periodical, to be sure) in 1764 that "This is the first reign ever known in the British annals, in which wit, learning, reasoning, and literary accomplishment of every kind, were almost entirely on the side of government" (vol. 17, p. 391).

There is suggestive evidence – and not just the testimony of enemies[84] – that Bute did not forget political considerations, or, to put it more precisely, did not separate literature from politics. In a 1761 letter to William Mure, his estate manager, who had apparently asked for a political favor, Bute responded that "in things of public concern" he "will neither regard your relation nor his own one minute, but turn his thought solely to a worthy subject ... merit and efficiency will ever weigh with me for publick office before private considerations."[85] In another letter he refuses to grant a place "from Parliamentary reasons" (*Caldwell Papers*, p. 147). It seems likely that "efficiency" means political usefulness, i.e., that dispensing of patronage will be an efficient way to achieve a political end. To decline patronage for "Parliamentary reasons" suggests that Bute was well aware of the need to avoid the sort of gift that might give offense to Parliament.

Another letter to Mure points to a piece of patronage that shows how the literary and the political realms were inextricably linked. Bute tells Mure to let the historian William Robertson know that he will help him to obtain "the Principal's chair either in Edinburgh or in Glasgow" (*Caldwell Papers*, p. 146). As Secretary of State for the Northern Department and *de facto* minister for Scotland, Bute was the head of what one contemporary called a "scheme of universal patronage" – the "disposal of places in the nomination of government" but also "an initiative, and always a controlling power in appointments [like the Principalship of the University of Edinburgh] which were nominally in the gift of corporate bodies and of individuals."[86] Bute had political reasons for promoting the career of Robertson: he hoped for a new "History of England" that would put

[84] Cf. Chesterfield on Bute: "He placed and displaced whom he pleased; gave peerages without number, and pensions without bounds; by these means he proposed to make his ground secure for the permanency of his power" (*Characters*, 473–74); and Lovat-Fraser: "To protect himself from attacks during his tenure of power, Bute had retained a body of political writers, who acted as his defenders and advocates ... A crowd of writers were induced by places and pensions to support the ministry" (*Bute*, 28–29). See also the discussion in Brewer, *Party Ideology*, 221–26.

[85] *Caldwell Papers*, II, I, 128.

[86] Thomas Somerville, *My Own Life and Times*, 379–80.

the reign of George III in the best possible light.[87] "Most of our best authors are wholly devoted to me," he wrote to a friend, "and I have laid the foundation for gaining Robertson, by employing him for the King in writing the history of England; he must be pensioned."[88] After protracted negotiations with Robertson, Bute gave his support, and Robertson was duly appointed Principal by the Edinburgh town council.

Even if political considerations were primary in the mind of the patron, they were discreetly concealed in any public announcements. This is nowhere clearer than in the best-known instance of Bute's patronage, the pension granted to Samuel Johnson in 1762. Sensitive to the thought that (given his notorious definitions of "patron" and "pension" in the *Dictionary*)[89] there was something embarrassing about accepting a pension, and to accusations that he was being bought off by the government, Johnson was anxious to be assured by friends that it was not dishonorable to accept a pension, and by the government that it was granted not for what he was expected to do for the ministry but for what he had already done for literature.

Most admirers of Johnson from Boswell onward have been as anxious as he was to conclude that the pension was simply a reward for merit and literary services to his country. But James Clifford has wondered whether the government may have thought that such a pension would contribute to political ends: "Did Bute and his ministers think they had bought a possible political supporter, or at least silenced a potential antagonist? It is hard to say."[90] Clifford notes too that it was suggested in Johnson's own day that the pension to sturdily English Johnson was in part designed to assuage anger at

---

[87] Cf. a July 1761 letter from Cathcart to Robertson: "Lord Bute told me the King's thoughts, as well as his own, with respect to your *History of Scotland*, and a wish his Majesty had expressed to see a History of England by your pen ... Great, laborious, and extensive as the work must be, he would take care your encouragement should be proportioned to it." Cited in Dugald Stewart, *Account of the Life and Writings of William Robertson*, in Stewart's *Collected Works*, x, 133.

[88] Quoted in Sher, "The Favourite of the Favourite," 203, who cites Lovat-Fraser, *Bute*, 30. But Lovat-Fraser, whose book is brief, semi-popular, derivative, and casually documented, offers no documentary evidence. For Bute's role in Robertson's appointment, see Jeremy Cater, "The Making of Principal Robertson," 60–84, and James L. McKelvey, "William Robertson and Lord Bute," 238–47.

[89] "Pension": "An allowance made to any one without an equivalent. In England it is generally understood to mean pay given to a state hireling for treason to his country." "Patron": "Commonly a wretch who supports with insolence, and is paid with flattery."

[90] "Problems of Johnson's Middle Years," 18–19. Cannon suspects the pension was part of Bute's program of "reconciliation" with the Tories (*Samuel Johnson*, 70).

Bute's profuse patronage of Scottish writers,[91] and concludes that this suspicion was "undoubtedly" correct. From Bute's point of view there was something else to be gained by pensioning Johnson. By 1762 the fame of the *Dictionary* was such that England could boast of its superiority over France, whose academy had yet to produce a dictionary of the French language. Anything that enhanced the glory of the nation would enhance the reigning government, which might implicitly take credit for it, particularly if a direct association could be demonstrated. To pension Johnson would, in the words of one anonymous petitioner writing to Bute, "fill up the proper measure of national and kingly glory."[92]

The anonymous writer, despite his claims to impartiality, is no more a disinterested party than any of the other participants, and his rhetoric (studded with conventional pieties) is designed to flatter. But his appeal suggests how a pension might be made to seem advantageous to the ministry. The writer knows that Bute has "the honour of being consulted by his Majesty oftener than most of those, who are about his person," and recalls too that "popular fame represents your Lordship as a man of letters and a patron of all useful arts." But the opening sentence makes the strongest appeal: a pension to Johnson "will redound not only to your own honour but to that of the whole kingdom." Bute can make the kingdom and the king look good. But he can also polish his own reputation: "how would both his Majesty's *and your character* be increased in the estimation of all who are the friends to learning and virtue [emphasis added]?"

Whether Bute also hoped for solid literary services from Johnson is indeed difficult to say, but evidence points to that conclusion. In 1763 Charles Jenkinson, a Treasury secretary and a sort of coordinator of press relations, left with Johnson some papers concerning the Peace of Paris, the terms of which were then being negotiated and much debated in the press.[93] Evidently Johnson was being asked to defend the government's position, just as Gibbon was to do some fifteen years later.[94] That Johnson apparently did not produce a defense

---

[91] Clifford ("Problems of Johnson's Middle Years," 9) cites a contemporary letter from Thomas Percy to Richard Farmer.

[92] An unidentified and anonymous letter to Bute, dated November 15, 1761, a copy of which was provided to Boswell (but not used in the *Life of Johnson*). Clifford cites the letter (*Dictionary Johnson*, 263–65). I have consulted a copy in the Boswell Papers at Yale.

[93] *The Jenkinson Papers*, 390–91.

[94] Johnson was not the only writer to whom Bute turned. Jenkinson also delivered similar papers to the pensioner John Campbell, who responded in 1763 with a pro-Bute pamphlet

may indicate that the ministers had mistaken their man, or merely that (as he did often enough) Johnson found it difficult to apply himself. He wrote to Jenkinson that he had "once hoped to have made better use of [the papers]" (*Jenkinson Papers*, p. 391). In later years the ministry again turned to their pensioner. *Thoughts on Falkland's Islands* (1771), were (Johnson himself said) written "upon materials furnished to him by the ministry." *The Patriot* (1774) was "called for by my political friends," and *Taxation No Tyranny* (1775) was "written at the desire of those who were then in power." Johnson told Boswell that the pamphlet had also been "revised and curtailed by some of them." Most observers, intent to defend Johnson against servility, have argued (disingenuously, it seems to me) that he was not simply toeing the administration's line but was in each case presenting his own opinions. At one point the requests apparently rankled. He complained to a friend that "his pension having been given to him as a literary character, he had been applied to by administration to write political pamphlets." He even thought of resigning his pension, until he was reassured that it would have been improper.[95] Johnson remained on the pension rolls, where he was listed among the "Writers Political" in 1782.[96]

I rehearse the facts concerning Johnson's pension not to try to determine whether it was granted for merit or with the expectation of some return, but to argue that it is quixotic to think the question could be settled. It is also unhistorical to try to distinguish between "merit" and "service," for it is improbable that Bute and his fellow ministers kept them separate. Regardless of what one said in public, everyone knew that writing and politics were inextricably mixed, and that it was impossible to look upon writing in a purely *disinterested* manner. In December 1760 the bookseller Robert Dodsley wrote to Shenstone about a campaign, then afoot, to get a pension for the poet. Shenstone, Dodsley assures him, of course has "Merit" but preferment is a matter of "Interest" – both the poet's and the patron's. "Come," Dodsley coaxes Shenstone, "and give the Ministry an Opportunity of doing themselves Credit."[97]

---

on *The Nature of the Sugar Trade*. For details, see Robert Rea, *The English Press in Politics*, 225–26. For Gibbon, see below, pp. 266–67.

[95] Boswell, *Life of Johnson*, ii, 134, 288, 317. In a March 1, 1775 letter Johnson referred quite bluntly to the ministry as "those for whom I write." See *Letters of Samuel Johnson*, ii, 184.

[96] Public Records Office, 30/8, vol. ccxxiv, Part i, fol. 77r, first cited in Korshin, "Types of Eighteenth-Century Literary Patronage," 470–71n.

[97] *The Correspondence of Robert Dodsley*, 445. For whatever reasons (and it seems plausible to

Just as it is unhistorical to separate the literary from the political in the minds of patrons, so it is unhistorical (despite the category under which Johnson is listed in the Treasury books, and despite polemical assertions by contemporaries) to assume that authors can be divided into the servants of art and the servants of political paymasters. Since the names of James Ralph, John Shebbeare, and William Guthrie rarely appear in literary histories without the tar of "hack" or "hireling," it is worth noting that to accept the label is to be unwittingly captured by their political opponents. According to one contemporary witness, they all had literary abilities. Smollett (not, of course, a disinterested observer) in a 1761 review of the current state of literature includes among the writers of history and biography not only Robertson and Hume but also Guthrie and Ralph, as well as Thomas Carte and Archibald Campbell.[98] Charles James Fox thought Ralph had "much less reputation as an historian than he seems to deserve."[99] Guthrie, in Boswell's view, was "a man who deserves to be respectably recorded in the literary annals of this country."[100] Shebbeare, pensioned in 1764, and reviled by Forster as "the most worthless of hack-partisans" (*Goldsmith*, vol. II, p. 388), was a friend of Johnson's. He had "knowledge and abilities," wrote Boswell, "much above the class of ordinary writers, and deserves to be remembered as a respectable name in literature" (*Life of Johnson*, vol. IV, p. 113). Although he was attacked as a suspected Jacobite, and resented as a pensioner, he established a reputation as a writer on political subjects in the 1750s,[101] and in the 1770s wrote on the same subjects that engaged Burke and Adam Ferguson.[102]

To set Ralph, Guthrie, and Shebbeare beside Burke and Ferguson might induce us to take the former more seriously, and to acknowledge that virtually all writers in the period – whether or not they are now in our canon – worked in a world of politics and patronage. By

suspect Bute's own "interest"), a pension for Shenstone was arranged – though he did not live to collect it.

[98] See the *Continuation* of the *History of England*, quoted in Basker, *Tobias Smollett*, 215.

[99] *DNB*, which also notes that Henry Hallam, a nineteenth-century historian, thought Ralph "the most diligent historian we possess for the time of Charles II."

[100] "His writings in history, criticism, and politicks, had considerable merit ... Johnson esteemed him enough to wish that his life should be written." Boswell, *Life of Johnson*, I, 116–17.

[101] He published a series of eight *Letters to the People of England* beginning in 1755. (He also published two novels – *The Marriage Act* in 1754 and *Lydia, or Filial Piety* in 1755, and an early medical treatise, *A New Analysis of the Bristol Waters*, in 1740.)

[102] He published a *Speech on American Taxation* in 1775 and *An Essay on the Origin, Progress, and Establishment of National Society* in 1776.

the same token, political programs were promoted by both govern-ment and opposition (and increasingly so in the 1760s) by means of the periodical press.[103] Were David Mallet, Arthur Murphy, and John Home granted pensions in the 1760s for "purely political" reasons? Why should we not assume that like Smollett and Johnson they had attracted attention *both* for the political acumen displayed in their writings *and* their literary abilities?

[103] See Brewer, *Party Ideology*, and Rea, *The English Press in Politics*.

CHAPTER 4

John Dryden

Dryden found a patron in most of the powerful figures of his day. The list of those to whom he dedicated works includes members of the royal family (the king, the queen, the Duke and Duchess of York, and the Duke of Monmouth), political leaders in office from Danby, Sunderland, and Clarendon to Clifford and Lawrence Hyde, statesmen out of place (Leicester, Chesterfield, and Halifax), and peers of some literary ability (Orrery, Newcastle, Rochester, Mulgrave, and Dorset), both Tories and (especially after 1688) Whigs, both Protestants (like Lord Haughton) and Catholics (Radcliffe, Salisbury, Clifford). For more than thirty-five years, from his early plays to the *Fables* in 1700 Dryden wrote dedications in which he heaped lavish praise on one patron after another.[1]

Johnson thought Dryden's dedications were deplorable exercises in nauseous flattery. *The State of Innocence*, he says, is dedicated to the Duchess of York "in a strain of flattery which disgraces genius, and which it was wonderful that any man that knew the meaning of his own words could use without self-detestation."[2] The nineteenth century inherited Johnson's judgment. Macaulay thought patronage led to a degrading "traffic in praise," and left a writer "in morals something between a pandar and a beggar."[3] Beljame writes of Dryden's "humiliating moral dependence": Dryden's dedication to Rochester is said to be remarkable for its "long-windedness," "insistent flatteries," and the "pains the poet takes to humble himself."[4] Wheatley thought Dryden "one of the greatest sinners"

---

[1]   Dryden provided dedications for twenty of his twenty-eight plays, the prose *Essay on Dramatick Poesie*, three volumes of prose translations in the 1680s, and four volumes of verse translations in the 1690s. He rarely provided dedications for his original poems, a point to which I will return.

[2]   *Lives of the Poets*, I, 359. Cf. 399.

[3]   *History of England*, ch. 3. repr. in Macaulay, *Selected Writings*, 320–21.

[4]   *Men of Letters*, 89, 107.

among dedicators who "sold their lying praises for money."[5] Twentieth-century admirers have not dislodged the judgment that Dryden's dedications are evidence of his regrettable dependence on the system of patronage, or (worse) of a censurable taste for "extravagant flattery."[6]

Of the great English writers perhaps no dedications exceed Dryden's in the insistence of the flattery and the professions of unworthiness. But Dryden is known too as one of English literature's proudest and – at least in print[7] – most self-assured of writers. A printed play by Dryden was typically preceded not only by a dedication but also by a critical preface.[8] And in the latter it was Dryden's usual practice, as Swift's narrator in *A Tale of a Tub* observes, to assure his audiences as frequently as possible that he was a great poet.[9] Swift's remark is hostile, but it points at a feature of Dryden's works that readers readily recognize, the bluff voice that speaks with self-assurance and conscious authority, confident that he has once again solved some technical difficulty, displayed a clear understanding of the literary issue at hand, and "excelled himself."[10]

How can we reconcile the image of servile dedicator and proud laureate and literary dictator? Leaving aside the idea of simple contradiction or inconsistency, and the idea that, as Pope would suggest later about Lord Hervey, pride and servility can be two faces of the same coin, we misread Dryden's dedications if we find in them nothing but servility and sycophancy. In defense of Dryden, one might point to the fact that the practice of dedicating was simply customary and the language of dedication conventional, not to be

---

5   Henry Wheatley, *The Dedication of Books to Patron and Friend*, 120.

6   As late as 1966 the California editors refer to the dedication of *The Indian Emperour* as "the first of many in which Dryden indulged his vein of extravagant flattery" (*Works*, IX, 295).

7   In his personal dealings, especially in his "Approaches ... to his Superiors," Dryden was said by Congreve to be "one of the most Modest [men] and the most Easily to be discountenanced." Kinsley, *Dryden: The Critical Heritage*, 265.

8   On some occasions Dryden combined dedication and critical preface in one text. In the dedication to *The Spanish Fryar* (1681) Dryden "must confess that what I have written looks more like a Preface than a Dedication" (in *Works*, XIV, 103).

9   *A Tale of a Tub*, 131. For examples of Dryden's practice of drawing attention to his own excellence, see the end of the Preface to *All for Love* and the beginning of the dedication to *The Spanish Fryar*.

10 Dryden in his dictator's chair, "magisterially presiding over the younger writers" (Johnson, *Lives of the Poets*, I, 396) is a familiar image. While serving as Poet Laureate and Historiographer Royal, Dryden (especially in his political poetry) writes as if he speaks for the nation. After the Revolution, when he lost his offices, Dryden speaks instead (as David Bywaters has argued) with authority derived from the long literary tradition represented in him. See *Dryden in Revolutionary England*.

taken literally, or that Dryden, with sons to raise and the standing of a gentleman to maintain, was driven by financial necessity. But very little of Dryden's total income was derived from private patronage.[11] And unlike writers of a later generation, Dryden, though he often complains about financial exigencies, never (as Johnson notes) seems to "lament the necessity" of dedication (*Lives of the Poets*, vol. I, p. 400).

The appeal to external circumstances as an explanation of Dryden's alleged "servility" is inconclusive. A reexamination of the language of Dryden's dedications provides other answers. One argument is that Dryden's dedicatory rhetoric offers praise as a disguised form of advice. The recipient is provided an image of ideal wit, grace, and generosity, and is urged – if he wishes to preserve his reputation – to make reality correspond with the image.[12] It can also be argued that Dryden's dedicatory language is not legislative but epideictic rhetoric, designed not to persuade an audience (of one) to follow a specific course of action but to delight that audience with the rhetorical skill of the speaker in what Dryden himself calls "the art of pleasing."[13] As Johnson says, Dryden "brings praise rather as a tribute than a gift, more delighted with the fertility of his invention than mortified by the prostitution of his judgement" (*Lives of the Poets*, vol. I, p. 400). Knowing what is required, Dryden is determined not simply to observe conventions but to demonstrate with what brilliance and originality he can observe them.[14] To write in this way is perfectly consistent with Dryden's magisterial assurance, and indeed only reinforces the patron's sense that Dryden deserves reward and the reader's sense that Dryden is the master of every literary occasion. Finally, critics in recent years have read the dedications for signs of Dryden's political allegiances. It has been argued that the dedications show Dryden to be a loyal adherent of the Stuarts, and

---

[11] Other income included copy money from booksellers, a partner's share from the King's Men for whom he had contracted to write three or four plays a year, his salary as Poet Laureate and Historiographer Royal, and rental income from property his wife brought into the marriage.

[12] "In the dedications ... Dryden is creating an ideal audience" (Eugene Waith, "The Voice of Mr. Bayes," 340). For an extension of the argument to Dryden's panegyrical poetry, see James Garrison, *Dryden and the Tradition of Panegyric*.

[13] Dedication of *Plutarchs Lives* (1684), in *Works*, XVII, 229.

[14] Cf. Burke's remark that the "extravagant panegyrics" in the Restoration were understood by the poets as occasions for competition, "the contest being who should go farthest in the most graceful way" (Sir James Prior, *Life of Edmund Malone* [London, 1860], 251, repr. in Johnson, *Lives of the Poets*, I, 400n).

particularly of the Duke of York,[15] and that after the Revolution Dryden sometimes used dedications to carry on a low-level crypto-Jacobite campaign, lamenting his own neglect, indirectly reflecting on the illegitimacy of the new king, and complimenting those peers who had wisely decided to retire from politics.[16]

Without denying that Dryden seems to deploy these strategies – urging his patrons to deserve the praise he brings them, showing off his rhetorical abilities, and intimating his political allegiances – I suggest that closer attention to the language of Dryden's dedications reveals another strategy consistent with the widely accepted idea of Dryden's self-assured authority. "Authority" is perhaps the key term here, and the nub of any dedication. It is mere politeness for a writer to acknowledge his gratitude for the patron's encouragement, protection, and material assistance. And it costs little for a dedicator to compliment the patron's splendid house, his accomplishments in the political world, or the nobility of the patron's family and lineage. The crucial step is for the dedicator to acknowledge that the patron justly exercises authority over the dedicator and his work, whether as a superior practitioner, a judge, or even as a kind of proprietor. In many of his dedications Dryden, in the very act of praising and of acknowledging the patron's authority, subtly resists that authority and lays countervailing claims of his own.

It is relevant to recall here that several of Dryden's panegyrical poems have been read ironically,[17] and that, as one critic has put it, Dryden engaged in "continual play with the admissions of dependency [on theatrical audiences] in his prologues and epilogues."[18] Dryden evidently found room, in the exercises of offering florid praise from a humble and obedient servant, for a variety of stances and tones. Johnson noted that Dryden's "modesty was by no means inconsistent with ostentatiousness," the California editors that in his prose it is sometimes "difficult to distinguish between modesty and pride."[19] I would go further and say that Dryden mastered the *art* of

---

[15]   For Dryden's persistent loyalty to the Stuarts (and especially the Duke of York), see George McFadden, *Dryden the Public Writer*.
[16]   See James Winn, *John Dryden*; Steven Zwicker, *Politics and Language in Dryden's Poetry*; and Anne Barbeau Gardiner, "Dryden's Patrons," 326–32.
[17]   See David Vieth, "Irony in Dryden's Ode to Anne Killigrew," 91–100; "Irony in Dryden's Verses to Sir Robert Howard," 239–43.
[18]   Paul Hammond, *John Dryden*, 48.
[19]   Johnson, *Lives of the Poets*, i, 396; Dryden's *Works*, XVII, 334.

combining modesty and pride, self-effacement and self-assertion, compliant civility and magisterial authority.

ACKNOWLEDGING THE PATRON

Acts of resistance, however, do not prevent Dryden from acknowledging, as he commonly does, the patron's right to judge the merits of the work at hand. "Who," Dryden asks rhetorically of his patron Orrery, himself a playwright, "could so severely judge of Faults as he, who has given testimony he commits none? your excellent Poems having afforded that knowledge of it to the World."[20] Dryden's language commonly emphasizes the patron's judicial function. He offers *The Conquest of Granada* to the Duke of York, appealing to him, in his capacity as both "Prince" and "Hero," as the highest judge of the merits of the play and of its hero, Almanzor: "I make my last appeal to your Royal Highness, as to a Soveraign Tribunal. Heroes shou'd onely be judg'd by Heroes; because they onely are capable of measuring great and Heroick actions by the rule and standard of their own" (*Works*, vol. XI, p. 7). King Charles is "the truest Judge" of Dryden's translation of the *History of the League*, because he is "so great a Master of the Original" (*Works*, vol. XVIII, p. 3). The authority of the Earl of Mulgrave, to whom Dryden dedicated his translation of the *Aeneis*, is based on his *Essay on Poetry*: "I submit my Opinion to your Judgment, who are better qualified than any Man I know to decide this Controversie [i.e., whether epic or tragedy is the higher form]" (*Works*, vol. V, p.273). Those whom Dryden hopes to please are the same judges Virgil chose to please, "the most Judicious: Souls of the highest Rank, and truest Understanding ... And therefore I appeal to the Highest Court of Judicature, like that of the Peers, of which your Lordship is so great an Ornament" (*Works*, vol. V, p. 328). As a writer who "excels all others, in all the several parts of Poetry which you have undertaken to adorn," the Earl of Dorset is "by an undisputed Title ... the King of Poets" (*Works*, vol. IV, pp. 5, 9). His "Authority" is based not on his rank but on his personal qualities, "inborn and inherent to your Person: What is produc'd in you by an Excellent Wit, a Masterly and Commanding Genius over all Writers: Whereby you are impower'd, when you

---

[20] Dedication to *The Rival Ladies*, in *Works*, VIII, 96.

please, to give the final decision of Wit; to put your Stamp on all that ought to pass for current" (*Works*, vol. IV, p. 10).

Dryden's strongest acknowledgments of the patron's judicial authority are typically reserved for gentleman-poets like Orrery, Rochester, Mulgrave, and Dorset, who as writers themselves are presumed to know whereof they judge.[21] But even before patrons who make no pretensions to literature Dryden presents himself in a subservient role. The Duke of Ormonde, to whom the *Fables* were dedicated, is the third generation of his family to offer patronage to Dryden, who presents himself as a kind of long-term tenant (*Poems*, vol. IV, p. 1439). With Mulgrave, Dryden is a family retainer. The earl has taken an interest in Dryden's career since the 1670s. By 1697 the relationship is an old and familiar – almost familial – one. Both Mulgrave and his kinsman Dorset had often "remember'd" Dryden in his difficult days after the Revolution (when he lost his royal salary): "So inherent it is in your Family not to forget an Old Servant" (*Works*, vol. V, p. 340).

In some dedications the patron's authority is not only that of the "head of the family," but that of a proprietor.[22] Rather than "dedicate" *The Conquest of Granada* to the Duke of York, Dryden thinks he more properly should "restore to you those Ideas, which, in the more perfect part of my characters, I have taken from you" (*Works*, vol. XI, p. 3). The poems in *Examen Poeticum* (1693) – a collection by several hands dedicated by Dryden to Lord Radcliffe – are "by many Titles yours" (*Works*, vol. IV, p. 363), because Radcliffe agreed to serve as patron to a collection before it was complete, and because he himself had probably contributed four poems of his own.[23] *The Rival Ladies*, says Dryden to Orrery, "was Yours, my Lord, before I could call it mine," since Dryden, inspired by his example, had resolved to dedicate it to him while it was still "only a confus'd Mass of Thoughts" (*Works*, vol. VIII, p. 95). In other dedications the patron is the proprietor not of the poem but of the poet himself. Having been patronized by Thomas, Lord Clifford in the 1670s,[24] Dryden says to

---

[21] In dedicating his *Don Quixote*, Part 2 to Dorset in 1694, Thomas Durfey called him "Best Judge of Men, and best of Poets too" (quoted in *Tatler* 214).

[22] For patron as originator and poet as executor of the patron's idea, see above, pp. 29–31.

[23] *Works*, IV, 696. Dryden refers to "your equitable claims to a Dedication" (i.e., your claims in equity as opposed to statute).

[24] In 1673 Dryden dedicated *Amboyna* to Thomas Clifford, the Lord Treasurer, who was instrumental in getting Dryden's salary as Poet Laureate paid to him, and in arranging for the repayment of Dryden's 1667 loan to the king.

his son Hugh in the dedication of Virgil's *Pastorals* in 1697 that he is in effect a household retainer, "your Lordship's by descent, and part of your Inheritance" (*Works*, vol. v, p. 7) – that is, part of his very property. In the dedication of *Marriage A-la-Mode* to Rochester in 1673 Dryden owns himself "your Creature" (*Works*, vol. xi, p. 223), one who owes his position (and, metaphorically speaking, his very life) to his patron. In dedicating *The State of Innocence* to the Duchess of York in 1677 he is simply "Your Poet."[25]

RESISTING THE PATRON

From the beginning of his career, however, Dryden in his dedications uses the form not only to declare his gratitude and – for whatever reason – to offer lavish praise, but also to assert his claims as a writer, and to redefine his position in the patronage system. That Dryden should do this is not a sign that the system itself was in decline – it would last for another century. It is a reflection instead of Dryden's anomalous position within it, in two different respects: class and economic dependency. As a university-educated gentleman, allied by marriage with the aristocratic Howard family, Dryden could mingle with the world of patrons in a way that a writer like Oldham could not. And as a nascent "professional," with an income from the King's Men, and as Poet Laureate (albeit with an irregularly paid salary) he was not wholly dependent on the generosity of private patronage. More important than these non-literary factors, however, is Dryden's sense that literature, as he defines it, is too serious a matter to be left wholly in the hands of the class of leisured aristocrats who traditionally bore responsibility for creating and overseeing it. This sense that practicing literature entailed serious study of the classics, wide reading in the English tradition and in modern European poetry, and disciplined attention to the craft of writing meant that a collision between Dryden and a figure like the Earl of Rochester was virtually inevitable. It is customary to assume that the collision took place between 1673, when Dryden dedicated his *Marriage A-la-Mode* to Rochester, and 1678, when Dryden made mocking allusions (only thinly veiled) to Rochester in the Preface to *All for Love*. But it appears that Dryden anticipated the falling out at the very moment when he was enjoying Rochester's favor. In

[25]　*Works*, xii, 81.

dedicating *Marriage A-la-Mode* to Rochester Dryden acknowledged both that he has been "admitted into your Lordship's Conversation" and that Rochester read the play "before it was Acted on the Stage," gave it some "amendment," and "commended it to the view of His Majesty ... and by His Approbation of it in Writing, made way for its kind reception on the Theatre" (*Works*, vol. xi, 221). In providing such favors Rochester acted the role allotted to him in the patronage system, just as Dryden did in formally offering thanks. But (from Dryden's point of view, anyway) Rochester did not content himself with his assigned role as patron, and this provoked a response from the client.

The dedication professes thanks for Rochester's "Protection and Patronage" and for his providing the very model of a gallant and witty courtier for the comic writers of the age. Instead of seeing Rochester as the glittering ornament of a court well disposed to favor writers, Dryden goes on – rather daringly, for a young writer who expects to be dependent on the collective generosity of the court – to develop a contrast between the ideal courtly patron and the kind of courtier too commonly found: "There are a midling sort of Courtiers, who become happy by their want of wit; but they supply that want, by an excess of malice to those who have it. And there is no such persecution as that of fools." Surrounded by rivals, Rochester might well be flattered to be distinguished from the herd of "midling sort of Courtiers." But he may have been disconcerted to find Dryden pointedly describe at such length how a bad patron displays envy of his clients, steals their wit, and stops the flow of royal favor, particularly since the dedication says that Rochester himself has not so much "avoided" such malice as somehow "surmounted" it – an ambiguous phrase at best. If Dryden is not hinting that Rochester cannot be counted on to have forsworn the practices of his fellow courtiers, then at least he is holding up for Rochester an expectation of how a patron is expected to behave. That Rochester has such a "frank Nature" as "to forget the good which you have done" may on the one hand be a sign of his modesty and his preference to do good by stealth; but on the other hand it may point to Dryden's fear that the fickle patron will "forget" the client and turn his inconstant favor some other way.

Later in the dedication Dryden is even bolder. Rochester is not only a generous patron but a forgiving judge who tempers his customary severity. In saying ironically that "I should have fear'd you, for my Critick, if I had not with some policy given you the trouble of being my Protector" (p. 223), Dryden may reveal that such fears are reasonable. Most tellingly of all, Rochester is himself praised as a witty writer. But even while acknowledging Rochester's preeminence, Dryden in effect discourages Rochester from devoting any serious attention to writing.

> Wit seems to have lodg'd it self more Nobly in this Age, than in any of the former: and people of my mean condition, are onely Writers, because some of the Nobility, and your Lordship in the first place, are above the narrow praises which Poesie could give you ... for my own part, I must confess, that I have so much of self-interest, as to be content with reading some Papers of your Verses, without desiring you should proceed to a Scene or Play. (p. 223)

Ostensibly Dryden concedes that a witty peer could easily outclass "people of my mean condition" – but why should they bother, since the rewards are so small? As he goes on to say, "'Tis a barren Triumph, which is not worth your pains." At the same time Dryden distinguishes between the gentleman amateur who spins "Papers" of "Verses" and the "Writers" who devote themselves to "Poesie." In an uneven battle – and an allusion to dueling[26] suggests that a nobleman has an advantage over a mere gentleman commoner – an aristocratic versifier could dominate the literary world if he chose: "Your Lordship has but another step to make, and from the Patron of Wit, you may become its Tyrant: and Oppress our little Reputations with more ease then you now protect them." This is elegant compliment, but it carries an edge. Later in his career, when Dryden was sure of his reputation, he could afford to call Dorset the "King of Poets" – and not be taken seriously. The young poet in search of patronage sees his patron as a potential "Tyrant." He in effect draws a line between the turf of the aristocratic patron and that of the commoner poet, and urges Rochester not to cross it. In so doing Dryden is redefining the literary field. Henceforth, he says, let patrons keep to the business of patronage and of idly composing "Verses." Leave the serious business of "Poesie" to the "Writers."

The same message – though expressed in politer words – may underlie the praise of the young Dorset (then called Buckhurst) in the dedication of the *Essay on Dramatick Poesie* (1668). Like Rochester Buckhurst was a young court wit. A handful of his satirical songs and

---

26 Dryden says he shares "the common prudence of those, who are worsted in a Duel, and declare they are satisfied when they are first wounded" (p. 223).

verse letters circulated in manuscript at court by the time Dryden addressed him, and he was credited with the fourth act of an English version of Corneille's *Pompée*, translated into verse couplets and published in 1664. In the dedication Dryden urged his young patron to write more, "which might be an honour to our Age and Country." But Buckhurst, in Dryden's view, is clearly headed for greater things than literature. As a young lord he will soon "enter into the serious and more unpleasant business of the world." Dryden indeed *wishes* that Buckhurst may be "soon call'd to bear a part in the affairs of the Nation, where I know the world expects you, and wonders why you have been so long forgotten" (*Works*, vol. XVIII, pp. 4–5). But as long as Buckhurst has some time to spare, Dryden urges him to think of "writing something, in whatever kind it be." The vagueness of the wish ("something, in whatever kind") and the plainly beckoning civic duties suggest that in Dryden's mind a young nobleman expected to leave versifying and playwriting behind him – and to leave that to the poets.[27]

Dryden's dedications to Rochester and Buckhurst represent not an open break with the patronage system, but a re-orientation of his own position within it, an essentially defensive maneuver. Nor was this the only strategy Dryden deployed in strengthening the writer's hand. In the exactly contemporaneous dedication to *The Assignation* Dryden tried a complementary strategy: instead of urging the patron not to cross the line, Dryden, in a kind of rhetorical sortie, crossed it himself. While the dedication to Rochester is addressed to "the Right Honourable, the Earl of Rochester," *The Assignation* is addressed "To My Most Honour'd Friend, Sir Charles Sedley, Baronet."[28] The difference in formality is not wholly accounted for by the difference in the rank of the addressees. Dryden's approach in the address to Sedley (Rochester's fellow court wit) is that of a "friend": "The Design of Dedicating Playes, is as common and unjust, as that of desiring Seconds in a Duel. 'Tis engaging our Friends (it may be) in a senceless quarrel, where they have much to venture, without any

---

[27] Compare the dedication of *The Rival Ladies* to Orrery in 1664, in which "Plotting and Writing" are "troublesome employments" requiring considerable pains. For Orrery, primarily a "Man of business," writing is "a Diversion of your Pain" (Orrery was known to write plays during fits of the gout that kept him inactive). "The Poet" is "but subordinate to the States-man in you" (*Works*, VIII, 96–97) – and Dryden implies that Orrery should keep it that way, would do better to devote himself to affairs of state.

[28] *The Assignation* and *Marriage A-la-Mode* were both entered in the Stationers' Register on March 18, 1673, advertised together on May 29, and listed together in the June 16 term catalogue. See *Works*, XI, 519.

concernment of their own" (*Works*, vol. XI, p. 319). Again borrowing
a metaphor from dueling (implicitly suggesting that the writer is a
gentleman rather than an artisan or servant), Dryden (with the
dedication to Rochester in mind) pointedly imagines his patron not
as his potential opponent but as his second.

The dedication goes on to describe the way in which Sedley serves
both as Dryden's "best Patron" and his "best Friend." Although
called a patron, Sedley is here cast primarily as a poet. Dryden
compares him not to Maecenas but to Tibullus. In the classical
parallel that Dryden develops, his own role is implicitly that of Ovid,
a fellow poet and fellow "*Roman* Knight." In a famous passage
Dryden paints a picture of their "Conversation and Friendship":

> We have, like them [i.e., like Ovid and Tibullus], our Genial Nights; where
> our discourse is neither too serious, nor too light; but always pleasant, and
> for the most part instructive: the raillery neither too sharp upon the present,
> nor too censorious on the absent; and the Cups onely such as will raise the
> Conversation of the Night, without disturbing the business of the Morrow.
> (pp. 320–21)

Here Dryden crosses the line that conventionally separates writer
from patron, affirming that he is the social equal of a court wit. He
also reverses the conventional relationship between patron and poet.
By dedicating his work to Sedley Dryden will procure fame not for
the patron but for himself: "they who ... wou'd forget me in my
Poems, wou'd remember me in this Epistle" (p. 320). Perhaps it
would be more apt to say that Dryden obliterates the line, with his
continual talk of how the pointedly informal "we" – boon companions! – conduct ourselves at table. Dryden's enemies, perhaps with
such passages in mind, liked to laugh at his awkward attempts to pass
himself off as a wit.[29] But they may have missed the implicitly
political point he was making. To present himself as the equal of a
friendly baronet may have been a calculated move as Dryden
jockeyed for position in relation to the "Great Persons of our Court"
(p. 320) whose favor he continued to seek.[30]

[29]   See, for example, Shadwell's *Medall of John Bayes*, and Rochester's "An Allusion to
       Horace."
[30]   We might read the early *Essay of Dramatick Poesie* (1668) – in which Sedley also figures – as
       another instance of Dryden promoting the poet to an equal level with the patron. The four
       speakers in the dialogue, Eugenius, Crites, Lisideius, and Neander, "three of them persons
       whom their witt and Quality have made known to all the Town" (*Works*, XVII, 8), are
       customarily identified as Dorset, Sir Robert Howard, Sedley, and Dryden himself (*Works*,
       XVII, 352–56).

The line between aristocratic patron and poet is redrawn even more clearly in the "Preface" to *All for Love*, in which Rochester again figures prominently. Perhaps not surprisingly, the play is dedicated not to a literary lord, but to the Lord Treasurer, the Earl of Danby, whose business as the king's chief minister so occupies him that, as Dryden says, you have "scarce any hour of your Life you can call your own." His "want of leisure" (*Works*, vol. xiii, pp. 8–9) means that, even if he had the inclination, he has no time for making verses. Dryden praises him for having "restor'd" and "advanc'd the Revenues of your Master," for providing the king with "the Means of exerting the chiefest ... of His Royal Virtues, his Distributive Justice to the Deserving, and his Bounty and Compassion to the Wanting" (pp. 4–5). The implication is that Danby's proper role, as minister and as patron, is to ensure the flow of funds and to direct them to the deserving and wanting – not least of whom are the country's poets.

In the substantial "Preface" to the play Dryden makes what is usually read as a thinly veiled attack on his former patron, Rochester, ridiculing him as little more than a man "of pleasant Conversation" who thinks himself a wit, so foolish as to expose his own "nakedness" (lack of wit), and primarily driven by vanity and malice (p. 14). Biographical critics focusing on the personal relationship between Dryden and Rochester point to the sharp contrast between the compliments in the dedication to *Marriage A-la-Mode* and the satire in the "Preface" to *All for Love*, and conclude primarily that the two had clearly fallen out between 1673 and 1678. But if we focus – as Dryden does – not so much on personal allusions to Rochester but on the relationship between writers ("We who write" – p. 14) and patrons ("they who should be our Patrons" – p. 16), we see continuity rather than contrast. Dryden is developing a theme he had announced earlier: the patron should be content to perform his assigned role in the patronage system, and leave writing to the writers:

We who write, if we want the Talent, yet have the excuse that we do it for a poor subsistence; but what can be urg'd in their defence, who not having the Vocation of Poverty to scribble, out of meer Wantonness take pains to make themselves ridiculous? (p. 14)[31]

It is understandable that poets might well want to be "rich," but it is

---

[31] As Paul Hammond has noted (*John Dryden*), Dryden slyly refers here to Rochester's "Satyr Against Mankind" (lines 137–38) in which man is said by "voluntary pains" to work his own distress out of mere "wantonness."

folly for the "rich" to want to be poets, and to be "discontented, because the Poets will not admit them of their number" (pp. 14–15).

Dryden goes on to distinguish on the one hand between Dionysius and Nero, notorious examples of bad patrons, and on the other Maecenas, the usual example of the good patron. While the former "proclaim'd themselves Poets by sound of Trumpet" and arranged to have themselves crowned laureates, Maecenas was witty enough to realize that poetry was not his talent. Nero perverted the office of patron, and goes down in history not only as a tyrant but also as a fool and a wretched poetaster. Maecenas is shrewder: "he thought it his best way to be well with *Virgil* and with *Horace*; that at least he might be a Poet at the second hand; and we see how happily it has succeeded with him; for his own bad Poetry is forgotten, and their Panegyricks of him still remain" (pp. 15–16).

Dryden's preface clearly signals to the Restoration patron – not only to Rochester but to any would-be patron – that Maecenas is the proper model to emulate: support a writer, but be content to remain in the background, and you will ensure your own fame. This implicitly challenges the patron's authority and limits his role to that of benefactor (provider of funds). Not only does Dryden reject the idea that the patron's relation to the client is that of "monarch" to "subject." He even challenges the patron's "right of judging." Dryden affirms, at the opening of the passage in question, that peers like Rochester, with only a "trifling kind of fancy, perhaps helped out by some smattering of Latin," lack wit and knowledge of the art of poetry, and are in fact not "qualified to decide sovereignly concerning poetry." And, after some barbed allusions to Rochester's poetic "Allusion to Horace," he returns to the same point. He will leave off, he says, "without farther considering him, than I have the rest of my illiterate Censors, whom I have disdain'd to answer, because they are not qualified for Judges" (p. 18). In the dedication to his *Essay of Dramatick Poesie* Dryden had declared that the court is "the best and surest judge of writing" (*Works*, vol. XVII, p. 4). He now refuses to accept the polite fiction that all men of noble education are possessed of true taste and thus qualified to act as literary monitors. This blow strikes at the heart of the aristocratic patron's traditional claim to preside over culture.

What is usually read, then, as an attack on a single patron should perhaps, in the context I am trying to develop, be also read as Dryden's assertion that the entire patronage system needs to be adjusted. The implication is that by insisting on being poets and judges the patrons are throwing the system out of proper balance; Dryden suggests that he is only restoring the traditional balance. But with the advantage of hindsight we can perhaps see that it is Dryden himself, increasingly aware of what Pope would later call the poet's "Dignity," who is trying to change the balance.

DRYDEN'S LATER DEDICATIONS

It is usually assumed that Dryden was in his later career simply happier in his patrons, especially Mulgrave and Dorset. My suspicion is that the falling out with Rochester was not just a turbulent episode but a kind of watershed. Although he would not again quarrel in print with a member of the patron class, in his dedications over the last two decades of his career Dryden found polite strategies by which to make claims for the rights and privileges of the poet over against those of the patron.

One strategy is in effect to put a limit on the patron's authority. Perhaps the best instance of this is found in Dryden's gracious tributes to Dorset in the "Discourse concerning the Original and Progress of Satire," prefixed to the 1693 translation of Juvenal and Persius. Dryden praises Dorset as the best of contemporary satirists – a pardonable exaggeration since by 1693 all of the Restoration satirists we remember (Butler, Rochester, Oldham, Marvell) except Dryden himself were dead. Dryden acknowledges Dorset's authority as Lord Chamberlain to regulate the "Decency and Good Manners of the Stage," and goes on to recognize not only the "Authority which is annex'd to your Office" but that which is "inborn and inherent to your Person: What is produc'd in you by an Excellent Wit, a Masterly and Commanding Genius over all Writers."[32] But at the same time Dryden subtly circumscribes that authority. If Dorset is the "King of Poets," then Dryden offers himself as an honest "Councellour":

as a Councellour bred up in the knowledge of the Municipal and Statute Laws, may honestly inform a just Prince how far his Prerogative extends; so I may be allow'd to tell your Lordship, who by an undisputed Title, are the King of Poets, what an extent of Power you have, and how lawfully you may exercise it over the petulant Scriblers of this Age. (*Works*, vol. IV, p. 9)

[32] On the conventional view of the patron's authority, see above, pp. 23–25.

In a literary world still organized according to the patronage system Dorset is "King" and Dryden one of his subjects.[33] But in a discourse about the legal limits of satire,[34] Dryden implicitly makes the important point that the patron's "Prerogative" is not unlimited, and that he too must exercise his "Power ... lawfully." Dryden is prepared to grant that as an "Excellent Wit" and a "Masterly and Commanding Genius," Dorset has the authority to "give the final decision of Wit" (p. 10), but this turns out to be a perfunctory gesture. It is Dryden's own very prescriptive "Discourse" that confirms the canon of ancient and modern satire he inherited from Casaubon and others, and details both the excellences and the deficiencies of the various practitioners. Dryden's own authority as judge derives not from his patron but from his learning, from the great satirists themselves (e.g. Boileau, "whose Example alone is a sufficient Authority" [p. 80]), and from his own practice. Dryden's polite fiction is that he is not instructing Dorset ("I will not burthen your Lordship with more [examples of "turns"]; for I write to a Master, who understands them better than my self" [p. 86]). He pretends that he is not telling Dorset anything he doesn't know already: "The quickness of your Imagination, my Lord, has already prevented me; and you know before-hand, that I wou'd prefer the Verse of ten Syllables, which we call the *English* Heroique, to that of Eight. This is truly my Opinion" (p. 82). Offering a judgment as his "own opinion" (a characteristic gesture) allows Dryden here and elsewhere to be both self-effacing (it's just my opinion, for what that's worth) and self-assertive (this is what I believe – and I am in effect my own authority).

Dryden's praise is subtly – and perhaps unconsciously – undermined too when he distinguishes between a learned poet, master of a high art, and a man with some natural gifts, by playing Jonson to Dorset's Shakespeare. Dorset's lyric poems, says Dryden, are "the Delight and Wonder of this Age" (p. 6). This echoes Jonson's well-known praise of Shakespeare, "The applause! delight! the wonder of our Stage," from a poem that seemed to many (including Dryden) an ambiguous tribute.[35] Within a sentence Dryden in fact names

---

[33] In the dedication of *Love for Love*, published two years later than Dryden's Juvenal, Congreve refers to Dorset's "*Monarchy* in *Poetry*" (*Complete Plays*, 209).

[34] Cf. Dryden's remarks about the lawfulness of lampoon (*Works*, IV, 59–60, 81).

[35] "To the Memory of My Beloved, the Author Mr. William Shakespeare: And What He Hath Left Us," line 18.

Jonson's "Verses to the Memory of Shakespear," not as an analogy to his own praise of Dorset but to Rochester's. Jonson's poem (like Rochester's passage on Dorset in his "Allusion to Horace") is "An Insolent, Sparing, and Invidious Panegyrick." This loud profession both condemns Rochester and covers up any guilt or embarrassment Dryden may feel in implying, as he clearly does, that Dorset writes happily, but without art or knowledge.

More generally, Dorset is accorded a position as a sort of honorary king and judge. It is implicitly understood that he will make no claim to actual rule, and has no interest in becoming – like Rochester – a "Tyrant of Wit." Rochester's name is in fact invoked in the "Discourse," ostensibly to cite – and to improve on – his praise of Dorset as satirist ("The best Good Man, with the worst-Natur'd Muse"). But Rochester also fulfills the rhetorical function of exemplifying Dorset's opposite, insolent, sparing, and invidious whether he is dispensing praise or patronage, his every act motivated by "self-sufficiency" (p. 6). And instead of having to persuade Dorset to confine himself to a few leisurely papers of verses, Dryden can complain that "your Lordship's only fault is, that you have not written more" (p. 11). But in the context of the "Discourse" as a whole, we can see that this is disingenuous. Although Dryden officially regrets that "because you need not write, you will not" and "out of a vicious Modesty will not Publish" (pp. 7, 11), he in effect accepts (and ratifies) the aristocratic patron's decision, and fixes Dorset in the traditional pose of the gentleman-amateur, content to write "Verses" and claims the field of "Poems" and satire for himself.[36]

Another strategy for shifting the balance of power – or, more properly, the balance of authority – is to make claims about the poet's "rights" in relation to those of the patron. "Rights" was a powerful term in late seventeenth-century discourse, especially after the passage of the Declaration of Rights in 1689. Dryden seems to have sensed that the idea of rights – more associated with the rising Whig tradition than with Dryden's own Tory tradition of support for Stuart authority, then in eclipse – might be wittily transferred from

[36] For a recent reading of the *Discourse* that pushes what I call Dryden's resistance much further, see Anne Cotterill, "The Politics and Aesthetics of Digression," 464–95. She reads the *Discourse* as a veiled attack on Dorset, a "court slave" (like Horace) in a tyrant's service. But as Cotterill herself acknowledges, Dryden continued to consider Dorset "a friend and patron" (p. 476) and finds much to praise.

the political to the literary sphere. At a time when the air was full of appeals to ancient English liberties guaranteed by Magna Charta, Dryden in the 1697 dedication of the *Aeneis* justifies his use of triplets (with an alexandrine final line) in heroic verse by appealing to the precedents set by Spenser, Chapman, and Cowley as the "*Magna Charta* of Heroick Poetry" (*Works*, vol. v, p. 331).[37] Indeed, as early as the 1679 dedication of *Troilus and Cressida* Dryden announced his intention to "reassume the ancient rights of Poetry."[38] The irony of a "Tory" poet pleading "ancient rights" was presumably not lost on his readers and patrons, both Whig and Tory.

For Dryden the idea of rights also carried implicit economic connotations, for in his dealings with booksellers, formalized by legal contract, he was concerned to protect his rights as a producer of verses.[39] In addressing a patron, however, a writer conventionally approaches not as a person with legal or economic rights, but as a supplicant. It is the patron who has rights. Thus Dryden tells the Earl of Danby in the dedication of *All for Love* that "your Lordship has the same right to favour Poetry which the Great and Noble have ever had" (*Works*, vol. XIII, p. 3). To speak of his own "rights" in an address to a patron, or to use related terms such as "title," "privilege," "estate," and "claim," even if there is a degree of banter in his tone, is to suggest that in any literary dealings, whether with a patron or a bookseller, Dryden does not consider himself merely the grateful recipient of largesse.[40] Dryden seemed to believe not only that the country had an obligation to support its great poets, and that the great patrons of the day bore the responsibility for supporting culture, but that the poet for his part had a "right" to such support.[41]

Thus, Dryden in 1693 says that having first addressed Dorset in his *Essay of Dramatick Poesie* in 1668, "and therein bespoke you to the World," he claims the "Priviledge" and "the right of a First Discoverer." Dryden wittily reverses the usual relationship between patron and poet. Rochester was famous for having "discovered"

---

[37] In the same paragraph Dryden speaks of taking "License in my Verses" and of "these priviledges of *English* Verses" – implicitly political language.

[38] *Works*, XIII, 221. The "rights" in question are prophesying and identifying heroes.

[39] The 1697 contract with Tonson does not explicitly refer to the "rights" of bookseller or poet.

[40] Dryden says he pretends to "no right" over the works by his fellow contributors to *Examen Poeticum* and does not assume the "Priviledge" of "Inscribing" them (*Works*, IV, 369).

[41] Cf. Rowe's dedication of *The Fair Penitent* (1703): "The privilege of poetry ... has given [poets] a kind of right to pretend ... to the favor of [the Great]."

Oldham living in obscurity, and Dorset himself was praised for having "discovered" Milton's works lying unread on a bookseller's stall and recommending them to Tonson for publication in the elaborate 1688 folio. Here Dryden claims to have "discovered" Dorset's talent and his patronage while the latter was still a young man.[42] The "first discoverer" of a new land – Dryden later says he was "sailing in a vast Ocean" without a "Compass" – was of course permitted in law to take title (in the name of the king), and presumably to be handsomely recompensed.

As early as the dedication of *An Evening's Love* to the Duke of Newcastle in 1671 Dryden had played with the idea of the poet's "title." Newcastle had earlier patronized both Jonson and Davenant, poets with whom Dryden wished to associate himself. By thanking Newcastle for his kindness to himself and to his predecessors, Dryden can "in some measure joyn my name with theirs: and the continu'd descent of your favours to me is the best title which I can plead for my success" (*Works*, vol. x, p. 200). Newcastle is clearly not expected to refer such language to his lawyers, but Dryden seems here to hint that to hold the "title" of legitimate successor (and heir) to Jonson would in turn entitle Dryden to *continued* support from Newcastle. Entitlement is often the subtext of Dryden's dedications. His repeated emphasis, as the years went by, on his "misfortunes" and his "ruin," the "unsettledness of my condition" and especially the encouraging "fair Words" that did not lead to solid support or to a "prospect of a future Subsistance," constitute not simply a complaint but a claim.[43]

The idea of the poet's "title" comes back again in the last decade of Dryden's career, when he has lost his salaried offices but can look back at the private patronage he has enjoyed – and to which he somehow feels entitled – after thirty years of honorable service.[44] In the dedication of Virgil's *Pastorals* to Hugh Lord Clifford, Baron Chudleigh, Dryden begins by recalling that Clifford's father had been "the Patron of my Manhood." When he returns to the theme of

[42] Etherege had in fact "discovered" Dorset earlier, by dedicating *The Comical Revenge* to him in 1664. See Dryden, *Works*, iii, 528.

[43] See the dedications to *Aureng-Zebe* and to *Juvenal* (*Works*, iv, 23). For other examples of Dryden's complaints of neglect and suffering, see the dedications to *Virgil's Pastorals* (1697), *Amphitryon* (1690), *Don Sebastian* (1690), and *Examen Poeticum* (1693).

[44] In the dedication of *Love Triumphant* to the Earl of Salisbury, a distant relation of his wife, Dryden refers to "the honour of my wife's relation to your noble house, to which my sons may plead some title, though I cannot" (*Works*, ed. Scott, rev. Saintsbury, viii, 372–73).

the virtues Clifford has inherited, Dryden also calls to mind the responsibilities, and gives a new twist to the idea of the patron's proprietorship:

You are acquainted with the *Roman* History, and know without my information that Patronage and Clientship always descended from the Fathers to the Sons; and that the same *Plebeian* Houses, had recourse to the same patrician Line, which had formerly protected them: and follow'd their Principles and Fortunes to the last. So that I am your Lordship's by descent, and part of your Inheritance. (*Works*, vol. v, p. 7)

By itself the final sentence conveys an elegant compliment: Clifford inherits a poet to serve and honor him. But in the context of "*Roman* History" he inherits the obligation to provide protection. Dryden claims his rights of "Clientship" give him "recourse" to patronage from the Clifford family.[45]

In the dedication of the *Fables* to the Duke of Ormonde in 1700 Dryden is even bolder: support from the Ormonde family is a kind of "estate" to which the poet makes claim. Dryden lays the groundwork for the claim in the dedication's opening sentence: "Some Estates are held in *England*, by paying a Fine at the change of every Lord: I have enjoy'd the Patronage of your Family, from the time of your excellent Grandfather to this present Day" (*Poems*, vol. IV, p. 1439). For the moment the patron might imagine that Dryden is referring to the Ormonde family estate, which passed into the hands of the present Duke in 1688. But as Dryden goes on his meaning becomes clearer: he means his own "estate" – the right to Ormonde's favor. Having honored two previous generations of the family Dryden has now "liv'd to a third Generation of your House; and by your Grace's Favour am admitted still to hold from you by the same Tenure." Dryden's right, so his metaphor implies, is as strong as a feudal tenure. Just as the Ormonde family "were cherish'd and adorn'd with Honours by two successive Monarchs," so Dryden (whose liege lord, so to speak, is Ormonde) has been "esteem'd, and patronis'd, by the Grandfather, the Father, and the Son." Although Dryden has delayed the "Payment of my last Fine," i.e., has not dedicated a work to the present duke since he succeeded to his title in 1688, he pleads that the "rigour of Law" does not require a "forfeiture of my Claim."

[45] Evidence recorded in *OED* suggests that "recourse" did not acquire its specifically legal meaning (a right to make a pecuniary demand) until the mid-eighteenth century, but Dryden's may be an unrecorded early usage.

The most significant of the poet's "rights," however, points not to his claim for support but to his ability to confer fame. In dedicating his translation of Virgil's *Georgics* to Chesterfield, Dryden honors the earl's "Principles of Generosity and Probity": "The World knows this, without my telling; Yet Poets have a right of Recording it to all Posterity. Dignum Laude Virum, Musa vetat Mori" (*Works*, vol. v, p. 140). The quotation from Horace (Ode iv, 8, 28) illustrates Dryden's meaning, but also exemplifies it: the praise that Horace offered has made the virtues of honest Romans known "to all Posterity." In claiming the "right of Recording" Dryden reminds the sympathetic Chesterfield – a Tory statesman out of place – and any other patrons or readers – that the poet has great powers, and an important role to play in a culture, a role just as important as that of the statesman.

"ONE TO PERFORM, ANOTHER TO RECORD"

One of Dryden's favorite themes throughout his career (in poems and in dedications) is what he called in the early *Astraea Redux* (1661) "the joint growth of Armes and Arts" (line 322, in *Works*, vol. 1, p. 31). England needs its Augustus, but it also needs its Virgil. Nearly forty years later Dryden found a way to make the same point at the end of an address to his honored kinsman, John Driden:

> Two of a House, few Ages can afford;
> One to perform, another to record.
> Praise-worthy Actions are by thee embrac'd;
> And 'tis my Praise, to make thy Praises last.
> (*Poems*, vol. iv, p. 153, lines 203–06)

The idea that the poet who confers praise has an important power and responsibility is as old as Horace and as recent as Milton, but Dryden goes further to declare that the recorder is as important as the performer. He could have found it in Milton's high conception (in his controversial prose) of his role as the recorder of English achievements and the defender of truth.[46] But Dryden seems to have adoped the theme as his own, and makes implicit and sometimes

---

[46] Cf. Milton's *Second Defense of the English Nation*: "If God willed the success of such glorious achievements, it was equally agreeable to his will that there should be others by whom those achievements should be recorded with dignity and elegance, and that the truth, which had been defended by arms, should also be defended by reason; which is the best and only legitimate means of defending it" (*Complete Poems and Selected Prose*, 819).

explicit use of it in dedications to his patrons. *Tyrannick Love* (1670) is dedicated to the dashing young soldier, the Duke of Monmouth. "Heaven has already taken care to form you for a Heroe" with the endowments of "Illustrious Birth" and "all the advantages of Mind and Body." But the work of making the hero is not complete: "the *Achilles* and the *Rinaldo* are present in you, ever above their Originals; you only want a *Homer* or a *Tasso* to make you equal to them" (*Works*, vol. x, p. 107). It is the poet, in other words, who finally makes the hero. In the dedication of *The Conquest of Granada* Dryden declares that the Duke of York has acted the part of hero – his "whole life has been a continu'd Series of Heroique Actions"(*Works*, vol. xi, p. 3). Dryden's role – which receives equal emphasis – is "to perform the part of a just Historian to my Royal Master," and to "fill the Annals of a glorious Reign." Each has his separate responsibility: "while your Royal Highness is preparing fresh employments for our pens [i.e., has been performing heroic actions that will later need to be written up]: I have been examining my own forces [the metaphor links the "forces" of "arts" with those of "arms"], and making tryal of my self how I shall be able to transmit you to Posterity" (*Works*, vol. xi, p. 6). Dryden's use of "tryal" suggests that his action too is implicitly heroic. Indeed, James enacts the part of hero, but Dryden has "form'd a Heroe" in inventing Almanzor.

The same theme (in the same language) appears in the dedication of *All for Love* to Danby, although Dryden takes more care to preserve modesty. "There is somewhat of a tye in Nature betwixt those who are born for Worthy Actions and those who can transmit them to Posterity: and though ours be much the inferiour part, it comes at least within the Verge of alliance; nor are we unprofitable members of the Commonwealth, when we animate others to those Virtues, which we copy and describe from you" (*Works*, vol. xiii, p. 3). Dryden deploys the conventional idea that the poet both transmits fame and animates readers to virtue (so that they in turn might win fame), but puts unusual emphasis on the importance of poets to those (like Danby) who are "the Fathers of their Country." The "Records" of fame produced by the poet-recorder even have a kind of quasi-legal status:

such who, under Kings, are the Fathers of their Country, and by a just and prudent ordering of affairs preserve it, have the same reason to cherish the Chroniclers of their Actions, as they have to lay up in safety the Deeds and

Evidences of their Estates: For such Records are their undoubted Titles to the love and reverence of After-Ages. (pp. 3–4)

The poets are more than not "unprofitable Members of the Commonwealth." In a society where preservation of status depends on continuation of "reverence" and where access to wealth and power is directly related to rank, the "Records" and "Titles" produced by the poets have a palpable economic and political value.

If the "perform vs. record" topos leads to the conclusion that the poet is in some sense equal to – or even superior to – the patron, this is a theme that Dryden in other ways hints at in his dealings with his patrons, especially in his later career. In the dedication of *Don Sebastian* (1690) Dryden observes in passing that Leicester has "more than once ... been offering him his Patronage" (*Works*, vol. xv, p. 63). To underline the point Dryden notes that while Leicester's ancestor Sidney gave patronage to Spenser in response to "the applications of a Poet," Leicester "offer'd it unask'd."[47] The implication is that as a poet of established reputation and by service to his country Dryden no longer need be a supplicant at preferment's gate: his patrons wait on him. In the same year Dryden boldly tells Sir William Levenson-Gower, dedicatee of *Amphitryon*, that "I have chosen you, with your permission, to be the Patron of the Poem" (*Works*, vol. xv, p. 233). And seven years later Dryden uses the same formula in dedicating the *Pastorals* to Clifford: "I could not possibly have chosen better, than the Worthy Son of so illustrious a Father" (*Works*, vol. v, p. 3).[48]

The strongest sign of the poet's control of the patronage relationship is of course his refusal to accept an offer of patronage. There is no record that Dryden turned down such an offer, but he did refuse Tonson's suggestion that the *Aeneis* be dedicated to King William, and offered the three parts of the Virgil translation to three men who had distanced themselves from the king.[49] When the country's poets poured forth elegies on the death of Queen Mary in 1694 Dryden was notable by his silence. It is probably significant too that although in 1693 he dedicated to her grieving husband an elegy on the death of the Countess of Abingdon, Dryden formally inscribed no other

---

[47] Winn, *John Dryden*, 437 also notices the importance for Dryden of the point that Leicester approaches *him*.

[48] Cf. the 1694 dedication of *Love Triumphant* to the Earl of Salisbury: "I have presum'd to make you my patron" (*Works*, ed. Scott, rev. Saintsbury, viii, 372).

[49] For details, see Winn, *John Dryden*, 484–85.

original poems – as opposed to translations – to any patron.[50] He
may have sensed that some work should be held back as wholly his
own.

An apparent exception, *Annus Mirabilis* (1667), is dedicated "TO the
Metropolis of Great Britain." True, many of Dryden's English
poems are cast as verse epistles – "To Sir Robert Howard," "To My
Lord Chancellor," "To Her Grace the Dutchess of Ormond"[51] –
and were thus implicitly dedicated to the addressee. Dryden may
have considered that his poetic labors during the years 1668 to 1688
– when he received a salary from the crown – already had a royal
patron. But on some important occasions, such as *Religio Laici* (1684)
and *The Hind and the Panther* (1687), Dryden appeared in print not as
the king's servant but as a "layman" and a private citizen. *The Hind
and the Panther*, he declares in a prefatory address "To the [anon-
ymous] Reader," was "neither impos'd on me, nor so much as the
Subject given me by any man" (*Works*, vol. III, p. 121), in language
that in effect declares that the poet was *independent of* the patronage
system and its assumptions. *Religio Laici* is not presented as a defense
of the king's church but as a "Confession of my own" (*Works*, vol. II,
p. 98).[52] For whatever reason then, Dryden over more than four
decades saw fit to publish his English poems without benefit of any
protection from a patron. For a poet working under the patronage
system to pass over in silence the opportunity of dedicating is itself
eloquent testimony to his claim that in some matters he is his own
master and the master of his own work.

The analogy of Sidney's generosity to Spenser in the dedication of
Don Sebastian provides Dryden with another opportunity to imply that
patron and poet are on a par. Though he modestly insists that "there
can never be another *Spencer*," Dryden encourages the idea that his
relationship to his patron is analogous to the relationship of Spenser to

[50] Dryden's contributions to *Examen Poeticum* (1693), dedicated to Lord Radcliffe, were
primarily translations. Two translations from Horace in his earlier *Sylvae* (1685) are
"inscribed" to Roscommon and Lawrence Hyde, Earl of Rochester.

[51] The last of these appeared as the first poem in the *Fables* (1700), a collection dedicated to
the duchess's husband, and might thus be regarded as a poetic continuation of the
dedicatory preface. It was apparently the duchess who, presumably on behalf of the duke,
presented Dryden with £500 (Johnson, *Lives of the Poets*, I, 408).

[52] In his "Preface" Dryden says that his "Verses" were written for and "address'd to" an
"ingenious young Gentleman my Friend; upon his Translation of *The Critical History of the
Old Testament*" (*Works*, II, 109). The gentleman in question, Henry Dickinson, is not even
named by Dryden, either in the "Preface" nor in the poem, even though Dryden at line
224 addresses a "Digression to the Translatour" (*Works*, II, 116).

Sidney. By the late seventeenth century, when they were both remembered as poets, the comparison clearly works in Dryden's favor. The same point is implicit in Dryden's making of Leicester a "second *Atticus*." By concluding his dedication "in the words of *Cicero* to the first of [the Attici]," Dryden confirms his own role as Cicero to Leicester's Atticus. What Dryden's reader remembers is not that Atticus was a great patron but that he was Cicero's friend.[53]

A similar jockeying for position goes on in Dryden's private correspondence with his patrons in the 1690s. In a very late letter to Charles Montague, seeking his "protection" of a proposal to translate the *Iliad*, Dryden assures the patron that "nothing ... shall stand without your permission," but finally insists on his own "conscience." The translation is undertaken, like the *Aeneis*, both for his country's honor [in which the patron would take an interest] and his own.[54] Chesterfield, acknowledging the dedication of the *Georgics*, speaks of Dryden's poem as an "unvaluable Present." Dryden, in return, politely and elegantly describes Chesterfield's cash as a "noble Present," thus implying that the patron-client relationship is really a ceremonious exchange of "presents" between equals.[55]

It is in his last decade, when Dryden had himself lost his official appointments, that he (perhaps by some obscure process of compensation) puts greatest emphasis on the poet's power and authority in relation to the patron. It is as if Dryden, having lost the sanction of royal authority in 1688, rediscovered authority in himself not only as the participant in a "venerable and transcendent literary tradition,"[56] but as a figure who could both confer fame and could – at least symbolically – act as performer too, and thereby enjoy the reward of fame. This is the period of *Alexander's Feast* (1697), in which the musician Timotheus, discharging the role of royal servant, not only praises his master Alexander and animates him to rage and desire, but is himself revealed as the "Mighty Master" (line 93) – not only music master but master of the puppet-like Alexander, who simply dances to Timotheus' tune. The poem celebrates not the power of Alexander (Dryden no doubt took some sly pleasure in

---

53 Cf. the dedication to *Aureng-Zebe* in which Dryden takes leave of Mulgrave by quoting the words of Cicero "which he sent with his Books *De Finibus*, to his Friend *Brutus*" (*Works*, XII, 58). Zwicker notes that Dryden emphasizes Leicester's Whiggish/Republican lineage to show him as a true, disinterested patron (*Politics and Language in Dryden's Poetry*, 183–85).

54 *Letters*, 121.

55 I take the last three sentences from my essay on "The Beginnings of Modern Authorship," 4.

56 Bywaters, *Dryden in Revolutionary England*, 22.

reducing the military hero – a stand-in for King William? – to a drunken amorous slave) but (in the words of the subtitle) "the power of music." The king at the end of the poem rushes off in a drunken revenge to burn the temples of the Persian gods, while Timotheus (whose pagan art had "rais'd a [mere] Mortal to the Skies") in effect supplants him: he divides the "Crown" of musical supremacy with St. Cecilia, patroness of Christian music. It is the name of Timotheus, not Alexander (never in fact named in the poem itself), that *Alexander's Feast* perpetuates.[57]

The poem enacts the symbolic supremacy of the artist over the patron. In various other ways during his final decade Dryden found occasions to make the same point. In the dedication to *Eleonora: A Panegyrical Poem Dedicated to the Memory of the Late Countess of Abingdon* (1692), for example, Dryden devotes most of his time not to the virtues of the deceased countess but to his own skill as a poet. He compliments himself on the "Happiness of the Execution," and pleads that "if I have not perform'd so well as I think I have, yet I have us'd my best endeavours to excel my self" (*Works*, vol. III, pp. 231–32). "Perform'd" is perhaps chosen deliberately: Dryden is not simply "recording" the virtues of the dead countess (whom, he says candidly, he had never met) but "performing" a public tribute. And in consequence he hopes for the reward that goes to great achievement:

as *Phidias* when he had made the Statue of *Minerva*, cou'd not forbear to ingrave his own Name, as Author of the Piece; so give me leave to hope, that by subscribing mine to this Poem, I may live by the Goddess, and transmit my name to Posterity by the memory of Hers. (pp. 233–34)

In a striking use of a phrase he had used before, Dryden hopes to "transmit to Posterity" not only the name of the poem's subject but the name of its author.[58] The poem's Latin epigraph (the lines containing Virgil's familiar "Hoc opus, hic labor est") makes the same point: it is only those few "of shining Worth, and Heav'nly Race" who are able to accomplish the "mighty Labour."[59] The lines

---

[57]　Some critics have argued that, although the poem on its surface delights in and marvels at the power of music, it in fact deplores Timotheus and his misuse of that power, and prefers the Christian music of St. Cecilia. But there is no reason to insist that Dryden's intentions were single or wholly consistent in a poem that devotes six stanzas to Timotheus and one to St. Cecilia.

[58]　As the California editors suggest, Dryden invites comparisons with Donne, whom he describes as "the great Wit, though not the best Poet of our Nation" (*Works*, III, 233).

[59]　*Aeneid*, VI, 128–31. I then cite from Dryden's own translation (*Works*, VI, 195–97).

may suggest that Eleonora has now mounted to the skies, but they say more emphatically that it is Dryden who has raised her to that eminence. The dedication not only redirects attention from the patron to the poet; it also suggests that in some sense the poet – as performing hero, whose name will descend to posterity – has occupied the patron's traditional space.[60]

There are other scattered hints in Dryden's final decade that in his mind the poet, while continuing to enjoy the patron's support, has as it were crossed the line and invaded his territory. In an aristocratic culture it had been the traditional role of the court and the great families to promote the country's glory, to increase its wealth, and to administer justice. (John Driden, a Justice of the Peace, is praised in that capacity.) Dryden's dedications in the 1690s increasingly imply that the poet in effect is (or ought to be) an officer of the state. In the "Discourse concerning . . . Satire" (1693) he suggests that satire has a quasi-judicial authority, punishing those whom the law cannot reach (*Works*, vol. IV, p. 59). To "make Examples of vicious Men" is "absolutely of a Poet's Office to perform" (p. 60).[61] In the dedication of the *Aeneis* in 1697 Dryden, while discussing the diction of the translation, describes himself as a kind of international trader in the office of the Lord Treasurer, importing "sounding Words" – like precious metal – from abroad:

I carry not out the Treasure of the Nation, which is never to return: but what I bring from *Italy*, I spend in England: Here it remains, and here it circulates; for if the Coyn be good, it will pass from one hand to another. I Trade both with the Living and the Dead, for the enrichment of our Native Language.

Perhaps to suppress the prejudices still attached to trade and commerce, Dryden appeals to older aristocratic ideals of "Magnificence": "if we will have things of Magnificence and Splendour, we must get them by Commerce" (*Works*, vol. V, p. 336).[62]

When he turned again to the fruits of translation in the "Preface"

---

[60] Cf. Congreve's contemporary "Epistle to the Right Honourable Charles Lord Halifax": "Honours which from Verse their Source derive, / Shall both surmount Detraction, and survive: / And Poets have unquestion'd Right to claim / If not the greatest, the most Lasting Name" (*Works*, III, 43). Congreve's ambiguous syntax suggests that both the honors conferred by and won by the poet are "most Lasting."

[61] Cf. the "Preface" to *Fables* (1700), where the satirical poet again plays a quasi-judicial role as "the Check of the Laymen, on bad Priests" (*Poems*, IV, 1454). Dryden's language in both passages (*crimes, punished, justice, innocent, guilty, condemnation*) suggests the judicial role.

[62] See Dryden's earlier use of the idea that the poet engages in a kind of "Commerce," in *Works*, IV, 12.. On magnificence, see above, pp. 35–39.

to his *Fables* (1700), Dryden again imagined himself as discharging a high function for the benefit of the nation. To modernize Chaucer and set him beside Ovid is to declare that the literature of England can stand comparison with that of classical Rome. The effect, Dryden hopes, is "to promote the Honour of my Native Country" which he says has "always" been his goal (*Poems*, vol. IV, p. 1445). The hopes of doing "honour" have been transferred to the translations from Dryden's earlier project of a native English epic. He had long harbored hopes of writing an epic as an "occasion to do honour by it to my King, my Country, and my friends" (dedication to *Aureng-Zebe* [1676], *Works*, vol. XII, p. 154). But the epic was never written – Dryden liked to imply that it was because he was never properly supported by patrons – and his references to the epic project in the 1690s are retrospective, though he still retains the high ambition of writing "chiefly for the Honour of my Native Country, to which a Poet is particularly oblig'd" (*Works*, vol. IV, p. 22). The *Aeneis* is "intended for the honour of my Country," and Dryden proudly claims that the translator preserves more of the spirit of Virgil than do the French or Italian versions (*Works*, vol. V, p. 325).

By imagining that as poet he might promote national honor, Dryden attempts to share the patron's authority or even to shift him into a secondary and supporting role.[63] At least one contemporary noticed the point Dryden was implicitly making. In his *Poetae Britannica* (1700) one Samuel Cobb praised Dryden's poetic conquests over French writers and suggested that poets had supplanted England's military heroes (then at war with France in a conflict whose outcome was yet unclear): "Now beyond our Arms, the Muse prevails,/ And Poets conquer, where the Heroe fails."[64]

Finally, there are hints that the poet plays a crucial role in maintaining the very foundation of a hereditary aristocracy – the perpetuation of the family line. One strategy is to suggest that the literary tradition, whether reaching back to Homer and Virgil or (in its native branch) back to Chaucer and Spenser, constitutes its own rival aristocracy. It is in these years that Dryden develops the theme that poets, like other families, have their own "Lineal Descents and

[63] Cf. the 1699 letter to Halifax, in which Dryden observes – in a matter-of-fact manner – that "'tis for my country's honour as well as for my own that I am willing to undertake the task [of translating Homer]" (*Letters*, 121).

[64] Cf. Aphra Behn on Bishop Burnet's praise of King William: "Your Pen shall more Immortalize his Name, / Than even his Own Renown'd and Celebrated Fame," in *Works*, I, 310.

Clans" (*Poems*, vol. IV, p. 1445).[65] Given the importance of poetic families, literary *succession* is as crucial as political succession, and Dryden's epistle "To My Dear Friend Mr. Congreve" (1694) dwells centrally on Dryden's concern that he have a proper successor on the "Throne of Wit" (an idea he first explored in the elegy on John Oldham a decade earlier).

Another strategy is to suggest that the scions of England's hereditary families depend on the poets for perpetuating their family lines. It is the muse, says Horace in a line quoted in the dedication of Dryden's translation of the *Georgics*, who "forbids men deserving of praise to die."[66] The poet can keep a name alive; he can also (in Dryden's favorite formulation) "transmit" it to posterity. The verb is more powerful and pointed than it appears. To "transmit" means to "pass on, *esp. by inheritance or heredity*."[67] This is of course the scion's own major responsibility – to pass on his name and substance, extending the blood lines (a point Dryden makes in the dedication of the *Fables* to the young Duke of Ormonde).[68]

Even when the scion somehow fails to produce an heir – a serious political problem in Restoration England – the poet can compensate. This perhaps explains the curious emphasis, in the epistle "To my Honour'd Kinsman," on Driden's bachelorhood. Dryden takes some pains to allude to his cousin's noble lineage. John Driden is himself descended from an "ancient Race" (*Poems*, vol. IV, pp. 1529–35, line 50), a "true Descendent of a Patriot Line" (line 195), but a "Second" rather than a first son (line 41) and thus "Heir" to his mother's rather than his father's lands. But the poet's cousin himself had no heir. Indeed, this was something of a problem in John Driden's family: none of his six brothers married. Dryden makes the best of it in the

---

[65] Cf. "Anne Killigrew" on the "Soul" that rolled through "all the Mighty Poets" (*Works*, III, 110), and the "Discourse concerning ... Satire" on Waller and Denham as "those two Fathers of our *English* Poetry (*Works*, IV, 84).

[66] Horace, Ode IV, 8, 28, quoted in the dedication of the *Georgics* (*Works*, V, 140). Dryden leaves Horace's Latin untranslated.

[67] *OED*, 2, emphasis added. In the dedication of the *Life of St. Francis Xavier* Dryden hopes that Queen Mary (wife of James II) may be "the chosen Vessel, by which it has pleas'd the Almighty goodness to transmit so great a blessing [i.e., a son]" (*Works*, XIX, 4).

[68] "The World is sensible that you worthily succeed, not only to the Honours of your Ancestors, but also to their Virtues. The long Chain of Magnanimity, Courage, easiness of Access, and desire of doing Good, even to the Prejudice of your Fortune, is so far from being broken in your Grace, that the precious Metal yet runs pure to the newest Link of it: Which I will not call the last, because I hope and pray, it may descend to late Posterity: And your flourishing Youth, and that of your excellent Dutchess, are happy Omens of my Wish" (*Poems*, IV, 1439).

poem, praising the serenity of the single life and invoking a little traditional misogyny. Even if cousin Driden is not "fruitful," his "Fields" are (line 44), and (like an Old Testament patriarch) he acts the role of generous benefactor to his neighbors and "Relations": "You feed with Manna your own *Israel*-Host" (lines 48–49). If not a *pater*, he is at least a "Patriot" (line 171). Dryden has been among the recipients of his generosity, and repays it in effect by performing for Driden what his cousin cannot do for himself: transmitting his name to posterity. " 'Tis my Praise," says Dryden in closing, "to make thy Praises last" (line 206).

It is Dryden's "Verse" that "preserves the Fame" (line 209), and Dryden himself seems aware that the fame is not only the kinsman's but the poet's too. In a contemporary letter (Ward, *Letters*, p. 120) describing the poem, Dryden once again emphasized, as he had in the dedication to *Eleonora*, his "own" enduring achievement, in language that will now seem familiar: "In the description which I have made of a Parliament Man, I think I have not onely drawn the features of my worthy Kinsman, but have also given my Own opinion, of what an Englishman in Parliament ought to be." Deploying the language of genealogical transmission, he goes on to say that he "delivers" the poem "as a Memorial of my own Principles to all Posterity."

CHAPTER 5

Jonathan Swift

As an ordained Anglican priest, with friends in both church and state to help him, Swift was inside the patronage system, and to some extent its beneficiary, in a way that his Roman Catholic friend and younger contemporary Pope was not. As a man of some real political influence, both during the Harley ministry in London and later as Dean of St. Patrick's, Swift was also empowered to act as a patron himself, and to smoothe the way for younger writers and churchmen. The irony is that Pope, the apparent outsider, in fact found more access to power and wealth than Swift, who had enough access to encourage him to dream of great rewards, and more than enough disappointment to make him bitter and resentful. Both Pope and Swift in their several ways were in fact provided comfortable support and reward; both liked to think of themselves as not only independent but "above" patronage: Swift would have endorsed Pope's mock-haughty claim that he was "above a patron," and might "condescend to call a minister my friend." Where they differ is in the strategies they constructed to assert and defend their independence and to soothe the sting of injured merit.

Among major writers of his day Swift is unusual, if not unique, in claiming to place himself firmly outside the patronage system. With the exception of *A Tale of a Tub*, no work of his own, in a writing career that extended from the 1690s to the 1740s, when patronage was at its height, is dedicated to a patron, and that dedication is riven with treacherous irony. In the *Tale* it is suggested that the dedication, as a worn out literary genre, can itself no longer please. The "Materials of Panegyrick being very few in Number, have been long since exhausted" ("The Preface").[1] But Swift's distaste clearly

---

[1] *A Tale of a Tub*, 49–50. "The utmost a poor Poet can do, is to get by heart a List of the Cardinal Virtues, and deal them with his utmost Liberality to his Hero or his Patron" (p. 50).

went deeper; there was something demeaning about the dedicator's posture. "I confess," he later wrote, "it is with some disdain that I observe great authors descending to write any dedications at all." *Descending* suggests that it is in effect the author rather than the patron who occupies the superior position. The young Swift had – without fanfare or obsequiousness – dedicated to King William his edition of the *Letters* of Sir William Temple (1700).[2] Years later Swift claimed he had once intended to "inscribe" his unfinished and unpublished *History of England* to Charles XII of Sweden, the only European prince who "might deserve that distinction from me" (*Prose Works*, vol. v, p. 11).

On the few occasions when he does write a dedication Swift carefully distances himself from any appearance that he is "descending." The dedication of *Tale of a Tub* to Somers is not only facetious; it nominally comes from the "bookseller" rather than the anonymous "author." The "author," in his equally facetious "Epistle Dedicatory" to "Prince Posterity," openly parodies the "usual Style of decry'd writers" both in offering "Reasons and Excuses for publishing their Works" and in appealing "to *Posterity*."[3] He also parodies assumptions of patronal authority underlying this or any other dedication. As patron, Prince Posterity, declares the dedicator, is the "sole Arbiter of the Productions of human Wit," and has an "inherent Birth-right to inspect" all modern writing. This doubly undermines the authority of patrons, not only by holding up to parodic ridicule the assignment of a right to judge, but by transferring that right from any mortal patron to "posterity" itself.

In the dedication "To the Right Honourable John Lord Somers," the bookseller's naive truth-telling exposes the reality beneath elaborate dedicatory compliments.[4] Dedications are mercenary devices, he notes innocently, designed to promote the sale of a book: "Your Lordship's Name on the Front, in Capital Letters, will at any time

---

2   The perfunctory dedication is reprinted in *Prose Works*, 1, 256. A copy of volume iii of Temple's *Letters* (1703) was inscribed in Swift's own hand to Count Magalotti, Councillor to the Grand Duke of Tuscany and a friend of Lord Somers (who had himself been a friend and political ally of Temple). See *Prose Works*, 1, 304. Swift may hint that, as a kind of counselor, he himself stands to Temple as Magalotti stands to the Grand Duke.

3   *A Tale of a Tub*, 30. The author consciously departs from dedicatory convention by pretending to praise his fellow writers Dryden, Tate, Durfey, Rymer, Dennis, Bentley, and Wotton.

4   The bookseller pretends to be "unacquainted in the Style and Form of Dedications" (*A Tale of a Tub*, 24).

get off one Edition" (*Tale of a Tub*, p. 23). They are written by hired pens, whose usual method is to recycle the materials from published dedications (p. 24) and to compile mere lists of virtues. Casting a cold eye on such unpromising materials, Swift in fact discovers a way to compliment Somers in an ingenious new way. The dedicator is reluctant "to ply the World with an old beaten Story of your Wit, and Eloquence, and Learning, and Wisdom, and Justice, and Politeness, and Candor, and Evenness of Temper in all Scenes of Life," for it is simply "the universal Report of Mankind" (p. 25), and the standard list of virtues conventionally attributed to all great men. (As Pope wrote in *Peri Bathous*, such men "have by their *Office*, a Right to a Share of the *Publick Stock* of Virtue."[5]) This is the old rhetorical device of preteritio, and its use here is unusually slippery and ironic, even for Swift. Is this "an old beaten Story" because it is a well-known and oft-told truth, or because it is merely conventional? Is Swift "reluctant" because he wishes not to appear merely conventional, because he cannot make the exhausted language of dedication convey the truth, or because he knows that the praise is no less false than the story of Somers' "Bravery, at the Head of an Army" or his "Lineal Descent from the House of *Austria*" (p. 25)? (Somers was of course a politician, not a soldier, and Swift elsewhere referred to his family background as "humble."[6])

Robert Martin Adams observes that Somers as the "quintessential money man" represented "everything against which Jonathan Swift stood most furiously opposed."[7] He goes so far as to find "covert hostility" throughout the dedication (p. 186). I suspect that, as in the case of both Temple and Harley, Swift's hostility was not incompatible with some desperate hope for further patronage. Whether or not Adams is right, the multiple irony of the dedication gives Swift some further protection. Somers as knowing man of the world need not take offense at the dedication. He can read the praise as witty compliment. In any case, Swift cancels the distance between dedicator and patron; both are urbane men of the world familiar with the clichés of dedication and the realities of politics, and can agree to

---

[5] Ch. 14, "How to make Dedications, Panegyricks or Satyrs," *Prose Works of Alexander Pope*, ed. Cowler, II, 227. "All Great Ministers, without either private or oeconomical Virtue are virtuous by their *Posts*; liberal and generous upon the *Publick Money*, provident upon *Parliamentary Supplies*, just by paying *Publick Interest*, couragious and magnanimous by the *Fleets* and *Armies*, magnificent upon the *Publick Expenses*, and prudent by *Publick Success*."

[6] *Prose Works*, x, 23. Cf. also *Examiner* 26, in *Prose Works*, III, 78–79.

[7] "In Search of Baron Somers," 192.

smile at them in bemused irony – though they may be smiling for different reasons.

A few years later Swift again appeared to reinforce the assumptions of the patronage system but in fact undermined them. He addressed to the Earl of Oxford (in the form of a "Letter") his *Proposal for Correcting, Improving and Ascertaining the English Tongue* (1712). Although Swift avoids *dedicating* the work to Oxford, he complies with the customs of dedication. He clearly expresses hopes that his lordship would respond both to the proposal and to Swift's praise of the "great Things done under your Ministry" (*Prose Works*, vol. IV, p. 18), and that the project "will owe its Institution and Patronage to your Lordship" (p. 16). Swift in effect proposes a "Society" (modeled on the French Academy) under the "Protection of a Prince" and under the "Countenance and Encouragement of a Ministry" (p. 5) to correct his native tongue. Such a project should appeal to the minister, Swift says, for it promotes the "Honour," the "Advantages," and the "Ornament of your Country," for which ministers (and the aristocracy generally) were, as Swift implicitly reminds Harley, traditionally responsible. More to the point, the proposal will ultimately promote the minister's own honor and fame. Swift appeals not for Oxford to provide private support, but for him to encourage the queen to follow Louis XIV's example in bestowing pensions on men of learning appointed to the "Society."

Swift's project has its origins in Restoration-era proposals, as does his appeal for royal patronage, which sounds traditionally deferential. But Swift in fact subverts the principles upon which such appeals are traditionally made. Although, he says, Charles I was a "great Patron of Learning" (p. 9), the English court, "which used to be the Standard of Propriety, and Correctness of Speech," has ever since the days of Charles II been "the worst School in *England*, for that Accomplishment, and so will remain, till better care be taken in the Education of our young Nobility" (p. 10). In other words, the traditional custodians of the language and of culture – the court and the nobility – are no longer qualified to perform that function. Members of the proposed "Society" would be chosen from those "best qualified ... without any regard to Quality, Party, or Profession" (p. 14). That is, "Quality" no longer "qualifies" a man to set cultural standards or to serve as a judge of correctness. Swift's dismissal of the rank-based authority of the traditional patron class could hardly be more complete.

Responsibility for fixing the language falls instead on men of learning. And to reinforce his appeal Swift reminds Oxford that monarchs and ministers alike are in fact dependent on such men. For a king's "lasting Monument" and a minister's very "Memory" cannot be entrusted to be preserved in the perishable "Hearts" of their loyal subjects. Durable fame can only be constructed by "the Pens of able and faithful Historians" (p. 17) writing in a language with the permanence of Latin. Risking affront, Swift warns Oxford that "if Genius and Learning be not encourag'd under your Lordship's Administration, you are the most inexcuseable Person alive" (p. 19). Even without irony Swift's appeals for patronage are imperious and unsettling.

In a much less known address to a patron, Swift near the end of his career again manipulated the dedicatory form so as to avoid "descending." He took an interest in promoting the poetical career of Mary Barber, who considered dedicating a collection of her poems to Orrery. Worried that dedicators cannot escape flattery, she asked Swift's opinion. He agreed that a "character" of Orrery could not properly come from her pen, and agreed to address a prefatory letter to Orrery on her behalf. It is a dedication, and yet not a dedication. Swift concedes the danger of being lumped with "the common Herd of Dedicators," and thus merely reviews for Orrery the various "Topicks" that she would have treated, had she written a dedication. This device, like that in the dedication to Somers, enables Swift to refer in an apparently matter-of-fact way to "Your Learning, your Genius, your Affability, Generosity," etc., without seeming to flatter. Barber, he concludes, has chosen a patron "justly." And, Swift advises Orrery, she "deserveth your Protection" (*Prose Works*, XIII, pp. 73–74). It is an ingenious rhetorical performance. Swift simultaneously plays the roles of dedicator, patron, and adviser to both.

Swift was well acquainted with the chief patrons of his day, including Somers and Halifax, and with the chief ministers, including Temple and Godolphin, Harley and Bolingbroke, and even, while still a very young man, had an audience with the king.[8] But with the exception of his early odes and *Proposal* addressed to Oxford, Swift provided no full-scale panegyrics to great men. Indeed, when he later provided characters of them in his prose works his words were

---

[8] For Swift's own brief account, see *Prose Works*, v, 194, where he reports that (presumably because he failed to persuade the king of the merit of his suit) "it was the first incident that helped to cure him of vanity."

carefully chosen to put in question their learning, their taste, or their liberality as patrons.[9] In Swift's *Examiner* 26 (February 1, 1710), Somers is said to lack even virtue. Halifax, he complained, provided "encouragements" to writers, but they were "onely good words and dinners."[10] Years later he was still wittily nursing the same grievance: "*Montague*, who claim'd the Station / To be *Maecenas* of the Nation, / For *Poets* open Table kept, / But ne'er consider'd where they Slept. / Himself, as rich as fifty *Jews*, / Was easy, though they wanted shoes."[11] Of his wit Swift wrote that he "never heard him say one good thing or seem to tast what was said by another."[12] Harley, he wrote, in words discreet enough to be shown to the subject himself, was concerned with "the generall welfare of His Country" and "perhaps" showed "too little regard to that of particular Persons."[13] In a later character, not published until after Swift's death, the criticism is somewhat sharper: Harley's "imperfections" included "Procrastination," especially "in the Disposall of Employments." And he was "heavily charged with the common Court vice of promising very liberally and seldom performing; of which I cannot altogether acquit him."[14] The reputed learning of the Earl of Dorset, another patron of great reputation, was "small or none."[15] Furthermore, the patrons of the day – especially those in the ministry – were in fact not performing their proper function of promoting real talent (rather than personal or political friends): "I never observed [a] Minister to use his Credit in the Disposal of an Employment to a Person whom he thought the fittest for it" (*Prose Works*, vol. IV, p. 246).[16]

---

9   "For Patrons never pay so well,/ As when they scarce have learn'd to spell" ("Directions for a Birth-day Song," in *Poems*, 463).

10 In his marginal "Notes on the Characters of Macky," in *Prose Works*, V, 258.

11 "Libel on Dr. Delany" (1730), lines 35–40.

12 *Prose Works*, V, 258.

13 See the manuscript character, in the *Journal to Stella*, II, 681–83. The character was later printed in the *History of the Four Last Years*, in *Prose Works*, VII, 73–75. Swift went on to provide some "allowance" for Harley's "Failing": "since he cannot be more careless of other Mens Fortunes than he is of his own" (*Journal to Stella*, 683).

14 Again Swift softened the blow: "Yet I am confident his Intentions were generally better than his disappointed Sollicitors would believe" (*Prose Works*, VIII, 137). Lady Mary Wortley Montagu thought Swift "ungratefull to the memory of his Patron the Earl of Oxford, making a servile Court where he had any interested views, and meanly abusive when they were disappointed" (*Complete Letters*, III, 57–58).

15 *Prose Works*, V, 258.

16 Of the covetous Duke of Marlborough Swift wrote: "None e'er did modern *Midas* [i.e., Marlborough] chuse,/ Subject or Patron of his Muse,/ But found him thus their Merit Scan,/ That *Phebus* must give place to *Pan*:/ He values not the Poet's Praise,/ Nor will exchange his *Plumbs* for *Bays*" ("The Fable of Midas," in *Poems*, 157).

Swift's public repudiation of the patronage system extended further: he refused money when it was offered him by Harley in acknowledgment of his work at the *Examiner*, perhaps because he did not like to think of himself a hired party writer; he was so embarrassed by the offer that he was driven to report it to Stella in cypher.[17] He refused to consent to a subscription edition of the *Examiner* papers, by which his friends said he might have made £500.[18] Money was corrupting: he joined the contemporary chorus of writers who lamented how "the Taste of *England* is infamously corrupted by *Sholes* of Wretches who write for their Bread."[19] Perhaps in order to place himself utterly above suspicion, he is reported to have accepted money for his writings only twice in his life.[20] To be sure, in Swift's case there were probably several motives for refusing money, but it is impossible to determine how much was gentlemanly pride, how much high principle, and how much a churchman's sense that a man of the cloth discharging his civic responsibilities should not be seen to profit from his pen.[21]

Swift not only refused to take money, he refused to consider himself a dependent of any man. His letters and journals not only from the years 1710–14 but throughout his life make clear that he prided himself as an equal to any minister, free to speak his mind before them and determined to preserve his dignity and independence.[22] He reported to Stella having "warned" Bolingbroke

Never to appear cold to me, for I would not be treated like a school-boy; that I had felt too much of that in my life already (meaning from sir William Temple); that I expected every great minister, who honoured me with his acquaintance, if he heard or saw any thing to my disadvantage, would let me know it in plain words, and not put me in pain to guess by the change or

17 See *Journal to Stella*, I, 208; and Harold Williams, "Swift's Early Biographers," 124.
18 See *Prose Works*, XIV, 3, and *Journal To Stella*, 399.
19 *Correspondence*, IV, 53.
20 See Johnson, *Lives of the Poets*, III, 50n. He sent his portion of the copy money for the Pope–Swift *Miscellanies* to a Dublin bookseller's widow (III, 38n). David Nokes says Swift received £40 in copy money for Temple's *Memoirs* (*Jonathan Swift*, 109). He received £200 for *Gulliver's Travels* (*Correspondence*, II, 152–55).
21 Curiously, in Swift's account of patronage in classical Greece and Rome, plebeians were dependent upon the patricians, "whom they chose for their Patrons and Protectors," supplying their patrons "with Money, in Exchange for their Protection." *Prose Works*, I, 212.
22 See for example the letter to Pope: "I have conversed in some freedom with more Ministers of State, of all Parties than usually happens to men of my level." *Correspondence*, II, 370.

coldness of his countenance or behaviour; for it was what I would hardly bear from a crowned head.[23]

He wanted it known that he was unwilling to defer or to beg, or even to approach, and seems to have made it a point of principle not to make the first advance. "I was at Court and church to-day," he wrote to Stella: "I generally am acquainted with about thirty in the drawing room, and I am so proud I make all the lords come up to me ... Duke Hamilton would needs be witty, and hold up my train as I walked up stairs" (*Journal to Stella*, vol. i, pp. 322–23). Such reports to Stella are difficult to interpret. On the one hand he is creating a little fiction in order to make innocent fun of himself, but on the other he is clearly pleased to be the center of attention, and glad of the opportunity to boast of his access. Delany was later to observe that Swift held it as a principle that "a man of genius was a character superiour to that of a Lord in high station,"[24] and thus lords should come to him. Orrery thought that Swift "assumed more the air of a patron, than of a friend. He affected rather to dictate than advise."[25] "I have taken Mr. Harley into favour again" (p. 191), he writes facetiously to Stella. But beneath the witty gaming lies a sense that his merit placed him not only above patronage, but above a patron. The heady atmosphere at court is perhaps responsible both for Swift's euphoria at being able to mix with the mighty, and for what probably lay beneath it – the anxious awareness that he was a kind of trained seal. But the determined hauteur seems to have become part of his character before he met Harley, as is suggested by the facetious *Decree for Concluding the Treaty between Dr. Swift and Mrs. Long* (1707–08), in which he stipulates that

Dr. *Swift*, upon the Score of his Merit and extraordinary Qualities, doth claim the sole and undoubted Right, that all Persons whatsoever, shall make such Advances to him, as he pleases to demand.[26]

And yet for all his pretense to be above or outside of the patronage system, Swift was very much in it, both as beneficiary and as patron. During his years in London (1710–14) Swift had no personal wealth to distribute and no places in his gift, but he was in a position to recommend to Oxford and Bolingbroke candidates for a variety of offices in church and state, or to "present" them at court – two of the

23 *Journal to Stella*, i, 230.
24 Patrick Delany, *Observations*, 29.
25 *Remarks*, 47.
26 *Prose Works*, v, 197.

traditional services of the patron. In the journal to Stella he pretends to complain about being "pestered" by "solicitors" seeking an introduction or a recommendation. Swift was in fact very active as a patron, especially for literary men. Among those he recommended to the ministers were Addison, Berkeley, Congreve, Diaper, Parnell, Ambrose Philips, Rowe, and Steele.[27] His motives seem a curious mix of generosity, vanity, and principle. Delany thought Swift "loved merit wherever he found it, and never seemed more delighted, than when he could draw it out from obscurity, into an advantageous light, and exalt it there."[28] But Swift was also clearly pleased to be able to display his power and to play the patron. Acting as a kind of broker between the worlds of power and wit, and sensing (so his language suggests) that he was engaged in a quasi-economic transaction, he imagined not one but two admiring and indebted audiences – both ministers and writers. For he insisted that each needed and valued the other. But he put an even higher value on himself: "I value my self," he wrote to Stella, "upon making the Ministry desire to be acquainted with Parnel; & not Parnel with the Ministry" (p. 612). And, in a society in which men were very sensitive about "obliging" and being "obliged" to each other,[29] recommending another writer was a way for Swift, always a scrupulous bookkeeper, to preserve and show a favorable balance in his social "accounts." After recommending Addison to the ministry, Swift says to Stella: "Well; he is now in my debt ... and I never had the least obligation to him" (p. 180).

But to recommend a writer is potentially to incur a debt with the ministry, or at least to expend a valuable asset – his "credit" with them. When Addison and Steele appear to "club" with each other (and to tend toward the Whigs?) Swift laments that he was "foolish enough to spend my credit" with the ministry on their behalf (p. 218). And the line separating economic transactions from matters of principle and conscience is a fine one. "I think I am bound," he says, "in honor & Conscience, to use all my little Credit towards helping forward Men of Worth [another quasi-economic term] in the world" (p. 659). The remark, like the others addressed to Stella, suggests once again that in fact Swift's admiring audience has at least two other parts – Stella and himself. After recommending Congreve to

[27] See *Journal to Stella*, I, 128–29, 180, 295; II, 586, 591, 612, 642.
[28] *Observations*, 27.
[29] Pope's Atticus is "so obliging that he ne'er obliged" ("Epistle to Dr. Arbuthnot," line 208).

Harley, Swift writes to Stella with obvious self-satisfaction: "I have made a worthy man easy, and that is a good day's work" (p. 295). In reporting that he has been ill used by all the Whigs whom he helped into places – "Steele I have kept in his Place; Congreve I have got to be used kindly and secured. Row I have recommended, and got a Promise of a Place" – Swift is complaining about ingratitude, but more plainly taking pride in his influence and his success: *I* have kept ... *I* have recommended ... Such remarks suggest that Swift fancied himself operating the very levers of power, and that Orrery was probably right in observing that "A man always appears of more consequence to himself, than he is in reality to any other person. Such perhaps was the case of Dr. Swift." Swift, he said, "enjoyed the shadow: the substance was detained from him. He was employed, not trusted" (Orrery, *Remarks*, pp. 46, 47).

Swift was not only a patron under the Harley ministry, he was also a petitioner. The original purpose for his trip to London was to plead on behalf of the Irish church. And one of his purposes for remaining was to secure a position for himself. Nor was this the first time that Swift had sought or enjoyed patronage. Sir William Temple had taken Swift into his household as a private secretary, and had later offered him a place in the office of Master of the Rolls, and then recommended him for the parish in Kilroot.[30] Lord Berkeley had given Swift a place as a chaplain and private secretary, and then recommended him for clerical posts at Laracor worth £260 per annum. Swift hoped for more, and curried favor with Halifax.[31] From an early point, and probably while still living with Temple, Swift developed a sense of injured merit, and of resentment that his would-be patrons failed to help him as much as they might. The paradox of his years in London is that he was much more successful as patron than as client: "I can serve every body but my self" (*Journal to Stella*, vol. II, p. 508).

In later years Swift continued to nurse his resentment, even while he established in Ireland a position of authority, and, as Orrery pointed out, "no inconsiderable ... power and revenue."[32] To "an ambitious mind," said Orrery, the promotion to the deanery at

---

30 *Prose Works*, v, 194. Temple had recommended Swift to the Secretary of State for Ireland for a clerkship and a fellowship at Trinity College (*Correspondence*, 1, 1–2).

31 *Correspondence*, 1, 142–44, 150, 157–60. On the complex negotiations leading to Swift's appointment, see Ehrenpreis, *Swift*, II, 7–13.

32 *Remarks*, 46–47.

St. Patrick's was "only an honourable, and profitable banishment ...
rather a disappointment than a reward" (*Remarks*, pp. 43, 46–47). As
Ehrenpreis remarked, his "rewards were greater than his bitterness
let him admit."[33] Even after he became the Hibernian Patriot, Swift
still sought and would have accepted church patronage in England in
the late 1720s.[34]

To some extent Swift's resentful sense of injured merit must have
been psychologically sustaining, but the costs may have been high.
Johnson speaks both of Swift's "pleasure of complaining," and of
"the rage of neglected pride, and the languishment of unsatisfied
desire." His resentment was not enabling, but ultimately disabling:
Swift, says Johnson, "wasted life in discontent."[35] As a proud and
independent writer, and as an acute student of neglected pride and
unsatisfied desire, Johnson might have been expected to approve of
Swift's resentments and his manly bearing in the company of great
men. But what Swift and his admirers regarded as independence
Johnson labeled servility:

> Much has been said of the equality and independence which he preserved
> in his conversation with the Ministers, of the frankness of his remonstrances,
> and the familiarity of his friendship ... No man, however, can pay a more
> servile tribute to the Great than by suffering his liberty in their presence to
> aggrandize him in his own esteem.[36]

Johnson invokes the principle of subordination – "between different
ranks of the community there is necessarily some distance" – and
suggests that any inferior who prides himself on his familiarity with a
superior is fooling himself. For the inferior is either present on
sufferance or because he is found temporarily useful. Swift, he
suspects, is guilty of "the pride of importance and the malice of
inferiority."[37] Swift at Harley's table was not displaying "magnanimity" or "greatness of soul." By encroaching on Harley's dignity
(and Johnson was no admirer of Harley) Swift in fact put himself in
Harley's power, to be "repelled with helpless indignity, or endured
by clemency and condescension" (*Lives of the Poets*, vol. III, p. 61). One

---

33 Ehrenpreis, *Swift*, II, xvii.
34 Swift's continuing search for patronage in England is a recurrent theme in the Ehrenpreis
and Nokes biographies.
35 *Lives of the Poets*, III, 61. Delany thought his "disappointments" and an "indulgence of his
passions" led to "sourness of temper" and thence a "decay in his understanding"
(*Observations*, 144).
36 *Lives of the Poets*, III, 21.
37 *Ibid.*, 22. Johnson goes on to note that Swift's "better qualities" overpowered his "childish
freedom."

of Johnson's recurrent themes is the "power" of Swift as writer. But as Harley's client, Swift, as Johnson saw it, was as impotent as Gulliver, for all his self-importance, at the court of the King of Brobdingnag.

This is a severe and perhaps unfair indictment. But there is reason to believe that Swift would have recognized the picture Johnson drew, and in some sense even anticipated it. If we read Swift's poems and prose satires with the patronage system in mind, we can see pictures of the patron–client relationship in which Swift confronts his painful awareness that the client has access but no real power and little likelihood of real reward. And yet Swift's poems and satires are not just oblique confessions of weakness. Some of them function too as strategies (or fantasies) of retaliation, in which the client finds a way to upstage the patron.

Swift confronted what he saw as the indignities of patronage at the very outset of his career. His early poems are usually viewed as attempts to work in uncongenial modes of praise (of Temple, Sancroft, et al.). In the last of them, the verses "Occasioned by Sir W— T—'s Late Illness and Recovery," Swift in the usual view bids "farewell to his youthful style."[38] At the same time, so I would suggest, he tries to bid farewell to his foolish hopes for patronage, and by exorcising the ghostly hope to steel himself against further disappointment. After taking note of its ostensible "occasion," the poem is cast as a complaint against the muse for having aroused the poet but eventually turned "bane to my repose,/ Thou universal cause of all my woes" (lines 81–82). The complaint is conventional – compare Oldham's poetic laments about the "hard fate of Writers" once they have become "possess'd with Muse"[39] – but Swift's poem is unusual in putting its emphasis on hopes raised and shattered:

> Wert thou right woman, thou shouldst scorn to look
> On an abandon'd wretch by hopes forsook;
> Forsook by hopes, ill fortune's last relief,
> Assign'd for life to unremitting grief...
> See Muse, what havock in these looks appear
> These are the tyrant's trophies of a year;

---

[38] Nora Jaffe, *The Poet Swift*, 74. Cf. Peter Schakel, *The Poetry of Jonathan Swift*, 28.
[39] "A Satyr. The Person of Spencer is brought in, Dissuading the Author from the Study of POETRY, and shewing how little it is esteem'd and encourag'd in this present Age," in Oldham, *Poems*, 242, 246; and "A Satyr. Address'd to a Friend, that is about to leave the University, and come abroad in the World" (226–32).

> Since hope his last and greatest foe is fled,
> Despair and he lodge ever in its stead. (lines 107–10, 125–28)[40]

The hopes of an aspiring poet in Swift's day, as in Oldham's, were for recognition and support. Swift had hopes that Temple would provide it, but as early as 1693, when this poem was written, seemed to have a sense that his hopes were misplaced. As Ehrenpreis suggests, the accusations against the muse are "ultimately addressed to his patron," although at this stage in his continuing dependency Swift cannot yet name Temple, even in an unpublished poem.[41] But the closing lines suggest both bitterness toward his patron and disgust with himself for having been taken in. His "ill-presented graces" did not win him "esteem." Perhaps because he had grown merely *familiar*, they "seem/ To breed contempt" (lines 145–46). The poem ends by formally – almost ritually – renouncing the witch-like muse and breaking the evil "enchantment" in which he has been trapped:

> There thy enchantment broke, and from this hour
> I here renounce thy visionary pow'r;
> And since thy essence on my breath depends,
> Thus with a puff the whole delusion ends. (lines 151–54)

In the context of patronage and dependence, the word "depends" has shocking force: the muse and the patron behind her in effect *depend* on the poet's breath to give them a kind of life. With a "puff" (an abrupt and unceremonious blast of air) Swift extinguishes the flame – and perhaps contemptuously both concludes and dismisses his ode of praise as a mere "puff" – the "undue or inflated commendation"[42] purveyed by a dependent poet.[43]

Near the end of his years in London, as Swift increasingly sensed that the promises of Harley and Bolingbroke were no more trustworthy than those of Temple, Somers, Sunderland, and Halifax,[44]

[40] At line 112, Swift's 1789 editor notes: "What a miserable state of mind must Swift have been in when he wrote this! which was owing to the state of dependence in which he had always lived from his birth to that time, with but little prospect of his being relieved from it. How grating this must have been to such a proud and generous spirit!" Reprinted in *Poems*, I, 54.

[41] *Swift*, I, 141. Cf. Nokes, *Jonathan Swift*, 26: "He complains of his Muse, since he cannot bring himself openly to complain of Temple."

[42] *OED*, sb., 6, not recorded before 1732. Swift's appears to be an early unrecorded use. Cf. the effusive commendatory letter from "John Puff, Esq.," in Fielding's *Shamela* (p. 1741).

[43] Cf. "puff" in Swift's punning poem to Sheridan (beginning "Poor Tom, wilt thou never accept a Defiance") in *Poems*, III, 1019.

[44] For promises of preferment from the Whig ministers, see *Prose Works*, VIII, 119.

and that his hopes would end in exile to Dublin, he could not yet permit himself to criticize his masters openly.[45] But he produced several poems which center on poet and patron, in which witty obliquity perhaps eased the pain. His imitation of the seventh epistle of Horace's first book, written in 1713, just after he was named Dean of St. Patrick's, casts Harley in the role of Maecenas. "My Lord" is "the Nation's great Support" (line 1), while Swift is just a poor priest. Harley takes him up and, for a jest, makes him a dean, promising a life of "Plenty, Power, and Ease" (line 92). The poem laughs at Swift's impressionable naiveté – Swift the "Gudgeon" takes Harley's bait (line 80) – and (in one common reading) conveys through its rallying tone of humorous grumbling the intimacy between cler- gyman and Lord Treasurer. I would argue that the poem in fact implies some real resentment and reproach for Harley's callous "jest" (a term used three times – and the third time with an edge of bitterness). An Irish deanery was not what Swift wanted, and it quickly proved costly and vexing. Instead of ruling as a "Tyrant" (line 90) over two dozen canons, Swift is obstructed and oppressed by tenants, farmers, and tithe collectors. His impotence is mocked by his patron's own commanding authority. In contrast to the hobbled dean, Harley needs but speak and his "Summons" (line 73) is obeyed, by servant and by client alike.

But the poem does not leave Swift humiliated. It contrives, in fact, to turn the tables on the patron by re-asserting the client's own power. That power consists in just saying no. The poem begins with Swift's refusal to accept Harley's invitation to dinner, and concludes with his symbolic resignation: "And Then since you now have done your worst," he says to Harley, "Pray leave me where you found me first" (lines 137–38). Just as Swift, before Harley found him, had "intended to retire" from the busy political world, so now too he claims to control his own fate, and to return to his original plan. Although only symbolic, the resignation serves as a means of discharging any obligation or repudiating a debt. Swift's strategy, in effect, is to deny that a patron–client relationship exists. Or rather, the relationship is displaced: Harley is the "patron" (line 23) not of Swift but of Erasmus Lewis, an undersecretary of state treated in the poem as Harley's "Errand"-boy (line 24). Swift himself is not to be

---

[45] After hearing that he was to be named dean of St. Patrick's, Swift told Stella he couldn't feel "Joy" at "passing my days in Ireld. and I confess I thought the Ministry would not let me go; but perhaps they cant help it" (*Journal to Stella*, 662).

considered an ordinary parson eager for preferment. He is a "Clergyman of special Note," and shuns his fellow clerics. *He* didn't approach Harley; Harley approached *him* – we recall Swift's boasts to Stella. The money in Swift's pocket is not a gift but a loan. The poem serves as a means for Swift to assert his own importance – he claims to go where he pleases and say what he thinks – but at the same time reveals that he shares Johnson's sense of the client's humble and humbling station. At Harley's table Swift "soon grows Domestick" (line 77). The term "Domestick" is loaded, suggesting both that Swift is one of the family, and that he has become a mere household chaplain, or domestic servant.

"The Author Upon Himself" (1714) is another response to the collapse of Swift's political ambitions. Again his strategy is to deny his client status and to represent the removal to Ireland as a kind of virtuous retirement (like Temple taking himself off to Moor Park). As in the imitation of Horace, Swift avoids presenting himself as a clergyman seeking preferment. More a man of wit than a parson ("Nor shew'd the Parson in his Gait or Face" line 14), Swift displayed the kind of grace that got him invited to "the Tables of the Great" (line 16). Writing for Harley was not his idea. He is advised to do so by his friends, and submits to their "better Judgments" (line 25). His allegiance is not to person or party but to principle. He wants to do what "Friendship, Justice, Truth require" (line 73) and feels the obligation – fostered (as Swift knew, though he does not say so) by scriptural parable – to employ his "Talents" for "nobler Ends" (line 24). He goes to court not to find a patron, but because he has been "invited" (line 28) by Harley. Once there he gains access and influence. Swift's tone combines pride and self-mockery – he is proud that he meets privately with Harley and St. John, and laughs at the rumors that exaggerate his importance. Swift's indirectness makes it difficult to decide how much power he actually lays claim to. It is said that Swift "oils many Springs which *Harley* moves" (line 40). As Pat Rogers notes, the syntax makes it unclear whether Harley moves the spring oiled by Swift, or whether Swift oils the spring which then moves Harley.[46] Is Swift merely an understrapper, or a manipulator of his master? He gains such influence as to become himself a patron, "caress't by Candidate Divines" (line 64) and solicited by the entire "*Scottish* Nation" that he might "be their Friend" (lines 69–70).

---

[46] *Jonathan Swift: The Complete Poems*, 670.

But all comes to nought. Enemies maneuver and faction divides his "great contending Friends" (line 72). Swift is still reluctant to blame Harley and St. John, and conveys no sense that he himself was simply used by the ministers. His own importance is suggested by the magnitude of the forces allegedly mobilized to defeat him. The "old redhair'd murd'ring Hag," the "Crazy Prelate," and the "Royal Prude" (lines 1–2) are larger-than-life villains, suitable for waylaying a heroic knight engaged in chivalric quest. The hag swears "Vengeance" (line 53) on him and becomes a monster, her mouth filling with venom distilled from her red locks, and then instilled into the "Royal Ear" (line 56). Although a proclamation spread "through the Realm" (line 59) puts a price on his head, he "scorns ignoble Flight" (line 61) and determines to make a stand. At this point, however, Swift undercuts his heroic pose. He escapes not by resisting but because "his watchful Friends preserve him by a Sleight" (line 62) – that is, by covering up Swift's authorship of a libelous pamphlet – and he subsequently endures trials more embarrassing than chivalric, as when the Treasurer of the Queen's Household "in S–t's ear thrusts half his powder'd Nose" (line 68). When Swift has done what he can, and what "Friendship, Justice, Truth require" (line 73), he finally abandons the campaign: "What could he more, but decently retire?" (line 74).

The question is neatly self-enhancing. It makes the point that Swift's departure from court was voluntary. He leaves not as a disappointed suitor but as a veteran diplomat (like his old patron Temple) who decides to "retire" – to a life of rural leisure and contemplation. Swift does not say that he was holed up in Berkshire, or that – a full twelve months before the poem was written – he had already been inducted as Dean of St. Patrick's. Indeed, the pretense is that the poem is written in 1713 – the date assigned to the poem in its first appearance in print in the 1735 *Works* – while Swift was still a part of the court, and not in 1714, when his Irish fate was sealed.

Once in Ireland Swift occupied himself with other interests, but his ambivalent quest for patronage continued, and he remained preoccupied with the relationship between those in positions of authority – kings, ministers, or hosts – and those who must depend on them. In this context it is worth recalling *Gulliver's Travels* (1726), in which Swift re-imagines the situation of the author and the noble patron to whom he must defer. The *Travels* are of course published without dedication, and the author in his prefatory letter addresses not a noble lord but "his Cousin Sympson," a fictional bookseller and publisher. According to the letter from "The Publisher to the Reader," the book might provide "Entertainment to our young Noblemen," but only if they managed to ignore Gulliver's account of English noblemen in his conversation with his Houyhnhnm master:

Nobility among us was altogether a different Thing from the Idea he had of it ... our young *Noblemen* are bred from their Childhood in Idleness and Luxury ... as soon as Years will permit, they consume their Vigour, and contract odious Diseases among lewd Females; and when their Fortunes are almost ruined, they marry some Woman of mean Birth, disagreeable Person, and unsound Constitution, merely for the sake of Money, whom they hate and despise. (Part IV, chapter 6)

"Ministers of State" do not come off any better. They are concerned primarily with attaining and retaining office; their chief skills are in "*Insolence, Lying,* and *Bribery.*" Although they have "all Employments at their Disposal," and are eagerly solicited, a prudent client will never believe their promises:

those he speaks worst of behind their Backs, are in the surest way to Preferment; and whenever he begins to praise you to others or to your self, you are from that Day forlorn. The worst Mark you can receive is a Promise, especially when it is confirmed with an Oath; after which every wise Man retires, and gives over all Hopes. (Part IV, chapter 6)

In this devastating account of "Ministers of State" from the dead-pan voice of Gulliver we can of course hear Swift's old complaints about "courtiers and court promises."[47] But "Ministers of State" are, as Swift liked to point out, themselves dependents, and the account of the "Diversions of the Court of Lilliput" works as merciless delight at the dangerous games that ministers must play in order to gain their appointments and preserve their power. The "Rope-Dancers" in Lilliput are not images of ordinary place-seekers (poets and churchmen), but of those "Candidates for great Employments, and high Favour, at Court" – i.e., men like Sunderland and Godolphin, Harley and St. John, swept in and then out of office with the tides of state. As Swift fantasizes the scene, these candidates are in effect obliged to demean themselves and act like acrobats – or musicians and poets – brought in to entertain their betters. What is

[47]   *Correspondence*, I, 150.

worse, the candidates in effect conspire in their own fate – they ask for it:

When a great Office is vacant, either by Death or Disgrace, (which often happens) five or six of those Candidates petition the Emperor to entertain his Majesty and the Court with a Dance on the Rope. (Part I, chapter 3)

As Gulliver goes on to record that these "diversions" and "entertain-ments" turn out to be attended with "fatal Accidents," we detect the political allegory about the rise and fall of great men at court, but can also see the episode as the fantasized revenge of a disappointed client: since they treated me as little more than an entertainer, and then threw me away, let them suffer, let them pay.

Elsewhere in the *Travels* there are other images of patronage, though they do not all work to demean the patron.[48] Indeed, the King of Brobdingnag, in his conversations with Gulliver about the manners and learning of Europe, may even serve as a kind of idealized patron. He is "a Prince of excellent Understanding," who "delighted in Musick," and Gulliver in fact attempts to "entertain" him with "an *English* Tune" on a giant piano. "His Apprehension was so clear, and his Judgment so exact, that he made very wise Reflexions and Observations upon all I said." Although his library is said to be small, "few things delighted him so much as new Discoveries in Art or in Nature." He embodies the dream that power and knowledge might be found in a single person, and that men of letters in a well-run state might have access to the sovereign and stand (for the moment) on equal footing. But Swift characteristically problematizes his utopia. Although Gulliver has the chance-of-a-lifetime occasion, he is no more successful in persuading the king to adopt a political expedient than the young Swift himself was in persuading King William to accept the Triennial Bill. The next time Gulliver appears before a king, he is put in his (accustomed) place. He is expected to "lick the Dust before [the] Footstool" of the King of Luggnagg. After doing so – the dust, he says, was "not offensive" – he is provided "a Lodging in the Court for me and my Interpreter, with a daily Allowance for my Table, and a large Purse of Gold for my common Expences" (Part III, ch. 9). Like a subservient client in a hierarchical system of authority and dependence, Gulliver – now more clearly a figure to be satirized – remains three months in the

---

[48]   Cf. the "original Institutions" in Lilliput, whereby those choosing candidates for "Employ-ments" have "more Regard to good Morals than to great Abilities" (I, 6).

country "out of perfect Obedience to his Majesty, who was pleased highly to favour me, and made me very honourable Offers" – which the vain and acquiescent Gulliver declines to specify. That Gulliver can so easily blink away the king's murderous tyranny makes him an image of the way patronage corrupts both the giver and the receiver.[49]

On distant and imaginary islands Swift re-invented a world of patrons and clients. On his own island of Ireland he also played with the idea that dependents can become masters, and vice-versa. Among Swift's Irish friends were Sir Arthur Acheson and his wife Anne (daughter of the Lord Chancellor of Ireland), who entertained him at their home at Market Hill, near Armagh, during three extended annual visits from 1728 to 1730. In the so-called "Market Hill" poems Swift playfully resisted the conventional compliments of the country-house poem tradition. Indeed, he so far refused the stance of grateful guest that several of the poems are written in the voice of Lady Acheson, the hostess who indulged his whims and quirks. She is made to complain in comical meters of his carping, critical, and imperious manner: "He loves to be bitter at / A lady illiterate; / If he sees her but once, / He'll swear she's a dunce." (*Poems*, vol. III, p. 854). "His Manners would not let him wait, / Least we should think ourselves neglected, / And so we saw him at our Gate / Three Days before he was expected." (p. 859)

He overstays his welcome, eats and swills enough to "swell" the household accounts; even his horses "eat all our Hay." Lady Acheson longs to be "rid / Of that insulting Tyrant Dean" (pp. 860–61). In another poem she composes an ironic "Panegyrick on the D–n, in the Person of a Lady in the *North*." Patron turned dependent poet, she resolves "my Gratitude to show,/ ... for all I owe," to offer her "Thanks delay'd" for all his "Favours left too long unpay'd" (p. 887). We can read the poem as another set of ironic "Verses" on Dr. Swift, or as an inverted comic complaint about a guest who was hardly the genteel parson of clean habits and "strict Decorum" that she pretends he is. But we can also read it as a

---

[49] For other images of patronage, see the "great Lord at Court" who "had performed many eminent services for the Crown" but received no reward (III, 4), and the survey of "modern History" in which three kings tell Gulliver that "they did never once prefer any Person of Merit," and called "Villains" to the "highest Places of Trust, Power, Dignity, and Profit" (III, 8).

bizarre fantasy about the reciprocal benefits of patronage, and the
patron's (rather than the client's) desire to "make suitable Returns,"
or to even the account:

> Impatient to be out of Debt,
> O, may I never once forget
> The Bard, who humbly deigns to chuse
> Me for the Subject of his Muse.
> Behind my Back, before my Nose,
> He sounds my Praise in Verse and Prose.
>
> My Heart with Emulation burns
> To make you suitable Returns;
> My Gratitude the World shall know:
> And, see, the Printer's Boy below:
> Ye Hawkers all, your Voices lift;
> A Panegyrick on D–n S—.   (p. 887)

"Suitable Returns" hints at a decorous exchange of presents (*OED*
III, 4), and also at the monetary gain that the client-poet hopes to
realize (*OED* II, 3b), but (in the light of what are presumably Swift's
sneaking poems "Behind my Back" and impudent poems "before my
Nose") also at retort (*OED* III, 5). When she declares that "the World
shall know" of her "Gratitude," one hears the conventional accents
of the grateful dependent, but also perhaps Swift's proud and
embittered determination (projected onto innocent Lady Acheson) to
publish the truth about an intimate patron–client relationship.

In other "Market Hill" poems Swift sets up as country squire
himself. He had actually entertained the idea of building, and went
so far as to buy land for the purpose from Acheson. At Acheson's
suggestion, the house was to be called Drapier's Hill, and in a poem
of that name Swift imagines that the house will survive when Swift's
name and all his works are forgotten or made mere "waste Paper"
(*Poems*, vol. III, p. 875). Whether enduring fame attaches to the poet
or to the hill and house he celebrates (and the patron that owns
them) is the troubling question that underlies this poetical squib, and
explains perhaps the choice of flattering historical analogues. Drapier's, the verse declares, will "vye with Cooper's Hill" (p. 875), and
(in a related poem) the name of the house "with Penshurst vies,/ And
wing'd with fame shall reach the skies" (p. 877). Does the fame
belong to Cooper's Hill or to Denham, to Sidney's Penshurst or to
Ben Jonson? When he pursues the fantasy of poet turning builder,
Swift characteristically slides downward: from immortal fame to

mortal flesh, from country house to a pair of outhouses – "Two Temples of magnifick Size," where "gentle Goddess *Cloacine*/ Receives all Off'rings at her Shrine./ In sep'rate Cells the He's and She's/ Here pay their Vows with *bended Knees*" (p. 893).

Swift's enthusiasm for building at Drapier's Hill soon dissipated, perhaps (as Scott suggested) because it was too far from Dublin and the larger world which he could not yet let go. The relationship between patron and client still engaged him, and in some late poems he continued to probe it. The "Libel on the Reverend Dr. Delany" (1730) is couched in the form of cynical advice from a veteran of the political wars. Occasioned by an epistle from Delany, Swift's fellow churchman in Dublin, to Lord Carteret, Lord Lieutenant, the "Libel" is a way for Swift to laugh at Delany's deluded dreams of patronage, dreams that Swift himself once shared. But in the end the real joke is not on the client Delany, but on his would-be patron, Carteret, and ultimately on *his* masters, Walpole and the king himself.

Swift begins with a picture of the aspiring clients, welcomed by the great as companions for their table, and boasting of their access and their intimacy with men in power. It is Swift at Harley's table all over again. This time Swift makes it painfully clear that the intimacy is in fact one-sided: it is the great who "Chuse" their companions (line 2), and who give "Leave" to let a client "sit when e'er you will" (line 4). If the client presumes on the familiarity to raise a matter of business, he "quite mistake[s] *Preferment*'s road" (line 12). Even Johnson's tart description of the self-important Swift in Harley's company pales beside Swift's own words, full of self-loathing, about the real relationship between patron and client.

> For, as their Appetites to quench,
> Lords keep a Pimp to bring a Wench;
> So, Men of Wit are but a kind
> Of Pandars to a vicious Mind;
> Who proper Objects must provide
> To gratify their Lust of pride.   (lines 21–26)

Swift provides a series of examples – gratifying his own bitter pride – of clients who either cynically complied with the lusts of great men (Congreve and Addison) or withdrew and starved (Steele and Gay). He notably omits his own case, and passes instead to Pope, who becomes the hero of the poem: "His Heart too Great, though

Fortune little,/ To lick a *Rascal Statesman*'s Spittle" (lines 81–82). Pope can afford to despise slaves "that *cringe* for Bread" (line 88) because he was "plac't," with Homer's help, "Above the Reach of Want." (Interestingly, Swift obscures the financial dimension of Pope's Homer project. Though he resented the dependence on patrons, Swift did not admire writers who wrote for bread).

Turning to Delany's situation, Swift suspects that his friend will rise no higher than domestic chaplain, fit for flattering, carving at table, and showing his wit. But the real force of Swift's satire is turned on Carteret, who would, "if he durst, be more your Friend" (line 114). The viceroy, though he dispenses Irish patronage, is himself not a free agent: he serves at the pleasure of the Prime Minister, and must submit to "W[alpole]'s more than R[oya]l Will" (line 122). By an ironic reversal, the patron turns out to be but a dependent upon a still greater man. Poor Carteret "must obey, or lose his *Place*" (line 160). Clients, then, from the deluded Delany to the unillusioned Swift, may take some comfort in the discomforts of dependence that plague their betters. Swift himself emerges as the second hero of the poem, able to "look on *Courts* with stricter Eyes" (line 175) and (in a stance that Pope was to find congenial in his own late satires) to base his judgment on "*Truth*" (line 194). Walpole is no better than the monarch of hell, the viceroy but a "V[iceroy] DEV'L" sent to do his bidding, and to spread "*Corruptions*" through courts and senates as he passes (lines 186–87). From Swift's almost-Olympian vantage, kings, ministers, viceroys, and their clients are all reduced to a single level.

In the context of Swift's poems on patronage, the famous "Verses on the Death of Dr. Swift" (1733) look like an elaborate self-justifying fantasy and a denial that he ever sought preferment. Thus, the characteristic passive verb in "the Dean was never ill receiv'd at Court" (line 308) both affirms that Swift had entrée to the court and conceals that his footing there was that of a client on his own behalf or that of the Irish church. When he claims that "He never courted Men in Station" (line 325), Swift must mean not that he never worked with and for Harley and others – this would be too blatant a lie – but that he never stooped to "court" them. In Swift's self-preserving fiction, he was sought out by the great: it was they who "courted" him. In turn, he "never thought an Honour done him,/ Because a Duke was proud to own him" (lines 319–20). Transferring pride from himself to the duke, Swift here answers in advance

Johnson's charge that he valued himself the more for his association with the great. Even "with Princes," says Swift, he "kept a due Decorum,/ But never stood in awe before 'em" (lines 339–40). Again Swift seems to be implicitly observing Johnson's rule about subordination, and to speak freely with a sovereign just as Johnson himself was to do some thirty years later. Elsewhere, however, Swift reduces the queen from majesty to meanness. She had once promised to send him some "Medals" and now forgets or cancels her promise (line 184). In explanatory footnotes Swift makes clear that he sent her a "Present" of Irish poplin. In return Swift was to receive not payment but some "Medals." He sees in the transaction not royal largesse promised and withdrawn, not an Irish merchant providing goods to the carriage trade, but (somewhat cheekily) an exchange of gifts between equals that one party has failed to fulfill.

If Swift had behaved prudently, he claims, he "might have rose like other Men" (line 356). But he refused to spare his "Tongue and Pen" (line 355). And after laboring "to reconcile his Friends in Power" (line 366) – the phrase is little changed from its appearance twenty years earlier in "The Author upon Himself" – Swift "left the Court in mere Despair" (line 370). Once again, that is, Swift was not dismissed, but took his own leave. He gained nothing by leaving – in Ireland he met only "continual Persecution" (line 400) – but finally evens the score by turning patron himself. He left his estate to "publick Uses" (line 156), and "gave what little Wealth he had,/ To build a House for Fools and Mad" (lines 479–80). By becoming a donor rather than a recipient, he symbolically turns the tables on the patrons who, as he saw it, failed to support him and his church.

Swift had one card left to play. As client he was dependent. But as clergyman charged with the care of souls, he had considerable power. Although all the evidence suggests that he performed his ecclesiastical duties scrupulously, he seems to have imagined, in some powerful fantasies left unpublished at his death, using his sacred authority to punish his enemies. The famous poem on the "Day of Judgment" may represent a dream of retaliation: sinners gather at the Last Judgment only to be told by an angry Jove (a stand-in for Swift himself) that it has all been a joke. More pertinent for my purposes are the "Verses Occasioned by the Sudden Drying up of St. Patrick's Well" (*c.* 1729). The "sacred Well" (line 65), located near Trinity College, Dublin, was said to have healing properties and to have been produced by St. Patrick himself, Swift's symbolic predecessor as spiritual leader of Ireland,[50] and namesake of his cathedral. In Swift's poem St. Patrick speaks and laments the "fatal Changes" (line 34) in Ireland since his time. The Irish are now drowned in vice and enslaved to the English. Aspiring clergymen must make slavish court to "foreign prelates," and for all their "Sweat" can only "procure a mean Support" (lines 75–76). St. Patrick foretells worse yet, and closes by withdrawing his care: "I scorn thy spurious and degenerate Line,/ And from this Hour my Patronage resign" (lines 101–02). "Patronage" here means primarily the guardianship by the patron saint of Ireland. But for the Dean of St. Patrick's the word has obvious links with the patronage or support he provided as champion of Irish rights,[51] and the patronage he himself sought all his life. By speaking as St. Patrick and by "resigning his patronage," Swift gains a kind of fantasized revenge. "Resign" is especially apt for a churchman who is both patron and client: it can mean to give up an office, or to give up a claim. Even in retaliation, Swift may here simultaneously and ruefully "resign" his hopes of preferment.

[50] Rogers, quoting Oliver Ferguson, *Jonathan Swift and Ireland* (Urbana: University of Illinois Press, 1962), 185, notes that a poem published in Dublin in 1726 referred to Swift as St. Patrick's successor (*Jonathan Swift: The Complete Poems*, 791).

[51] Johnson refers to Swift's efforts to "patronize" the Irish and to Swift as their "benefactor" (*Lives of the Poets*, III, 50).

CHAPTER 6

Alexander Pope

Pope has long been regarded as the first "professional writer" in England able to make a living by his pen, without depending on the support of aristocratic patronage. Ever since Beljame, literary historians have noted with a kind of pride that Pope's *Iliad*, which made his fortune, was dedicated not to the Earl of Halifax or Dorset, but to a fellow writer, William Congreve. This image of proud independence is one that Pope himself cultivated: "But (thanks to *Homer*) since I live and thrive,/ Indebted to no Prince or Peer alive ... Un-plac'd, un-pension'd, no Man's Heir, or Slave."[1] His sympathetic biographers have largely accepted the claim. Mack goes so far as to suggest that Pope's 1714 contract with Bernard Lintot to provide an English *Iliad* "foretells the end of the patronage system more effectively than Johnson's famous letter to Chesterfield."[2] Recent commentators, from Mack to David Foxon, have also made clear how successful Pope was at manipulating the economic levers – floating a hugely profitable subscription, driving hard bargains with his booksellers, setting up a printer and a bookseller to produce his works, and retaining control of his copyrights – that established the financial foundation of his proud independence.[3]

But Pope presents another image to the historian of literary patronage as well. More perhaps than any other writer of his day, Pope lived, as he himself put it, "among the Great" (Imitations of Horace, Satire II, 1, line 133). Johnson too locates Pope squarely within the patronage system. Pope, he says, "seems to have wanted neither diligence nor success in attracting the notice of the great; for from his first entrance into the world ... he was admitted to

---

[1] Imitations of Horace, Epistle II, 2, 68–69, Satire II. 1, 116. Cf. also Pope's *Correspondence*, II, 469, and Spence, *Observations*, I, 160.

[2] Maynard Mack, *Alexander Pope: A Life*, 863.

[3] David Foxon, *Alexander Pope and the Early Eighteenth-Century Book Trade*.

familiarity with those whose rank or station made them most conspicuous" (*Lives of the Poets*, vol. III, p. 90). Pope often chose to present himself in letters and poems not as a painstaking craftsman or a brilliant entrepreneur but as a gentleman who wrote for his leisure and for the pleasure of a few noble friends, to whom he addressed many of his poetic epistles both early and late. His literary rivals and enemies were acutely aware of his powerful social connections, and were no doubt envious of his ability to cultivate and apparently mix freely with members of an aristocratic patronal class. Johnson implies that Pope was a bit of a social climber, "ambitious of splendid acquaintance" (p. 90) and rather too given to "enumerating the men of high rank with whom he was acquainted" (p. 204). Other aristocrats, like John Lord Hervey, for whom Pope had expressed ridicule or contempt, looked on him with the prejudices of their class as a fawning sycophant of mean spirit and low birth. One of Pope's greatest antagonists, Lady Mary Wortley Montagu, declared that his success was in effect wholly dependent on his great friends. Recalling the satirical sallies of Pope and Swift against "the great," she thought it "pleasant to consider that had it not been for the good nature of those very mortals they contemn, these two superior beings" – i.e. Pope and Swift – "were entitle'd by their Birth and hereditary Fortune to be only a couple of Link Boys." Imputing to Pope meanly mercenary motives, she claimed that he "courted with the utmost assiduity all the old men from whom he could hope a legacy: The Duke of Buckingham, Lord Peterborough, Sir G Kneller, Lord Bolingbroke, Mr. Wycherley, Mr. Congreve, Lord Harcourt etc."[4]

Lady Mary is no disinterested witness, but she put her finger on something significant when she noted that Pope on the one hand "contemned" the patronal class and on the other benefited from it. For Pope may be said to have resisted the traditional claims of patrons throughout his career and to have asserted his own claims, but to have managed the matter so well as never to seem to bite the hand that fed him, and to have remained a part of the patronage system, both as supplier of services and as beneficiary, even as he worked to undermine it.

The famous subscription to Homer, in which Pope derived income both from Lintot and from a glittering array of noble subscribers, is

---

[4] *Complete Letters of Lady Mary Wortley Montagu*, III, 57–58.

only the most brilliant instance of Pope's ingenious triumph. His subscription lists include many of the traditional patrons of literature.[5] Burlington, Bolingbroke, Halifax, Lansdowne, and others all signed up for multiple sets,[6] and in many cases apparently did not claim all the sets for themselves, in effect making of them a gift for Pope to re-sell.

The success with Homer among the fashionable world is well known, but it is worth recalling that not only in 1715 but throughout his career Pope in fact received many of the traditional benefits of private patronage. As a young writer he had the good fortune to make the acquaintance of a number of older writers, from whom he gained encouragement, suggestions, approval, invitations, and introductions. Although Pope does not present them as such, these are the typical fruits of patronage, and more valuable than gifts or pensions to a writer who was aiming at a public career in poetry. How some of Pope's early friends – Trumbull, Lansdowne, Halifax, the Marquis of Wharton, Talbot, Sheffield, Lord Somers – served as a kind of literary network that connected him with other potential supporters can be illustrated with a brief example. Trumbull, who had himself been a patron of both Wycherley and Dryden, probably introduced Pope to Wycherley, who in turn introduced him to William Walsh, a sort of late Restoration man of wit. Walsh provided flattering attention and valuable criticism, hosted Pope for six weeks at his family seat near Worcester during the summer of 1707 – the first of Pope's many "summer rambles" – and introduced him to old Jacob Tonson the bookseller, who (prompted no doubt by spreading reports about Pope's talent) declared an interest in publishing his *Pastorals* (which he was to do in 1709). That the young Pope's network extended from patrons to booksellers is suggestive of the way in which he straddled the old and the new literary worlds. Also emblematic of Pope's participation in both a manuscript culture and a print-oriented culture is a holograph of his *Pastorals*, prepared for circulation among a group of aristocratic friends. The manuscript's title, noted the printer Jonathan Richardson, is drawn "in printing capitals so perfectly beautiful, and so exactly imitated, that one can hardly believe they are not really from the press."[7]

---

5   Matthew Hodgart notes that "Nearly 30% of the subscribers belong to the peerage." See "The Subscription List for Pope's *Iliad*, 1715," 26.
6   For details, see R. H. Griffith, *Alexander Pope: A Bibliography*, I, 41–42.
7   Richardson at one time owned the manuscript. Words which would have been printed in

Once he had become a published author Pope maintained his connections with a circle of figures who were interested in promoting his career or in various ways making his life easier. Although he usually preferred not to consider them his "patrons,"[8] they in effect performed that function, as brief examples may suggest. John Caryll, after recommending that riding would be good for Pope's health, gave him a horse. James Craggs, Secretary of State, made Pope a gift of South Sea "subscriptions," and offered to provide a pension of £300 out of Secret Service funds – Pope declined, but said he might call on Craggs if need arose.[9] In 1728 Burlington loaned Pope the services of his lawyer and of some lesser servants, and in 1733 offered some building stone for use at Twickenham.[10] Others provided dinners and more extended hospitality. Pope was a frequent guest at Walpole's dinners in the 1720s and enjoyed summer visits at country seats throughout southern England – Caryll's Ladyholt, Oxford's Wimpole Hall, Burlington's Chiswick, Cobham's Stowe, Bathurst's Cirencester. Lord Harcourt provided a kind of private writer's retreat for Pope at Stanton Harcourt in the summers of 1717 and 1718, a house for his exclusive use in which he was able to work without interruption on his Homer. Still others, by associating themselves with Pope as his addressees or his subscribers, or (like Walpole) presenting his work at court, helped attract the attention of booksellers and bookbuyers.[11]

Such support did not distinguish Pope from many other beneficiaries or private patronage. What makes Pope unusual is the way in which he made use of patrons to procure new services.[12] He put his eminent subscribers (especially Caryll, Trumbull, and Harcourt) to work as salesmen to solicit still other subscriptions. He secured an

italics are "in common printing character, the general being in italics, beautifully formed, so as in all to imitate a printed book." See Pope's *Works*, I, 239.

8   But on occasion Pope facetiously accepted the term, as in a 1728 letter to Burlington: "I beg my Lady Burlington's Patronage of the Ass & the Dunciad, me and my burden" (*Correspondence*, III, 4). The frontispiece of the 1729 *Dunciad Variorum*, then planned, represents an ass bearing a burden of dull books.

9   Spence, *Observations*, I, 99.

10   *Correspondence*, II, 532; III, 4, 341. Sir William Fortescue, who later rose to be Master of the Rolls, apparently provided Pope legal advice "without a Fee" (see Pope's "Epistle to Fortescue," line 10).

11   Pope's gain was sometimes indirect. The presence of distinguished subscribers on his list added to his reputation and to the value of future copy. But by the terms of his contract with Lintot, Pope did not share in the profits of the general sale to buyers attracted by noble subscribers.

12   Sherburn remarks on Pope's "amazing gift for getting services even from noble friends" (*Correspondence*, III, 26n).

updated form of "protection" by having the copyright of the potentially libelous *Dunciad* registered in the names of the Earls of Bathurst, Burlington, and Oxford, all exempt from prosecution. And in the 1730s, when Pope followed a more dangerous path that ultimately led him into the political Opposition, he was able, if he needed it, to count on the political protection of well-placed friends, not only Tories and Opposition Whigs, but friends of the ministry as well.

Pope responded to these various benefits by providing the sort of literary services normally expected of clients, including dedications, complimentary addresses, and verse epitaphs. The *Pastorals*, *Windsor Forest*, and *The Rape of the Lock* all carry dedications. The Preface to the *Iliad* acknowledges the support of many "great" names. In his later years Pope was more likely to compliment not by formally dedicating a work to its addressee, but by means of a verse epistle to Bolingbroke, Cobham, Bathurst, Burlington, and others, which no less effectively reaffirmed, and advertised, Pope's connection with the patronage class.

Although we usually think of the revisions of Betterton's Chaucerian imitations and of Wycherley's poems as part of the young Pope's poetic apprenticeship, we should also see them as the sort of literary services provided by clients to patrons. Pope wrote two "Choruses" for a play by John Sheffield, Duke of Buckingham in 1716,[13] and some complimentary verses in 1717 in response to Sheffield's own compliment. His posthumous edition of Sheffield's poems, with his own revisions, should be seen in this light not simply as the editorial labor of a literary professional but also as the gratitude of a recipient of the duke's patronage. In 1735 he wrote an epitaph on Sheffield's son. This was only one of many epitaphs produced for the families of noble friends and patrons, including Dorset, Caryll, Trumbull, Craggs, Harcourt, and Digby.[14] Pope was never too busy to offer professional services – advice on landscape gardening is another example – to his prestigious friends.

Maintaining friendly relations with those in a position to help him and yet preserving independence – that was the trick. The proceeds

[13] Pope printed them in his 1721 edition of Sheffield's *Works*, where he noted that they were "Written at the Command of his Grace, by Mr. Pope" (*Poems of Pope*, Twickenham Edition, VI, 155).

[14] The epitaphs were well enough known to attract the attention of Johnson, who wrote "A Dissertation on the Epitaphs Written by Pope" for *The Visiter* in May 1756.

from the Homer translation only provided the economic base. Trimming this delicate balance was a lifelong effort. Pope's success was no doubt due in part to his personal skills as an ingratiating and witty companion and houseguest. But it also depended on his ability to define by means of his writing the relationship between himself and his supporters. Pope implicitly challenges the subordination of writer to patron, and though he lacks high birth and inherited wealth emphasizes on the one hand his affinities with the traditional patron class, and on the other the sharp differences that separate him from other writers, the ones who are dependent, as Pope is not, on patrons or booksellers.

We can see indications of Pope's means of resistance to the traditional claims of patronage throughout his career. One strategy was to think of patrons as personal "friends," and to treat them as such, implicitly asserting an equality with them. A 1711 letter to Caryll, his generous neighbor and fellow Catholic, reveals Pope's practice almost nakedly. Caryll had apparently already begun making gifts to Pope, and was about to make another. Pope writes to him:

I could wish you would not oblige too fast. I love to keep pace with a friend if possible; and 'tis a rule, you know, in walking to let the weakest go foremost: Let me first prove my self your friend ... and then, sir, do what you will.[15]

Caryll was a wealthy landowner from an old and well-connected family, and was himself old enough to be Pope's father, and yet Pope is here concerned to level the differences between them. As soon as Pope finds a way to reciprocate, he will have proved himself Caryll's "friend," and then may accept favors freely. But he remains concerned about any suggestions of an asymmetry in their relationship. Indeed, in a letter to Caryll just six months earlier Pope had noted that Caryll's "present" of oysters is matched by his own "present" of a drawing (*Correspondence*, vol. 1, pp. 114–15). To some extent this is what any friend would try to do, and in Pope's case it is understandable that he would make what gifts he could, but would remain sensitive about the impossibility of "keeping pace" with such friends as Caryll, who had far greater resources. In later years Pope found it convenient to minimize still further any debt to his early

---

[15] *Correspondence*, 1, 128–29. The letter was first printed in 1735, but the passage I quote was omitted in this and all later editions printed by Pope, perhaps to cover his tracks.

patron Caryll. In the 1735 edition of his *Letters* some letters originally sent to Caryll were re-addressed to Wycherley and Addison, perhaps because these literary luminaries cast more light on Pope, perhaps because he wanted to draw attention away from his early connections with a Catholic (and Jacobite) family, perhaps because, at a point when he had attained greater independence, he wanted to minimize his earlier reliance on patronage.

By the 1730s even more than before Pope seems to want to even the score, to pay off old debts, to be as little obliged as possible, even to close "friends." He accepted invitations to grand country houses, for example, so long as he could invite his host to his more modest villa at Twickenham and keep accounts even. He was likewise anxious that his reading public not conclude that he was indebted to any great men. When it was rumored that the Duke of Chandos had made a gift to Pope of £500, he took pains to deny it in print, and to declare that "Mr. P. never receiv'd any Present farther than the Subscription for *Homer*, from him, or from Any Great Man whatsoever."[16] Any suspicion of indebtedness to members of the court, whether Stuart or Hanoverian, was likewise insistently refuted in the notes to the *Dunciad*: "our Poet never had any Place, Pension, or Gratuity, in any shape, from the said glorious Queen, or any of her Ministers. All he owed, in the whole course of his life, to any court, was a subscription, for his Homer, of 200 *l.* from King George I, and 100 *l.* from the prince and princess."[17] Pope had in fact been granted £200 in 1725 as "his Matys Encouragement" of the translation of the *Odyssey*. But he converted the grant into a subscription by crediting Walpole (the king's Lord Treasurer) with ten sets, and publicly disclaiming any debt. Bearing in mind both the flattery of a court in which Dryden engaged, and the writers hired and pensioned by Walpole in his own day, Pope proudly sets himself apart.

POPE'S DEDICATIONS

Although Pope wrote at a time when published poems and plays often carried formal dedications, with an epistle or preface compli-

[16] "Epistle to Dr. Arbuthnot," Pope's own note to line 375. A "Present" confers an obligation, but a subscription (and Chandos [then called the Earl of Caernarvon] had subscribed for twelve sets) is a kind of contract, fulfilled as soon as the books are delivered.

[17] "Testimonies of Authors," in *Poems of Pope*, v, 45. The four-times-repeated "any" suggests the intensity of Pope's protest.

menting the patron's taste and generosity, he only wrote two such
dedicatory addresses in his long career.[18] One is the dedication of
the *Rape of the Lock*. The other is a mock-dedication by "The
Author" to "Himself," published in an essay "On Dedications" in
the *Guardian* in 1713. The latter, which appeared about a week after
Windsor Forest (inscribed, as we shall see, to Lansdowne), shows that
the young Pope, like his friend Swift, found the form to be suspect
even if he was not ready to abandon it. Because the praise offered
in so many dedications is only a kind of "Prostitution," and
because fame is "promiscuously bestowed on the Meritorious and
undeserving," the poet who might wish to express his true opinion
of his patron's value is reluctant to use language that has been
"rendered suspected by Flatterers": "Even Truth itself in a Dedication is like an Honest Man in a Disguise or Vizor-Masque, and will
appear a Cheat by being drest so like one." And yet the temptation
to stretch the truth is great, because the writer addresses the
patron "with a Prospect of Interest." If he exaggerates the patron's
merit, he's either "dishonest" or (if he stands to gain nothing) he's
a fool.

After observing that most dedicatory praise actually reflects what
the author most desires be said about himself, Pope closes with a
"new kind of Dedication," in which he simply makes explicit what is
usually only implicit. In "The Author to Himself" the dedicator
declares that the "Honour, Affection and Value" he has for himself
is "beyond Expression." We should not over-interpret Pope's little
jeu d'esprit, but it is significant that his parody, while its wit is directed
against dedicators rather than patrons, confesses that he finds no real
role for the patron in the production and reception of literature. In
acting as his own patron, Pope's mock-dedicator recognizes no
authority beyond himself. He in effect authorizes himself, in ironic
anticipation of Pope's subsequent attitude toward the authority of
the patron class. We might see this mock-dedication as a forerunner
of the "Letter to the Publisher, Occasioned by the present Edition of
the Dunciad," a document signed by "William Cleland" but written
by Pope himself, which (appearing with editions of the *Dunciad*
beginning in 1729) declares the writer's "great regard to a person

[18] Unless we count the verse epistle to Oxford prefixed to Pope's edition of Parnell's *Remains*
(1721), which Pope misleadingly called "the only Dedication I ever writ" (*Correspondence*, II,
90) and the mock-dedication of *Sober Advice from Horace* (1734), addressed by "the author" to
"Alexander Pope, Esq."

[i.e., Pope himself] whose friendship I shall ever esteem as one of the chief honours of my life."

A year later, in his only other formal dedication, Pope used the form for unconventional purposes, not to secure the patron's generosity and to confirm the patron's role as judge and sponsor of literary merit, but to extricate himself from a ticklish situation in which the Fermor family had become offended at the public attention prompted by the two-canto version of the *Rape of the Locke* (1712). Both the dedication and the poem implicitly reassert the poet's power to satirize the conduct of his social betters or to confer "Fame" upon them.

The tone of Pope's teasing dedication has been much discussed, as have the equivocal phrases that allow room for some satire at Arabella Fermor's expense. But the opening of the dedication deserves more notice. Pope's first sentence – "It will be in vain to deny that I have some Regard for this Piece, since I Dedicate it to You" – is a sly revision of the traditional patron-client relationship. Pope in effect removes from the patron the right of assigning value. Arabella's opinion of the piece is not being solicited: Pope (and the public) have already determined that it has merit. The patron should be flattered that the poet has chosen to honor her by associating her with one of his best poems. Pope's words were not casual, but carefully and deliberately chosen. "I have managed the dedication so nicely," he wrote to Caryll, "that it can neither hurt the lady, nor the author" (*Correspondence*, vol. 1, p. 207). And he managed the poem so as to make himself look good. The same cannot be said about Arabella, as she and her family apparently came to realize.

With the exception of the five-canto *Rape of the Lock*, Pope dispensed with such epistles dedicatory in those of his own early works which he formally dedicated. His *Pastorals* carry simple inscriptions on their separate title pages: "To Sir William Trumbull," "To Dr. Garth," "To Mr. Wycherley," and "To the Memory of Mrs. Tempest." The first three of the four poems extend compliments to their addressees near the beginning of each poem. As is the case in most of Pope's early dedications, the addressee is praised not as patron but as poet: "O let my Muse her slender Reed inspire, / 'Till in your Native Shades you tune the Lyre" ("Spring"); "Accept, O *Garth*, the Muse's early Lays, / That adds this Wreath of Ivy to thy Bays" ("Summer"); "Thou, whom the Nine with *Plautus*' Wit inspire / The Art of *Terence*, and *Menander*'s Fire" ("Autumn").[19]

Although Pope modestly acknowledges the addressee's implicitly superior literary merit, he in effect puts himself on the same level – as a fellow poet. And when in later years Pope added notes to the poems, this attitude is made even clearer. His addressees are presented as the poet's "friends". "Our Author's friendship with this gentleman [Trumbull] commenced [when Pope was] under sixteen." Garth is "one of the first friends of the author."[20] To declare that such eminent men are his "friends" is of course a means to advertise his own early distinction. But it also serves notice that there is nothing mean or servile in his own conduct, and announces that in his relationships with anyone eminent for birth or talent he will ignore apparent inequalities, just as he did by commencing a friendship with Trumbull "at very unequal years."

Windsor Forest is dedicated to George Granville, Lord Lansdowne, Secretary of War in Queen Anne's Tory Cabinet and recently raised to the peerage and appointed a Privy Counsellor.[21] Again, what Pope selects to emphasize is not what separates him from the minister and peer but what joins them: their poetry. Lansdowne is called upon by Pope not to continue serving the queen as a statesman but to "sing" as a poet: "'Tis yours, my Lord, to bless our soft Retreats, / And call the Muses to their ancient Seats, / To paint anew the flow'ry Sylvan Scenes, / To crown the Forests with Immortal Greens, / Make *Windsor* Hills in lofty Numbers rise" (lines 283–87).

Granville's title as poet is a courtesy. As Johnson noted, when a man "illustrious by his birth ... declared himself a poet ... his claim to the laurel was allowed."[22] By promoting Granville's poetic claims, Pope engages in Dryden's familiar dedicatory tactics. We do not need to suppose that he thought any higher of Granville's verse than Johnson did. But we should also look at his praise from the point of

---

[19]   The dedications were apparently an afterthought. Neither the inscriptions nor the dedicatory couplets appear in Pope's holograph manuscript.

[20]   Mrs. Tempest was "particularly admired by the Author's Friend Mr. Walsh." The notes on Garth and Mrs. Tempest first appeared in 1736, the note on Trumbull not until 1751. The note on Wycherley passes on the criticism that he had "too much wit" and not enough "correctness."

[21]   Pope may have intended to dedicate the poem to Trumbull, who had proposed the subject. See Pope's *Works*, I, 324, and Frances Clement, "Lansdowne, Pope, and the Unity of *Windsor-Forest*," 44–53.

[22]   *Lives of the Poets*, I, 294.

view of the poet. By complimenting not Granville's birth, high office, taste, or right to sit in literary judgment, but his poetry, Pope sets the terms by which the writer meets the patron – not as dependent but as equal, as fellow writer. The polite fiction that pastoral Pope must defer to heroic Granville is just that – a polite fiction that everyone (including Granville) is meant to see through.

Six years later Pope again dedicated a major work to an older writer, when he inscribed the completed *Iliad* to Congreve. Most commentators simply assume that such a dedication marks Pope's independence from the patronage system, and do not observe that in some respects Pope was continuing in an old pattern. Nor have they remarked how the Homer project, enmeshed in the patronage system, both confirmed that system and subtly modified it.

It was apparently Trumbull, acting like a traditional patron, who first suggested to Pope that he undertake a translation of Homer. When Pope completed his specimen translation of the "Episode of Sarpedon," he sent it to Trumbull, who responded with high approval.[23] The proposals for a subscription edition were published in October 1713, and the contract with Lintot not signed until March 1714 – it was clearly important for Pope to determine and establish his support among wealthy subscribers before closing with a book-seller. After the proposals were announced, Pope received offers of support from friends, including Lord Lansdowne, who wrote in October that Pope could "depend upon the utmost services I can do in promoting this work, or anything that may be for your service."[24] Pope in turn called upon other friends to "promote" his work by soliciting subscriptions. He also sought their critical opinions. "I have," he writes in a letter to Caryll in November 1714, "been perpetually waiting upon the great, and using no less solicitation to gain their opinion upon my Homer than others at this time do to obtain preferments."[25]

Thus far, Pope's venture sounds like the sort of project tradition-ally sponsored by the patronage system. The work was proposed, encouraged, subscribed for, and criticized by the literary patrons of the day. Among the patrons whose opinion Pope solicited was the Earl of Halifax. But the famous story of Pope's visit is often cited as a sign that even as a young writer he was becoming discontent with the deference toward patronal authority that the system required. The

[23] *Correspondence*, I, 45.   [24] *Ibid.*, 195   [25] *Ibid.*, 267.

story is worth examining once again, since it by no means indicates a clear break with the patronage system.

In May 1714, when Halifax had apparently subscribed for ten sets, Pope proudly wrote to Caryll that he had been "honoured" with Halifax's "patronage."[26] (Fourteen years later, as we have seen, it suited Pope's interests to regard an equal sum from the king not as "patronage" but as mere "subscription".) Later that year Pope was invited to read from his translation-in-progress at the house of his lordship, who had gathered some literary friends for the occasion, including Addison, Congreve, and Garth. As Pope read, Halifax interrupted him "very civilly" several times to comment: "I beg your pardon, Mr. Pope, but there is something in that passage that does not quite please me. Be so good as to mark the place and consider it a little at your leisure. I'm sure you can give it a better turn." These "loose and general observations" apparently left Pope puzzled about how to proceed, and upon quitting the house he asked Garth what he should do. Garth laughed, and said that this was just Halifax's "way," that Pope should in effect ignore the "observations," and "call on Lord Halifax two or three months hence, thank him for his kind observations on those passages, and then read them to him as altered." Pope follows Garth's advice, and Halifax responds, "Ay, now they are perfectly right! Nothing can be better."[27]

Johnson thinks that in this second interview Halifax has been "despised or cheated."[28] Mack suspects that from this moment Pope began forming his portrait of proud, full-blown Bufo.[29] But these suspicions seem unwarranted. Pope's initial visit to Halifax and his readiness to return do not suggest that he was rebelling against the conventions of the patronage system. He apparently accepted the idea (which Johnson himself articulated) that Halifax, "having been first a poet, and then a patron of poetry, had acquired the *right* of being a judge."[30] Pope's complaint is not that Halifax offered criticism, but that he did not provide *specific* criticism that Pope could use, or at least react to (of the sort Walsh had provided on the unpublished *Pastorals*). And indeed by returning and by resubmitting

---

[26] See Pope's letter to Caryll of May 1, 1714, in *ibid.*, 220, where his purpose seems to be to preserve the appearance of political impartiality by showing that he has friends in both parties.

[27] Spence, *Observations*, I, 87–88.

[28] "Life of Pope," in *Lives of the Poets*, III, 127.

[29] *Alexander Pope: A Life*, 271–72.

[30] *Lives of the Poets*, III, 126. My emphasis.

his work to Halifax's eyes, Pope was acting prudently but also publicly confirming the earl's authority as judge (although perhaps privately resolving to trust his own judgment in future). Garth's laughter at Pope's puzzled "embarrassment" is not the conspiratorial ridicule by a fellow writer of a pompous patron but the hearty delight at the young Pope's naiveté on the part of an older writer (twenty-seven years senior to Pope, and Halifax's exact contemporary) who had apparently often witnessed such scenes in the past and did not think the less of Halifax for it (as fellow Whig loyalists and members of the Kit-cat Club, they had known each other for more than twenty years).

Pope continued to acknowledge both Halifax's position and his favor, and apparently left a copy of some part of the translation in his hands, with what seems to have been a cover letter apparently asking for Halifax's criticisms and any suggested last-minute revisions. Like any author would, Pope assures Halifax that he attends his lordship not "out of expectation, but out of gratitude." Halifax had, however, apparently offered to provide a pension if Pope "cared to accept it"[31] – an "easy fortune" – large enough to enable Pope to "live agreeably in the Towne." Pope had evidently not determined whether to accept this provisional offer. He cautiously notes the "high Strain of Generosity in you to think of making me easie all my Life, only because I have been so happy as to divert you an hour or two" – but Pope's response is hardly "faint" or "frigid," as Johnson calls it. Johnson seems not to know about the offer of a pension (his knowledge come only from the 1735 edited version of Pope's letter, which makes no explicit reference to a pension). And it seems hasty to conclude (as Johnson does) that Pope was holding back, and "would not dedicate [the *Iliad* to Halifax] till he saw at what rate his praise was valued."[32] For whatever reason, the delicate negotiations between author and patron did not lead to a formal dedication to the earl. One complicating factor may have been that Halifax was probably also negotiating with Thomas Tickell, who was known to be preparing a rival translation of the *Iliad*; it appeared only one week after Pope's and was indeed dedicated to Halifax.

There is no evidence that relations between Halifax and Pope were ever broken off. When Halifax died in May 1715 – before either Pope's or Tickell's translation appeared – Pope remembered him

---

[31] Spence, *Observations*, I, 99.   [32] *Lives of the Poets*, III, 127.

warmly as a patron of the arts in some otherwise high-spirited verses (about leaving London for the summer) he circulated among friends.[33] When Pope published the first volume of the *Iliad* in June, his printed "Preface" publicly acknowledged his gratitude to Halifax, and honored him as both poet and patron: "The Earl of *Halifax* was one of the first to favour me, of whom it is hard to say whether the Advancement of the Polite Arts is more owing to his Generosity or his Example."[34]

If Pope's private opinion of Halifax had begun to change, he did not make it public for many years. It is quite possible that his opinion did not change until the 1730s, by which time Pope had more firmly separated himself from the patronage economy. In 1735 Pope printed a version of his 1714 letter to Halifax, but revised it to omit a sentence in which he politely begs Halifax not to "forget" Homer, and reduces the subscription from the full-scale "Your most obliged, most obedient, & faithful humble Servant" to plain "I sincerely am yours, &c."

The conversation with Spence, our source for the story of Pope's visit to Halifax, did not take place until twenty years later, when Pope, looking back in 1734 on a long career, and on his acquaintance with great men of a former age, could say that "The famous Lord Halifax was rather a pretender to taste than really possessed of it." And it was not until 1744 that Pope told Spence of Halifax's offer of a pension, in effect glossing the letter to Halifax as his response to the patron's offer.[35] Pope is not necessarily to be trusted as a witness. He was recounting events up to thirty years after the fact, and he had a strong motive to separate any offer of a pension from any thought of a dedication. As with the edition of his letters, Pope may be engaged here in the rewriting of history in order to suggest that his attitude toward patronage in 1744 was already in place some thirty years earlier.

But there are signs even in 1715 that Pope was beginning to think more like an independent literary entrepreneur and less like an author who accepted his traditional place in a fixed hierarchy. One indication is that Pope drove a hard bargain with his bookseller.

---

[33] "A Farewell to London. In the Year 1715."
[34] "Preface," in *Poems of Pope*, VII, 24.
[35] He told Spence that, having heard nothing after the offer for three months, he wrote, saying (in part) that "All the difference I could find in having or not having a pension was that if I had one I might live more at large in town ..." etc. Spence, *Observations*, I, 99.

Another is more subtle: the way in which Pope made use of the conventions of introducing a book to his reader and of acknowledging the kindness he received.

The first volume of Pope's translation (1715) is introduced not by the dedication to Congreve – that does not appear until 1720 – but by a critical "Preface." Pope takes from Dryden the idea of a critical preface, but transforms it from a dedicatory epistle to a "discourse" or "preface" directed implicitly to the anonymous reader. The "Discourse on Pastoral Poetry" addressed an unspecified "you." The Homer translation begins with a "Preface" addressed not to Congreve but to a generalized reader. Pope's recurrent pronoun is "we" – "We come now to the Characters of his Person," "If in the next place we take a View ..." – and in closing the "Preface" he submits his work "to the Publick, from whose Opinions I am prepared to learn." This represents a significant shift from the practice of a Dryden, whose dedicatory prefaces close with compliments to the patron and a submission, implicit or explicit, to *his* judgment.

Pope does go on, however, to offer acknowledgments to those who have encouraged or supported him. And those he names are significant: first the "best Poets" of the day, a careful blend of Whigs and Tories – Addison, Steele, Swift, Garth, Congreve, Rowe, and Parnell. Only then come the "First Names of the Age," those "distinguish'd Patrons and Ornaments of Learning" who appear as his "chief Encouragers" and are listed among his subscribers. Pride of place in this group is given to "those who have done most Honour to the Name of Poet": Buckingham, Halifax, Bolingbroke, Lansdowne. Finally come other great men – the Earl of Caernarvon (later made Duke of Chandos), Stanhope (Secretary of State), and Harcourt (son of the former Lord Chancellor), men distinguished not for their poetry but their rank and their generosity. The order is significant. Pope assigns priority among his encouragers to fellow writers; eminence in writing is valued more highly than birth or political accomplishment or patronage. His language of compliment more closely resembles a modern-day "acknowledgments" page than a Restoration-era dedication. And although Pope readily calls his encouragers his patrons – "I have found more patrons than ever Homer wanted"[36] – what he emphasizes is not their condescension in stooping to honor him but his delight in the "Friendship of so

---

[36] Earlier he notes that Bolingbroke "has not refus'd to be the Critick of these Sheets, and the Patron of their Writer."

many Persons of Merit." Where Dryden's practice assigns authority
to his patrons, Pope's assigns it to Homer himself, to Homer's critics,
and to the "best Poets" of his own age, the "judges most to be
feared."

The actual dedication to Congreve does not come until the end of
the final volume, where it is nearly buried.[37] But the dedication was
not an afterthought, nor was its placement casual. Pope's Homer
manuscripts include an annotation in his own hand reading "End of
the notes with a dedication to Mr. Congreve, as a memorial of our
friendship occasioned by his translation of this last part of Homer."[38]
Again Pope modifies the conventions of dedication to suggest a
different kind of relationship between author and dedicatee. Pope's
brief dedication is not actually addressed to Congreve; it is presented
as the last of his "Notes." Nor does Congreve's name appear in the
heading, which reads simply "The Dedication of the Iliad." In fact,
the dedicator begins by acknowledging debts to two other writers
with whom Congreve must share the spotlight. They are Pope's
"Friends," Broome, who had supplied "Extracts from Eustathius"
for the notes, and Parnell, who wrote up the "Essay" on Homer's
life. Only then does Pope turn to the as-yet-unnamed Congreve.

The choice of addressee is noteworthy. Macaulay thought Congreve was politically safe – "on terms of civility with men of all
parties"[39] – at a time (just after the triumphal return of the Whigs)
when politics were especially partisan. It has been widely assumed
that by selecting Congreve Pope was transferring to an author the
sort of status usually reserved for a noble patron. But Congreve may
have been chosen for other reasons. By 1720 he was long retired from
the stage. Although only fifty, he had published nothing for twenty
years, and had in effect adopted the character of "gentleman" rather
than author, a man "whose manners were polite, and his conversation pleasing."[40] He seems to have met Pope as early as 1709, and to
have begun a correspondence with him.[41] When Voltaire sought him
out, Congreve "spoke of his Works as of Trifles that were beneath

---

[37] As Ault says, it is "unassumingly printed at the very end of the notes to the sixth and last
      volume." *Prose Works*, cxxiv.
[38] "This last part" refers to Bk. 24, which Congreve had translated in 1693. Perhaps the idea
      of dedicating to Congreve occurred to Pope while he was translating Bk. 24, and
      borrowing a Congreve couplet (see his note to Bk. 24, line 934). But in the dedication itself
      Congreve's importance is broader.
[39] *Critical and Historical Essays*, III, 45.
[40] Johnson, *Lives of the Poets*, II, 224.
[41] Pope writes in 1729 of "a long 20 years friendship" (*Correspondence*, III, 10).

him," and "hinted" that he should be visited "on no other Foot than that of a gentleman, who led a Life of Plainness and Simplicity."[42] Both Voltaire and Johnson found such posturing to be "despicable foppery,"[43] but Pope may well have been both charmed by the older man's attentions and attracted to the aristocratic role that he played. By dedicating the *Iliad* to Congreve Pope may be signaling both to the general reader and to the patronage class that he too is to be regarded in the character of gentleman-writer, one who hopes to be valued as a man as well as a writer, and one who can freely mingle – and not only because of his wit – with "men of fashion" and with the great.[44]

Pope's plain-speaking pose stands in calculated contrast to the elaborate rhetoric of conventional dedications. He will avoid any "Ceremonies of taking leave," and instead of "endeavouring" through an apology for his work "to raise a vain Monument to my self," Pope offers to Congreve and to posterity "a Memorial of my Friendship, with one of the most valuable Men as well as finest Writers, of my Age and Countrey." The emphasis – not on Congreve alone but on Pope's friendship with him – again marks Pope's departure from the conventional ways of the dedicator. Congreve is acknowledged as a *fellow* translator of Homer and thus as Pope's equal in rank. The dedication closes by producing at last the name of the dedicatee. Pope has "the Honour and Satisfaction" of "placing together ... the Names of Mr. CONGREVE, and of

A. POPE."

No "humble, obedient servant." Just plain "A. Pope."[45] The design of the printed page – the two names set in all caps, and Pope's name set below on a separate line – shows once again how Pope found ways to manage the rhetoric of patronage to serve his purposes. The dedicatee is named first. The dedicator deferentially names himself second, and does not presume to place his name on the same line. But by leaving his name to stand alone he has contrived, after all, to produce a kind of "Monument to my self."

The dedication of the *Iliad* in 1720 suggests then that although

---

42 *Letters concerning the English Nation*, 96.
43 *Lives of the Poets*, II, 226.
44 One may speculate that Congreve was not simply Pope's second choice, a fall-back after negotiations with Halifax failed. If Pope's intent were to declare a parity between author and patron, or the author's priority to the patron, Congreve was more useful to him than Halifax.
45 This was Pope's normal signature on a personal letter.

Pope remained part of the patronage system, he had claimed for himself a role considerably stronger than that of the traditional client. As I have suggested, from his earliest published works Pope had been laying the groundwork for this claim. We can see it not only in those poems, like the *Pastorals* or *Windsor Forest*, which carry dedications, but also in those works which pointedly do not. I will focus on two, the *Essay on Criticism* in 1711 and the edition of Pope's *Works* in 1717.

The absence of a dedication for the *Essay on Criticism*, at a time when dedications were still common, is itself a signal, particularly since Pope's poem asks a crucial question about the literary system: who has the right and the competence to serve as a judge of literary merit? In Dryden's day it had been assumed that gentlemen of education and leisure, particularly if they had some literary inclinations, were the natural judges, since they possessed true taste.[46] Pope's *Essay* implicitly challenges that old assumption. Although he begins with the notion that some are "*born* to Judge" (line 14) – apparently endorsing the traditional view – he quickly moves to a more democratic idea: "Yet if we look more closely, we shall find / Most have the *Seeds* of Judgment in their Mind" (lines 19–20). "Most" people, indeed, anyone, in other words, might become a critic. And although Pope concedes the necessity of innate taste and good sense, he regards criticism as an art that must be learned by careful study of the ancients: "Be *Homer*'s Works your *Study*, and *Delight*, / Read them by Day, and meditate by Night" (lines 124–25). If we read these lines in the context of the patronage system, we can see more clearly that Pope has in mind the inadequacy of the typical gentleman's education of the day. To be a true critic requires more than picking up a smattering of Greek and Latin at school. (This may account for Pope's remark that the *Essay* would not be understood by one gentleman in sixty.)[47]

It also requires skill in the art one professes to judge. "Let such teach others who themselves excell, / And *censure freely* who have *written well*" (lines 15–16). Pope's couplet implicitly nods at the carping censurers, rule-bound pedants, and coffee-house witlings –

---

[46] Cf. Dennis: "Nothing is more certain than that supposing equal Talent and equal application, a Man of Quality has great Advantages over the best of Men," even (Dennis makes clear) in poetry (*Critical Works*, I, 414).

[47] Pope wrote to Caryll that he feared the poem was one that "not one gentleman in three score even of a liberal education can understand." *Correspondence*, I, 128.

usually said to be the targets of the *Essay* – who had discredited criticism, but they equally point to the gentleman writer with a *"little Learning"* who occasionally pens a song. Later in the poem Pope sharpens the satire at the expense of a *"Lord"* who produces *"woful stuff"* – and yet is praised by servile critics (lines 414–23) – and the *"Honourable* Fool / Whose Right it is, *uncensur'd* to be dull" (lines 588–89).[48] Pope makes clear that by "writing well" he means not simply a gentleman's accomplishment, but *"Nature's chief Master-piece"* (line 724), a high calling and a life's work. Criticism too requires highly developed skills and judgment. The consequences of this argument for literary politics are radical. Pope implicitly calls for a shift of power from the traditional patron class to the writers themselves.[49]

In practice, however, the effect is not revolutionary. The true critic needs *"Good Breeding"* (line 576) and a *"Courtier's Ease"* (line 668). And the ideal critics of Pope's own day turn out to be not John Dryden (whom Johnson was later to call "the father of English criticism") but three Restoration gentlemen, the Duke of Buckingham, the Earl of Roscommon, and William Walsh – in other words, members of the traditional class of patrons and judges. To be sure, Pope's compliments – which in Dryden might have taken the form of a formal dedication[50] – are offered to men who had significant reputations as *writers* (at least in his own eyes). Pope offers his praise not at the beginning of his poem but only at the end. And his footnotes, added in 1751, bring out that Pope regarded the figure of highest rank, Buckingham, less as a "Nobleman" who "patroniz'd" writers (Dryden's view of him) than as a familiar friend.[51]

Pope's cautiously hinted resistance to the traditional claims of the patronage class is more open in the "Preface" to his *Works* of 1717.

[48] Dennis, professing traditional respect for "People of Quality who have applied themselves to Poetry," recognized the force of Pope's strictures. He claimed (intemperately) that Pope "happens to have a very great Contempt ... for the Authors [of quality]." *Critical Works*, 1, 414.

[49] When Dennis drew attention to Pope's "contempt," he sought to soften the impact, writing to Caryll in June 1711 that he was no "despiser of Men of Quality" (*Correspondence*, 1, 123).

[50] Pope's footnote to Buckingham points out that he (Pope) is "not the only one of his time who complimented [Buckingham's 1682 *Essay on Poetry*], and its noble Author. Mr. Dryden had done it very largely in the Dedication to his translation of the Aeneid" (*Poems of Pope*, Twickenham Edition, 1, 323–24).

[51] While relations between noble patron and Dryden cooled after 1685, "Our Author" (says Pope) "was more happy, he was honour'd very young with his friendship, and it continued till his death in all the circumstances of a familiar esteem."

Again, the absence of a dedication is itself significant. (In the same year Congreve dedicated his edition of Dryden's *Dramatic Works* to the Duke of Newcastle).[52] In the first sentence Pope addresses not an individual patron, nor even his friends, but the "readers" of his book. He appears before his readers as a well-known writer engaged in "collecting [his] pieces" – most of which had already appeared separately – and bidding for "the favour of the publick."

Most accounts of the "Preface" note not his direct appeal to the public but the implicitly aristocratic stance that Pope adopts.

Poetry [is] by no means the universal concern of the world, but only the affair of idle men who write in their closets, and of idle men who read there.

There are indeed some advantages accruing from a Genius to Poetry, and they are all I can think of: the agreeable power of self-amusement when a man is idle or alone; the privilege of being admitted into the best company; and the freedom of saying as many careless things as other people, without being so severely remark'd upon.

I writ because it amused me; I corrected because it was as pleasant to me to correct as to write; and I publish'd because I was told I might please such as it was a credit to please.

One may be ashamed to consume half one's days in bringing sense and rhyme together; and what Critic can be so unreasonable as not to leave a man time enough for any more serious employment, or more agreeable amusement?

Poetry, by this account, is a matter of private "agreeable amusement," a diversionary game which one can take or leave, but in no sense an "employment" or an attempt to make a demand upon public attention. Pope claims to be indifferent to the success of his works.

But the "Preface" is not simply a manifesto of gentlemanly detachment. Mack has pointed to an attitude in Pope's prose that regards literature not as trifling but as serious business, "a professional activity to which, at least by serious practitioners, only the highest standards of performance should be brought."[53] This attitude is not absent from Pope's "Preface." The true poet must indeed "have the constancy of a martyr, and a resolution to suffer for its sake," when he dedicates himself to the task of reading, composition, judgment, and self-correction.

---

[52] Young and Dennis were still writing lavish dedications at this time.
[53] *Alexander Pope: A Life*, 335.

the Ancients ... had as much Genius as we ... to take more pains, and employ more time, cannot fail to produce more complete pieces. They constantly apply'd themselves not only to that art, but to that single branch of an art, to which their talent was most powerfully bent; and it was the business of their lives to correct and finish their works for posterity. If we can pretend to have used the same industry, let us expect the same immortality.

In Mack's opinion, such a view of literature, while "diametrically opposed" to the older aristocratic notion, somehow enjoys a "curiously peaceful co-presence" (*Alexander Pope: A Life*, p. 335) with it in his "Preface." In my view the two attitudes are not so peacefully conjoined; they constitute a glaring and unresolved contradiction. Both here and elsewhere Pope is aware of what is at stake in the general cultural shift from one attitude to the other, and in effect dramatizes it in his "Preface." Each attitude serves him in a different way. To claim that poetry is a matter of "self-amusement" – in the context of the patronage system – is in effect to declare that Pope himself belongs to the class of gentlemen-writers who trifle for their own pleasure, and not to the herd of hacks who desperately scratch out a living. This stance enables Pope to distinguish himself self-enhancingly from Grub Street (perhaps the success of his commercial venture with Homer made him feel uncomfortably close to the commerce of literature). But it also enables him to *displace* the traditional patrons of literature: I don't need you because I'm independent. I constitute myself as my own authority: it is enough that I simply wish to write and print. To declare on the other hand that poetry requires lifelong service and maybe martyrdom is to elevate the writing of verse to a calling, thus marking off distance between himself and most producers of literature. By comparison, the hack is engaged in sordid trade and the "holiday writer" (Pope's term for the gentleman-poet)[54] who writes "for diversion only," can't be considered "a true Poet."[55] The "true" poet is on a plane where the patron can neither help nor hurt him.

It is notable that Pope does not define himself as what we might call a "professional writer" – where professional suggests not writing for money but a skilled service requiring specialized intellectual

---

[54] He could have found it in Dryden's description of the noble translators of Virgil who "writ for Pleasure" (*Works*, v, 340).

[55] See Pope's early letter to Caryll about Crashaw as gentleman-poet (*Correspondence*, I, 109–10) and his late conversation with Spence about Dorset and Rochester (Spence, *Observations*, I, 201).

study and training. Such a notion, implying both high status and independence, would require many decades to develop, and was not yet available to Pope. What were available were the older ideas of writer-as-gentleman and (to a lesser extent) of the writer's quasi-religious vocation. In adopting these images of the writer Pope may well have been sincere, but could have adopted them simply because they enabled him to claim a kind of independence.

But there is yet a third attitude toward literature (on which Mack does not remark) embodied in Pope's language. The "Preface" assumes a world of fellow "authors" who will "print" and "publish" their work, "booksellers" who will buy them, and "readers" in the "publick" whom Pope seeks to "please." In the context of the patronage system, such a vocabulary sends a signal. To situate oneself squarely within the world of booksellers and readers is in effect to go over the heads of the patrons and appeal directly to the "public," signaling to the world of patronage that the poet has other sources of support, and is not completely dependent on their bounty. But as always Pope tries to have it both ways. Although he appeals in the "Preface" for "the favour of the publick," he also assumes that he already enjoys their favor. Not only that, he assumes that he already enjoys the support of the "great" and "eminent." In the final sentence of the "Preface" Pope manages to combine a seemly modesty and seeming diffidence about his prospects for fame[56] with a bold confidence. If his volume should perish, he says,

let it serve as ... a *Memento mori* to some of my vain contemporaries the Poets, to teach them that when real merit is wanting, it avails nothing to have been encourag'd by the great, commended by the eminent, and favour'd by the publick in general.

These words (and the "Preface" as whole) do not leave real doubt about Pope's opinion of his own "real merit." More important, the final phrases ("encourag'd by ... commended by ... and favour'd by ...") declare that Pope already enjoys what any aspiring dedicator seeks. And he enjoys them without having to resort to the bribery of "unjust praise." The *Preface* in effect asserts that Pope need no longer stoop to the indignity of dedication.

The dedication to Homer was the last dedication that Pope would write, unless we count the "Epistle to Oxford," composed as part of

---

[56] Some critics have been persuaded by Pope's professions and diffidence. For an example, see my own *Alexander Pope: The Poet in the Poems*, 71–99. The "Preface" now seems to me to be quite audacious in its claims.

the posthumous edition of Parnell's poems that Pope published in 1722.[57] As Pope's later note indicates, the epistle "was sent to the Earl of Oxford with Dr. Parnell's Poems published by our Author, after the said Earl's Imprisonment in the Tower and Retreat into the Country, in the year, 1721."[58] The "Epistle" thus functions as a kind of "epistle dedicatory" – Johnson calls it a "very elegant Dedication"[59] – though it falls short of explicitly dedicating the edition to Oxford, and in that respect again provides Pope with an opportunity to redefine the traditional relationships between authors and patrons.

Another poet might have identified more with Parnell – a fellow poet. Pope clearly identifies with his addressee, Oxford, as friend and fellow mourner. Rather than "love me, as you loved him," Pope's poem says "we both lament his loss." Parnell is "thy once-lov'd Poet" (line 1), adorned with "softest Manners" and "gentlest Arts" (line 4), and "dear to the Muse" (line 5), a delicate and feminized spirit. The possessive pronouns (cf. "thy *Parnell*," line 16) almost make of the dead poet a dependent member of the household, a child or a favorite pet. By contrast, Pope is himself "The Muse" who "attends" Oxford "to the silent Shade" of his retreat. But he "attends" rather as "Friend" than as the attendant on a great man. His function, significantly, is to "trace" brave Oxford's "latest Steps," to "Re-judge his Acts, and dignify Disgrace" (line 30). "Re-judge" both refers back to Oxford's trial for treason – Pope will in effect preside over an appeal or retrial – and firmly suggests, in the context of a dedicatory epistle, the traditional poetic powers to which Pope lays claim. It is the poet's power, as Johnson said later, to confer true fame, to bestow "the honours of a lasting name" (*Rambler* 136).[60] Parnell may now forget that Oxford "e'er was Great" (line 18) – i.e., was a "great man" (a man of high rank), but Pope will fearlessly proclaim that Oxford is "truly Great" (line 39). Implicitly too Pope reclaims a power customarily assigned to the patron. It is traditionally the patron's power and right to "judge" literary merit.

57 The last in his own name, that is. When Richard Savage published his *Collection of Pieces of Verse and Prose which have been published in occasion of the Dunciad* in 1732, Pope wrote a dedication for him, addressed to the Earl of Middlesex. See Johnson's *Lives of the Poets*, II, 360, III, 147.

58 The note was first published in an edition of Pope's poems in 1740.

59 *Lives of the Poets*, III, 137. See the exchange of letters between Pope and Oxford in October–November 1721, just before the edition appeared (*Correspondence*, II, 90–91).

60 Cf. Pope's "Honour not confer'd by Kings" (*Epilogue to the Satires*, Dialogue II, line 243).

Oxford's role in the poem is simply to "love"; Pope remains the only "judge" – and as Parnell's editor he quite literally acted in the capacity of judge (deciding which poems to include) and patron (presenting Parnell's work to the world).

No work of Pope's after 1722 contains a dedication of any kind (the *Dunciad* contains an invocation to Swift – "O thou! whatever Title please thine ear,/ Dean, Drapier, Bickerstaff, or Gulliver!" – but is not dedicated to him). The absence of dedications in itself suggests that Pope has adopted a stance of independence. And yet – as I remarked earlier – Pope remained a beneficiary of the patronage system to the end of his life. But he set the terms: he would not formally dedicate his poems, though he might address them to men of high rank. As Johnson noted, to his later works (more than in his early career) Pope "took care to annex names dignified with titles" (*Lives of the Poets*, vol. III, p. 205). The difference is plain enough to any reader: a dedicator humbly offers a poem to a patron who deigns to notice, but Pope frankly addresses his later poems to men he considers his friends and equals, men like Bolingbroke, Cobham, and Bathurst who can be rallied as well as complimented.[61]

The little-cited "Epistle to James Craggs, Esq; Secretary of State," written about 1718 but not published until the 1735 *Works*, is an apt instance. The poem was presumably sent to Craggs shortly after he had been named to succeed Addison as Secretary of State, and about the time he offered Pope a pension. Its opening lines draw a picture that might be a self-portrait as well as an image of its addressee:

> A soul as full of Worth, as void of Pride,
> Which nothing seeks to show, or needs to hide,
> Which nor to Guilt, nor Fear, its Caution owes,
> And boasts a Warmth that from no Passion flows;
> A Face untaught to feign! a judging Eye,
> That darts severe upon a rising Lye,
> And strikes a blush thro' frontless Flattery.
> All this thou wert.   (lines 1–8)

Pope urges Craggs, now in high office, to continue in the same path: "candid, free, sincere, as you began, / Proceed – a Minister, but still a Man" (lines 12–13). Pope hopes that the new minister will not be

---

[61]   Cf. the revealing August 1723 letter to Swift, who helped Pope to learn "how to gain, and how to use the freedoms of friendship with men much my superiors" – without falling into flattery (*Correspondence*, II, 183–86).

ashamed of his old "Friend." Or else, presenting himself now as Craggs' conscience – and his equal, "'tis I must be ashamed of You" (line 17). When it was published in 1735 – Craggs himself had died of smallpox in 1721 – Pope's "Epistle" substantiates his claim (to which I will return) that he condescends to call a minister his friend.[62]

POPE'S LATER CAREER

Although one might look to a number of Pope's poems of the 1730s to see how he positions himself as an independent writer living "among the great," the "Epistle to Dr. Arbuthnot" is probably the clearest example. In the context of Pope's relations to his patrons, it is possible to see that Pope's "Epistle" not only defines his own stance but also – in its three famous portraits of Atticus, Sporus, and Bufo – anatomizes the corruptions of the patronage system.

Before turning to the well-known "Arbuthnot," however, it is instructive to recall the image of the patron in Pope's later poems. In the games in Book II of the *Dunciad* dedicators compete for the favor of a patron: "He wins this Patron who can tickle best" (Book II, line 188). The "lordly master" is a crude caricature of a patron: brainless (he "looks broad nonsense with a stare"), tight-fisted, and corruptible (the winning dedicator offers his sister to his Grace). In Book IV patrons "With-hold the pension" and only patronize "for pride" (lines 95, 102). Timon in the "Epistle to Burlington" (1731) is not only an exemplar of false taste but of the misuse of a patron's riches, like Virro and Bubo, each dismissed as a "wealthy fool" (line 17). In the "Epistle to Augustus" (1737) George II is saluted ironically as "great Patron of Mankind" (line 1).

It is also instructive to look briefly at the lesser-known "Letter to a Noble Lord" (1733). Both the poetic epistle to Arbuthnot and the prose "Letter" contain sharp attacks on Lord Hervey. Both were prompted by the Lady Mary–Lord Hervey "Verses Address'd to the Imitator of Horace" (1733) and by Hervey's "Epistle from a Nobleman to a Doctor of Divinity" (1733). The title – "Letter to a Noble Lord" – invokes the traditional patronage system and those many addresses, under such a title, by deferential authors to men of

---

62 Cf. the *Epilogue to the Satires*, where Pope recalls his attachment to worthy statesmen in disgrace: "Thus SOMMERS once, and HALIFAX were mine" (Dialogue II, line 77). Note the telling reversal of the typical address to a patron – "I am yours (to command)," "I am your humble servant," etc.

rank. But as a letter of rebuke to a lord it belongs to the proud tradition that includes Johnson's letter to Chesterfield.[63]

Pope draws a crucial distinction "betwixt the [high] rank your *Lordship* holds in the *World*, and the [low] rank which your *writings* are like to hold in the *learned world*." That Pope draws the distinction at all, or that he conceives of two different hierarchies of "rank," indicates how far he has moved away from the patronage system, and how ready he is to place himself on a level with "a person of your quality and power." For Dryden, Mulgrave and Dorset are equally eminent for rank, taste, and wit. Their rank itself virtually guarantees their eminence in taste and wit. And if it happened not to in particular cases, it was simply good manners in the dedicator to assume that the rule held. In reflecting satirically on Hervey's bungled grammar, Pope invokes a contrary example from the Restoration period: "May not I with all respect say to you, what was said to *another Noble Poet* by Mr. Cowley, *Pray*, Mr. Howard [Edward Howard, son of the Earl of Berkshire], *if you did read your* Grammar, *what harm would it do you?*" Pope's ridicule of Hervey's writings (while acknowledging his rank) gains special force when we set it against the customary compliment that Hervey might still expect from more compliant authors,[64] and against the tradition of ridiculing what passes among noblemen for wit.

Pope also implicitly acknowledges that he lives in a world in which men of "quality" are men of "power." He depends for both "Protection" and "Comfort" on the queen and the prime minister (to whom Hervey has access), and he urges Hervey not to seek to discredit him in their eyes:

Above all, your Lordship will be careful not to wrong my *Moral Character* with THOSE under whose *Protection* I live, and thro' whose *Lenity* alone I can live with Comfort.

Pope's tone combines deference to the authority of what he later calls the "GREATEST PERSONS" with a warning to Hervey himself that he is prepared to satirize any "rich and noble knave" – including Hervey – in public:

This, he thinks, is rendering the best Service he can to the Publick, and even to the good Government of his Country; and for this, at least, he may

---

[63]   One might also include Dryden's ambiguous dedication of *Marriage A-la-Mode* to Rochester.

[64]   Cf. Conyers Middleton's dedication of the *Life of Cicero* to Hervey in 1741 – parodied by Fielding in *Shamela*.

deserve some Countenance, even from the GREATEST PERSONS in it. Your Lordship knows of WHOM I speak. Their NAMES I should be as sorry, and as much asham'd, to place near *yours*, on such an occasion, as I should be to see *You*, my Lord, placed so near *their* PERSONS, if you could ever make so ill an Use of their Ear as to asperse or misrepresent any one innocent Man.

Mention of the royal "Ear" is calculated to recall another image of Hervey (as Fannius, or Lord Fanny) that Pope had invoked in his imitation of Donne's fourth satire, also published in 1733: "Not *Fannius* self more impudently near,/ When half his Nose is in his Patron's Ear" (lines 178–79),[65] and in the "Epistle to Dr. Arbuthnot."[66] Hervey, in other words, is himself the favorite of a courtly patron. While Pope pointedly has "neither *Place, Pension*, nor Power to reward for *secret Services*," and has been "excluded from all *posts* of *Profit* or *Trust*," Hervey – as was widely known – had a pension of £1,000 a year from the king. He had used flattery, so Pope and others claimed, to win high places at court as Privy Councillor and Lord Privy Seal: it is "to your art at court, not your art of poetry, that your Lordship must owe your future figure in the world." By inserting his nose in his patron's ear, a quasi-obscene gesture Pope would recall in his character of Sporus, Hervey figures the corruption of the patronage system, in which advancement depends on malicious whispers and the gratification of the patron's appetite. When he took up his pen and especially when he published, Hervey (so Pope writes) "put himself upon a level with me" and is subject to attack. Part of Pope's retaliation is ironically to underline that they are both dependents. Hervey threatens to misuse his courtier's arts to promote himself and to harm his enemies in the ears of "the GREATEST PERSONS." Pope depends only on his "Genius," his "Industry," and his "Moral Character" to win him the favor of "many friends, who will be always remember'd as the first Ornaments of their Age and Country."

Pope's "Letter" was in fact not published in his lifetime. He had it printed, as if he intended to publish it, and sent it privately to Hervey, perhaps as a warning. Contemporary accounts suggest that it circulated among Hervey's friends and enemies (Fielding apparently knew

---

[65] In his *Letter* Pope pretends disingenuously that Fannius should not be construed as Lord Hervey – the common assumption – but merely as "a foolish Critic, and an enemy of *Horace*."

[66] "At the Ear of *Eve*, familiar Toad" (line 319). See below, p. 153. Hervey's well-known bisexuality made him an apt emblem of the ways in which patronage can corrupt both parties.

of it),[67] and reached the eyes of both Queen Caroline and Walpole, who succeeded in persuading Pope to suppress it. Why he agreed has been debated,[68] but among the reasons may have been Pope's sense that the letter might be even more effective as a deterrent if it were displayed privately but held back from public circulation.

Pope's mature stance – and in some ways a summation of his relationships (as he liked to see them) to the patronage system – can be seen at its most effective in the "Epistle from Mr. Pope to Dr. Arbuthnot" (1735). We usually think of the poem as Pope's apologia pro vita sua, a defense of his character before the court of public opinion, and an attack on his enemies. But we should consider also that the audience contains a number of Pope's titled supporters, and that the poem is also in effect designed to confirm their support. As was clear in the "Letter to a Noble Lord," Pope was very much aware of the special conditions under which he lived, the "protection" and "leniency" of the court which might be withdrawn, the power of his enemies, and the importance of his friends.

But he took pains to make clear that he was no dependent, and enjoyed a relationship with "the great" on relatively equal terms. Thus Pope distinguishes himself from most of the denizens of the "Castalian state" of poetry. Other writers are "oblig'd by hunger" (line 44). They deploy a "venal quill" (line 151) or turn "a *Persian Tale* for half a crown" (line 180) because they are "in debt" (line 154), the constant condition of every "hireling Scribler" (line 364). By contrast Pope, pressed by no financial need, writes for private pleasure – "to ease some Friend" or "To help me thro' this long Disease, my Life" (lines 131–32) – and consults his own "Dignity and Ease" (line 263). If his writings appear in print, it's almost without his cooperation ("This prints my Letters," line 113) and if his name is a household word ("What tho' my Name stood rubric on the walls?", line 215) it wasn't his doing ("I sought no homage from the Race that write," line 219). Other poets may solicit subscriptions (line 114), write dedications (line 109), need patrons (lines 97–100), and serve them as a grateful dinner guest or private secretary. But Pope pays no court to "full-blown *Bufo*, puff'd by ev'ry quill" (line 232). Instead he has the warm encouragement and approval of "*Granville* the polite ... Courtly *Talbot, Somers, Sheffield* ... *St. John*'s self" (lines 135–41) and other members of the traditional patron class. Pope avoids the

---

67 See *Joseph Andrews*, 188, n. 2; 313, n. 2.
68 See Mack, *Alexander Pope: A Life*, 609 and note.

slightest suggestion that he received any material support. These great men are simply his "friends," as they were Dryden's friends before.

"Friends" is the key word here, and it carries significant weight. To declare that Granville and Sheffield are your "friends" rather than your "patrons" (and that you don't need their help) deploys in a public forum the same strategy Pope had earlier deployed in his private correspondence. It erases the social and political difference between patron and client. (When a Grub Street hack calls himself his "friend" [line 112], Pope finds it "abusive".) We are equals, Pope says, and we are bound by "love" (lines 138, 144) rather than obligation or money, and we in effect belong to the same class. Other writers "pay their court" (line 115) to *him*, submitting to his judgment ("what you'd have it, make it" – line 46), writing dedications (line 109), asking him for a patron, and pursing him to "Twit'nam" (Pope contrives to name his "country seat" in his poem.) Repeated use of the word "friend" – it appears some twenty times in the poem – might suggest a contrast between the private or personal sphere (assigned a high value in the poem) and the public world of venality and treachery. But in the public world of eighteenth-century literature "friends" – so long as they are not "timid" (line 343) – could in fact be of considerable public value. They could intercede for you (as with a theater manager – see line 60), or defend your honor (as a false friend would not – see line 206). Indeed, "friends" in eighteenth-century public discourse typically refers to political supporters and associates. By emphasizing that he has many such friends (including the well-known "Dr. Arbuthnot," so prominently addressed and named in the title), Pope not only refutes the charge flung at him in the "Verses Address'd to the Imitator of Horace" (1733) – "'Twill make thy Readers few, as are thy Friends" – but also hints that they are in a position to protect him and to use their influence to support him.

The intended audience is not only Pope's enemies, who are to take such claims as a veiled threat, but Pope's own friends, who can see from his poem what is expected of them. This perhaps helps explain the extraordinary couplet in which Pope declares himself to be "Above a Patron, tho' I condescend/ Sometimes to call a Minister my Friend" (lines 265–66). Taken straight, the lines seem offensively boastful of Pope's "splendid acquaintance." And yet their arrogance, though designed no doubt to provoke his enemies, seems to be comical, half-facetious. His friends – including ex-ministers and wealthy patrons of the arts – can take them knowingly as Pope's little joke. Still, the bantering wit and the winking eye don't prevent Pope from standing on his "Dignity and Ease," and – without offense – claiming the poet's equality with (here masking as superiority to) the great.

At some level Pope, like Dryden before him, seemed to think that, in a properly ordered society, a great writer deserved "protection" from "the great." "Much freer Satyrists than I," he observed to Arbuthnot in a contemporary letter, apparently with Horace in mind, "have enjoy'd the encouragement and protection of the Princes under whom they lived" (*Correspondence*, vol. III, p. 420). Unspoken is the question: why shouldn't I? Shakespeare too had – in strikingly similar language – enjoyed the "protection of his Prince" and the "encouragement of the Court," and had responded by producing the higher achievements of "his riper years."[69] By implicitly claiming that he has "friends" in high places Pope manages to display the benefits of patronage without incurring any of the indebtedness.

Bolstered by his "friends," Pope stands free of a patronage system which no longer serves the purpose for which it was designed. In one way or another each of the poem's chief satirical targets – Atticus, Sporus, and Bufo – embodies a system in which the power of the patron has been corrupted. Atticus represents the man of letters functioning as a patron in a position to judge, commend, encourage, and if not to provide support himself then to procure it. He is "born to write, converse, and live with ease" (line 196). By means of his "Talent" and his "Art" he has risen to a place of influence. But instead of helping others to rise, he shows "hate for Arts that caus'd himself to rise" (line 200). Whereas the patron under the ideal patronage system was qualified to judge and prepared to exercise his authority, Atticus is evasive and ambiguous, "Alike reserv'd to blame, or to commend,/ A tim'rous foe, and a suspicious friend" (lines 205–06). In an earlier version of the portrait – perhaps deleted because it seemed to reflect too obviously on the rival Pope and Tickell *Iliads* – Atticus like a potential patron listens to "two Wits on rival Themes contest." He "Approves of each, but likes the worst the best."

[69] "Preface to Shakespeare," in *Prose Works*, II, 16. Shakespeare's "production," says Pope, "improved, in proportion to the respect he had for his auditors." By implication, if Pope himself can write for worthy judges and patrons, he will write better.

Bufo more obviously displays the perversion of the patron's role. Instead of feeding poets he starves them, while he himself is "fed" a rich diet of "soft Dedication" by those seeking "his judgement" and "a Place." Undiscriminating in his taste, he receives the addresses of "an undistinguish'd race" of wits both true and false. He is less likely to help the living than honor the dead, by paying funeral expenses and displaying busts in his library. And Sporus, though not a patron himself, can corrupt the system at its very source. Bearing out Pope's worst fears in the "Letter to a Noble Lord," Sporus (Hervey) has access to the "Great," and like a toad at the ear of Milton's Eve acts as "Prompter" to the "Puppet." While true patrons, as Dryden says, have "the liberality of kings in their disposing" and direct it to the deserving,[70] Sporus spits out "Politicks, or Tales, or Lyes," poisoning the very fount of royal bounty. While Sporus rises by flattery, by worshiping fortune and following fashion – and implicitly teaches others to rise by the same route, Pope refuses such servility, despises the malicious "Whisper" that "Perhaps, yet vibrates on his SOVEREIGN's Ear" (line 357), and condemns alike – from his vantage of independence – the "hireling Scribler" and "hireling Peer" (line 364).

Despite Pope's lifelong resistance to the claims of patronage, and his redefinition of the relationship between himself and members of the patron class, it cannot be said that – in Beljame's words – his example led directly to the "emancipation" of the writer. Thomson, Young, and Fielding among Pope's contemporaries continued to offer lavish dedications to their patrons in the 1740s, and no other self-made writer in the century enjoyed the degree of Pope's financial success. The system of literary patronage continued relatively intact – in theory, as well as in practice – to the end of the century. Pope's achievement was dependent upon his extraordinary genius, indefatigable industry, and unique ability to manipulate the traditional patrons, the subscription system, and the emerging literary marketplace.

But Pope did leave behind a legacy that over time established an image of the independent writer, free from the chains of patronage. The image was highlighted by his friends Spence and Warburton, the former in his collection of manuscript *Anecdotes* and his *Apology for*

---

[70] See above, pp. 28, 81.

the Late Mr. Pope (1749) and the latter in his notes to the authorized
1751 edition of Pope's *Works*. Warburton had himself talked to
Spence, and took many opportunities to bring out what he saw as
Pope's fearless independence as a writer and satirist. Early biographers burnished the heroic image brighter. William Ayre's *Memoirs of
Alexander Pope* (1745) reaffirms Pope's own claims that he "has liv'd
with the Great without Flattery, been a Friend to Men in Power
without Pensions, from whom as he ask'd, so he receiv'd no Favour,
but was done him in his Friends" (vol. 1, p. 303). Owen Ruffhead's
1769 *Life* elaborates the point:

> though he lived among the great and wealthy, he lived with them upon the
> easy terms of reciprocal amity, and social familiarity. But his familiarity
> with them never so far corrupted his manners, or influenced his writings, as
> to induce him to flatter or dissemble. He courted none on account of their
> honours or titles ... Not only his principles but his spirit, excluded him
> from all views of employing their influence to procure for himself either
> place or pension. (pp. 488–89)[71]

Ruffhead's own note draws the moral of other writers: "men of
worth and abilities should rely solely on their own industry, as the
most effectual means to attain that sure and noble independence,
which renders them superior to the neglect and insolence of exalted
baseness." Brave and inspiring words, but in disseminating them
Ruffhead and others were taken in by Pope's assiduous mythmaking
efforts to leave behind an idealized image of the "independent"
writer.

---

[71] Cf. Pope's disingenuous letter (*c.* 1739) in which he declines a request to write an
inscription for a monument for the Prince of Wales: "I ... who have received so few
favours from the great myself, that I am utterly unacquainted with what kind of thanks
they like best" (*Correspondence*, IV, 170).

CHAPTER 7

Edward Young and Richard Savage

Patronage flowed not only to the great writers of the day, but to those whom we now think of as marginal. The careers of Edward Young (1683–1765) and Richard Savage (1697–1742) are worth reexamining, if only to revise the myths, fostered by the poets themselves, that they were neglected by the patrons of the day. In fact, though they complained bitterly, both were well rewarded. Furthermore, Young was in fact rather less obsequious than we have thought, and Savage rather more fawning.

EDWARD YOUNG

Young is often described as the archetypal literary careerist – opportunistic, self-promoting, shamelessly ready to provide lavish praise in exchange for pension or preferment. Long before George Eliot's famous attack in 1857, in "Worldliness and Otherworldliness: the Poet Young," he was damned for hypocrisy, for pretending to celebrate unworldly retirement and otherworldly hopes while desperately soliciting worldly advantage.[1] That he was an avid solicitor of the patrons of the day is undeniable. But it is too hastily assumed that he was unusual in his obsequiousness. In fact, Young's practice as a dedicator is consistent with the standards of his day. When he made his literary debut during the last years of Queen Anne's reign, both Whig and Tory writers found numerous paths to preferment. Young chose the Tory rather than Addison's Whiggish route, publishing the panegyrical *Epistle to the Right Honourable George Lord Lansdowne* in 1712 and *The Last Day*, dedicated to the queen, in 1713.

---

[1]   Herbert Croft's narrative of Young's life, printed as part of Johnson's biographical preface in 1782, anticipates Eliot's judgment: Young is a "ready celebrator," "despicable" in his "servility of adulation" and "extravagant" praise of his patrons. John Mitford's life, in his 1844 edition, frequently paraphrasing from Croft, sees "fulsome and hyperbolical flattery." See Johnson's *Lives of the Poets*, 111, 366, 372, 384, 385.

155

Both poems, as Croft points out, praised the recently concluded Peace of Utrecht, and thus promoted Tory interests.[2] Like Pope, whose *Windsor Forest* had on the same occasion praised both queen and Lansdowne, Young also thought it fitting to remain in good communication with the Whigs, Pope with a "Prologue" to Addison's *Cato* and Young with commendatory verses prefixed to the play in 1713. And he solidified his links to the triumphant Whigs by inscribing to Addison a poem in 1714, *On The Late Queen's Death, and His Majesty's Accession to the Throne*, thus reassuring his patrons that just as he saw continuity between his own praise of Anne and his praise of George I, so his rewards should continue.

Under George I Young thrived, supported both by the crown and some of the leading political figures of the day. His *Paraphrase on Part of the Book of Job* (1719) was dedicated to the Lord Chancellor, Thomas Parker, and his *Busiris* (1719) to the Lord Chamberlain, the Duke of Newcastle.[3] By 1719 the Duke of Wharton had taken Young into his somewhat uncertain protection, and received the dedication of *The Revenge* (1721).[4] But by 1723 Young had to sue Wharton (unsuccessfully) to try to compel him to honor his financial pledges, and he turned to Bubb Dodington, to whom he dedicated in 1725 the third of what were later collected as his *Love of Fame* satires. Each of the satires was published separately, and Young intended to find a separate patron for each one. (The practice was not unusual; Thomson in the same decade was to find four patrons for the four poems that were eventually published as *The Seasons*, and Dryden in the 1697 *Works of Virgil* had dedicated Virgil's three poems to three different patrons.) In the end Young's plan to dedicate the second satire failed, but the others found patrons in the Duke of Dorset, Spencer Compton (Speaker of the House of Commons), Lady Elizabeth Germain, and Sir Robert Walpole, whose attention to Young had probably been drawn by Dodington. Walpole was no doubt instrumental in arranging for a pension of £200 a year, granted in May 1726, and for Young's appointment as chaplain to

---

2   The *Epistle* "seems intended ... to reconcile the publick to the late peace." The dedication of *The Last Day*, praising the peace, is "clearly political" in "complexion" (Croft, in Johnson, *Lives of the Poets*, 111, 365, 366).

3   For Young's service in the household of the Earl of Exeter in 1719–20, see Harold Forster, *Edward Young*, 62–64.

4   Young received a life annuity of £100 pounds a year from Wharton in 1720 (*ibid*, 61) and another £100 pounds a year in 1722. But the reckless Wharton was by then deeply in debt, and Young had to sue him (to no avail) to recover what he claimed his due. For details, see *ibid*, 75–78.

the Princess of Wales.[5] When Walpole was initiated into the Order of the Garter two months later, Young gratefully saluted him with a panegyrical poem entitled *The Instalment.*[6]

When the Prince of Wales succeeded to the throne in 1727 Young took appropriate steps to consolidate his position. Having served as chaplain to Princess Caroline (now queen), he dedicated a sermon to her,[7] and was duly appointed chaplain to the king in April 1728 (the position carried no salary, apparently because Young already had a pension). He greeted his new monarch and master with *Ocean: An Ode, Occasion'd by his Majesty's Royal Encouragement of the Sea Service. To which is prefixed an Ode to the King; and a Discourse on Ode* (June 1728).[8] Young apparently hoped that the king might do still more for him, and in particular might make him a bishop. But George was not interested, perhaps because, as he is quoted as saying, "Young has a pension."[9] When Laurence Eusden died in September 1730 Young was reported to have been offered the Laureateship, but declined it, having by then decided to take up a fat living as Rector of Welwyn, worth £300 a year, offered him by his Oxford college. When his pension was added in he was worth £500 a year. He was one of the best paid men of letters in the country.

Young's receipts from booksellers are difficult to estimate. His most popular poem, *Night Thoughts*, went through a total of forty-eight authorized editions in his lifetime (counting separate publication of individual "Nights" as well as collected editions). He must have shared in the initial financial success of each edition. According to Tierney, the editor of Dodsley's correspondence, Young sold

---

5   It is possible that Young was at that time named Chaplain to the Princess of Wales. See *ibid,* 98. In 1727 Gay was offered – no doubt with Walpole's approval – a post as Gentleman Usher to another princess. Young sought the same rewards that Gay did – but was more successful.

6   For Young's pursuit, during these years, of the Duke of Chandos (he wrote a poem on the death of the Duke's son in 1727) and Carteret, who controlled church patronage in Ireland, see *ibid,* 106–07, 131.

7   *A Vindication of Providence; or, A True Estimate of Human Life ... Preached in St. George's Church, near Hanover Square, soon after the late King's death* (November 1727).

8   A sermon in 1729 entitled *An Apology for Princes, or the Reverence due to Government,* was dedicated to the House of Commons. In 1730 Young published anther "naval lyric," the *Imperium Pelagi,* dedicated to the Duke of Chandos.

9   Biographers since Croft have wondered why George II did nothing more for Young. Speculations include the claim that Young's worldly youth made him an inappropriate candidate for a bishop, that his professions of contented retirement were taken at face value, and that he had attached himself to the Prince of Wales – with whom the king was at odds. See Croft, in Johnson, *Lives of the Poets,* III, 390–91, and Forster, *Edward Young,* 249–50.

Dodsley his remaining rights to the first five "Nights" for 260 guineas
in 1743. He got another fifty guineas for Night VI in 1745. Nights
VII–IX went to Andrew Millar for sixty guineas in 1749, but Millar
did not acquire permanent rights.[10] *Busiris* brought him three
"author's nights" and another eighty guineas for the copy in 1719.
The Revenge brought only £50 when it was published in 1721, but *The
Brothers* was sold to Dodsley in 1753 for 140 guineas (*Correspondence of
Dodsley*, p. 529). Adding in two "author's nights," Young "realized"
£400 (*Complete Works*, vol. I, p. lxix). Dodsley also bought *The Centaur
Not Fabulous* in 1755 for £200.

Young seems to have understood that the economics of literature
depended on a network of friends and supporters, who could defend
your reputation, introduce you to a patron or a bookseller, and sign
up subscribers. He may not have had Pope's head for business, but
he knew the importance of maintaining good relations with both
fellow poets and patrons. And he was more successful than Pope at
avoiding making enemies. A snapshot of Young in the years around
1730 shows him corresponding with Thomas Tickell (with whom
Pope had quarreled), collecting subscriptions for the *Dunciad*, writing
two poetic epistles to Pope on the writers of the age (thus perhaps
securing the alliance with Pope, who could be a dangerous enemy),
favorably mentioned (as a leading writer) in poems by Pope and
Allan Ramsay, helping introduce young James Thomson (in search
of patronage) to Bubb Dodington, and subscribing to the collected
edition of *The Seasons* (1730). Young was well connected to the chief
Whig patrons of the day – Dodington, Walpole himself, Chesterfield
– and through them was linked to writers outside Pope's circle,
including Thomson and Fielding.[11]

For the remainder of the decade of the 1730s Young largely
devoted himself to his parish duties at Welwyn. But he had not
abandoned poetry;[12] nor had he abandoned his hopes for higher
ecclesiastical preferment, as his letters abundantly demonstrate.
When he returned to poetry in 1742 with the first of what would be

10 For details see the editors' notes in *Night Thoughts*, the *Correspondence of Robert Dodsley*, and
    Young's *Correspondence*.
11 Years later both Thomson and Fielding would compliment Young and Dodington for
    having patronized him. See Thomson's address to Dodington in "Autumn" (line 667,
    added in 1744), and Fielding's epistle to Dodington "Of True Greatness" (1741). Fielding
    also compliments Young in his *Miscellanies*, 78, 136.
12 He produced two more "naval lyrics," *Sea-Piece* (1735), dedicated to Voltaire, and *The
    Foreign Address* (1734), addressed to the members of Parliament: "Nor mean the song, or
    great my blame:/ When such the patrons, such the theme" (*Poetical Works*, 11, 393).

Night Thoughts, he at first published anonymously, but when it was clear that the poem was a success and the second edition appeared, a poem entitled *The Complaint. Night the First* was dedicated to Arthur Onslow, Speaker of the House of Commons. Later "Nights," published separately, were dedicated to other patrons, most in a position (so he thought) to help him: the Prime Minister (Spencer Compton, Lord Wilmington, who had already patronized the *Love of Fame*); the Duchess of Portland; Philip Yorke, the son of the Lord Chancellor; Henry Pelham (First Lord of the Treasury); and finally Pelham's brother, the Duke of Newcastle.[13] Further ecclesiastical preferment of the sort he sought, however, was not forthcoming. Young never rose to a higher position in the church than Rector of Welwyn.

After *Night Thoughts* his works (with one exception) appeared without dedication or were addressed "to a friend." And when Young in 1757 published his own edition of his *Works* he not only passed up the opportunity of dedication, but omitted a number of his early poems (e.g., the *Epistle to Lord Lansdowne*), and omitted the dedications of those of his early works that he chose to reprint. It is as if Young had publicly turned his back on the patronage system that in the end had (so he felt) failed him. Ironically, when George II was succeeded by his grandson in 1760, a place worth another £200 a year as Clerk of the Closet to the widow of the Prince of Wales was found for Young by Newcastle (now Prime Minister). His long courtship of Newcastle – reaching back nearly forty years to *Busiris* – paid off again. When Young died in 1765 he was worth £14,000, and was able to leave £1,000 to his housekeeper and to leave his son and heir "a very handsome fortune."[14] Thus for all his own laments, and all the attention paid by his biographers from Croft to Forster to his alleged "neglect" and his "worldly failure," Young prospered as a

---

[13] The first printing of the *Night the Ninth* included verses dedicated to Newcastle entitled "Some Thoughts, occasioned by the Present Juncture" (and later printed as "Reflections on the Public Situation of the Kingdom"). *Night the Fifth* was dedicated to the Earl of Lichfield, nephew of Young's wife. It is not known why "Nights" 7 and 8 have no dedicatee.

[14] As described by Young's trustee, in Forster, *Edward Young*, 375. For a copy of the will, see *Correspondence*, 601–04. It is not clear how Young amassed such a fortune. He did not marry money. His wife apparently brought with her only a pension of £100 a year (see Forster, *Edward Young*, 141). There are apochryphal tales that he received vast sums (£2,000 from Wharton for *The Revenge*, £3,000 for *Love of Fame*), and that he likewise lost "thousands" in the South Sea debacle. Company records show that Young subscribed £3,500 in the South Sea Company at the height of the fever in 1720 (see the note in *Night Thoughts*, 332.)

writer, both from the booksellers and the patrons, ministerial, ecclesiastical, and private. He simply failed to win the bishopric to which he aspired.

Another misconception about Young's career in patronage is that he was derided by his contemporaries as a pensioner. Perhaps because Pope and Swift so freely ridiculed the writers whom Walpole generally chose to favor, it is assumed that Young – who had a pension from Walpole – was subject to the same charges of literary prostitution. In fact, the major attacks on Young as a flatterer come after his death. During his own lifetime Young was sometimes the subject of mild ridicule but not moral censure. To Pope he was "the sport of peers and poets"[15] – not because he sought the brass ring of patronage (and succeeded) but because he was apparently absent-minded, surprisingly unworldly, and (in some instances, e.g., Wharton) rather unlucky in his choice of patron, and unskilled in securing his own interests.[16] Swift's "On Reading Dr. Young's Satires" rather inoffensively identifies a contradiction in *Love of Fame*: on the one hand the poem praises the king and his ministers, presumed to be responsible for setting the moral tone for the realm, and on the other it directs satire at the universal vices of "the present age."[17] Young in fact remained on reasonably good terms with Pope and Swift, even after his Whiggish ties to the court would have left an increasing divide between him and his Tory friends in the 1730s. He seems to have escaped charges of worldly opportunism that were directed against a fellow royal chaplain.[18] When he is attacked in his own lifetime as a toady, it comes from a partisan source, William Shippen, a staunch Tory, a Jacobite, and an outspoken critic of Walpole, and should be largely discounted as political polemic.[19] Likewise, old cranky Thomas Hearne, who thought Young's oration dedicating the Codrington Library in 1716 "very vile and miserable,"

---

[15]   Owen Ruffhead, *Life of Alexander Pope*, 291n.

[16]   Joseph Warton observed that "To drive a bargain, was not the talent of this generous and disinterested man" (*Essay on the Genius and Writings of Pope*, 11, 471).

[17]   The "Verses on the Revival of the Order of the Bath" refer to "Younge" as "empty" (line 10), but Swift's latest editor considers it "most unlikely" that this is the poet. He proposes Sir William Yonge. See *Jonathan Swift: Complete Poems*, 748–49.

[18]   On the "self-seeking clerical vultures" of the day, see Edmund Pyle, *Memoirs of a Royal Chaplain, 1729–1763*, vii.

[19]   After Young's *Instalment* appeared, Shippen published *Remarks Critical and Political upon a late Poem, entitled the Instalment* (1726), attacking "the most abject spirit of flattery and prostitution, as well as the grossest indelicacy and want of address, that perhaps ever appeared in any writer." In Forster, *Edward Young*, 99.

had already dismissed Young as one of the young Oxford poets, "all bad."[20] Steele, by contrast, thought even the dedication of *The Last Day* to Queen Anne displayed "a noble magnanimity."[21]

Young's character remained in good repute at the time of his death. While the anonymous memorialist of the *Annual Register for 1765* (1766) freely criticizes the weaknesses in Young's poems, he makes no mention at all of his dedications, probably because he was working from the 1757 edition, in which they did not appear.[22] Instead, Young is still considered a neglected poet, who wrote during a former reign (that of George II) when "the arts of poetry ... were but little promoted or encouraged from the throne" (vol. II, p. 32). The account of Young in the *Biographia Britannica* (1766) makes no mention of Young's patrons or dedications, except for a brief reference to his "noble patron," Wharton.[23]

The attacks on Young's dedications seem to begin with Croft in 1780, who (oddly enough) implies that he is *defending* Young from some of the charges against his character.[24] What may have prompted Croft to write was the appearance, in 1778, of a posthumous sixth volume of Young's works (in an edition that began appearing in 1762). In this volume, compiled by Isaac Reed, there appeared the poems that Young had deliberately omitted from his own collected edition in 1757, together with all the prose dedications to his works, that had not seen the light since their first appearance.[25]

---

20   Hearne's *Remarks and Collections*, 11 vols. (Oxford: Oxford Historical Society, 1885–1921), IV, 151, VI, 12, and Young seems to have thought the learned Hearne a pedant (see the mock-footnote to the Codrington oration, Young's *Complete Works*, II, 314n).

21   *The Englishman*, for October 29, 1713, quoted in Forster, *Edward Young*, 33.

22   He promises to comment on "all" of Young's poems "as they are to be found in the last edition of his works" (*Annual Register for 1765*, 2 vols. [London, 1766], II, 33).

23   VI, 2, Supplement, 256. This author seems to be working from the 1762 selected edition of Young's works.

24   E.g., "Young was certainly not ashamed to be patronized by the infamous Wharton .... But [if] virtuous authors must be patronized only by virtuous peers, who shall point them out?" (in Johnson, *Lives of the Poets*, III, 364). "Should justice call upon you to censure this poem [the epistle to Lansdowne], it ought at least to be remembered that he did not insert it into his works ... Shall the gates of repentance be shut only against literary sinners?" (p. 365). Croft could have found such charges in Reed's 1778 biographical account. See below.

25   Reed's motives seem somewhat mixed. As an editor he may simply have been eking out an additional volume to pad the bookseller's receipts. He claims that his volume "must be allowed to contain pieces which will not reflect any discredit on their author ... The slightest performances of a great master are always highly esteemed" (*Complete Works*, ed. Nichols, I, viii). But he also appeared as the poet's biographer with a damning account of Young's life in an article in the 1782 edition of the *Biographica Dramatica*: "Dr. Young (who never failed to discover virtues in a coach and six, and without a blush could balance 'Heaven' against Lord 'Wilmington'), on the score of profane flattery may need

The reprinted dedications made Croft think Young "more despicable as a dedicator" (Johnson, *Lives of the Poets*, vol. III, p. 384), but he is plainly uncomfortable that Young omitted them in 1757. He pointedly notes, in the course of his narrative, each dedication that Young wrote and later "suppressed" – his verb itself suggests bad motives. "If Young thought the dedication contained only the praise of truth, he should not have omitted it in his works. Was he conscious of the exaggeration of party? Then he should not have written it" (p. 367). Either way Young loses. Later Croft acknowledges that the dedications at least show Young was a grateful client. Perhaps, he concludes, Young had "no right to suppress" them. A dedication, he implies (with slender knowledge of literary convention and practice), is a kind of oath or solemn public declaration: "I know not whether the author, who has once solemnly printed an acknowledgement of a favour, should not always print it" (p. 384).[26]

Croft's attack was not unanswered. One respondent even defended Young's dedications as honest and sincere at the time he wrote them, and properly suppressed when Young later realized that he had misjudged the merit of his dedicatees.[27] But by Croft's day the elaborate dedications that preceded many literary works were less common than they had once been. Croft furthermore was writing just a few years after Ruffhead's 1769 biography, which, however impractically, had proposed Pope as the model of the "independent" writer. Young himself seems to have sensed as early as the 1750s that his youthful dedications, written while he was still a man of the world, did not reflect credit on an elderly clergyman. Indeed, the title of his edition, *The Works of the Author of Night Thoughts in Four Volumes* (1757), suggests that he is quite consciously presenting a particular image of himself – as "the author of Night Thoughts," a meditative, moral, and pious poet who has written other works that such an author might appropriately own.[28] His subtitle, *Revised and Corrected by Himself*, hints that his works were popular enough to be

---

forgiveness, and we hope he will receive it (I, 766). Young's "addiction to licentious flattery has induced him to dress up his patrons in the attributes of a Being whose greatness and whose goodness admit of no approximation" (I, 768). Although Croft's account of Young is dated September 1780, one wonders (from his references to "the censurers of Young") whether he had seen Reed's 1782 work in manuscript.

26 In his first collected *Seasons* (1730) Thomson dropped the prose dedications and added complimentary lines in the text of the poems.

27 *Gentleman's Magazine*, 52 (1782), 70–71.

28 And yet he seemed to think it not unfitting to republish the very worldly *Love of Fame* satires.

widely (and carelessly) printed, and that the author was not content to leave the corrections to his bookseller. The headnote suggests that he may have thought readers would find his poems more "pardonable" if they lacked compliments to monarchs, ministers, and peers, or obtrusive marks of the partisan political enthusiasms of the 1710s and 1720s. But it is just possible that Young, all along, was a somewhat reluctant participant in the patronage economy. John Doran, claiming that Young's "true vocation" was satire, goes so far as to "question if the stupendous flattery of his dedications be not themselves pure satire" (*Complete Works*, vol. I, p. xxxviii). It is perhaps impossible to fully substantiate Doran's suspicion, but it is notable that throughout his career the language of his dedications reveals some ambivalence about his role as client.

Young's dedications

As early as the dedication to the Latin Codrington *Oratio* in 1717 Young is already self-conscious about the practice of dedicators, and sustains a facetious irony, rather like Swift's tone in the dedication of *A Tale of A Tub* to Lord Somers. A dedication "void of commonplace" has never been "published before by any author whatsoever." For his part, the patrons' "common fate" is "inconveniences" – of having to listen to the dedication and read the work being offered to them. Young's over-ingenious solution is to present to his patrons – "the Ladies of the Codrington Family" – a work which they (not being Latinists) cannot read. Walking the fine line between raillery and compliment (like Pope, in addressing Arabella Fermor) Young says he writes "in a learned tongue ... not because you understand it, but because, I hope, you do not." (For if you did, he says with conventional modesty, you would discover the oration's defects.) The instability of Young's irony is suggested by the fact that he insists on mentioning his patrons' illiteracy twice more.[29]

The brief dedication of *Busiris* to Newcastle in 1721 acknowledges that most dedications are justly ridiculed as "shameful prostitution of the pen":

Addresses of this nature, through a gross abuse of praise, have justly fallen under ridicule. How pleasant it is, to hear one of yesterday [i.e., an upstart]

---

[29] The ladies, he says, are "the first that received the patronage of what you did not understand." He later mock-formally "absolves" them "from any obligation of reading what is presented to you." We might even suspect some gentle satire at their expense.

complimented on his illustrious ancestors! a sordid person, on his magnificence! an illiterate pretender, on his skill in arts and sciences! or a wretch contracted with self-love, on his diffusive benevolence to mankind!

Young again adopts the Swiftian strategy of declaring that, although dedications have fallen into disrepute through abuse and excess, they can still convey true praise.[30] Young's reclamation project – first produce a conventional dedication, and then find a name to which it might be addressed – is ingenious, but hardly a ringing defense of panegyric.

He retained doubts about the form. In the "Preface" to the *Love of Fame*, for example, applying a Platonic fable of the birth of love, he suggests that "modern poetry" is the daughter of "the god of riches" and thus has an "affectation of preference and distinction." But her mother is "the goddess poverty." This makes her "a constant beggar of favours" and it accounts for "flattery" and "servility." She is also "a little subject to blindness," and this "makes her mistake her way to preferments and honours." Does this little fable not suggest Young's misgivings about having chosen "flattery" of his patrons as the route to preferments and honors? In the opening lines of the first satire (duly dedicated to the Duke of Dorset) immediately following the preface Young wonders whether the indiscriminate panegyric of modern poetry is any better than a corrupt legal system:

> Shall poesy, like law, turn wrong to right,
> And dedications wash an Aethiop white,
> Set up each senseless wretch for nature's boast,
> On whom praise shines, as trophies on a post?
> Shall fun'ral eloquence her colours spread,
> And scatter roses on the wealthy dead?
> Shall authors smile on such illustrious days,
> And satirize with nothing – but their praise?
>
> (*Poetical Works*, vol. II, p. 60)

By 1725 (when the first satire was written) Young's patron Wharton had already fallen into disgrace, and it seems plausible to imagine an oblique confession of shame. He calls for "instructive satire" to "sharply smile prevailing folly dead," but at the same time (perhaps wary of who pays the piper) calls for a satirist only "Discreetly

---

[30] "It gives the grace of novelty and peculiarity to a dedication that shall reclaim panegyric from its guilt, and rescue the late-mentioned sublime distinctions of character from absurdity and injustice, by applying them to a Duke of Newcastle. It is a kind of compliment paid to panegyric itself, to use it on so just an occasion."

daring." Indeed, Young's *Love of Fame*, which won *him* great fame, is just that: although his satires are full of character types (Codrus, Hippolytus, et al.), none are given historical identities. When he names names, it is to compliment Dorset, Chesterfield, Dodington, et al.[31] And yet the suspicion nags at him that poets proffering praise are only holding "shameless auctions" (vol. II, p. 92). If not so mercenary as a tradesman, a dedicating poet is worse, a "prostitute" or a "beggar": "All other trades demand, verse makers beg;/ A dedication is a wooden leg" (p. 93). That is, the poet exposes his spineless dedication in the way a beggar exposes a wooden leg – "to move compassion."

Misgivings about patronage are hinted at too in the 1730 verse epistles to Pope. In the first of them Young laughs at the duplicitous commerce degrading to both patron and poet:

> O how I laugh, when I a blockhead see,
> Thanking a villain for his probity;
> Who stretches out a most respectful ear,
> With snares for woodcocks in his holy leer:
> It tickles thro' my soul to hear the cock's
> Sincere encomium on his friend the fox,
> Sole patron of his liberties and rights!
> While graceless Reynard listens – till he bites.
>
> (*Poetical Works*, vol. II, p. 316)

As a soliciting poet Young already had experience of vulpine patrons. But the folly of naive expectations is only part of the problem. Patronage, Young suggests, corrupts both the poet and the patron:

> The richest statesman wants wherewith to pay
> A servile sycophant, if well they weigh
> How much it costs the wretch to be so base;
> Nor can the greatest powers enough disgrace,
> Enough chastise, such prostitute applause,
> If well they weigh how much it stains their cause.
>
> (p. 314)

In the second epistle Young warns against betraying the pen for "lucre ... the sacred threat of gold," for

---

[31] Doran observes "how heartily" Young "could lash the vices of all excepting his patrons" (*Complete Works*, I, xxxix). One might accuse Young of shameless hypocrisy, of illogically exempting his patron from the general satire. Alternatively, one might suspect subtle satire at the expense of these very patrons.

> [Apollo's] sacred influence never should be sold,
> 'Tis arrant simony to sing for gold:
> 'Tis immortality should fire your mind;
> Scorn less a paymaster than all mankind.
>
> (p. 318)

Doran notes that "for a poet, ever seeking a patron; for a pensioner, ever looking for increase of income; and for a clergyman, who was sharply inquiring after preferment, there is more than an usual display of independence in these poems." He thinks Young can't be "serious" in warning against "arrant simony," since "he who professed to give in song a praise unpurchaseable by gold, sang for a pension" (*Complete Works*, vol. 1, pp. xlix–l). But it is just as plausible to read the line as self-criticism on the part of a poet who like Johnson's Savage knows the difference between vice and virtue even if he fails to honor it in his practice.

Young continued to supply dedications to his works, and panegyrics for his paymasters. But he contented himself with simply "inscribing" the individual "Nights" with a single line of the title page (and, in some cases, direct address in the text of the poem), rather than supplying a prose dedication, as had been his initial practice. In a famous passage in the fourth "Night," Young seems to reflect with regret and misgivings on his years of chasing patronage. Although he has a royal pension, "My very Master" (apparently King George), "knows me not" (IV, line 55).

> I've been so long remember'd, I'm forgot.
> An Object ever pressing dims the Sight,
> And hides behind its Ardor to be seen:
> When in his Courtiers Ears I pour my Plaint,
> They drink it, as the Nectar of the Great;
> And squeeze my Hand, and beg me come to-morrow;
> *Refusal*! canst thou swear a smoother Form?
>
> (lines 57–63)

His concern now is not the prostitution of the pen, but the futility of the pursuit.

> Twice-told the Period spent on stubborn *Troy*,
> Court-Favour, yet untaken, I besiege;
> Ambition's ill-judg'd Effort to be rich.
> Alas! Ambition makes my Little, less;
> Imbittering the Possess'd: why wish for more?
>
> (lines 66–70)

Although he can see the futility of it, he concedes that his efforts persist: he continues to "besiege" court-favor. And although the following lines censure the folly of "*Wishing*," and give thanks for the contentment of a simple "rural Life," the reader may doubt that Young has reconciled his contrary attractions toward "worldliness" and "other-worldliness."[32] By the same token, it would appear that Young had not sworn off the pursuit of patrons.

In the ninth and final "Night" (dedicated to Newcastle) Young piously remembers that the great "PATRON" is God himself (line 2347). The rhetorical gesture is perhaps perfunctory because the idea of God's patronage receives very little elaboration – God like a long-suffering patron obliged to listen to a clumsy poet "canst not 'scape *uninjur'd* from our *Praise*" (line 2350). But patronage is clearly on his mind.[33] The "final Effort" of Young's muse is sustained not by a pension but by a "Spirit of Support," rewarded not by cash but "CONSOLATION" (line 2377). Henceforth, "Thy *Patron*, HE, whose Diadem has drop'd / Yon Gems of Heaven; *Eternity*, thy *Prize.* / And leave the Racers of the World their Own, / Their Feather, and their Froth, for endless Toils" (lines 2388–91). It is Young's palinode to earthly patronage.[34]

After *Night Thoughts* Young's dedicatory practices change. Even before he published his dedication-free edition in 1757 he had evidently reconsidered the place of dedication in his works. His tragedy *The Brothers* (1753) was published without a dedication. In preparing to publish his *Centaur Not Fabulous* (1755), cast in the form of "Six Letters to a[n unnamed] Friend," he corresponded with his printer, Samuel Richardson, about the form which its dedication should take.[35] The work was ultimately dedicated "To the Lady ******" (Audrey Harrison, Lady Townshend). The prose dedication

---

[32] The same might be said about many eighteenth-century literary churchmen from Swift and Burnet to Hoadly and Warburton. The established church in the period was very much an institution of "this world."

[33] Cf. IV, lines 661–62, where Death (because it opens the door to immortality) is "glorious Patron of the Past and Present!", and IX, line 271, where at Judgment there is "No Patron! Intercessor none!"

[34] Young's critics have been skeptical. Croft thinks that at the conclusion of *Night Thoughts* Young is "weary perhaps of courting earthly patrons" and turns to a divine one (Johnson, *Lives of the Poets*, III, 382). Eliot notes that Young has a "fervid attachment to patrons in general, but on the whole prefers the Almighty" (*Essays*, 337).

[35] At this time Young also discussed with Richardson the four lines of verse addressed "To the Speaker" which accompanied his gift to his former patron, Speaker Onslow, of a locket containing a lock of Milton's hair. The lines and locket were sent privately "in a letter" to Onslow (*Correspondence*, 407), but were apparently never published.

is, as Young described it, "pretty long," consisting of a humorous and risqué account of the old fable of the centaurs, with a modern application to "our modern Centaurs" (the "men of pleasure" against whom Young's satire is directed). Young promises to offer "not one word of compliment" to the lady – he reminds her that she always frowns "at praise", and the tone is marked not by humility or reverence but by sustained raillery.[36]

In 1758 Young's sermon on *The Truth of Religion*, preached by the royal chaplain before the king, was printed with a prose dedication "To the King," in which the author plainly addresses George II in his capacity as Defender of the Faith. He signs himself simply "Your Majesty's most dutiful subject, and ancient servant" – as if to indicate that he is only performing his duty. "Ancient" suggests not only that Young is nearly eighty, but perhaps also that he has served his king (with little reward) for more than thirty years.[37]

In his final years Young dispensed with dedications altogether. When *Conjectures on Original Composition* appeared in 1759 it was addressed "in a letter to the Author of Sir Charles Grandison" – Richardson was Young's friend and printer – but it carried no dedication. Young's praise is reserved for those who display "original genius." Indeed, though he refers gracefully at the opening to Richardson's "worthy patron, and our common friend" (evidently Sir Arthur Onslow, to whom Young had dedicated "Night the First" of *Night Thoughts*),[38] it is not patrons but "originals" who, in his view, are the "great Benefactors," performing what amounts to a political act in the realm of culture: "they extend the republic of letters, and add a new province to its dominion."[39] When Young was named Clerk of the Closet to the Princess Dowager in 1761 he responded with a letter of thanks to his friend and patron, the Duchess of Portland, who had interceded on his behalf. But there is no record of a letter to the Earl of Bute, who granted the place.[40] And Young

---

[36] Doran was surprised at "the figure of lascivious centaurs and salacious nymphs" in the dedication (*Complete Works*, 1, lxvii).

[37] In a letter to the Duchess of Portland (July 9, 1758) Young notes that the dedication of the sermon was designed "to put his Majesty in mind of my long service, but, I take for granted, without any manner of Effect" (*Correspondence*, 475).

[38] Forster, *Edward Young*, 303. Young in 1757 no longer claims Onslow as his own "patron," but as his "friend."

[39] *Conjectures on Original Composition*, 45.

[40] In a postscript to a letter to the Duchess of Portland (c. February 1761) he simply asks her to let Bute know, if he "falls in your way," that he "was to pay my duty to him before I left Town" (*Correspondence*, 524).

addressed no verses to the Dowager Princess or to his new royal master, as he had done to his two predecessors in 1714 and 1727. The old poet either considered himself under no obligation, or he saw no prospect of further reward, and thus no need to cultivate the crown. His final published work, *Resignation* (1762), although written at the request of his friend Mrs. Montagu, in order to offer private comfort to the widow of Admiral Boscawen, and perhaps intended (in a public version) to be dedicated to Mrs. Boscawen, was ultimately published (in an expanded form) with a brief "Advertisement" but no dedication.[41]

Young's practice in the years after *Night Thoughts* suggests that he found the dedicatory style of his youth no longer appropriate, not because he had abandoned his hopes for further reward (he continued writing to friends to ask for their support as late as 1758[42]), but because he thought that public dedications did not suit the dignity of an accomplished poet and a man of the cloth, or because he sensed that, in the changing literary climate of the 1750s, dependence on a private patron was less to be counted on and less to be advertised. But it would be a mistake for us to conclude that, simply because he was never made a bishop, Young was unfortunate in his patrons. He was in fact rewarded by private, state, and ecclesiastical patronage virtually all his writing life. His career provides evidence that the patronage system continued relatively intact well past mid-century.

RICHARD SAVAGE

Like Edward Young, Richard Savage (some ten years his junior) tirelessly pursued literary patronage, enjoyed a considerable level of support, and lamented that he never received the recognition he so deeply desired and deserved. But while Young as he grew older achieved some measure of resignation, and tried to look back on his pursuit of patronage as youthful folly, Savage nursed his resentment until his early death. Even his most sympathetic biographer concludes that he was "never made wiser by his Sufferings," and continued always "to amuse himself with Phantoms of Happiness, which were dancing before him."[43] Although such "Phantoms" were

---

[41] See *ibid.*, 529, 542.
[42] See Young's letter to Newcastle dated July 12, 1758 (*ibid.*, 476–77).
[43] Samuel Johnson, [*An Account of the*]*Life of* [*Mr. Richard*] *Savage* (1744), 74.

not limited to elusive benefactors, Savage's pursuit of patronage is a leitmotif of Johnson's account, and an inquiry into Savage's dealings with a string of patrons and would-be patrons can serve as a reminder that during the very years when a poet with Pope's talent and entrepreneurial skill seemed to rise above patronage, there were lesser talents who – whether for choice or necessity – could make a kind of career of moving from one uncertain patronage to another. Indeed, as I will suggest, Savage – a friend, admirer, understrapper, and finally beneficiary of Pope – in some ways seems Pope's dark parody.

In Savage's career can be seen a kind of parable about the conditions of authorship at a time when the patronage system was beginning to be supplemented by another economy. Savage was born under one dispensation and grew up under another. In 1697 court gentlemen still wrote with ease, and manuscript satires made the rounds of a relatively confined literary world. The traditional association between men of rank and men of wit was still a close one. After 1714, as Pope sensed, a poet who hoped to prosper would increasingly have to become adept at dealing with booksellers as well as patrons, and would have to master the new techniques of print publicity. When Savage came of age as a writer in the 1720s he in fact met with considerable success, and won substantial if not continuously comfortable support from patrons and subscribers – and at least one of his works (*The Bastard*) enjoyed a very good sale, about which, so Johnson reports, Savage was particularly proud and pleased (*Life of Savage*, p. 72). But he didn't realize that continued success would require some entrepreneurial energy and application. Failing to adapt to an emerging market economy in which writing was something to be sold for a good price, he deployed an old rhetoric of entitlement, and wrote obsessively all his life about false patrons and deserving authors. In his fantasies he was not only the son of the Earl Rivers, but he was a poet whose merits were richly rewarded.

He considered himself a neglected genius, but during the course of a twenty-five year career from about 1718 to 1743 Savage was more successful than most of his contemporaries, procuring rather bountiful support from private patrons (nobility, gentry, merchants, and even other writers), from the ministry, and from the court. From them he enjoyed most of the forms of support traditionally provided: introductions, intercessions with the court on his behalf, a subscription edition, regular lodging and maintenance, gifts of money, and a pension.

Savage's efforts to secure patronage began early. After failing to convince the players to accept his first play, he found a patron for his second. *Love in a Veil* was dedicated to Lord Lansdowne (the patron of Pope and Young) in 1719. While there is no record of Lansdowne's response, the play attracted the attention of Steele and of Robert Wilks, an actor and theatre manager, both of whom were in a position to help an aspiring dramatist. Johnson, consciously citing the traditional benefits for which clients thank their patrons, reports that Steele "declared in his Favour with all the Ardour of Benevolence which constituted his Character, promoted his Interest with the utmost Zeal, related his Misfortunes, applauded his Merit, took all Opportunities of recommending him" (*Life of Savage*, p. 13), and even promised an allowance.[44] If Johnson can be believed, Savage had a valuable friend and promoter. Whether through Steele's efforts or those of other friends, word of Savage's case reached the Duke of Dorset, the "universal patron," who thereupon provided encouraging words, allegedly telling Savage that "in his Opinion, the Nobility ought to think themselves obliged without Solicitation to take every Opportunity of supporting him by their Countenance and Patronage" (p. 20). Meanwhile, the solicitous Wilks "took an unfortunate Wit into his Protection, and not only assisted him in any casual Distresses, but continued an equal and steady Kindness to the Time of his Death" (p. 18). Wilks persuaded Mrs. Brett to give Savage £50 and to promise an additional £150 (Tracy, *Artificial Bastard*, p. 43). His next play, *Sir Thomas Overbury*, was dedicated to Herbert Tryst, who seems to have provided unspecified "past Favours," and who now responded with a gift of £10 (the going rate) and later enrolled as a subscriber to Savage's *Miscellany Poems and Translations* (1726). A key promoter of Savage's collection was Aaron Hill, who had helped him revise the play on Overbury. He went on to become Savage's champion, supplying money as well as introductions, and conducting a campaign on his behalf in the *Plain Dealer*, the periodical journal he edited. The collection of *Miscellany Poems* succeeded in winning a number of subscribers, including three members of the family of the Duke of Rutland (to whom Savage addressed two poems).[45] It was dedicated

---

[44] Clarence Tracy, *The Artificial Bastard*, 44.
[45] See *ibid.* 64–66, who says Rutland had become Savage's patron by 1724.

to Lady Mary Wortley Montagu, who provided, through Edward Young as intermediary, "a present of money."[46] In later years Savage repeatedly announced proposals for a subscription edition of his own works.[47] Although he never delivered copy to the press, he managed to persuade subscribers to stake him.[48]

By about 1726, though he had failed to persuade Mrs. Brett, the former Countess of Macclesfield, to own him as a son, Savage succeeded in winning an annuity of £50 a year, apparently from Mrs. Brett and her nephew, the Earl of Tyrconnel (Tracy, *Artificial Bastard*, p. 77). Tyrconnel was to be Savage's most important patron, not only because he later petitioned the king for Savage's pardon in 1727, sought to get him appointed Poet Laureate in 1730, and presented Savage's second *Volunteer Laureat* poem to the queen at court in 1733 (Tracy, *Artificial Bastard*, pp. 115–16), but also because he provided a substantial allowance (£200 a year) from about 1728 until the two men quarreled and irrevocably broke in 1735. From 1726 to 1730 Savage also enjoyed a pension of £50 a year from Anne Oldfield, the celebrated actress who lived (and loved) among the great.[49] Savage may have always been short of funds, but it was not for lack of support.

In 1727 he began mining the vein of court and ministerial patronage. When George I died Savage joined the elegiac chorus with *A Poem, Sacred to the Glorious Memory of our Late Most Gracious Sovereign Lord King George*, and inscribed it to Bubb Dodington. Further patronage from all sides was forthcoming after Savage was arrested for murder. An extraordinary and well-organized outpouring of support was orchestrated by Savage's friends and patrons: what we would now call a public relations campaign (the anonymous *Life of Savage*, in which Hill and other friends were involved), appeals to the king for pardon, and gifts of money. Pope sent £5 in 1727 (Young again serving as courier).[50] The Countess of Hertford, who, like Dorset, patronized a number of the poets of the day, is said to have taken up Savage's cause, and insisted on an audience with the queen,

46   See Johnson's *Lives of the Poets*, 11, 343n.
47   See the *Gentleman's Magazine*, 7 (1737), 128, for the only surviving proposals.
48   Johnson reports that he "for many Years continued his Solicitation, and squandered whatever he obtained ... whenever a Subscription was paid him he went to a Tavern" (*Life of Savage*, 103). The Duke of Chandos was among the subscribers.
49   Johnson says it was paid until her death in 1730 (*ibid.* 19). Tracy thinks the initial gift of £10 "may have become an annuity" (*Artificial Bastard*, 47).
50   Spence, *Observations*, 1, 216.

when, so Johnson claims, she was instrumental in winning the pardon.[51] Tracy reports that others, including Wilks and Mrs. Oldfield, interceded to appeal for a pardon (*Artificial Bastard*, p. 91).

After receiving the king's pardon in January 1728 Savage worked indirectly to ingratiate himself. The dedication to *The Bastard* in 1729, inscribed with mock "due reverence" to Mrs. Brett, acknowledges the king's "Mercy," "Royal Pity," and "great Goodness," and pointedly resolves that the author's life, "which has so graciously been given me, shall become considerable enough *not to be useless* in His Service, to Whom it was forfeited." The italicized words plainly suggest that he looks forward to some appropriate governmental employment. In the dedication of *The Wanderer* in 1729 to Tyrconnel (whom Johnson describes as an "implicite Follower of the Ministry," *Life of Savage*, p. 51), Savage hopefully predicts that Tyrconnel's patronage will pave the way for recognition from higher authority: "that I live, my Lord, is a Proof that Dependance on your Lordship, and the present Ministry, is an Assurance of Success," and he suggested that, like Tyrconnel, he too was attached to "Liberty, and the Royal, Illustrious House of our Most Gracious Sovereign" (Tracy, *Artificial Bastard*, p. 96). By 1732 Savage felt bold enough to address the court directly, and on the queen's birthday published the first of his *Volunteer Laureat* poems, dedicated to the queen. Later that year he addressed Walpole, whether as part of his own campaign for preferment or because (as Johnson says) he was "enjoined" by Tyrconnel, "not without Menaces, to write in Praise of his Leader" (*Life of Savage*, p. 51). *Religion and Liberty* (1733), an epistle addressed to Walpole, implies that Walpole was instrumental in the royal pardon, and reminds his patron of a "fair Promise."[52] Perhaps in response Walpole promised "the next Place that should become vacant, not exceeding two hundred Pounds a Year" (Johnson, *Life of Savage*, p. 88, Tracy *Artificial Bastard*, p. 118). Although the place never materialized, Walpole sent twenty guineas (Johnson, *Life of Savage*, p. 51), an unusually generous response, though Johnson thought that a man of his wealth could have done better. Six months later Tyrconnel presented the second of Savage's *Volunteer Laureat* poems at court, and the queen responded by awarding Savage a pension of £50 a year (which was paid until her death in 1737). While serving as the queen's pensioner, Savage apparently saw nothing inappropriate

---

[51] See Johnson, *Life of Savage*, 38, and Tracy, *Artificial Bastard*.
[52] "Nor can the Prison 'scape your searching Eye." Savage, *Poetical Works*, 174.

in soliciting the support of her estranged grandson with *Of Public Spirit*, a poem addressed to the prince on his birthday in 1736.

The prince did not smile, and in 1737 when the queen died Savage's pension was not renewed. But patronage had not completely dried up. In 1739 Pope organized a "subscription" (from untitled friends) whereby Savage would be provided with an allowance of some £50 a year,[53] which might enable him to live modestly – if he retired to Wales. This he did, though with ill grace enough to provoke his subscribers, and the pension was apparently cut in half, but it seems to have been continued until his death in 1743. Even in his last years, though he never received the support he thought he deserved, a trickle of patronage continued to flow – £5 here, £30 there, an offer from his friends to attempt a reconciliation with Lord Tyrconnel. Even his keeper in Bristol's Newgate prison poured out "Benevolence" – Savage was "supported by him at his own Table without any certainty of Recompense" (Johnson, *Life of Savage*, p. 126).

This unadorned record of the support Savage received – separated out from Johnson's sympathetic narrative – might suggest that, for an author with a rather modest rate of production, he was very well rewarded.[54] For almost all of the last twenty years of his writing career, Savage was the recipient of a pension. More than most writers of the day, he "lived among the great." For some ten years, what Johnson calls "the Golden Part of Mr. *Savage*'s life," he lived like a lord, a man of magnificence and taste, indeed, like a patron himself: "His Appearance was splendid, his Expences large, and his Acquaintance extensive. He was ... caressed by all who valued themselves upon a refined Taste ... His Presence was sufficient to make any Place of publick Entertainment popular; and his Approbation and Example constituted the Fashion" (*Life of Savage*, p. 44). What is most striking about Savage's reaction to his good fortune (despite the conventional professions of gratitude to his patrons) is that he considered a comfortable income simply to be his due. In

---

53   Johnson says it "did not amount to fifty Pounds a Year" (*Life of Savage*, 114). Tracy suggests
     that Pope himself contributed £10, and secured equal sums from Ralph Allen, Erasmus
     Lewis,and Moses Mendes, and lesser sums from Thomson and Mallet (*Artificial Bastard*,
     138) – only one of them (Allen), notably, drawn from the traditional patronal class.
54   Johnson does not shrink from pointing out that a pension of £50 a year, "though by no
     Means equal to the Demands of Vanity and Luxury, is yet found sufficient to support
     Families above Want, and was undoubtedly more than the Necessities of Life require"
     (*Life of Savage*, 96).

Johnson's biting words, which cut to the heart of the matter, he assumed that he was "born to be supported by others" (*Life of Savage*, p. 137).

Savage (unlike Pope) gave little thought to the idea that his writings constituted literary *property* that might be sold advantageously. Indeed, he did not much recognize the difference between "mine" and "thine" – especially when he was in Tyrconnel's house. And yet in his own eyes Savage's life is the story of dispossession – dispossessed as a son, and dispossessed as an author – and he devoted his life to regaining what he thought was rightfully his, not money but title and regard.[55] Furthermore, his attempt to reclaim his birthright and his *patrimony* was intimately linked, in his own mind and in that of his friends, with his obsessive claim on *patronage*. No dedication by Savage, appealing for patronage, failed to mention his alleged noble birth and dispossession. But he was not simply asking for the restoration of his legal birthright, although there is some evidence that such an appeal found sympathetic listeners.[56] It seems likely that Savage mingled in his own mind the legal and moral precept that a son deserves to inherit from his parents with the traditional idea (shared by Dryden) that a poet deserves to be supported by men of position and wealth. Thus, in an early dedication he declares that "My Play, and my Self, my Lord, are equally Orphans"[57] – and both play and writer are in search of a parent to own and support them. In the preface to his *Miscellaneous Poems and Translations* (1726) his birth and his writing are again linked. Having been left with no legal father or mother, Savage is in effect dead at law, and therefore "Born," as he says, ironically appropriating a colloquial phrase, to "live by my Wits" (*Poetical Works*, p. 266). But he never abandoned the idea that his "Wits" would in some way restore his birthright, and that he would one day be acknowledged as both lord and laureate. In a poem written near the end of his life Savage imagined a day when "Me, to some nobler sphere, should fortune raise, / To wealth conspicuous, and to laurel'd praise"

---

[55] It should be remembered that Savage thought himself *doubly* dispossessed as a son, for he considered himself the legal son of the Earl of Macclesfield (until the marriage was annulled by special act of Parliament) and the natural son of the Earl Rivers, who died without knowing that he had left a child out of his will. That he bore the same name – Richard Savage – as his putative natural father no doubt made him feel even more acutely that he had lost his birthright as a son and heir.

[56] See above, p. 171.

[57] *Love in a Veil*, A2v.

(*Poetical Works*, p. 256). "Conspicuous" is apt: Savage not only wanted to be wealthy, he wanted to be able to live like a lord, and be known to be one. His desire knew no bounds: not only praise but the Laureateship as well.

It might also be said that Savage discovered (or declared) himself to be a lord and a poet at virtually the same moment. Shortly after he was informed that he was the natural son of the Earl Rivers – whether truly or falsely does not matter here[58] – Savage made his first public appearance, at the age of 18, as a *writer* of some Jacobite pamphlets. (Was it only a coincidence that he chose to write about a *dispossessed* monarch?) A year later dispossession and writing were again brought together, when a play on which he was laboring (*Woman is a Riddle*) was staged and later published, as his own, by Christopher Bullock (Tracy, *Artificial Bastard*, p. 39). After Savage had for some years been advertising himself as the "son of the Earl Rivers," he began to call himself the "Volunteer Laureate," since the Laureateship, to which he thought himself entitled, had gone to Cibber. Both Cibber, who resented the "Usurpation," and Johnson, who reported the incident, seem to be aware that Savage's new ploy was logically no different from – and in effect an extension of – his original claim. Savage "assumed the Title of *Volunteer Laureat*," just as he had earlier assumed the title of son of an earl. Cibber observed with both justice and *ad hominem* wit that one might "with equal Propriety stile himself a Volunteer Lord, or Volunteer Baronet" (Johnson, *Life of Savage*, p. 79). Functionally, of course, the claims to noble rank and to great abilities are the same: both are designed to prompt what Savage wanted – "Deference and Regard" (p. 100).

Because Savage considered himself *both* a nobleman *and* a genius, he illustrates with peculiar vividness the condition of the aspiring author under a system of patronage: conscious of his merit and of what Johnson called the "natural Dignity of Wit" (p. 99), but condemned to deference which he found humiliating,[59] and therefore determined one way or another to mitigate the humility. Dryden's way was to insinuate the rival authority of the poet himself, Pope's to declare proudly to his aristocratic friends and protectors

---

[58] After a careful review of the evidence, Tracy argues that "Whatever the truth may have been, Savage believed what he said" (*Artificial Bastard*, 27).

[59] "He was ready to lament the Misery of living at the Tables of Other Men ... He now began very sensibly to feel the Miseries of Dependence ... he could not bear to conceive himself in a State of Dependence" (Johnson, *Life of Savage*, 52, 111, 138).

that he was nobody's placeman or slave. Savage's was to declare that he was literally the social equal of any patron in the land.

Johnson's remark that Savage thought himself "born to be supported by others" is probably based on Savage's own preface to *Miscellany Poems* (1726). There he presents himself as one of the "Natural Children" of a nobleman, now "thrown, friendless, on the World, without Means of supporting *myself*, and without Authority to apply to Those, whose Duty I know it is to support me" (*Poetical Works*, p. 266). Savage's words nicely point toward two different supporters: his mother, who refuses to acknowledge him and thus provide him "Authority," and patrons like Lady Mary Wortley Montagu, to whom the volume is dedicated, and to whom Savage makes an unauthorized approach – since he does not "have the Honour to be known to your Ladyship."[60] Indeed, Savage makes of her a surrogate mother, for she eminently possesses the "Goodness, Tenderness, and Sweetness of Disposition" which his own biological mother lacked, the very "natural Qualities, from the Breast, He was born to depend on." What is remarkable here is not simply that Savage appeals to his noble birth, but that in effect he appeals to his childlike helplessness: he is still an infant at the breast in need of nourishment. The child/poet's status under parentage/patronage is thus double: on the one hand an equal, on the other a dependent. Perhaps not surprisingly, it is in addressing *female* patrons that Savage can without embarrassment declare his dependence. Thus in *The Bastard*, ironically dedicated to his mother, he presents himself as a kind of orphan, and wittily presumes on that basis to be a kind of ward of the state. "As I was a *De-relict* from my Cradle, I have the Honour of a *lawful Claim* to the best Protection in *Europe*. For being a *Spot* of Earth, to which no Body *pretends* a *Title*, I devolve naturally upon the King, as one of the *Rights* of His *Royalty*" (*Poetical Works*, p. 88).[61] The king inherits "Title" or "Right" to the abandoned property, along with the responsibility of providing for him (while the poet, correspondingly empowered, holds a "lawful Claim"). In the poem itself the role of surrogate is assigned not to the king but to the queen, a more explicitly maternal figure:

[60] Savage's "Preface" was addressed to his "Readers" (among whom he knew were several potential patrons), "to whom I have not the Honour to be known" (*Poetical Works*, p. 265).

[61] Savage puns on the legal terms, *relict* – a surviving widow and inheritor – and *derelict* – abandoned property.

> Lost to the life *you* gave, *your* son no more,
> And now *adopted*, who was *doom'd* before,
> *New-born* I may a nobler mother claim;
> But dare not whisper her immortal *name*.
>
> (lines 103–06)

Savage's language suggests that the patronized poet is not only a child in need of protection, but that in winning patronage (being "adopted") he in effect becomes an infant again – a new-born at the breast.

Without the protection of patrons, Savage implies, the poet will not survive, not just because he is "neglected" but because – in a recurrent and characteristically lurid metaphor – he is in effect deliberately *exposed*. The "Preface" to his *Miscellany Poems* begins with an image of a child dead in law – the poet is "Nobody's *Son* at all." After perfunctory remarks about the *Miscellany* itself, and about the kind encouragement of his subscribers and friends, Savage compulsively returns to his mother's murderous cruelty, comparing it to the account in Locke's *Essay* of ostensibly "civilized" peoples, "amongst whom, the Exposing their Children, to perish by Want or wild Beasts, has been a Practice as little condemn'd, or scrupled, as the begetting them."[62]

In later years Savage apparently continued to think of himself as an unfortunate child. In the first of his *Volunteer Laureat* poems he is like the infant Moses set adrift and fortunately found by "a Pharaoh's Daughter":

> Hated by Her, from whom my Life I drew,
> Whence should I hope, if not from Heav'n and You?
> Nor dare I groan beneath Affliction's Rod,
> My Queen my Mother, and my Father God.
>
> (No. 1, lines 25–28)

In the fourth he is a victim who has never escaped the "Wrongs" that haunted and pursued him from infancy

> In Youth no Parent nurs'd my infant Songs,
> 'Twas mine to be inspir'd alone by Wrongs;
> Wrongs, that with Life their fierce Attack began,
> Drank Infant Tears, and still pursue the Man.
>
> (No. 4, lines 1–4)

---

[62] *Poetical Works*, 268–69. Savage also cites Locke on a Christian people who buried their children alive, and "another Sete of People, that dispatch their Children, if a pretended Astrologer declares 'em to have unhappy Stars."

And in a letter to the *Plain Dealer* in 1724 there appeared over Savage's signature (but written by Hill) an extraordinarily melodramatic poem in which the wretched poet is again an exposed child:

> Hopeless, abandon'd, aimless, and oppress'd,
> Lost to Delight, and, every way, distress'd;
> Cross his cold Bed, in wild Disorder, thrown,
> Thus, sigh'd Alexis, Friendless, and alone –
> Why do I breathe? – What Joy can Being give,
> When she, who gave me Life, forgets I live!
> Feels not these Wintry Blasts; – nor heeds my Smart.
> But shuts me from the Shelter of her Heart!
> Saw me expos'd, to Want! to Shame! to Scorn!
> To Ills! which make it Misery, to be born!
> Cast me, regardless on the World's bleak Wild:
> And bad me, be a Wretch, while yet, a Child![63]

If the idea of poet as exposed child came from Hill, it was warmly adopted by Savage. In "The Friend. *Address'd to* Aaron Hill, *Esq*," (1726 – but surely shown to Hill earlier) Savage describes himself as "thwarted and expos'd,/ By Friends abandon'd" (*Poetical Works*, p. 59). And in the late poem "To John Powell, *Esq; Barrister of Law*" (1742) the image of the exposed child still obsessed Savage: "Me still should ruthless fate, unjust, expose/ Beneath those clouds, that rain unnumber'd woes" (*Poetical Works*, p. 256).[64]

But the poet/son is not only a helpless dependent; he is also a proud equal, born with "a *Heart* that is as *proud* as my Father's" (*Poetical Works*, p. 264). His dedications and his poems insist unequivocally and tirelessly that he is "Son of the late Earl Rivers."[65] This was a pose that he maintained even in the darkest days of his poverty and imprisonment. Most commentators focus on the truth or falsity of his claim, or on the fantasizing mind that could drive him to imagine himself a nobleman. What is sometimes overlooked is that the idea that the poet is a gentleman, even an aristocrat, was a

---

[63] The lines appeared in *Plain Dealer*, no. 28 (June 26, 1724), and were reprinted as Savage's in the anonymous *Life of Mr. Richard Savage* (1727), p. 15. They were later printed in the *Works of the Late Aaron Hill* (1753) as "Verses Made for Mr. S-v-ge; and sent to my Lady M-ls-d, his Mother."

[64] Johnson's observation, that Savage "may be considered as a Child *exposed* to all the Temptations of Indigence, at an Age when Resolution was not yet strengthened by Conviction, nor Virtue confirmed by Habit" (*Life of Savage*, 75), is based (as is so much else in the *Life*) on Savage's own words and his recurrent image of himself.

[65] As Tracy notes (*Poetical Works*, 265), *each* of his contributions to the *Miscellany Poems* is headed with the words "By Richard Savage, Son of the late Earl Rivers." It is with these words too that he begins his "Preface" to his readers.

cultural convention still honored in Savage's day (although under pressure from the expanding class of authors) and within living memory a matter of fact.

To declare that he is a gentleman is to claim that the poet too has (or hopes he has) a certain rank and dignity. (Johnson's reference to "the natural dignity of wit" and to Savage's "eminent Rank in the Classes of Learning" may reflect not only a meritocratic point of view but a little nostalgia for the old world of aristocratic culture.) Savage's notorious insolence, negligence, and fits of poetic vigor (often satirical), followed by bouts of dissipation, suggest that one of his implicit models is the witty rake at the Restoration court of Charles II. His usual disregard of the business of making a living by his pen (meeting deadlines, fulfilling obligations, dealing with booksellers) and of practical needs in general suggests that he considered it somehow beneath the attention of a gentleman.[66] His remarkable generosity – even if we discount the probably apocryphal story of dividing his last guinea with the woman who accused him of murder – suggests not just that he had a charitable and forgiving heart but that he imagined that he lived in an economy of gift-giving, a world in which if one had money one bestowed it on those in need. Such benefactions are probably related to his own modest – or symbolic – acts of literary patronage. In 1730 he subscribed a guinea to Thomson's *Seasons*, and in 1731 put himself down for twenty copies of a new poetical miscellany.[67] Tracy, noting Savage's interest as poet in the figure of the "scholar-gentleman ... generous with his money in the encouragement of arts and letters," suggests that he "always conceived of himself as by rights a dispenser of [patronage]" (*Artificial Bastard*, p. 69).[68]

He could imagine himself a gentleman who simply devoted himself to his private studies and wrote for pleasure. Even in his Newgate cell he could write of the "Tranquillity" that permitted him to pursue "the Amusement of my poetical Studies, uninterrupted and agreeable to my Mind." Now "collected in myself ... tho' my Person is in Confinement, my Mind can expatiate on ample and

---

[66] This is not to suggest that he didn't lay schemes for a subscription edition, or complain from Wales that his friends had cost him "the Profits" of a play he had wanted to bring to London (Johnson, *Life of Savage*, 125).

[67] See G. C. Macaulay, *James Thomson*, 31, and A. L. Reade, *Johnsonian Gleanings*, v, 12.

[68] Tracy's mild psychologism also suspects unconscious depictions of Savage's "ideal self" in the portrait of the landed gentleman John Joliffe (*Artificial Bastard*, 71), and on the evidence of *The Bastard* suspects that Savage saw himself "as the founder of a noble family" (p. 82).

useful Subjects, with all the Freedom imaginable" (Johnson, *Life of Savage*, p. 125). Savage's words may seem to us forced cheerfulness or deluded ravings, but they resemble the language of an eminently sane poet, Pope, casting himself in his 1717 "Preface" as a private gentleman writing for his own pleasure, or imagining the "soul Supreme" of the imprisoned Harley, or the imprisoned Bolingbroke to be "free, tho' in the Tower."[69] By the same token Savage's public claims that he was the son of an earl may be pathological, but they would not have seemed anomalous in his day. Pope advertised (or invented) aristocratic connections: the Earl of Downe, he claimed in a note to the "Epistle to Dr. Arbuthnot," was the "head" of his father's "family."[70]

Savage's self-serving appeals were also being encouraged by the rhetoric of entitlement deployed by his friends, who blurred the distinction between the deserving poet and the disenfranchised nobleman, and let "merit" slip via "desert" into "entitlement." Steele wrote anonymously in the *Plain Dealer* in 1724 that the "Cruelty" of Savage's mother had "intitled him to a Right of finding Every Good Man his Father."[71] Aaron Hill argued that Savage's talents "Intitle him to the *Favour* and *Adoption* of some great *Personage*" – "adoption" blurs the distinction between foster-parent and patron – and that his "Merit" and "Wrongs ... entitle him to the Hope, of finding Better Parents, among Strangers."[72] Savage himself adopted this rhetoric of entitlement. His "ill-fortune," he claimed in the Preface to his *Miscellany Poems* of 1726, is a "Merit, that entitled me to [the] Notice [of my subscribers]" (*Poetical Works*, p. 267). Later, when Stephen Duck's subscription edition won the endorsement of Queen Caroline, Savage asserted that his own "Birth," "Misfortunes," and "Genius" gave him "a fairer title" to her favor (Johnson, *Life of*

---

69 "Epistle to Robert Earl of Oxford, and Earl Mortimer" (pub. 1722), "The First Epistle of the First Book of Horace, Imitated" (pub. 1738). Savage's language elsewhere – "expatiated," "Collected in myself" – probably echoes Pope: "The soul, uneasy and confin'd from home,/ Rests and expatiates in a life to come" (*Essay on Man*, I, 97–98), and *Iliad*, XI, 511, where Ulysses is "collected in himself".

70 Dryden let it be known that he was related by marriage to the Howards. Fielding claimed descent from the Hapsburgs, and used their imperial eagle on his seal. See Battestin, *Henry Fielding*, 7–8. Fielding's first cousin was the Earl of Denbigh.

71 November 30, 1724.

72 *Plain Dealer*, No. 15, 28. Cf. No. 73: "Both *Merit*, and *Ill Fortune*, join, to recommend the Proposer." In a letter to Thomson Hill argues that because Savage was "born ... to inherit the estate and title [of Earl Rivers]," and subsequently deprived of it by parliament, he now has "the most equitable right in the world to a pension from the Crown" (quoted in Johnson, *Lives of the Poets*, II, 406n).

Savage, p. 103). Johnson's *Life of Savage* is pervaded with the same
rhetoric of "Merit and ... Distresses" (p. 98) and "intitle[ment]" (pp.
63, 80), suggesting that Savage's conversation was studded with such
language. Johnson's observation that Savage's writings "entitle him
to an eminent Rank in the Classes of Learning" (p. 4) – as opposed
to the social order – both derives from Savage's rhetoric and gently
but firmly corrects it.

To be "entitled" to patronage makes the poet metaphorically
possessed of a kind of right or estate to which he holds "title," and
sets him on a level with his patrons. In some other traditional ways
too Savage as recipient of patronage found ways to declare himself
equal to his benefactors. He is said by Johnson to have asserted that
his allowance from Tyrconnel did not make him obliged or indebted
to his patron. On the contrary, it was Tyrconnel who owed a debt:
Savage considered that his "Subsistence"[73] was "not so much a
Favour, as a Debt, since it was offered to him upon Conditions,
which he had never broken" (p. 61). When Tyrconnel withdrew the
"Subsistence," Savage, in his curt and contemptuous letter (addressed to "the Right Honourable Brute, and Booby") reminded
him of the "debt" he was now trying to deny: "I find you want ... to
swear away my life, that is, the life of your creditor, because he asks
you for a debt."[74] Unless we are familiar with the rhetoric of
patronage, this might seem preposterous, and yet Dryden lodged
"claims" on behalf of the poet, and Johnson, in discussions of
patronage in the *Rambler,* assumed that a patron's "promise" conferred a "claim," and that a writer who writes well has a "right" to
honor.[75]

But unlike Dryden and Johnson, who emphasized both what was
due *to* the poet and due *from* him, his rights but also his powers and
responsibilities, Savage seemed to think that he had no obligations.
He rarely emphasizes the poet's role as recorder of heroic deeds, or
as bestower of fame and honor.[76] He seems not to have been
troubled by his failure to produce the volume of poems for which he

---

[73] Savage (or Johnson) puns on "subsistence" – means of support – and "subsistence money"
      – a kind of expense account. See *OED.*
[74] Reprinted in Boswell, *Life of Johnson,* I, 161–62n. Hobbes provides an account of why
      Savage might have found it galling to be indebted: "For benefits [from one 'to whom we
      think ourselves equal'] oblige, and obligation is thraldom; and unrequitable obligation
      perpetual thraldom; which is to one's equal, hateful" (*Leviathan,* Pt. 1, ch. 11).
[75] See below, p. 235.
[76] But see *The Wanderer,* III, lines 211–14, V, lines 329–30, and "the recording Muse" in
      Religion and Liberty, lines 19–22.

accepted subscriptions. He viewed his dedications as exercises, in which – unlike Dryden, say, or Swift – he made little attempt to be artful, witty, or original.[77] Praise is perfunctory, and Savage usually regards the dedication as a rhetorical occasion for him to plead his miseries rather than his patron's merits.[78] In the dedication of the *Collection of Pieces relating to the Dunciad*, a dedication Savage probably did not write but agreed to sign, he assumes that the patron has no more interest in the dedication than he does: "I will not pretend to display those rising Virtues in your Lordship, which the next Age will certainly know without my Help."[79] Instead, he narrates the circumstances of the work's publication, for which he offers no apology: "I believe your Lordship will pardon this Digression, or any other which keeps me from the Stile, you so much hate, of Dedication." It seems clear that the hatred is Savage's own. By the same token, even the *Volunteer Laureat* poems are rather mechanical exercises. As Johnson noted, Savage "did not appear to consider these Encomiums as Tests of his Abilities [as, in Johnson's judgment, Dryden did], or as any thing more than annual Hints to the Queen of her Promise, or Acts of Ceremony, by the Performance of which he was intitled to his Pension, and therefore he did not labour them with great Diligence" (*Life of Savage*, p. 80).[80]

Savage's poems

Savage may not have troubled himself with the niceties of flattery in the poems addressed to patrons, but the conditions of the proud poet under a patronage system were never far from his mind, and it is

---

[77] Of his dedications Johnson observes that "his Compliments are constrained and violent, heaped together without the Grace of Order, or the Decency of Introduction" (*Life of Savage*, 29–30).

[78] The dedication to *The Wanderer* begins with an account of the poem's composition and reception, when Savage catches himself from falling into what he perhaps recognized as his common tendency: "But my Intention is not to pursue a Discourse on my own Performance; No, my Lord, it is to embrace this Opportunity of throwing out Sentiments that relate to your Lordship's Goodness" (*Poetical Works*, p. 95). "Throwing out Sentiments" suggests the degree of artfulness that he seems to think required.

[79] Quoted in Johnson, *Life of Savage*, 47. Compare Swift's witty version of the same topos in his dedication of *A Tale of a Tub* to Somers.

[80] It might be argued that Savage's several poems of praise in *Miscellany Poems* addressed to fellow writers – Hill, Dyer, Eliza Haywood, and Mrs. Hill – serve to close the gap, in his mind, between writer and patron. Of that volume Hill's biographer observes (with some exaggeration): "Most noticeably frequent are the compliments interchanged among the authors themselves. All the flattery usually at the service of noble patrons is here poured out on one another." Dorothy Brewster, *Aaron Hill*, 185.

possible to discern throughout his poems a virtual obsession with the topic. The details may vary, but the same figures appear again and again: the bountiful patron, the ungenerous tyrant of rank and wealth, the rewarded hack and the suffering true poet. In a recurrent fantasy, compensating perhaps for the humiliation of dependence, the honest poet finds a generous patron or even becomes one himself.

It is not surprising that when Savage addresses a noble patron, he is full of compliment, both in the dedication and frequently in the poem as well. But when Savage considers "the Great" as a class, they are commonly "vain," "Monsters" of pride and "tyrannic Power," and yet eager to be flattered, and therefore "vulgar." If the flatterers' arts are "mean," the patrons (who accept them) are "meaner."[81] But they call forth most censure when they fail to provide support. For patrons have an obligation to use their power to aid the worthy:

> Ill fare the *Man*, who, robed in purple pride,
> To wounded *Worth* has no relief apply'd!
>   . . .
> Why has he pow'r, and why no heart to chear,
> Unseeing Eyes, and Ears that will not hear?
> ("A Poem Sacred to King George," lines 55–56, 65–66)

Savage does not elaborate an "economy" of patronage. He simply assumes that the wealthy have an obligation to be generous. Why else were they favored by fortune?[82]

When "the Great" consent to distribute their bounty, Savage mocks the ignorance of "unletter'd Pride" (they praise from "custom" rather than "knowledge" – *The Wanderer*, Book v, line 310). And he impugns their motives with conventional accusations: they give only to raise their own "self-Renown" (line 315). Rather than assist the living, they extol a poet after he has died, and build a "sculptur'd Tomb, and labour'd Bust": "Vain Pomp! bestow'd by ostentatious Pride, / Who to a Life of Want Relief deny'd" (lines 287–88).[83] The "squand'ring Peer" in *The Wanderer* "smiles" only on "Slaves of Guilt." For those in need he throws "the frequent Slight,

---

81   "The Picture," line 48, "Verses on *Gideon*, lines 2, 5–6, "Verses on the Vice-Principal of St. Mary Hall," line 1.

82   "What's Pow'r, or Wealth? Were they not form'd for Aid,/ A Spring for Virtue, and from Wrongs a Shade?" (*The Wanderer*, Canto 5, 11, lines 147–48).

83   Compare Pope's "He help'd to bury whom he help'd to starve" ("Epistle to Dr. Arbuthnot," lines 247–48) and Johnson's "To buried merit raise the tardy bust" ("Vanity of Human Wishes," line 162).

and ruthless Taunt" (Book III, lines 110–11). What is yet worse, the manner of dispensing bounty poisons the gift. "Dependance on the Great, in former Times," Savage says discreetly to Tyrconnel in the dedication to *The Wanderer*, "generally terminated in Disappointment; nay, even their Bounty (if it could be called such) was in its very Nature ungenerous. It was, perhaps, with-held through an indolent, or wilful Neglect, 'till those, who lingered in the Want of it, grew almost past the Sense of Comfort. At length it came, too often, in a Manner, that half cancell'd the Obligation, and, perchance, must have been acquired too by some previous Act of Guilt in the Receiver, the Consequence of which was Remorse and Infamy" (*Poetical Works*, pp. 95–96). Did Johnson have Savage's words in mind when he wrote to Lord Chesterfield of the earl's long-deferred offer of assistance?

But the Great will always find venal bards ready to provide whatever flattery they require, and ready to accept whatever indignities are offered. In "The Authors of the Town," the poet "Johnny" (probably John Gay), whose "fine Works at Court Obtain Renown," flatters his patron ("How Grand the Verse which *My Lord's* Feats declares," line 199) and even agrees to put his name to my lord's play ("fosters ... his Patron's Wit," line 215).[84] In "The Progress of a Divine" the upwardly mobile priest agrees to foster his patron's child: he marries the patron's pregnant mistress in order to win "*fat-goose Living*" (line 194).

In response to charges that he himself was guilty of selling compliments, Savage sometimes confesses and sometimes denies. In an early poem he offers a contorted apology for his "meaner Views," denying that he meant "to swell vain Minds" ("The Friend," lines 17–19), and in the later *Wanderer* – in lines that that might have served as an epigraph to Johnson's *Life* – admits the charge but tries to disarm censure:

> Oh, let none censure if, untried by Grief,
> If amidst Woe untempted by Relief!
> He stoop'd reluctant to low Arts of Shame,
> Which then, ev'n then he scorn'd, and blush'd to name.
>
> (Book III, lines 269–72)[85]

---

84 As Tracy notes, there is no evidence that Gay was "in the habit of fathering other people's literary bastards" (*Poetical Works*, 75).

85 Johnson remarks that "it is probable that these Lines ... were occasioned by his Reflections on his own Conduct" (*Life of Savage*, 97).

In his poem in praise of Walpole three years later Savage fends off the charge of flattery by reassigning any meanness to the "low Wits" who "Sneer at all Gratitude, all Truth disguise" ("Religion and Liberty," lines 1–2). If "Truth" is his "Guide" (i.e., if he simply praises real Worth), he pointedly insists, "This, nor the Poet, nor the Patron shames" (line 18). But the fact that he even feels the need to deny shame suggests that he feels its pressure.

In marked contrast to the proud, ungenerous great are the ideal patrons – most of whom turn out to be the ones whom Savage addresses. Endowed with power, the true patron knows what it is for: "He (truly great!) his useful pow'r refines, / By him discover'd *Worth* exalted shines" ("A Poem Sacred to King George," lines 71–72). But rather than emphasize the good patron's sense of obligation or responsibility, Savage more commonly imagines, as did some contemporaries, that he finds *pleasure* in being generous. His very "Joy" is "Bounty," and, like God himself, "Smiles o'er the *Beings*, which his Bounty rais'd" (line 76). Dodington (Savage's addressee) and his "Royal Master" (whose recent death the poem laments) are said to be just "such" patrons. So is Tyrconnel, whose "Delight" is "to forgive Injuries, and confer Benefits" (dedication to *The Wanderer*).[86]

Just as the vulgar great serve to set off the few good patrons, so the venal hack serves as a foil to the "honest" poet. Savage's own are "honest Lays" ("Religion and Liberty", line 15). The "Bard" in *The Wanderer* struggles in poverty but never stoops to "sooth Vice, or venal Strokes betray/ In the low-purpos'd, loud, polemic Fray." Never did his verse "immodest Worth contain, / Or ... heav'nly Truths prophane" (Book v, lines 297–300). In "A Poet's Dependance on a Statesman" (1736) those who rise to "posts" through low means are contemptible – even in their own eyes:

> Themselves, in secret, must themselves despise;
> Vile, and more vile; till they at length disclaim
> Not sense alone of glory, but of shame.

(lines 48–50)

The tell-tale intensity suggests that Savage intimately knew the shame. But in the poem he righteously refuses to stoop to low arts:

---

[86] Other ideal patrons are quasi-divine. "The honourable Mrs. Knight" is a frankly unreal figure, "in whose transcendant mind, / Are wisdom, purity, and truth enshrin'd" ("Verses [on] the Vice- Principal of St. Mary's Hall," lines 3–4). The Duke of Rutland is "godlike" ("The Animalcule," line 36).

> Be posts dispos'd at will! – I have, for these,
> No gold to plead, no impudence to teize.
> All *secret service* from my *soul* I hate;
> All dark intrigues of pleasure, or of state.
> I have no pow'r, election votes to gain;
> No will to hackney out polemic strain;
> To shape, as time shall serve, my verse, or prose;
> To flatter thence, nor slur a *courtier*'s foes;
> Nor *him* to daub with praise, if I prevail;
> Nor shock'd by *him*, with *libels* to assail.
> Where *these* are not, what claim to *me* belongs;
> Though *mine* the *muse* and *virtue, birth*, and *wrongs*?
>
> (lines 21–32)

Savage's poem anticipates the accents of Pope's own late satires, in which a righteous poet stands single against a world of vice triumphant.[87] But at its most gratifying Savage's fantasy extends even further into visions of triumph and revenge.

"The Friend" (1726, revised 1736) compliments Aaron Hill as true friend (who offers advice, encouragement, and assistance) and independent poet (of the sort Savage clearly wished to be) – "To equals free, unservile to the great," ready to honor "Greatness" when it is "by worth, acquir'd" but to scorn it "when titles insult speak" (lines 40–43). More than that, Hill is the idealized patron whom Savage always sought:

> When some, with cold, superior looks, redress,
> Relief seems insult, and *confirms* distress;
> You, when you view the man, with wrongs besieg'd;
> While warm you act th'obliger, seem th'oblig'd.
>
> (lines 33–38)

For a poet who wanted to think of himself as his patron's equal, to be "obliged" is to suffer an indignity. The perfect patron, whom Savage celebrates in Hill, provides support but magically confers no obligation – indeed, takes the obligation upon himself.

Savage goes on to imagine not only a private patron but a "publick friend" who if wealthy will provide his bounty, if wise will

---

[87] At the end of "A Poet's Dependance on a Statesman," Savage asks that after his death he be remembered for what he was – i.e., what he wanted to be:

> Say, when in death my sorrows lie repos'd,
> That my past life, no venal view, disclos'd!
> Say, I well knew, while in a state obscure,
> Without the being base, the being poor!
>
> (lines 65–68)

supply advice, if powerful will justly distribute places. "To no *one*, no *sect*, no *clime* confin'd," he will be the *"friend* of *human race"* (lines 82–83). In part an idealized figure, the portrait of the "publick friend" may also be an oblique appeal to the Prince of Wales, then cultivating the image of the disinterested patriot king – the following year Savage was to address his poem "Of Public Spirit" to the Prince. At the end of "The Friend" Savage returns to Hill, who is said to share the spirit of the "publick friend" (i.e., the Prince) and to deserve his bounty: "Through fortune's cloud thy genuine worth can shine; / What wou'dst thou not, were wealth and greatness thine?" The lines implicitly focus not on Hill but on Savage: if Hill had wealth and greatness, what would he not do for me? The poem celebrates most deeply the fantasy-patron.

CHAPTER 8

Mary Leapor and Charlotte Lennox

Recent attention has been directed at the efforts of professional playwrights like Aphra Behn and early novelists like Delariviere Manley to earn the rewards of authorship. Some attention has been paid as well to the peasant poets of the mid- and late-eighteenth century (such as Ann Yearsley) who were taken up by female patrons. But little work has been done on the role of women in the patronage system.[1] Some women may have hesitated to enter into an arrangement whereby they implicitly engaged to exchange "benefits" with a patron – especially a male patron – or to accept his "protection" at a time when "protection" was a euphemism for sexual "keeping."[2] (This may have promoted the emergence of female patrons.) On the other hand, the traditional dependent status of women may have in fact made it easier for patrons to agree to protect them and for women writers to become literarily dependent upon a patron. But even if a patron chose to "protect" a female writer, there were fewer benefits he could confer upon her than upon a man: a woman in the eighteenth century would not be named private secretary to a peer, or set up as a political journalist, or appointed to a church living. Isobel Grundy notes that some of the functions of the patron – introductions, public endorsements, collecting subscriptions – were during the course of the century taken over by other writers. She goes on to observe that men would more easily benefit than women from the "mutual helping-hand system among professional colleagues" – if only because there were fewer established professional women to provide assistance to their peers.[3] Still, evidence survives to demonstrate that the emergence of the female "professional" writer did not have to await the decline of the patronage system.

---

[1] Cheryl Turner briefly considers the topic in *Living by the Pen*, 87–98.
[2] See *OED*, 1b, with examples from 1677.
[3] "Samuel Johnson as Patron of Women," 63.

Women in fact participated in the patronage system, both as patrons and authors, from the beginning of the century, and (especially if subscription publication is considered) benefited from patronage in increasing numbers as the century ended.

Women were active as patrons as early as the Restoration, when, as I have already noted, "the ladies" – especially the two princesses and the prominent duchesses – were both an essential part of the audience in the playhouse and an important source of court patronage.[4] Queen Caroline had more interest in learning and letters than did her husband George II, and she distributed patronage to a number of writers, including Stephen Duck, Richard Savage, and others.[5] (Savage, as I have suggested earlier, had more women than men patrons). Many of the better known private patrons in the eighteenth century were titled women: the Countess of Hertford, the Duchess of Newcastle, the Countess of Northumberland.[6] Elizabeth Montagu and the other Bluestockings performed many of the traditional functions of patrons.

Women authors (like their male counterparts) had most access to the patronage system through subscription publication. Analysis of the information gathered by the compilers of eighteenth-century book subscription lists shows that women writers (and especially women poets) are well represented among recipients of this form of patronage. Women writers whose poems were published by subscription include Mary Masters and Jane Adams (1733), Mary Barber (1734), Sarah Dixon (1740), Jane Brereton (1744), Mary Collier (1762), Mary Darwall (1764), Philippina Hill (1768), Clara Reeve (1769), Priscilla Pointon (1770), Anne Penny (1771), Elizabeth Ryves (1777), and Ann Merry (1779). Rather than decreasing, the number of women poets who published by subscription in fact increased in the latter part of the century. In 1787, the fifty-two books of all kinds published by subscription included volumes of poems by seven

---

[4]   See above, pp. 27–28, and the extended discussion in David Roberts, *The Ladies*. Roberts notes that during the period 1660–1700 plays were dedicated to fourteen different female patrons (p. 96). Even if, as he argues, they provided "little practical assistance" (p. 99), court ladies could make a play and playwright fashionable.

[5]   Chesterfield noted that George "had a contempt for the *belles lettres*, which he called trifling," but that Caroline, though a lover of money, "could occasionally part with it, especially to men of learning, whose patronage she affected." *Characters*, 6, 10.

[6]   The Countess of Hertford (1699–1754) was married to the seventh Duke of Somerset; her daughter Elizabeth married the seventeenth Earl (and first Duke) of Northumberland; Henrietta Duchess of Newcastle was married to the first Duke (and Prime Minister). Newcastle and Northumberland were active patrons in their own right.

women (Elizabeth Cobbold, Anna Maria Williams, Charlotte Sanders, Elizabeth Smith, Eliza Thompson, Jane Timbry, and Ann Yearsley). During the 1780s there were twenty such volumes, and in the 1790s fifteen.[7] Indeed, it appears that the system of subscription publication made it *more* likely that a woman writer's poems would see print. Had women had to depend solely on copy money from booksellers, far fewer would have entered the ranks of published authors.

Women writers might hope for patronage from three different sources: (1) the traditional class of patrons in the court and the aristocracy, (2) local members of the gentry and the professional classes who are prominent on subscription lists, and (3) the male literary establishment of editors (such as George Colman), printers (such as Richardson), and authors (such as Johnson) who took an interest in promoting the careers of particular women. Rather than providing a comprehensive survey of women writers and their patrons, I offer two case studies: Mary Leapor and Charlotte Lennox. Both began their careers as admirers and imitators of Pope, and both came to maturity in the post-Popean literary world. Each illustrates the range – and the limits – of patronage opportunities. Both appeared first with volumes of poetry, but Leapor died before her poems appeared in print. Lennox turned to translation and to fiction-writing, and became well established as a professional writer, but died in poverty after a long career. Each of them apparently found her engagement with the patronage system to be embarrassing and difficult. Each left a record – sometimes oblique, sometimes direct – of those difficulties in her writings.

MARY LEAPOR

Mary Leapor was one of a surprisingly large number of peasant or working-class poets in the eighteenth-century who managed not only to compile a body of work but to find patrons who took them up and saw their work into print.[8] Leapor spent her short life in the vicinity

---

[7]   See the series of pamphlets published by the Book Subscription List Project, the latest of which is *A Check-List of Eighteenth-Century Books Containing Lists of Subscribers*, comp. R. C. Alston, F. J. G. Robinson, and C. Wadham.

[8]   Other "peasant poets" taken up by patrons include Stephen Duck (patronized by the queen), Mary Collier, Ann Yearsley (patronized by Hannah More), James Woodhouse (patronized by Elizabeth Montagu and by Shenstone), Elizabeth Hands, Elizabeth Bentley, and Robert Bloomfield. Poets with working-class origins taken up by patrons

of Brackley, in Northamptonshire. She was the daughter of a gardener who made a very modest living in the employ of local landowners and later as a nurseryman in business for himself in the service of the local gentry. The poet was at one time employed as a kitchen-maid in at least two large houses in the neighborhood, and after 1742 as her father's housekeeper. Having attended the local free school, she apparently "delighted in reading" while still a child, and somehow managed to accumulate a small collection of books (including the poems of Dryden and Pope), and to write verses in the scraps of time she could save from the daily drudgery of domestic labor. Eventually her poems came to the attention of one of her former employers, and at the time of Leapor's early death from measles in 1746 (at the age of twenty-four) plans had been laid, with the help of Samuel Richardson and some of his literary circle in London, which led to the posthumous appearance (by subscription) of two volumes of her poems in 1748 and 1751.[9]

Those critics who have aided in the recent rediscovery of Leapor have presented her as a kind of victim, prevented from realizing her potential by the systems of class hierarchy and patriarchy. One has argued that her history is evidence of the failure of the patronage system:

Despite the presence in her village of several people [such as the local schoolmaster, vicar, bookseller, and gentry], capable of recognizing and sympathizing with her struggle, without the help first of an unliterary and unusually determined country gentlewoman and then of Samuel Richardson she would have remained unnoted. (Rizzo, "Mary Leapor," p. 313)

Rizzo is surprised that Leapor was not noticed earlier. But the real surprise, I would argue, is that she was noticed at all. The odds against *any* obscure author in the 1740s appearing in print are very high. A young woman poet, deep in Northamptonshire, with only a rudimentary education and almost no access to people of learning (or even to people who had a taste for reading), is very unlikely to

include Robert Dodsley (footman), Robert Tatersal (bricklayer), Henry Jones (bricklayer), and William Falconer (sailor). For an early biographical discussion of their work see Rayner Unwin, *The Rural Muse*. For more "political" readings, see Moira Ferguson, "Resistance and Power in the Life and Writings of Ann Yearsley," 247–68, and Donna Landry, *The Muses of Resistance*.

9   For biographical details, see two essays by Betty Rizzo, "Christopher Smart, The 'C. S.' Poems, and Molly Leapor's Epitaph," 21–31, and "Mary Leapor: An Anxiety for Influence," 313–34, and the full-length biography by Richard Greene, *Mary Leapor*, esp. 1–37.

publish a volume of poems in London. A kitchen-maid with a taste for poetry is almost surely going to remain mute and inglorious. And yet Leapor acquired a reputation that lasted for the remainder of the century as a poet of real ability. It seems likely that without the subscription edition she never would have been printed. And her career demonstrates that the patronage system in effect had its agents everywhere: it served to discover and encourage talent, even in Brackley.

Leapor benefited from two distinct kinds of patrons, members of the local gentry who first noticed her work, and a network of literary figures in London who had the means of bringing her poems into print and into a certain reputation. As Rizzo and Greene have shown, the key figure was probably one Bridget Freemantle, the daughter of a country rector who had been a fellow of Lincoln College, Oxford. It was she who first noticed her poems, and who, together with Susanna Jennens (a local gentlewoman who wrote verses, and Leapor's first mistress) helped bring them to the attention of Richardson's circle. Freemantle seems to have performed several of the traditional functions of the patron – providing Leapor with a gift (a writing bureau which she valued highly), sending her verse tragedy, *The Unhappy Father*, to John Rich at Covent Garden, writing a brief account of Leapor's life for the second volume of her poems, and soliciting subscriptions. Jennens may have been the one who conveyed the manuscript of Leapor's poems to London. Freemantle in particular, although apparently a generous and disinterested friend, was clearly conscious that in bringing Leapor forward she was working within the traditions of patronage, whereby literary merit is recognized and validated by gentle persons of "rank" and "taste." In a letter "To the Reader" prefixed to the second volume of Leapor's poems, Freemantle assured subscribers that Leapor was no presumptuous and ambitious servant girl seeking to climb her way into higher life. She was, Freemantle said, "contented in the Station of Life in which Providence had placed her" (*Poems upon Several Occasions*, vol. II, p. A2v). Her "Papers" were "communicated to several Persons of Rank and of distinguished Taste and Judgment, who were pleased to express a great Satisfaction in the View they had of promoting a Subscription for their being printed." Once her merit had been assayed by the traditional well-born judges, she in effect had permission to move into a "higher Sphere, to which in all Probability, if it had pleased God to spare her Life, her own Merit would have raised

her." But since Leapor had already died, she could represent no
threat to the social order: the subscription was organized not for her
own benefit but for that of her impoverished father.

Once the manuscript was brought to the attention of literary
London, a number of established figures played a role in promoting
the subscription edition.[10] Written proposals were prepared and
subscriptions had to be secured.[11] The poems were edited (by Isaac
Hawkins Browne, himself a poet and MP), and printed (volume one
by John Watts and volume two by Richardson, who published works
by a number of women writers), praised (by John Duncombe in his
Feminiad, 1754), reprinted (in the *Monthly Review* for November 1749)
and anthologized (by Bonnell Thornton and George Colman in their
Poems by Eminent Ladies, 1755). Richardson tried to get Christopher
Smart to write an epitaph. Another of Richardson's friends, Susanna
Highmore, seems to have attempted to commission Elizabeth Carter
for the same purpose on behalf of a poet who was known as "her
favourite."[12] It is appropriate to think of such services as a form of
patronage, for they were apparently offered without concern for any
immediate material return, and yet need not be thought of as purely
disinterested service to literature: if Leapor were to win reputation
her literary supporters would stand in some reflected glory. Without
such promotion and assistance (regardless of the underlying merit of
her work), Leapor would very likely have remained unknown.

Leapor's rediscoverers have not surprisingly wanted to hear hers
as an original voice, regarding the world from her own unusual
perspective, and to see her as an enemy to the systems of oppression
that almost kept her silent, and have looked to her poems to find
evidence of an author who resented her dependent status.[13] But a
critic not predisposed to find an independent and subversive voice
will find instead that Leapor, although she reflects on the situation of
the dependent poet, often adopts a point of view she could only have
known through her reading, and that the resistance to dependence is

[10] Rizzo ("Mary Leapor," 326–27) notes the "predominance of the Richardson circle"
among the subscribers to vol. ii.

[11] The author of the proposals for the 1748 volume is unknown; Garrick wrote the proposals
for vol. ii. Duncombe in 1784 wrote that the proposals were "drawn up by Mr. Garrick
under the patronage of several persons of rank and taste." See *Gentleman's Magazine*, 54
(1784), 806, quoted in Greene, *Mary Leapor*, 23.

[12] See the letter from Carter to Highmore, quoted in *ibid.*, 28.

[13] Landry in particular has asserted that Leapor was an enemy of "patriarchal oppression"
(*Muses of Resistance*, 104). Greene, *Mary Leapor*, 51–52, in fact doubts this claim, but argues
that Leapor was bitter about female subordination.

more muted than one might expect. Her stance seems resignation and bemused ironic deference rather than resentment and anger.

It is understandable that critics should look to Leapor's *Crumble-Hall* as an index of her socio-political stance as a poet, for it is here that she regards the English country house, long celebrated as a symbol of an aristocratic social order, from her peculiar vantage – below stairs. It seems likely that in such a poem Leapor might reflect on the systems of dependence in which she participated, as a woman, as a servant, and as a poet. Landry has read the poem as a "class-conscious plebeian country-house poem that undeniably mocks and seeks to demystify the values of the gentry, whose social power in large part depends upon the deference – and the continued exploitable subservience – of servants and laborers" (*Muses of Resistance*, p.107). But the servants' labor is not described as oppressive, and the contrast between the grand reception rooms and the dark, dirty, and dangerous back stairs works not to expose and "demystify" but offers a comic glimpse of what no reader should be shocked to discover. Yet even Greene, who doubts Landry's highly ideological reading, sees the poem as "bold" and "angry," and suspects that its omission from the first volume of Leapor's poems was "a substantial concession to patronage" (*Mary Leapor*, p. 153).[14] Patronage in fact does not figure directly in the poem, nor does Leapor have much to say about the landowner at all, or even about the social hierarchy in the house. A less tendentious reading of *Crumble-Hall* would find not so much "anger" as ironic observation of country-house poem conventions in a manner already made familiar by Pope's "Epistle to Burlington," a poem which Leapor clearly knew and imitated – the unread books in the library recall Timon's study. The shift of perspective from landowner to kitchen servant sounds not like class solidarity but traditional mock-heroic:

> "Ah! *Roger*, Ah!" the mournful Maiden cries:
> "Is wretched *Urs'la* then your care no more,
> That, while I sigh, thus you can sleep and snore?
> Ingrateful *Roger*! wilt thou leave me now?
> For you these Furrows mark my fading Brow:
> For you my Pigs resign their Morning Due:
> My hungry Chickens lose their Meat for you.   (lines 137–43)

---

[14] I would argue for a more detached Leapor than Greene, who thinks that her "most angry works," reflecting "rebellious thought" (*ibid.*, 153) and resisting the influence of patronage, were deliberately held back from the first volume.

And the dramatized scene in the servants' hall recalls Swift's comic
tone and the humble domestic detail of "Baucis and Philemon," "A
Description of the Morning," and his "progress poems" (such as
"Phillis, or, the Progress of Love"):

> Thus she – But now her Dish-kettle began
> To boil and blubber with the foaming Bran.
> The greasy Apron round her Hips she ties,
> And to each Plate the scalding Clout applies:
> The purging Bath each glowing Dish refines,
> And once again the polish'd Pewter shines.   (lines 150–55)

Pope and Swift are predecessors she clearly admires and whose work
she adapts but sees no need to subvert.[15]

In other poems Leapor deals more directly with the system of
patronage in which she was to become implicated. Her most explicit
treatments of the topic, however, do not attempt to reinterpret it from
her particular point of view as an aspiring working-class poet buried
in Northamptonshire. The very title of her "The Way of the World"
is ironic, a view of the great world that she could only know from her
reading. One of her topics is the hypocrisy of false promises, and her
example the proud and self-concerned "Patron" who pretends to be
"the humble Slave of all Mankind" (*Poems*, vol. 1, p. 92):

> But the worst Flatterer that wears a Tongue,
> Is him whose Power aggravates the Wrong:
> To whose grand Levee Crowds of Suppliants run,
> And bow like *Persians* to the rising Sun:
> Where starv'd Dependents linger out their Days,
> Yet proud to share his Snuff-box and his Praise,
> Grow stiff with Standing and with Staring thin,
> To watch the Dimple on their Patron's Chin:
> Who with a Nod can make the Wretch believe,
> And smiles on Hunger which he'll ne'er relieve.   (pp. 93–94)

Leapor makes no claim to have observed the levee herself, with its
stock elements, the "Crowds of Suppliants" and the smiling and
nodding proud patron on whom all eyes focus. She in effect
reimagines the scene that Pope and others had described. The detail
of the "Dimple on their Patron's Chin" is her own, although it

---

[15] For Leapor's appropriation of Swiftian style in *Crumble-Hall* and in other mock-pastoral
poems, see Margaret Doody, "Swift Among the Women," esp. 79–82. For Leapor's
allusions to and appropriations of Pope, see Claudia Thomas, *Alexander Pope and his
Eighteenth-Century Women Readers*, 152–57, 199–204.

strikes me as characteristically "Popean," as if Leapor were in fact an expert ventriloquist, speaking in Pope's manner,[16] and producing passages that can withstand comparison with Pope's account of Bufo. The patron's smile is especially chilling, turning as it does within a single line from the promised offer of favor and relief to well-fed and complacent disregard.

In a well-realized dramatic scene, the patron "Virginius" is found "Surrounded thick with Bus'ness and with Gold." The suppliants approach to ask his favor. He distributes promises, and invites one of the dependents to return later. But the patron avoids him, and when finally "seiz'd and boarded" by the lurking client, Virginius

> Smooth'd up his Face and with a leering Eye
> Began. "Oh, Mr. What-d-ye-call, Is't you?
> I'm glad to see you: Yet I'm sorry too,
> Sure some ill Stars presided o'er your Fate,
> I cou'd have serv'd you, but you're come too late."
>
> (pp. 95–96)

Here and elsewhere Leapor has mastered Pope's characteristic devices – the zeugma, the snatches of colloquial conversation – to produce a scene that asks to be read as a kind of set-piece on a standard theme. The poem ends, as do some of Pope's poems, with an idealized portrait (recalling Pope's "Man of Ross") of a good patron, an "honest Soul" who does good quietly, but is "too grand a Being for the soothing Trade" (p. 96).

The "Advice to Myrtillo" is another skeptical look at the promises of patrons, and what is required of the dependent who would hope to prosper. Again Leapor ventriloquizes, casting the poem as a letter of advice from a man of some experience to a young poet about to set up as an author:

> Since you, *Myrtillo*, will devote your Time
> To the lean Study of delusive Rhyme:
> Since you're content to slumber out your Days,
> To dream of Dinners, but to feed on Praise;
> Receive this Counsel, e'er your Flights begin,
> From one long practis'd in the darling Sin.
> Now Fame's broad Ocean lies before your Way,
> Yet, Friend, be careful; 'tis a dang'rous Sea.
>
> (*Poems*, vol. 1, p. 167)

---

[16] I borrow the term from Doody, who notes how Leapor is adept at "ventriloquizing" masculine voices ("Swift Among the Women," 80).

Again Leapor probably has in mind literary models, Pope's Bufo, who feeds "some Bards with Port, and some with Praise," and Oldham's poems on literary ambition, "A Letter from the Country to a Friend in Town, giving an Account of the Author's Inclinations to Poetry," and "A SATYR, Address'd to a Friend, that is about to leave the University, and come abroad in the World."[17] As ambitious "author" Oldham too confesses a "darling Sin" (his phrase) – the "vile and wicked lust of Poetry" ("A Letter from the Country," lines 87–89) – and as chastened man of experience warns his young friend:

> How many men of choice and noted parts,
> Well fraught with Learning, Languages, and Arts,
> Designing high Preferment in their mind,
> And little doubting good success to find,
> With vast and tow'ring thoughts have flock'd to Town,
> But to their cost soon found themselves undone,
> Now to repent, and starve at leisure left,
> Of miseries last Comfort, Hope, bereft?
>
> ("A SATYR," lines 11–18)

Leapor's advisor warns of the flattery that patrons expect, and the price that a proud poet who refuses to flatter must pay:

> Do you the Levee of his Grace attend,
> And (like most Poets) shou'd you want a Friend,
> Make not its Worth the Measure of your Song;
> But learn his Humour, and you can't be wrong:
> Perhaps this Maxim must offend the wise;
> But you must flatter, if you mean to rise:
> Observe what Passions in his Bosom roll,
> And watch the secret Motions of his Soul:
> Mind what false Guard has left a Breach within,
> For some choice Folly, or some darling Sin:
> These you must hide – but draw his Virtues nigh,
> Lest the rude Picture shock the gazing Eye.
>
> (*Poems*, vol. 1, p. 169)

> But shou'd your Pride the common Track refuse,
> You'll find small Pensions for your haughty Muse.   (p. 170)

The double-ventriloquism – Leapor speaks as a man who knows the

---

17 *Poems of John Oldham*, 149–56, 226–32. Cf. also the "SATYR. The Person of Spencer is brought in, Dissuading the Author from the Study of Poetry, and shewing how little it is esteem'd and encourag'd in this present Age." Oldham's poems were known to those interested in the trials of dependency. See above p. 8.

world, and speaks through the forms of Oldham – once again suggests that if she is obliquely reflecting her own experience with small-town country patrons, Leapor is disguising it in conventional satire and commonplaces about the miseries of dependence.

Elsewhere her poems more closely adapt themselves to her situation as a rural poet with little access to audiences, much less patronage and fame. "An Epistle to Artemisia. On Fame" (apparently addressed to her friend and local patron Bridget Freemantle, the "Artemisia" of the poems) pays "Tribute" to Artemisia among "the Patrons of my early Song,"[18] but goes on to offer a comic lament for the poet ("Mira," as Leapor often called herself in her poems) who must endure the condescending (but vacuous) criticism of her social betters:

> Once *Delpho* read – Sage *Delpho*, learn'd and wise,
> O'er the scrawl'd Paper cast his judging Eyes,
> Whose lifted Brows confess'd a Critic's Pride,
> While his broad Thumb mov'd nimbly down the Side.
> His Form was like some Oracle profound:
> The list'ning Audience form'd a Circle round:
> But *Mira*, fixing her presuming Eyes
> On the stern Image, thus impatient cries:
> Sir, will they prosper? – Speak your Judgment, pray.
> Replies the Statue – Why, perhaps they may.
> For further Answers we in vain implore:
> The Charm was over, and it spoke no more.
>
> (*Poems*, vol. II, pp. 46–47)

Delpho may be a local gentleman who sets up for a judge of poetic merit, but he is of no more help than Halifax was to Pope. Other friends and critics come in, but they only dispense insincere praise, or prove to be more interested in gossip: "Preferment great! To beat one's weary Brains,/ To find Diversion only when it rains!" (p. 53). That is, her only "preferment" is the tiresome conversation of local friends who while away the damp afternoon by laughing at her "idle Play."

Another poem, "The Disappointment," treats of encouraging (but

---

18 One poem, "The Genius in Disguise," is spoken in the voice of a writing bureau in which Leapor apparently kept her poems (see "Epistle to Artemisia. On Fame," in which her "Babes" [Leapor's footnote identifies them as "Her Poems"] are put to rest "in their tiny Chest," and Leapor's letter about the "Papers" kept in her "Buroe," printed in *Poems* II, xxviii). It offers "Gratitude" to "our Patron yours and mine" (p. 134). The writing bureau was evidently a gift from Bridget Freemantle.

hollow) words from one "Sophronia." Like many Leapor poems, it shows a preoccupation with false promises.

> When you, *Sophronia*, did my Sense beguile
> With your Half-promise, and consenting Smile;
> What Shadows swam before these dazled Eyes!
> Fans, Lace, and Ribbands, in bright Order rise.
>
> Such Phantoms fill'd these giddy Brains of mine;
> Such golden Dreams on *Mira*'s Temples shine;
> Till stern Experience bid her Servant rise,
> And Disappointment rubb'd my drowsy Eyes.
> Do thou, *Sophronia*, now thy Arts give o'er,
> Thy little Arts; for *Mira*'s Thoughts no more
> Shall after your imagin'd Favours run,
> Your still-born Gifts, that ne'er behold the Sun.
>
> (*Poems*, vol. II, p. 80)

Leapor's lines form a kind of palinode, a farewell to trust in false promises. She goes on to compare such promises with the elegant praise of a male critic who is more interested in displaying his own wit:

> Your Nods, sly Glances, and soft Whispers, are
> Like well-bred *Vido*'s Friendship to the Fair,
> So fine, 'tis melted at th'Approach of Air ...
> ... when he chuses for his skilful Tongue
> A Theme so low as *Mira*'s simple Song,
> 'Tis not his Comment on the artless Lines,
> But his own Genius in the Lecture shines;
> And when he bows, 'tis that the World may see
> His own good Manners, not Respect to me.
>
> (pp. 80–81)

Other poems shadow the efforts of the provincial poet to gain access to London. "To a Gentleman with a Manuscript Play" constructs an extended comparison between the rural matron who sends her daughter into domestic service in London with the rural poet who exposes her play to the wits and critics of the metropolis:

> Tho' unassur'd, yet not in deep Despair,
> I trust this Infant to its Patron's Care:
> Ah let your Roofs this simple Vagrant[19] shield,
> I ask no more than Charity may yield,
> Some little Corner in the friendly Dome,
> (Lest this loose Varlet be induc'd to roam).

---

[19] Leapor's text here reads "Vagrants," an obvious printer's error.

This poem ends too with another portrait of an idealized patron of "Good-nature" and "gen'rous Mind" (*Poems*, vol. I, pp. 269–70).

A more ambitious work based on the same writerly anxieties is "Mopsus: or, the Castle-Builder." By far Leapor's longest poem – running to thirty-two pages in her second volume – it treats a farm boy (an "aspiring Youth") who dreams of fame and fortune in London. The poem is a kind of allegory: Leapor left hints that it concerned her own literary ambitions. In a letter published with her poems and entitled by her editor "On her Verses being sent to London," she notes that "*Mira* has her gay Intervals, and an excellent Knack at Castle-building" (*Poems*, II, p. 312). In a later letter she confesses that in *Mopsus* "I have drawn my own Picture in many Places where I have described this unlucky Hero" (p. 316). Freemantle confirmed that her "mentioning a Subscription [edition of the poems], I believe, occasioned her Poem, call'd *Mopsus, or, The Castle-Builder*" (p. xx).

Mopsus is sent to the local school, where he fills his head with "discontented Thoughts": "He loaths the Country, and his Fellow Swains;/ For mighty Projects fill his working Brains" (p. 13). While plowing the fields "musing *Mopsus*" dreams of being a prince. He sees (or dreams he sees) a band of gypsies; one tells his fortune. After he fees her, the gypsy dame "bless'd her Patron" (p. 14) – an ironic use of a word that otherwise hovers unspoken in the poem – and he goes off to win the hand of the local heiress. But he is told he must slay giants and accomplish other Herculean tasks. Disappointed, he steals money from his father and goes off to London, where he is taken in by two women of the town, Chloe ("A wise Director in the Bank of Sin") and Celia ("A young Proficient in the School of Shame"), who rob him. He ends up in jail, and after sending for more money from home he gains his freedom. Viscount Simper then tricks him into marrying his cast-off pregnant mistress, who gives birth five days later, abandons him and the child, and conveniently dies. Mopsus returns home and receives the prodigal's welcome. He resolves to live in the country with "calm Virtue, and a peaceful Mind": "No more Delusions in his Fancy rise,/ Grown grave by Sorrow; by Experience wise."

If we read the poem with dreams of literary fame and fortune in mind, Leapor is admitting ambitions only to repress them severely. It is her education that gives rise to "discontented Thoughts" – precisely the sort of discontent in the lower orders that would arouse nervousness in Leapor's subscribers and had to be allayed by Free-mantle's denial in her biographical sketch. The story of the aspiring provincial poet has the effect of an old morality tale, and suggests that Leapor taught herself to have grave misgivings about her poetic aspirations. Those misgivings continued even as friends in her last years encouraged her subscription edition. One of her letters concerns the imminent printing of her poems and the proposal (which Leapor resisted) from an unnamed gentleman that they be supplied with a biographical portrait of the author, like the poems of Stephen Duck: "as to what he observes concerning *Stephen Duck*, I am of Opinion, that it was not his Situation, but the Royal Favour, which gained the Country over to his Side; and therefore I think it needless to paint the Life of a Person, who depends more upon the Curiosity of the World, than its Good-nature. Besides, the seeing myself described in Print would give me the same Uneasiness as being stared at" (*Poems*, vol. II, p. 314). Displaying an almost instinctive delicacy, she was also uneasy at the suggestion that she solicit the favor of some ladies whom she apparently did not know:

I have great Apprehensions, that the Ladies won't think it worth their Care. In this Temper of Mind I cannot help sighing, to think that my Way of Life obliges me to seek the Approbation of a giddy World, and People whose manner of thinking I am a Stranger to, as well as to their Friendship. Those lines of Mr. *Pope* now occur to my Memory, where he professes only to consult the End of his Being, and resolves to
> Maintain a Poet's Dignity and Ease,
> And see what Friends, and read what Books I please.
But this Quotation will not serve for me. (pp. 317–18)

That is, I cannot afford such luxuries. Quite apart from my duties as a housekeeper, my dependent status requires that I be prepared to please. But far from displaying a strong "class consciousness" (Landry, *Muses of Resistance*, p. 98), Leapor shows no "solidarity" with the below-stairs world, and in her various literary gestures associates herself with letters, leisure, and independence. A poet who calls herself "Mira" and addresses her friends and patrons as "Artemisia" and "Parthenissa" is not a figure whose texts offer many "radical possibilities" to ideologically minded interpreters.

Leapor displayed the same reluctance when she was advised to dedicate her poems to some "great Lady." But again the objection does not seem to be class-oriented. Freemantle reported that "I gravely told her, I thought we must endeavour to find out some great

Lady to be her Patroness, and desir'd her to prepare a handsome Dedication" (*Poems*, vol. II, p. xxiv). There follows in Freemantle's letter – which, printed with the poems, serves to present Leapor to the reading public – a deft satire on the patronage system: L: "But pray, what am I to say in this same Dedication." "Oh, a great many fine Things, certainly." L: "But, Madam, I am not acquainted with any great Lady, nor like to be." "No matter for that; 'tis but your supposing your Patroness to have as many Virtues as other People always have: You need not fear saying too much; and I must insist upon it." "She really seemed shocked," Freemantle continued, "and said: But Dear Madam, could you in good Earnest approve of my sitting down to write an Encomium upon a Person I know nothing of, only because I hope to get something by it?" (pp. xxvi–xxvii). Leapor plays the role of innocent truth-teller in Freemantle's little dramatic vignette, a piece that suggests its author was familiar with the satiric commonplaces rehearsed in works like Thomas Gordon's well-known *A Dedication to a Great Man Concerning Dedications* (1718).[20] In the end, indeed, Leapor wrote no dedication, and her poems came forth without the protection of some "great Lady" as their "Patroness," though they were escorted by a list of more than six hundred subscribers, including many names – two dukes and five earls (including Chesterfield) – that would have caught the eye of impressionable readers. But by the time the poems appeared, Leapor had been dead nearly two years, and she had no opportunity to move into a "higher sphere" or to pursue a literary career.

CHARLOTTE LENNOX

Leapor's early death leaves us wondering what she might have gone on to do: would she have been taken up by the fashionable world? Would she have gone on to write another volume of poems? Or (like many other women poets) would she after a moment in the sun have returned to the obscurity of Northamptonshire village life?[21] The career of Charlotte Lennox provides a kind of continuation of Leapor's story. Lennox was an almost exact contemporary of Mary

---

[20] E.g., "Dedicators are a Sort of *Intellectual Taylors*, that cut out Cloaths for a Great Man's Mind without ever taking Measure of it" (p. 4). Gordon's work reached a fourth edition by 1719.

[21] Rizzo, avoiding sentimentality and critical overestimate, guesses that she would have been "happy and productive" but would not have written "the work expected of her" ("Mary Leapor," 329).

Leapor. Born probably five years later than Leapor in 1727, and raised like her in provincial obscurity (the daughter of an army officer in the colony of New York),[22] she was introduced to the literary world at almost the same moment: Lennox's *Poems on Several Occasions* appeared in London in 1747, just one year before the first volume of Leapor's *Poems upon Several Occasions* in 1748. And like Leapor she benefited from the encouragement and support of a number of London writers, including Richardson, who helped her into print and praised her work after it was published. While Leapor died at twenty-four with a single book to her name, Lennox went on to become a hard-working professional writer with some sixteen titles in her bibliography, and survived to the age of eighty-four. Like many writers of the day, she labored for the booksellers, deriving most of her income from copy money, but also took part in the economy of patronage, dedicating at least seven of her works to private patrons. And yet though Lennox was one of the most productive writers of her day, she serves as a reminder that steady publication and the "favour" and "protection" of the great were no guarantee of independence or even a competence. Lennox struggled with debt, and ended her life as a charity case.

While Leapor found support from local patrons, Lennox took what seemed the more promising path to fame and fortune: as a young woman – possibly as young as fourteen or fifteen – she came to the attention of the "great Ladies" whom Leapor never knew. Details of her early life are sketchy, but it appears that she was sent to England, perhaps for her education, where she was to come under the care of her mother's sister, a Mrs. Lucking "of Messing Hall, the widow of a gentleman of an honourable family and good fortune in Essex"[23] – who might be thought of as Lennox's first patron. But when Mrs. Lucking and her only son suddenly died, shortly before or after her arrival, Lennox came to the attention of several women of rank attached to the court. She was taken up,

---

22   The traditional date and place (1720, in New York) have been challenged by Philippe Séjourné in *The Mystery of Charlotte Lennox*. Duncan Isles, on the authority of the "Memoirs of Mrs. Lenox" published in the *Edinburgh Weekly Magazine* in 1783, suggests that she was born *c.* 1729–30, possibly in Gibraltar. Isles' monograph on "The Lennox Collection,", 18 (1970), 317–44, and 19 (1971), 36–60, 165–86, 416–35, is an essential supplement and corrective to the only complete biography, Miriam Small's *Charlotte Ramsay Lennox*. Isles' monograph was announced as a prelude to a new biography and a projected edition of Lennox's letters – but both remain unpublished in 1995.

23   *Edinburgh Weekly Magazine*, 58 (1783), 34. Isles gives the family's name as "Luckyn" – though without explanation ("The Lennox Collection," 326).

probably as some kind of higher servant, perhaps a child's companion, by the ladies of the Finch family. Her first volume of poems was dedicated to Lady Issabella (*sic*) Finch, "First Lady of the Bedchamber to their Royal Highnesses the Princesses" (i.e., Amelia and Caroline, the daughters of George II), and a lady with sufficient literary interest to have a library. Isabella Finch was well connected: the daughter of Daniel Finch, second Earl of Nottingham, and sister of the Duchesses of Roxburgh and of Cleveland, as well as Lady Mansfield (wife of the future Chief Justice) and Lady Rockingham (mother of the future Prime Minister). Lennox may have spent time with both Lady Finch and her sister the Dowager Marchioness of Rockingham.[24] There followed a falling-out for reasons that remain obscure.[25] She seems to have married in 1747 (Alexander Lennox does not appear to have had any connections with the great world), but remained close enough to the court to presume to offer a "Birthday Ode" to the Princess of Wales in 1750.[26] It was advertised as "presented to her Royal Highness by the Earl of Middlesex" (who was to serve her as a patron again), though how she met him is not known.

Although her next work, a novel entitled *The Life of Harriot Stuart* (1751), was not equipped with a dedication – for reasons I will return to – she by then had made contact with a second source of patronage, Samuel Johnson and other London writers who celebrated the publication of her novel with a festive dinner at the Ivy Lane Club, where she was literally given a "crown of laurel" to recognize her triumph.[27] The support provided to Lennox by Johnson, Fielding, and Richardson in the writing, publication, and promotion of her next novel, *The Female Quixote* (1752), is well enough known that it does not need recounting here.[28] Johnson's efforts on

---

[24] *National Cyclopedia of American Biography* (New York: White, 1896), VI, 51. Whether she passed from the protection of Lady Finch to Lady Rockingham, or vice-versa, is unclear. The *National Cyclopedia* is not reliable: it passes on the story that Lennox was the daughter of the Lieutenant-Governor of New York.

[25] Perhaps because of some sexual indiscretion or some sexual jealousy (as Small [*Charlotte Ramsay Lennox*, 7] suggests, following the *National Cyclopedia of Biography*, which notes that an "obscure love-affair ... ended her friendship" with Lady Rockingham), or perhaps because she had contracted an imprudent marriage as early as 1747 with a man of "no fortune" (as the "Memoirs of Mrs. Lenox" suggests, p. 34).

[26] It was published in the *Gentleman's Magazine*, 20 (Nov. 1750), 518.

[27] For an account of the dinner, see Sir John Hawkins' *Life of Samuel Johnson*, 286–87.

[28] Except to note that Isles has challenged the traditional attribution of chapter 11 of Part 9 to Johnson. See the Oxford English Novels edition of the novel (ed. M. Dalziel), 414–15, 418–27.

her behalf in later years have also received recent attention.[29] It is tempting to think of the dinner as the symbolic moment, complete with official bestowal of honors, when Lennox passed from aristocratic patronage to that of fellow professionals in the republic of letters. But in fact Johnson himself was instrumental in subsequently reintroducing Lennox to the *traditional* source of patronage, the peerage. He not only introduced Lennox to the literary peer, the Earl of Orrery (who was to help get *The Female Quixote* into print, and was to assist her in compiling her next book[30]), but wrote the first of a series of dedications to private patrons for Lennox to sign.

The Female Quixote was supplied with a dedication, very probably written by Johnson,[31] to the Earl of Middlesex (a well-established patron who had earlier accepted a dedication from Richard Savage). Throughout the following decade Johnson was to provide Lennox with other dedications. Her *Shakespear Illustrated* (1753) was dedicated to the Earl of Orrery. She then turned to translations from the French. The *Memoirs of Maximilian de Bethune, Duke of Sully* (1756) appeared with a dedication (again by Johnson) to the Duke of Newcastle, then Prime Minister, who responded (according to the 1783 "Memoirs of Mrs. Lenox") with "a most liberal present" and "declared that he would recommend her to the king as a person who well deserved a pension."[32]

The reported offer – if true – is a kind of turning point in Lennox's career in patronage. Newcastle is said to have "kindly" observed that "her birth and merit entitled her to royal notice" – perhaps he accepted the story that she was the impoverished daughter of a royalist governor. (The situation recalls the appeal that Dorset made in the 1720s on behalf of Savage as "injured nobleman," and suggests that some eighteenth-century patrons responded as much to "birth" as to "merit".) Although there is no evidence of the amount of the proposed pension, royal pensions paid to other writers in the 1750s and 1760s commonly amounted to £200 to £300 per annum, and at this point Lennox would probably have found such an amount sufficient to support herself and her husband. But Lennox is said to have "very politely declined" the offer to secure her a pension "in

29 See Gae Holladay and O. M. Brack, Jr., "Johnson as Patron," 172–99, and Isobel Grundy, "Samuel Johnson as Patron of Women," 59–77.
30 See Isles, "The Lennox Collection," 18: 335 and 19:36, and *Letters of Samuel Johnson*, I, 63.
31 For a recent challenge to the traditional attribution to Johnson, see David Marshall, "Writing Masters," 105–35.
32 "Memoirs of Mrs. Lenox," 35.

favour of her husband, for whom she solicited a place, which the Duke promised to procure him the first opportunity" ("Memoirs of Mrs. Lenox," p. 35). Perhaps because a pension was paid during the lifetime of, and at the pleasure of the king, and George II was then seventy-three years old, Lennox gambled that a salaried place for her husband might be safer and more lasting – for who knew if the next king would renew a pension? Newcastle must not have been offended (it was not uncommon for clients to ask for a place instead of a pension), for Alexander Lennox is later recorded as holder of several minor places in the 1760s and 1770s.[33] Given the marital discord she later suffered, and her husband's spendthrift ways, she would probably have done better to take the pension.

Lennox herself continued to look for patrons. Although the *Memoirs of the Countess of Berci* (1756) carried no dedication, another volume of French memoirs the following year, the *Memoirs for the History of Madame de Maintenon and of the Last Age* was dedicated (with Johnson's help) to the Countess of Northumberland, another active patron of the arts.[34] In 1758 her "Dramatic Pastoral," *Philander*, was dedicated (with Johnson as ghost) to James Caulfeild, fourth Viscount Charlemont.[35] And in 1759 Lennox apparently thought that the time was right for her to look to the next court. Her translation of *The Greek Theatre of Father Brumoy* was dedicated (by Johnson) to the Prince of Wales (soon to become George III), who is said to have responded with "a munificent present."[36] Just after the accession of the new king Lennox wrote to Henrietta, Duchess of Newcastle acknowledging past favors, and requesting permission to dedicate to her the second edition of her novel *Henrietta*.[37] The request was accepted,

---

[33] In an October 1760 letter to the Duchess of Newcastle, Lennox thanks her for "Your favourable intentions with regard to Mr. Lennox" (quoted in Small, *Charlotte Ramsay Lennox*, 28). Isles summarizes the evidence that Mr. Lennox held places, perhaps procured for him by the Duchess, in the 1760s and 1770s ("The Lennox Collection," 59).

[34] From her bookseller she received £86.17.6 in copy money (Séjourné, *The Mystery of Charlotte Lennox*, 29).

[35] Charlemont was a key political supporter of Rockingham. According to the *DNB*, his "literary and artistic tastes found gratification in the society of Burke, Johnson, Reynolds, Goldsmith, Beauclerk, and Hogarth, and he acted as chairman of the committee of the Dilettanti Club."

[36] "Memoirs of Mrs. Lenox," 35. The memoirist reports that the prince's advisor, the Earl of Bute, played a key role (as usual, it might be added) by making "generous representations" about Lennox – i.e., probably advising patronage, and that Lady Bute took some interest in the matter.

[37] The letter, in the Newcastle Papers in the British Library, is reproduced in Small, *Charlotte Ramsay Lennox*, 27–28.

and a dedication dated November 20, 1760, appeared in the new edition of the novel in March 1761.

Lennox then for a decade made repeated and successful appeals, with Johnson's assistance, to the highest-ranking patrons in the country, including the Prince and Princess of Wales, the Prime Minister and his influential wife, and a pair of earls. Why Lennox needed Johnson's help has not been satisfactorily explained. Lennox had herself demonstrated sufficient versatility as a writer that she would have no doubt been equal to the task of writing formal dedications. Her early novels show that she had sufficient command of the polite formulas of courtly speech, and both the veiled autobiographical portraits in her novels and the anecdotes surrounding her early life suggest that she was equipped with the necessary self-confidence – and even boldness – to approach her superiors. Perhaps she was overworked, struggling to complete long works of translation, or burdened with illness. Perhaps she recognized, along with his contemporaries, that Johnson was unusually adept at writing dignified dedications.[38] Perhaps as a female author she sensed a need to draw on the superior literary authority of Johnson (well known by 1752 as "Mr. Rambler"), in the same way that she imitated Johnson's prose style and sententiousness to provide the climactic (penultimate) chapter of *The Female Quixote*, in which Arabella yields to the advice of a learned "Divine."

Another puzzle is why Lennox, so active a participant in the patronage system throughout the 1750s, should subsequently have had so little benefit from it, at the very moment when, as Johnson put it in his dedication of Brumoy's *Greek Theatre* to the future George III, a "more illustrious period of letters and of patronage" was on the horizon.[39] One possible explanation is that she was in effect caught in the political crossfire of the first years of the new reign. Bute (from whom she had received encouragement) had helped see to the removal of Newcastle (another of her patrons), and the Rockingham Whigs (to whom Lennox had connections through Charlemont and the Dowager Marchioness of Rockingham) were in the wings, waiting to take over. Perhaps, with links to several factions, she was not considered politically reliable. Having accepted patronage from the Duchess of Newcastle in 1761,

38 See below, pp. 283–85.
39 Quoted in Allen Hazen, *Johnson's Prefaces and Dedications*, 94. For discussion of the substance of the dedications Johnson wrote on behalf of Lennox, see below, pp. 258, 272.

she may in effect have forfeited any further opportunity of winning favor from Bute.[40]

In any case, it is striking to note that after 1761 Lennox in effect stood outside the patronage system. Over the next fifteen years, although her earlier works were frequently reprinted, she was to produce a good deal less new work than she had in the previous ten, and none of it carried a dedication. *The Lady's Museum*, a periodical designed for female readers, appeared from March 1760 to January 1761, when it was published bound in two volumes. A stage comedy, *The Sister*, had one performance in February 1769,[41] and was published the following month. At one point Lennox seems to have considered dedicating the work to a "great personage" – perhaps the Duchess of Newcastle again, or Lady Gower, but the work as published has no dedication.[42] A translation of the *Meditations and Penitential Prayers* of the Duchess de la Vallière appeared in 1774. And another stage comedy, *Old City Manners*, her adaptation of the Jonson–Chapman–Marston *Eastward Hoe*, was performed and published in 1775. She apparently asked permission to dedicate the play to Lady Bute, but the request was rejected.[43]

Lennox had thus not given up on the possibilities of patronage. In 1773 she engaged Sir John Hawkins and Sir Joshua Reynolds to help her bring out an illustrated subscription edition of *The Female Quixote*, but the project was abandoned.[44] In 1775 Johnson wrote for her a set of even more ambitious *Proposals*, dedicated to the queen, for a collected edition of her works. The language of the *Proposals* suggests that her motive was wholly economic. They ask not for the protection and "approbation" of the subscribers, for the works are said to have been successfully published already. But they were "of no great advantage to the writer," and the author plainly now hopes to realize some "profit." Perhaps the booksellers were unwilling to bring out a collected edition without (in effect) a subsidy or some assurance of a good sale. But the proposal for a subscription must not have attracted enough interest, for the edition never appeared. (An earlier set of proposals in 1752 to reprint her 1747 *Poems on Several Occasions* had likewise failed.) Although Lennox's

---

[40] See a 1769 letter from James Murray to Lady Gower, quoted in "The Lennox Collection," 58.

[41] Thus she did not even benefit from the traditional author's "third night."

[42] "The Lennox Collection," 58.

[43] *Ibid.*, 176–77.

[44] *Ibid.*, 168–70, 172.

name remained before the public thanks to reprintings of *The Female Quixote* and the *Memoirs of Sully*, she may have seemed in 1775 – when she was fifty-five – a writer of the last age.[45] On the other hand, she may have simply proven that the patrons of the day were not ready to support an edition of the *Works* of a female writer: no such collected works by a female writer appeared in the eighteenth century. She tried again, with a scaled-down plan. Boswell wrote a set of proposals in 1793 for a new edition of her *Shakespear Illustrated*, to be dedicated to the Duchess of York, but this time even the proposals, though printed, were not published.[46] And a contemplated subscription edition, sometime after 1793, of an "Opera" (probably an operatic version of her *Philander*) never got off the ground.[47]

Why the patronage system failed her after 1760 must perhaps remain a mystery. It cannot have helped that, in Mrs. Thrale's words, "nobody liked her."[48] Biographers have speculated what qualities in her character might have given offense, particularly to women – personal uncleanliness, aggressiveness, bad temper, vanity.[49] If this was indeed her reputation among women contemporaries, it is not surprising that she failed to find more support. In a world in which patrons expected ingratiating deference, Lennox was a strong-minded and independent young woman, as she would have had to be to make her own way as a girl from New York (or even Gibraltar) to London. She must have had enough personal charm to make her way into the inner circles of the court, and she seems to have been able to cross the usually impermeable barrier that separated the world of the patron from that of the client/author. Once admitted to the world of great ladies, and permitted more "familiarity" than writers could expect, she seems to have been a sharp-eyed observer of foibles, and perhaps sharp-tongued too – if we may judge by her earliest writings. A potential patron who, not deterred by her reputation, looked into her writings, might have

---

[45] In the final twenty-eight years of her life she published only one work, the novel *Euphemia* (1790, and not reprinted). The 1783 "Memoirs of Mrs. Lenox" suggest that the main reason was ill health: "This lady's ill state of health forbids us to expect many future productions from her elegant pen" (p. 36).

[46] "The Lennox Collection," 183 and n. For a transcript of the Harvard copy of the proposals, see *ibid.*, 421–25. See also *The Correspondence and Other Papers of James Boswell*, 461.

[47] "The Lennox Collection," 184.

[48] Fanny Burney, *Diary and Letters* (I, 86).

[49] Séjourné, *The Mystery of Charlotte Lennox*, 24–26. He also suspects jealousy of her success on the part of other women.

been troubled by its collective portrait of the polite world and the patronage system.

Her volume of *Poems on Several Occasions. Written by a Young Lady* is dedicated to Lady Finch, with the usual acknowledgment of "Obligations," "Favour and Indulgence," etc. Most of the volume consists of conventional love songs, pastorals, and light Horatian odes. But several of the poems verge on satire, and hint that she may have witnessed in her time with Lady Finch more than a little "Envy," "Deceit," and "Scandal." "Envy. A Satire" paints the throne of "Pale Envy," where those "who to Virtue, Wit, and Beauty lost; / Here strive to blast the Fame they cannot boast." The "Votaries" appeal to "Envy" for a boon:

> If by the happy Force of fraudful Lies,
> Sunk in Oblivion the bright Merit dies;
> If spotless Chastity to Shame betray'd;
> If charms, when blasted, in the blooming Maid,
> Deserve thy Smile, – the pleasing Mischief Aid. (p. 21)

One of the "Votaries" then steps forward, concealing her aims even from her associates with "Friendship's soft Disguise" (p. 22). Perhaps the poem is little more than a conventional social satire. It might be regarded as a creative imitation of Pope's Cave of Spleen.[50] But the subtext of Lennox's poems often seems to be false friendship. "The Rival Nymphs. A Tale" (pp. 7–11) hints at the perils of a court lady: envy, rivalry, the falling out of friends. "Ardelia to Flavia, an Epistle" appeals to a disaffected friend, confessing a "fatal Crime" which merits her friend's "Anger" (p. 46). Elsewhere, "In Answer to Consolatory Verses wrote by a Friend" – the title hints at some personal matter – she suggests the difficulties of being a bright girl in the fashionable world with talent but no fortune: "Virtue in Rags," even if endowed with the "Gifts" of "Nature," can't disarm "Contempt and Scorn": "By Fortune favour'd Fools may rise to Fame, / Without it Virtue is an empty Name" (p. 85).[51]

There is no evidence that Lennox's poems were read by her

---

50 Lennox often seems to have Pope in mind. Cf. "The Art of Coquettry," a poem which takes Ariel's instructions to Belinda and makes them into a kind of didactic poem: "Attend my Rules to you alone addrest,/ Deep let them sink in every female Breast,/ ... How to enslave, and keep the vanquish'd Heart,/ When the stol'n Sigh to heave, or drop the Tear,/ The melting Languish, the obliging Fear." Later lines in the poem clearly recall Pope: "Power all your Wish, but Beauty all your Arms" (*Poems*, 61), "conscious of her Face" (p. 62).

51 Cf. Pope's "Epistle to Bathurst," line 334: "Virtue! and Wealth! What are ye but a name!"

contemporaries as oblique commentaries on the world of high life to which she had been admitted. But there is clear evidence that one famous reader – Lady Mary Wortley Montagu – saw very thinly disguised depictions of real life in her next work, *The Life of Harriot Stuart.* The episode in question, located prominently at the mid-point of the two-volume novel, concerns the relationship between Harriot, a young girl with high spirit but no fortune, and Lady Cecilia, a fine lady who promises to get her a place at court. Harriot is given to writing poems – indeed, several of her poems are recycled from Lennox's 1747 volume[52] – and it is probably not unreasonable to see her as a kind of stand-in for Lennox herself.[53] A friend puts Harriot's "manuscript-poems ... into the hands of a lady of great distinction about court, remarkable for the brilliancy of her wit, and her taste for the Belles-Lettres," as well as an impressive library. Lady Cecilia herself "holds one of the first employments at court; and her generosity is so diffusive, that she is said to seek out persons, to whom her interest may be useful. I have heard [says a friend of Harriot's] of a number of people, who have an intire dependence upon her." But Harriot, so she says, did not at that time hear "the sarcastic turn of these words" (vol. i, pp. 233–34). Lady Cecilia takes her up, promising to her "the care of making your fortune; and you may depend upon the absolute promise I now give you, to procure a genteel place about the princess" (p. 239) – Lady Finch herself was at that time Lady of the Bedchamber to the princesses.

"Absolute promise" serves to warn anyone familiar with the discourse of patronage – or with Swift – that there is less here than meets the ear.[54] Lennox may be said to be dramatizing, in prose fiction, an almost archetypal scene of disillusion, in which the Patron utters a promise to the credulous Author, a promise that is soon to be forgotten. To write the scene Lennox of course need not have experienced such a promise herself, though she hints that she may have. What is significant is that Lennox develops the situation, which earlier writers had used for satiric

---

[52] Including "To Death. An Irregular Ode," "An Evening Ode," "To Flavia," "To Delia, Inviting her to a retreat in the Country," a poem beginning "Oppress'd with every anxious woe," and "On Reading Hutchinson on the Passions."

[53] Lennox later named her only daughter Harriot (b. 1765).

[54] As Gulliver explains to the Houyhnhnm master concerning offers of preferment, "The worst Mark you can receive is a Promise, especially when it is confirmed with an Oath; after which every wise Man retires, and gives over all Hopes" (*Gulliver's Travels*, "A Voyage to the Houyhnhnms," ch. 6).

purposes, into an extended sequence more characteristic of Richardson than Fielding.

Less than a decade before *Harriot Stuart*, Fielding had presented a similar situation in Book II, chapter 16 of *Joseph Andrews*. Parson Adams and Joseph meet an apparently affable and generous "gentleman" who expresses his delight in Adams, and offers him a church living worth £300 a year – upon the decease of the incumbent. Adams overflows with gratitude, and Fielding sets about exposing both the emptiness of the distant promise and the credulity of Adams. If only Adams had no children, the gentleman would make him his chaplain; if only Mrs. Adams understood a dairy, he would offer him a house, etc., etc. The final promise of fresh horses the next morning of course proves also to be empty, once again surprising the foolish Adams, still confident of the gentleman's generous intentions, but not Joseph, who tells him that "it is a maxim among the gentlemen of our cloth" – i.e., footmen – "that those masters who promise the most perform the least."

Lennox, although she exposes Lady Cecilia's hypocrisy, focuses equally on Harriot's increasing anxiety and spirited resentment. Offering in effect a rudimentary analysis of the psychological and political dynamics of patronage, she provides her promissory patron with plausible motives for taking up a client and then breaking off the relationship. Lady Cecilia evidently derives pleasure from having inferiors wholly dependent upon her, and from displaying such power before her friends. She not only shows off her protégée ("she took a pleasure introducing me to her acquaintance" – *The Life of Harriot Stuart*, vol. II, p. 3) but prevents anyone else from offering assistance. Harriot realizes that such introductions provide a client with "an opportunity of strengthening interest, by the addition of very powerful friends." But Lady Cecilia realizes this too, and resolves "no one should interpose in an affair she had taken the management of," and "prevented any solicitation for a provision from the government for me, by declaring, in all companies, she would procure me an establishment herself" (pp. 3–4). Harriot writes poems in praise of Lady Cecilia, who reads them aloud "to all her acquaintance," but, though she is ready enough to hear herself praised, ironically (says Harriot) "began to grow weary at the flattering compliments that were paid me [i.e., to the poet rather than the patron] in her presence" (p. 15). Lady Cecilia then begins to scheme to free herself from her "obligation" to provide for Harriot a "settlement at court" (p. 21). To get her out of the way, Harriot is made "companion" to her niece, and in effect removed from the drawing room to the nursery. There, Harriot attracts the attention of three different young men (one of them nominally attached to the niece and another to her mother), and falls afoul of her friends, accused of being a jilt, a prostitute, and a traitor. Harriot confesses a delight in being noticed – Lennox perhaps hints here at the pleasures of successful clienthood – and returns to Lady Cecilia, only to meet renewed accusations, which she resists with high-spirited sarcasm, and then leaves the house.

The sequence evidently bore sufficient resemblance to Lennox's own experience in the households of Lady Finch and Lady Rockingham that Lady Mary Wortley Montagu was scandalized: "I was rouz'd into great surprize and Indignation by the monstrous abuse of one of the very, very few Women I have a real value for, I mean Lady B. F. [i.e., Bell Finch] who is not only clearly meant by the mention of the Library (she being the only Lady at Court that has one), but her very name at length, she being christen'd Caecilia Isabella, tho she chuses to be call'd by the Latter."[55] From her story the sympathetic Lady Mary, expressing class solidarity, draws the harassed patron's moral that courtiers will always attract enemies: "I allwaies thought her conduct in every light so irreproachable, I did not think she had an Enemy upon Earth; I now see 'tis impossible to avoid them, especially in her Situation. It is one of the misfortunes of a suppos'd Court interest ... even the people you have oblig'd hate you if they do not think you have serv'd to the utmost extent of a power that they fancy you are possess'd of, which it may be is only imaginary." In the tight world of the Georgian court, one can imagine that word soon spread that Charlotte Lennox was not a properly grateful recipient of patronage.

Harriot draws a different moral. When, after leaving Lady Cecilia's house, she is introduced to yet another noblewoman who has been shown her poems, Harriot is dubious about the proffered admiration: "The behaviour of the countess and Lady Cecilia had taught me to fear, rather than hope for, the friendship of persons of high rank" (p. 149). If Lady Mary's reading is to be trusted, we can probably conclude that Lennox herself came to the same conclusion. In this light it is not surprising that *Harriot Stuart* was published

---

[55] March 1, 1752 letter to her daughter, the Countess of Bute. *Complete Letters of Lady Mary Wortley Montagu*, III, 8.

without a dedication, and that Lennox, although she published a number of works carrying dedications in the 1750s, never wrote another dedication herself: perhaps she accepted Johnson's offers of assistance in part because she could not bring herself to deploy the formulas of gratitude and obligation with any conviction.

Her early exposure to the risks of the patronage system may have induced her at the end of the 1750s to take up a literary project in which she in effect became her own patron. *The Lady's Museum* was introduced in 1760 with an editorial preface: "I shall usher in my pamphlet," Lennox wrote (in reference to the first number of her periodical), "with the performance of a lady, who possibly would never have suffered it to appear in print, if this opportunity had not offered" (p. 1). The opening "performance" is the introductory essay in a series to be called "The Trifler." Although Lennox received several contributions to *The Lady's Museum* from friends, the "Trifler" essays appear to have been written by Lennox herself. While it is a common device in periodical essays for an "editor" to claim to have received contributions from correspondents, Lennox may have found the device especially fitting, since it allowed her as it were to patronize herself. "The Trifler" turns out to "a woman young, single, gay, and ambitious of pleasing" (p. 3), but fearful of being considered a coquette. Lennox, as her poem on "The Art of Coquettry" suggests,[56] had long been interested in the figure of the coquette, who here becomes a figure for the aspiring writer, seeking only to please: "The desire of fame, or the desire of pleasing ... in my opinion, are synonimous terms ... The poet's inspiration, the patriot's zeal, the courtier's loyalty, and the orator's eloquence. All are coquets, if that be coquetry" (p. 3).[57] Like Harriot Stuart, the writer – and perhaps especially the female writer – takes pleasure in pleasing, and runs the risk (in a world where patrons have power) of pleasing too little or too much.

Later in *The Lady's Museum* Lennox returns to the subject of false patrons, this time in a serialized narrative entitled "The History of Harriot and Sophia." The title characters begin as minor dependents within the patronage system; they are the daughters of a gentleman with the "moderate salary of a place at court" (p. 17).[58] Sophia is the

---

56 The poem was first published in the 1747 volume, and was republished, with some slight changes, in the *Gentleman's Magazine*, 20 (1750), 518–19.

57 In her dedication of her *Poems*, Lennox had referred to them as "the following trifles."

58 Curiously, Arabella in *The Female Quixote* is also the daughter of a man who loses his place

more serious of the two sisters, devoted to reading, and (unprovided with an income) prepared to become a governess. Two men take an interest in her, providing books and some education. One, whom she considers "my dear benefactor" (p. 646), is an idealized figure of the patron. But he is a shadowy figure, far less realized than Mrs. Howard, another detailed portrait of the self-interested and finally treacherous patron. Mrs. Howard is "a widow lady of a very affluent fortune, who had established such a character for generosity and goodness, that [Sophia] hoped that if she could be induced to take Sophia under her protection her fortune would be made" (pp. 650–51). For her part Mrs. Howard claims to see Sophia as an opportunity for doing good: "You have obliged me infinitely by putting it in my power to gratify the unbounded benevolence of my heart upon a deserving object" (p. 651). But her initial words give her away: patronage (as Lennox sees it) is commonly an occasion for exercising power and gratifying one's own appetites.

Lennox goes on to provide an analysis of the patron's complex motives, making clear that patronage in practice was sometimes far from disinterested benevolence. Indeed, patrons found their own "advantage." Initially the focus remains on one particular patron:

Mrs. Howard indeed always prevented those on whom she conferred favours from incurring the guilt of ingratitude; for she took care to be fully repaid for any act of benevolence; and having a wonderful art in extracting advantage to herself from the necessities of others, she sometimes sought out the unfortunate with a solicitude that did great honour to her charity, which was sure to be its own reward. A few ostentatious benefactions had sufficiently established her character. (p. 652)

Lennox's thumb is on the scale: not only is Mrs. Howard a bad patron, determined to extract full "credit" for her benefactions, but she violates the old expectations of hospitality (like the misers in Pope who fail to stock a good kitchen and table) and racks her tenants.

She is given prominence in the narrative not because she is essential to the plot, but because Lennox wants to use her to make a more general point. From Mrs. Howard Lennox turns, in Rambler-like reflections, to what she calls "the vanity of giving":

Nothing is more certain than what is called liberality is often no more than the vanity of giving, of which some persons are fonder than of what they

at court. Did Lennox, who encouraged the story that she was the daughter of a colonial governor, somehow think that she was *entitled* to some preferment? *Euphemia*, her last novel, also begins with the heroine's loss of her inheritance.

give. But the vanity of giving publicly is most prevailing; and hence it happens, that those who are most celebrated for their charity are in reality least sensible to the feelings of humanity: and the same persons from whom the most affecting representation of private distress could not force the least relief, have been among the first to send their contributions to any new foundation. (p. 653)

Like Lady Cecilia, Mrs. Howard enjoys playing the role of patron. But Lennox's analysis of her is pushed further. Lady Cecilia evades the performance of her promises. Mrs. Howard makes "ostentatious benefactions" with no real regard for the persons whose distresses she is relieving.[59] She maximizes her reputation for liberality by a minimum of outlay, wishing to help Sophia "as far as she could, consistent with her prudent maxims, which were to make other persons the source of those benefits, the merit of which she arrogated to herself" (p. 653). The "prudent maxims," as Lennox probably knew, are in fact those of Machiavelli, who advises the prince to gain a reputation for "liberality" by giving away other people's money.[60]

Lennox exposes the degeneration of patronage, in the hands of "some persons," into self-interested calculation in which the benefactor takes "care to be repaid for any act of benevolence." But the generality of the reflections suggests that Lennox also sensed that patronage, even in Senecan tradition, is always an *exchange* of benefits. It only requires a slight shift of emphasis to transform *beneficiae* into profitable investments.

But, like the typical subjects of Johnson's moral analysis, Mrs. Howard turns out to be less a hypocrite than self-deceived: "that lady had been so used to disguise herself to others, that at last she did not know herself; and the warmth and vehemence with which she delivered her sentiments imposed as much upon herself as her hearers" (p. 653). By comparison with the imperious Lady Cecilia, Mrs. Howard is a bundle of confused motives – vanity, prudence, and sentiment. But from this moment of Johnsonian empathy Lennox again pulls back. When her son falls in love with Sophia, Mrs. Howard is enraged and (like Lady Cecilia) tries to destroy Sophia's reputation.

After a series of romantic adventures Sophia is at last rewarded with a rich husband, Sir Charles Stanley, who had much earlier

---

[59] She has something in common with Pope's Narcissa, who "Gave alms at Easter, in a Christian trim,/ And made a Widow happy, for a whim" ("Epistle to a Lady," lines 57–58).

[60] See above, pp. 36–37.

made her a gift of books. Now he again acts in effect as her patron on her behalf and in her name: "He took upon himself the care of rewarding her friends; he presented Mr. Lawson to a very considerable living: he procured Dolly's husband a genteel and lucrative employment; and married her younger sister to a relation of his own" (p. 826). Sophia herself tastes "the good fortune which heaven had bestowed upon her" and in effect becomes a patron herself: "her chief enjoyment of [her fortune] was to share it with others, and Sir Charles, who adored her, put it amply in her power to indulge the benevolence of her disposition" (p. 825). Although the language unnervingly recalls Mrs. Howard (who delights to "gratify the unbounded benevolence of my heart"), it gratifies a notable fantasy, one shared by Swift and by Richard Savage before her: the patronized (and victimized) client becomes the ideal patron.

Lennox's narrative was published separately in 1762 as *Sophia*. It carried no dedication; nor did any of Lennox's subsequent works. Paradoxically, although she could not secure the patronage of her works, she was able to gain some financial assistance to maintain herself and her family. Someone – perhaps the Duke or Duchess of Newcastle – arranged for her to have "apartments" in Somerset House from 1768 to 1773, until she was evicted when the building was remodeled.[61] In her last years she was given small grants of money not by her old aristocratic patrons but by the Literary Fund, established in 1790 by a group of middle-class London professional men. The Fund was a modestly endowed literary society: it charged its subscribers one guinea a year, and made small grants to needy writers. Lennox received some assistance virtually every year from 1792 until her death in 1804.[62] Lady Frances Chambers (wife of the judge for whom Johnson wrote law lectures), who helped bring Lennox to the attention of the Literary Fund (Small, *Charlotte Ramsay Lennox*, p. 57), apparently provided her lodging in her final years, not as a benefaction and encouragement to a promising writer but in effect as charity to a broken veteran of the literary wars who was old and ill and "in great distress for the common necessaries of life." Her burial expenses were reportedly borne by George Rose, who had

---

[61]   See J. W. Croker's 1848 edition of Boswell's *Life of Johnson*, 83. Somerset House, which belonged to the queen, has been described as (in those days) "a sort of aristocratic almshouse" ("The Lennox Collection," 60n).

[62]   For details, see Small, *Charlotte Ramsay Lennox*, 57–58. Even the Royal Literary Fund was interested in, and perhaps moved by, the story that Lennox was "daughter of Colonel Ramsay, Royalist Governor of New York," for that is how she was listed in their records.

earlier sponsored her application to the Literary Fund. Rose, one of Pitt's senior ministers, was a wealthy man with literary interests and some reputation for benevolence, a new-style patron not from the aristocracy but from the wealthy middle class.[63] It was a bleak end for a writer who had begun more than half a century earlier as a fashionable poet with good connections at court. If we were to judge the patronage system solely by the way it treated Charlotte Lennox, we would have to conclude that it performed poorly even at mid-century, and was simply not in place at the century's end, when she was the beneficiary of a much more modest system of charitable relief.

[63] Rose, who wrote some political and economic tracts, is said to have had "considerable literary pretensions" (*Gentleman's Magazine*, 88 [Jan. 1818], 1, 82). He was named a trustee of the British Museum in the year in which Lennox died. In an obituary notice the *GM* observed that "the lists of subscribers to the patriotic and charitable institutions of the county [of Hampshire] are the best proofs of his benevolence" (*GM*, 88 [July 1818]), 11, 93). Small, *Charlotte Ramsay Lennox*, 62 notes that Lennox may have been introduced to Rose by the printer William Strahan, Alexander Lennox's one-time employer.

CHAPTER 9

Samuel Johnson

Standard accounts of the rise of modern authorship love to dwell on
Johnson's famous letter to Chesterfield, and have (from Carlyle
onward[1]) assumed that this incident in 1755 may stand as a symbol of
the proud Johnson's determination to reject the patronage system
and make his way by his wit. The traditional view survives in Alvin
Kernan's remark that the letter is "the Magna Carta of the modern
author."[2] But the significance of the incident in Johnson's own life is
still misunderstood, despite some careful reconstruction and analysis
twenty years ago by Jacob Leed and Paul Korshin.[3] They make it
clear that Johnson in the famous letter was not so much coldly
declining an offer from a would-be patron as complaining that,
having agreed to serve – at Johnson's request – as patron, Chesterfield had not lived up to his part of the bargain.[4] This argument
seems not to have compelled assent or even much attention, and
most observers dismiss the topic of "Johnson on patronage" with a
ready allusion to the famous definition of patron in the *Dictionary* –
"Commonly a wretch who supports with insolence, and is paid with
flattery," to the equally famous line in *The Vanity of Human Wishes*
(revised after the 1755 Chesterfield incident) about the miseries of
authorship, "Toil, envy, want, the patron, and the jail," and to
Johnson's apparently dismissive remark to Boswell: "We have done
with patronage" (*Life of Johnson*, vol. v, p. 59).

But the letter to Chesterfield and these displays of witty severity do

---

[1] See Carlyle's review of Croker's 1831 edition of Boswell's *Life of Johnson*, in *Fraser's Magazine*, 5 (1832), 396–98.

[2] *Printing Technology, Letters, and Samuel Johnson*, 105.

[3] See Jacob Leed, "Johnson and Chesterfield," 1677–90, and "Johnson, Chesterfield, and Patronage," 2011–15; and Paul Korshin, "The Johnson–Chesterfield Relationship," 247–59, and "Johnson and Literary Patronage," 1804–11.

[4] Leed argues that the letter is "a reproach to an avowed and accepted patron," and not a "complaint that no patronage was ever offered." See "Johnson and Chesterfield," 1684.

not by any means tell the whole story of Johnson's complicated relationship with and attitude toward the patronage system. It is true that Johnson took pride in the thought that "no man ... who ever lived by literature, has lived more independently that I have done,"[5] and that he considered the booksellers, who more than once served in effect as underwriters of his literary efforts, to be the real "patrons of literature."[6] But Johnson was also a participant in the traditional patronage system. While still in Lichfield the young Johnson was given encouragement, lodging, introductions to "the best company," recommendation letters, and perhaps his appointment at Stourbridge Grammar School through the offices of Cornelius Ford and Gilbert Walmesley, who in effect functioned as his first patrons.[7] He sought direct private patronage (from Chesterfield – he only received £10 and several compliments in *The World*), published three works by subscription, was offered a church living,[8] enjoyed a pension from His Majesty for more than twenty years (as one of several "Writers Political"), and wrote at least twenty dedications for other writers.[9]

My immediate concern is not with Johnson's career as a dependent or client, or with his career *as* a patron (which has received attention)[10] but with his attitude toward the form of patronage which attracted the most notoriety in both his day and in later generations – the direct support of struggling writers by the titled and wealthy. And to determine Johnson's response we need to consider a wide range of evidence – not just the Chesterfield episode and not just the *Life of Savage* (1744) with its sympathetic account of the miseries of dependence. The full record shows that Johnson was much less critical of the private patron than we have heard, that his attitudes changed significantly from the 1740s to the late 1770s, that his understanding of patronage as a cultural practice in the early eighteenth century was subtle but limited, and that his deepest interest is not in the economic or political dimension of patronage, but in the

---

[5] Boswell, *Life of Johnson*, 1, 443.

[6] *Ibid.*, 305. Cf. "Doddy [Robert Dodsley the bookseller], you know, is my patron" (1, 326).

[7] See James Clifford, *Young Sam Johnson*, 87, 159–64; and W. J. Bate, *Samuel Johnson* 45–58, 78–86. See also Boswell, *Life of Johnson*, 1, 81, 102. Hawkins refers to "the patronage of Mr. Walmesley" (*Life of Samuel Johnson*, 36). Johnson praised Walmesley in terms usually reserved for patrons: "he was one of the first *friends* that literature procured me, and I hope that, at least, my *gratitude* made me worthy of his *notice*" (Boswell, *Life of Johnson*, 1, 81, my emphasis).

[8] By the father of Bennet Langton about 1757–58 (Boswell, *Life of Johnson*, 1, 320).

[9] See below, pp. 272–75, 283–85.

[10] See above, pp. 205–06.

moral aspects – the ways that the client writer exposes his own pride or his vain hopes of comfort and preferment. Finally, it will put in new light some of Johnson's notoriously "hostile" remarks about the greatest of his immediate literary predecessors – Dryden, Swift, and Pope.

Reconsidering Johnson's *Lives of the Poets* also provides apt reminders that the patronage system encompassed not only the leading poets of the Restoration and early eighteenth century but other major figures as well – Thomson, Gay, and even such small fry as Elijah Fenton. Furthermore, Johnson's attitude toward the patronage system is an important index of the climate of opinion during the mid- and late-eighteenth century. Johnson himself lived through most of the massive cultural transition in early modern England in which a commercial nation gradually emerged alongside an aristocratic culture of rank and privilege. That an "independent" writer could regard patrons and patronage even-handedly, and that Johnson became more implicated in the system as the century wore on, not more but less critical of it, suggests that we need to revise our idea of the rise of the professional author. Even for Johnson, pride in one's "independence as a literary man" was in no way inconsistent with "reverence for rank and respect for wealth" (*Life of Johnson*, vol. I, p. 443).

PATRONAGE IN *THE RAMBLER*

By Jacob Leed's count forty-two of the *Rambler* essays (roughly 20 percent) "in some sense" touch on the subject of patronage.[11] Although he acknowledges that Johnson's attitude in the *Rambler* is "by no means uniformly adverse," his thesis is that Johnson delivers "serious warnings" about the "dangers" of patronage ("Patronage in the Rambler," p. 7). Johnson is indeed eloquent on the difficulties of solicitation, the corrupting effects of flattery (on both parties), and the "drudgeries of dependence" (*Rambler* 104). However, it is worth underlining Leed's point that Johnson warns not against the patronage system as a whole but against its perversions and its "particular dangers." Only five years later, in the *Dictionary*, Johnson was to define an (ideal) patron as "One who countenances, supports, protects" – to which he added the more often cited satiric reflection.

[11] "Patronage in the Rambler." But only some eight essays discuss the subject at any length.

It is the false patron Johnson has in mind in *Rambler* 105: "For what ... is the end of patronage but the pleasure of reading dedications, holding multitudes in suspense, and enjoying their hopes, their fears, and their anxiety, flattering them to assiduity, and, at last, dismissing them for impatience?"[12] But not all dedications are "adulatory and servile." In *Rambler* 136 men of merit have a "right" to our "honor" and "respect." It is appropriate for an author to dedicate his work in "hope" of future "benefit" as well as "gratitude" for past favors. What is more, the dedication (so long as it is directed toward men of "merit") is one of the writer's means of teaching: "To encourage merit with praise is the great business of literature." Johnson even goes so far as to say that the writer has a *responsibility* to praise well, preserving the "distinction" between good and evil so as to maintain the "force of praise." If the value of praise is kept up – if praise does not become "cheap," evil men will remain in fear of infamy. And touching on a favorite theme, Johnson notes that by praising well the writer makes proper use of the abilities and powers with which he has been entrusted.

Even when lamenting the "vexations of dependence" and the "shackles of patronage" (*Rambler* 163) and affirming the dignity of the independent writer (*Rambler* 208), Johnson is not so much attacking the patron as reminding the writer of his responsibilities. 163 denounces the "cruelties exercised by wealth and power," but its real concern is to warn the writer against the vain hope of reward from promising patrons. Writers tempted by such promises are, like Tantalus, to be punished for their servility. The point of 208, which closes the *Rambler* series, is not to attack the patronage system, despite the ringing claim that, "having laboured to maintain the dignity of virtue," Johnson will not "degrade it by the meanness of a dedication." Rather it is to insist on the writer's responsibility. A patron might have provided "protection," or have enabled the writer insolently to "overbear" the "censures of criticism." Johnson insists that as a writer he himself must do without such "protection": "I must remain accountable for all my faults." We should not conclude from Johnson's epigrammatic wit that all dedications spring from meanness, but rather that evasions of moral responsibility are evidence of meanness.

To qualify Leed's argument is not to assert that Johnson in the

---

[12] Compare the famous words to Chesterfield: "Is not a Patron ... one who looks with unconcern," etc. See Boswell, *Life of Johnson*, I, 262.

Rambler is a *defender* of the patronage system. Patronage in these essays of the early 1750s is treacherous but it is not an institution beyond redemption. Though easily corrupted and often corrupt, it has a proper place. Johnson's real concern is not with patrons but with young writers, whose vain hopes need to be suppressed.[13] Furthermore, as a young writer himself, Johnson probably shares those hopes, and writes out of the very uncertainties and dependencies that he warns against in the essays. Later in his career he would provide a more balanced – and detached – view of the patronage system.[14]

PATRONAGE IN THE *LIVES OF THE POETS*

It has been occasionally noted in passing that in his later years Johnson was no outspoken critic of the patronage system. Both Leed and Korshin remark that in the *Lives of the Poets* Johnson's comments on patronage are not "adverse," but "mild and uncritical ... noncommittal and neutral."[15] It is perhaps somewhat surprising that nobody has thought it necessary to say more. My claim is that it is in the *Lives of the Poets* that Johnson provides his most sustained discussions of the topic of literary patronage. Although he does not set down a systematic theory, we can go beyond characterizing his remarks in negative terms – "no adverse comment," "uncritical," "noncommittal" – to see that they can be assembled into a coherent view of a practice that was not only necessary but could ideally be a system of what in Senecan fashion he called "reciprocal benefits." And a full account of Johnson's mature thoughts on patronage must attend not only to the famous discussions of Dryden, Swift, and Pope and their traffic with the great, but to the minor lives as well – of writers such as Edmund Smith and Isaac Watts and of patrons such as Halifax, Granville, and Lyttelton.

To begin with, Johnson acknowledges that the writer is typically a dependent, that he will naturally seek encouragement from his friends and support from those who can provide it. Such a situation is not deplored, but simply accepted as a given. Elijah Fenton, for example, though born "of an ancient family," was the "youngest of

---

13   When he does consider the patron's point of view, Johnson finds that patrons might refuse support because of "honest indignation" (*Works*, IV, 357).

14   While the *Rambler* focuses on the pressing duties of the present-day reader, the *Lives of the Poets* focuses on the completed lives of writers and patrons who lived and died in earlier generations.

15   *SBHT*, 13 (1971–72), 2012; *ECS*, 7 (1974), 471 and n.

twelve children," and therefore "necessarily destined to some lucrative employment" (vol. II, p. 257) – Johnson puns on "destined to" (which can mean both "intended or designed for" and "predetermined by unalterable decree"). Human intentions are superseded by a larger force: the young man was in fact "destined" to become nothing more than an impoverished poet. Having spent some time at Cambridge without taking a degree, and refusing to take the oath of allegiance to King William, Fenton was "excluded from the regular modes of profit and prosperity, and reduced to pick up a livelihood uncertain and fortuitous." He passed his life honorably, but "in penury." His career is typical: secretary to the Earl of Orrery, then tutor to the earl's young son, then a schoolmaster. He wrote in praise of Queen Anne and of the Duke of Marlborough, and was noticed. Bolingbroke offered "promises of a more honourable employment," but in fact nothing ever came from them, or from the queen and duke. He was befriended by other wits, among them Pope, who helped by hiring Fenton (to translate for him) and by recommending him to Craggs (just named Secretary of State) as a sort of private tutor. Here would have been a safe harbor, "a prospect of ease and plenty" (p. 259). But Craggs soon died of the smallpox. Still, Fenton found another friend. Pope, acting in effect as a patron, again recommended Fenton, this time to the widow of his old friend Sir William Trumbull, as a tutor for her son. Fenton's last years were thus "calm and pleasant" (p. 262). His duties did not prevent him from continuing his literary efforts or mixing, in the metropolis, with his literary friends. Throughout his brief account Johnson presents Fenton's progress without reflecting on the miseries of the learned or the injustice of unrewarded merit. Fenton was in no way degraded by his dependence, and he apparently discharged his responsibilities honorably. On the whole he fared well, supported by his friends and rewarded by a comfortable position in an aristocrat's household.

James Thomson, who won greater fame, made a similar progress through the patronage system that by and large served him well. One of the nine children of a Scots clergyman, while still a schoolboy he won a "patron" who helped supervise his education and planned for him a career in the church. Thomson had other ideas, and, determining to be a poet, set off "to seek in London patronage and fame" (vol. III, p. 283). His expectations are amusingly naive – that in a great city he will escape "petty competition and private malignity," and that "merit" will quickly become "conspicuous."

But in fact within a year he does gain the "notice" of Aaron Hill. The dedication of *Winter* (1726) to Sir Spencer Compton then produces (after a little prompting from Hill)[16] a gift of twenty guineas – and Thomson is launched. *Summer* is dedicated to Bubb Dodington, "who had power to advance the reputation and fortune of a poet," and *Spring* to the Countess of Hertford, who invited "every summer some poet into the country" (p. 287).[17] Thomson makes "friends" who recommend him to their friends, and get him appointed to hold a minor public office in the gift of the Lord Chancellor and to accompany the Lord Chancellor's son on the grand tour. His patron dies, but is succeeded by another, Lord Lyttelton, who recommends him to the Prince of Wales (who provides a pension of £100 a year), and later (after Lyttelton joined the ministry) "conferred upon him the office of surveyor-general of the Leeward Islands" (p. 293). Remaining in England (of course), and assigning the work to his deputy, Thomson clears £300 a year.

Although Johnson's summary is laced with irony – Thomson's "ease and plenty" lead him not to prosecute his labors but to "suspend" his poetry; the Prince of Wales, "struggling for popularity," with some calculation "professed himself the patron of wit"; the lazy Thomson, having taken the pension, is "now obliged to write" – it does not in any way indict the system of patronage that provided comfortably for a man like Thomson and rewarded his genius with recognition and moderate riches. Thomson's story (like Fenton's) happens to be a story of success, and thus perhaps does not provide an occasion for Johnson to condemn the cruelty of patrons and the indignity of the system. But their stories need to be set against those better-known stories of Savage and Dryden in order for us to arrive at Johnson's assessment of patronage as a whole.

In a number of respects Johnson implicitly endorses the system as an appropriate means of providing support to needy writers. He understands that dependence is the normal situation for a writer, even for a writer as well known and able as Swift. The only writer of the fifty-two in the *Lives of the Poets* who is in any sense "independent" is Pope, and Johnson emphasizes the considerable support that Pope enjoyed from his titled friends. It is foolish pride (or worse) for a writer not to pay court to a potential patron. Edmund Smith "by

16   About the same time Hill "promoted" the subscription to Savage's *Miscellany*. See Johnson's account of his "generosity" in the *Life of Savage*.
17   She also helped Savage. See above, pp. 172–73.

pride, or caprice, or indolence, or bashfulness, neglected to attend [Halifax] ... and at last missed his reward by not going to solicit it" (vol. II, pp. 15–16). Thomson's "bashfulness, or pride, or some other motive perhaps not more laudable, withheld him from soliciting [a place from Lord Hardwicke]; and the new Chancellor would not give him what he would not ask" (vol. III, p. 290). William King is "again placed in a profitable employment, and again threw the benefit away" (vol. II, p. 30). It is by no means degrading for a poet to accept a sinecure, as Congreve (Commissioner for Licensing Coaches, and places in the Post Office and Customs Office) and Thomson do. It is fully expected (and meets with Johnson's implicit approval) that "friends" will seek to help "friends." So too a new government will want to reward its "friends." When the Hanoverians take over in 1714, Granville loses the "favours" he had won from Queen Anne and her government, but Garth's "merits" are "acknowledged and rewarded" (vol. II, p. 61) and Rowe "at the accession of King George ... [is] made poet laureat" (vol. II, p. 72). There are exceptions, as in the case of Ambrose Philips, which Johnson uses to reflect on the folly of great expectations: "When upon the succession of the House of Hanover every Whig expected to be happy, Philips seems to have obtained too little notice: he caught few drops of the golden shower, though he did not omit what flattery could perform" (vol. III, p. 321).

Individual patrons are on the whole presented rather favorably in the *Lives*. Dorset is the "universal patron" (vol. II, p. 42), "celebrated for patronage of genius" (p. 181), "a man whose elegance and judgement were universally confessed, and whose bounty to the learned and witty was generally known" (vol. I, p. 306). In other words, Dorset was both a good judge and a generous supporter of literature; he deserved his fame as the Maecenas of the age. Halifax, patronized by Dorset, became himself "the general patron" (vol. II, p. 15), and scattered his bounty on "almost all" the poets of his day, and let no dedication go "unrewarded" (p. 47). He was widely praised (by poets whom he patronized) and Johnson takes the trouble to dissent from Swift's "slight censure" and Pope's "acrimonious contempt" (p. 46). Nor does Johnson withhold from Halifax "the right of being a judge." He seems not to agree with Pope that Halifax was "rather a pretender to taste than really possessed of it" (vol. III, p. 126). In reporting the famous story of Pope's puzzlement at Halifax's "loose and general observations" on the *Iliad*, Johnson allows Pope his laugh but will not allow that his "scorn and hatred" (p. 128) are just. Halifax makes "voluntary offers" of support, but Pope responds with "frigid gratitude." Halifax hopes for praise and Pope for money, but the relationship is broken off "because Pope was less eager of money than Halifax of praise" (pp. 127–28). Johnson concedes that Halifax probably felt no "personal benevolence" toward Pope, but neither in this nor in any other respect does he suggest that the patron was acting improperly.[18] Of other patrons, Johnson gives generally favorable (if brief) representations of Somers, Lyttelton, and the Duke and Duchess of Queensberry (Gay's patrons). Like Dorset and Halifax, they are not guilty of pride or cruelty, and treat their dependents neither as slaves nor spaniels.

Even some of the patrons of Richard Savage emerge from Johnson's early *Life* (1744) – written when he was young and bitter about his own dependence – as rather more sinned against than sinning. Steele was a well-meaning "Benefactor" who proposed to set up Savage "In some settled Scheme of Life," and paid him an "Allowance." But Steele "had many Follies" – not vices, but follies, – and was "seldom able to keep his Promises, or execute his own Intentions." When Savage ridiculed him, Steele withdrew the allowance. Johnson does not find this unreasonable: "who is there that can patiently bear Contempt from one whom he has relieved and supported, whose Establishment he has laboured, and whose Interest he has promoted?"[19] After a quarrel, Lord Tyrconnel banishes Savage and withdraws his patronage, but Johnson treats the matter with even-handed justice: "it was undoubtedly the Consequence of accumulated Provocations on both Sides" (pp. 65–66). Savage's friends in Bristol raise money for him, but understandably lose interest: "as Merchants, and by Consequence sufficiently studious of Profit, [they] cannot be supposed to have look'd with much Compassion upon Negligence and Extravagance" (pp. 120–21). Johnson's kindest words are reserved for those of Savage's patrons who do not belong to the traditional patronage class – actors like Wilks and Mrs. Oldfield, or Dagg his Newgate jailer, who "supported" Savage "at his own Table without any certainty of Recompense" (p. 126). Those patrons with power and hereditary wealth are dismissed by Johnson with some coldness, the queen, whose generosity was "avaricious"

---

[18] See above, pp. 134–35.   [19] *Life of Savage*, 15–16.

(p. 79), Walpole, who broke his promise to Savage "without Regret" (p. 109).[20]

Johnson is indeed careful to note that not all patrons deserve the honor and respect heaped upon them by clients and historians. The Duchess of Monmouth was "remarkable for inflexible perseverance in her demand to be treated as a princess" (*Lives of the Poets*, vol. II, p. 268). Some are merely proud (without even pretending to be kind). The Duchess of Marlborough was "a woman without skill or pretensions to skill in poetry or literature" (vol. II, p. 89). It was just as well that neither she nor her husband "desired the praise, or liked the cost of patronage" (p. 259). The Countess of Suffolk remained deaf to all pleas on behalf of Gay: "solicitations, verses, and flatteries were thrown away; the lady heard them, and did nothing" (vol. II, p. 275). King William's reputation as a patron was misleading. He cared little for poetry himself, but his ministers did. They "pleased themselves with the praise of patronage" (vol. II, p. 298), and thus William "procured without intention a very liberal patronage to poetry" (p. 85). The villain in Johnson's account is perhaps the Earl of Oxford, who (like several of William's ministers) "desired to be thought a favourer of literature," and becomes representative of the patron who takes and promises but does not give.[21] He admitted Swift "to familiarity," but there is doubt that he took Swift into his "confidence" (vol. III, p. 15). Likewise, he admitted Parnell "as a favourite companion to his convivial hours, but, as it seems often to have happened in those times to the favourites of the great, without attention to his fortune" (vol. II, pp. 50–51). He encouraged Rowe to study Spanish, but then (when Rowe did so) insultingly "dismissed him with this congratulation, 'Then, Sir, I envy you the pleasure of reading *Don Quixote* in the original'" (vol. II, p. 71). Despite his access to the king, he "never proposed a pension" for his friend Pope (vol. III, p. 118).[22] Oxford is the one figure in the *Lives of the Poets* who matches the cruel imperiousness of Aurantius in *Rambler* 163. For the most part the lordly patrons of English letters deserve praise both for

---

[20] Johnson does not offer direct criticism of the king or the Prince of Wales. He implies, in the traditional complaint, that Savage's "Prospects" of help from them were "intercepted" (*ibid.*, 109).

[21] Lyttelton, otherwise generous, pays for James Moore's "apologetic poem" with "kind words, which, as is common, raised great hopes, that at last were disappointed" (*Lives of the Poets*, III, 448).

[22] He "lamented" that Pope's genius should be "wasted" on translation, "but proposed no means by which he might live without it" (*ibid.*, 110).

their judgment and their bounty. Granville, "illustrious by his birth ... elegant in his manners," deserving "reverence for his beneficence" (vol. II, p. 294), is the more typical patron in Johnson's *Lives of the Poets*.

PATRONAGE AND SUBORDINATION

The relation of the aristocratic patron and the dedicating client in the literary system, as Johnson represents it, is an aspect of that broader system of "subordination" which for Johnson was the foundation of the social and political order and the guarantor of security and happiness. The role of the dedicating poet, by the same token, is not simply one of servile flattery. To be sure, Johnson defines "dedicator" in the *Dictionary* as "One who inscribes his work to a patron with compliment and servility," and he speaks with obvious distaste of one of Addison's dedications ("an instance of servile absurdity," *Lives of the Poets*, vol. II, p. 89), of Thomson's "servile adulation" of Hill (vol. III, p. 284), and of Dryden's "meanness and servility" (vol. I, p. 399). In all of Savage's dedications the "Compliments are constrained and violent, heaped together without the Grace of Order, or the Decency of Introduction: he seems ... to have imagined ... that Flattery would make it's Way to the Heart, without the Assistance of Elegance or Invention" (*Life of Savage*, pp. 29–30).

But dedications in themselves are not corrupt. Johnson's remark implies that in a properly written dedication compliments would be graceful, decent, and elegant, and in a dedication properly directed, compliments would be deserved. Flattery of fortune's favorites is self-degrading: "He that has flattery ready for all whom the vicissitudes of the world happen to exalt must be scorned as a prostituted mind that may retain the glitter of wit, but has lost the dignity of virtue" (*Lives of the Poets*, vol. I, p. 271).[23] But as Johnson notes when he takes the time to consider the matter carefully, even when they are not wholly deserved, compliments are not necessarily hypocritical flattery. Dedicators are not likely to fool anybody. "The known style of a dedication is flattery: it professes to flatter"[24] – the emphasis here belongs on *known* and *professes*. Readers know how to interpret a

---

[23] Cf. *Rambler* 104: "There is no character so deformed as to fright away from it the prostitutes of praise" (*Works*, IV, 193).

[24] Boswell, *Journal of a Tour to the Hebrides*, in *Life of Johnson*, V, 59.

dedication. One does not expect complete "veracity" from "a poet professedly encomiastick". And Johnson does not "accuse" Prior of "flattery" in a poem praising William III so extravagantly that he "exhaust[s] all his powers of celebration." For Prior "probably thought all that he writ" (vol. II, p. 185).

The "Life of Halifax" concludes with a characteristically Johnsonian reflection on accusations of flattery: "To charge all unmerited praise with the guilt of flattery, and to suppose that the encomiast always knows and feels the falsehood of his assertions, is surely to discover great ignorance of human nature and human life. In determinations [such as determining the merit of a patron] depending not on rules, but on experience and comparison, judgement is always in some degree subject to affection. Very near to admiration is the wish to admire" (vol. II, p. 47). One can understand, Johnson goes on, why patrons like Halifax are often praised – unjustly – for their poetry. If we admire the "understanding" of a friend, "we admire more in a patron that judgement which, instead of scattering bounty indiscriminately, directed it to us; and, if the patron be an author, those performances which gratitude forbids us to blame, affection will easily dispose us to exalt."[25] If we understood human nature better, Johnson in effect says, we would be less hasty to blame a dedicator when gratitude and interest, together with the respect due to rank, combine to produce expressions of encomiastic praise.

"The great system of subordination" – "very necessary for society," and tending "greatly to human happiness" – is of course based on inequality, and the operative inequalities are not those of "merit" but of rank and wealth. "A man is born to hereditary rank; or his being appointed to certain offices, gives him a certain rank" (*Life of Johnson*, vol. I, p. 442). With rank and wealth come certain privileges and the power of serving as governors and judges of their inferiors. As it happens, Johnson also thought that those with high "rank" tended to be "better": "the higher in rank, the richer ladies are, they are the better instructed and the more virtuous" (*Life of Johnson*, vol. III, p. 354). Or – like the Earl of Chesterfield (whose morals were questionable) – they were more likely to have "elegant" manners and to be proper judges of literary merit. Johnson in his later years spoke of Chesterfield with respect – "His manner was exquisitely elegant, and he had more knowledge than I expected."

---

25   *Lives of the Poets*, II, 47. By the same token, it is understandable, and harmless, that Granville is praised for genius (*ibid.*, 293–94).

Writers occupied their own lower rank, and in general Johnson
expected them to yield to the superior judgment of a titled patron.
True, Johnson insisted proudly that, on matters of "philology and
literature," he himself had "the best right to superiority" in conversation with Chesterfield,[26] but we should hesitate to generalize
from this instance in characterizing Johnson's attitude toward
patronage.

If a writer owed deference to those of higher rank, his genius
enabled him to mix with them. Savage, because of "the Reputation
of his Abilities, the particular Circumstances of his Birth and Life,
the splendour of his Appearance, and the Distinction which was for
some time paid to him by Lord *Tyrconnel* [his patron]", was "intitled"
to "Familiarity with Persons of higher Rank, than those to whose
Conversation he had been before admitted" (*Life of Savage*, pp. 63–
64). The textual form of this crossing of class lines is the "letter to a
noble lord" – Johnson offered high praise to several examples of the
form, which remained in use through the eighteenth century.[27] To
address a lord does not oblige a poet to sink into obsequiousness. It
may encourage him to rise to elegance (as with Addison's "Letter to
Lord Halifax")[28] or even a corresponding *nobility* – Ambrose Philips'
letter to Dorset is "the production of a man 'who could write very
nobly'."[29] But it was also important that writers maintain their *own*
"dignity" – their "rank" – and not simply comply with the wishes of
the great: "Nothing has so much degraded literature from its natural
rank, [emphasis added] as the practice of indecent and promiscuous
dedication" (*Works*, vol. v, p. 356). By dedications crammed with
"abject adulation" Dryden permitted the "degradation of the dignity
of genius" (*Lives of the Poets*, i, p. 398). "Degradation" is here both a
moral and a political category. To degrade is to "diminish the value
of" but also "to deprive one of an office, dignity, or title."[30] The
writer's power is in bestowing "the honours of a lasting name and
the veneration of distant ages," and he thus serves as a check on "the
active and ambitious." It is the "authority" of the writer – whose

---

26 *Life of Johnson*, IV, 332–33.
27 Robert Folkenflik notes its persistence up through Burke's "Letter to a Noble Lord" in
    1790. "Patronage and the Poet-Hero," 367–68.
28 Better known as the "Letter from Italy," it is "justly considered as the most elegant, if not
    the most sublime, of his poetical productions" (*Lives of the Poets*, II, 86; cf. *ibid.*, 128).
29 Johnson is seconding Pope's "high praise" of Philips' "Poetical Letter from Copenhagen"
    to the Duke of Dorset (III, 31).
30 *Dictionary*.

praise confers fame or infamy – "by which greatness is controlled" (*Works*, vol. v, p. 355).

In such a socio-political system it follows that patrons should occupy positions of authority – not absolute but limited authority – in the literary world, even in the mind of someone who was proud of having fought his way by his wit. While Johnson did not cede the exclusive right to judge and reward literary merit to aristocratic patrons, and while he seems pleased to see the power of the booksellers increase to the point that they had become "the patrons of literature," we should not conclude that he challenged the "rights" of the traditional class of literary patrons. (In the related area of lay-patronage in the church, Johnson firmly defended the traditional right of patrons to name the ministers of the churches in the local parish. Although Johnson's primary argument is that the "right" of patronage was "dearly purchased by the first possessors, and justly inherited by those that succeeded them," he also assumes that the patron will be an "acknowledged superior" and the best – perhaps the only – judge of learning in the parish.[31])

Johnson's remarks on the writer's power to confer fame serve as a reminder that the patronage system, when properly managed, is not simply a means whereby the rich and highborn can dominate their inferiors. Just as the "great system of subordination" provides for "a reciprocal pleasure in governing and being governed" (*Life of Johnson*, vol. I, p. 408), so the patronage system (as Johnson perceives it) ideally involves reciprocity. He notes the "reciprocal kindness that had been exchanged" between Pope and his one-time patron Chandos (*Lives of the Poets*, vol. III, p. 153). In his "Life of Watts" Johnson, remembering the Senecan tradition of *beneficiae*, especially commends the relationship between Watts and the patron, Sir Thomas Abney, in whose household Watts found "friendship," "kindness," and "attention" for thirty-six years.[32] "A coalition like this," he says, "a state in which the notions of patronage and dependence were overpowered by the perception of reciprocal benefits, deserves a particular memorial" (vol. III, p. 305). It is clear from Johnson's account what "benefits" Watts received. Johnson quotes an earlier biographer:

[31] *Life of Johnson*, II, 243–46. See above, p. 7.
[32] Abney made his fortune in the City as a dealer in fish, money, and land. He was a friend and Hertfordshire neighbor of Lord Somers. For details see R. M. Adams, "In Search of Baron Somers," 180–81.

"Here [Watts] had the privilege of a country recess, the fragrant bower, the spreading lawn, the flowery garden, and other advantages, to sooth his mind and aid his restoration to health; to yield him, whenever he chose them, most grateful intervals from his laborious studies, and enable him to return to them with redoubled vigour and delight." (pp. 305–06)

Watts apparently was "without any care of his own," and without any particular responsibilities – as tutor or chaplain – in the household. About the benefits received by Sir Thomas, or offered by Watts, Johnson is not explicit, but we may assume that they consist of the many sermons and books that Watts provided to "the church and world," and perhaps the beneficent effect of a pious and exemplary life.[33] The "Life of Addison" provides a more concrete exchange of "benefits." In a transaction brokered by Halifax, Godolphin sends "encouragement" to Addison to celebrate the battle of Blenheim. Addison produces *The Campaign*, which does "honour" to the "country," and is subsequently rewarded with "ample recompense" (vol. II, p. 88) – appointment as Commissioner of Appeals. The country then gains the devotion of a skilled civil servant who ultimately rises to become Secretary of State.

It cannot be said that Johnson works out in any detail, either in Watts' case or in the case of other writers and patrons, how patronage may be said to involve "reciprocal benefits."[34] And although Johnson rarely imagines the patron's point of view,[35] his scattered comments in the *Rambler* and the *Lives* suggest that he was intuitively aware of the ways in which the writer's and the patron's engagements with the world always involved a complex exchange of claims and debts. If a writer uses his abilities well, he can "claim ... regard" (*Rambler* 136). As we have seen, this is an old idea, sustained into the eighteenth century by the popularity of Senecan morals and by the insistence, on the part of writers from Dryden to Thomson, that a poet has certain "rights," can lodge certain quasi-legal

---

33 Even Macaulay a hundred years later senses the "benefits" Watts provided. Such a man "of pure and exalted character ... may much more than repay by his example and his instructions the benefits which he receives" (*History of England*, ed. C. H. Firth, 6 vols. [London: Macmillan, 1914], IV, 1730).

34 But the idea clearly appealed to him. Cf. *Rambler* 137, on "reciprocation of benefits," and *Rasselas*, ch. 12, where Rasselas, imagining himself a patron, thinks of "the soft reciprocation of protection and reverence."

35 In the *Life of Johnson* he thinks how a patron may be "harassed with solicitations" (II, 168), and in the "Life of Halifax" that he, like every man, "willingly gives value to the praise which he receives" (*Lives of the Poets*, II, 47). Cf. also the discussion of Steele and Tyrconnel in the *Life of Savage*.

"claims."[36] To *claim*, as Johnson's *Dictionary* notes, is to "demand of right ... Not to accept or beg of favour, but to exact as due."[37] If a writer has "distinguished himself by any publick performance," he has a "right" to honor for which he need "pay" nothing (*Rambler* 136); praise will be paid to him as a "debt" (*Rambler* 155), or he may "claim" it as a "tribute" (*Rambler* 136), so long, that is, as it acknowledges "those virtues on which conscience congratulates us" (*Rambler* 155), i.e., those we know we have. By the same token, if a writer misuses his abilities, he may be "charged with misapplication" (another quasi-legal verb) and become "contemptible" (*Rambler* 136). If a writer writes well, he deserves to be rewarded, just as the patron's merit deserves praise.[38] If a patron makes a "particular" promise to a writer, he confers a "claim" on him (*Rambler* 163).

It is clear that the (ideal) relationship between patron and writer is for Johnson a complex moral calculus of claim, desert, right, debt, tribute, and gift that he did not fully articulate in a single essay. Perhaps he came closest in *Rambler* 136 where he notes that the patron offers the writer "encouragement" in his efforts and is repaid when the writer "encourage[s] merit with praise" and "pays ... respect." This, says Johnson (quietly punning), is "the great business of literature." But praise and patronage involve no simple *quid pro quo*. Indeed, in the subtle exchange the poet becomes the patron. It is "only the sons of learning" who have "the power of bestowing" the "honours of a lasting name." In Johnson's economy the poet in "the great republick of humanity" becomes analogous to the king himself. To *bestow* is to give bounty (*Dictionary*), as a monarch bestows gifts, honors, and even (when conferring an hereditary title) a lasting name. Like a king the writer is charged with "fixing the stamp of literary sanction" (i.e., minting the coin of true praise) and is "entrusted with the distribution of the ... rewards of merit." The act of dispensing "honours" and "rewards of merit" is of course, in a society organized around status, typically that of the monarch or his ministers, who are "intrusted with the distribution of the Prince's

[36] On Dryden and "rights", see above, pp. 85–89. Thomson, dedicating "Spring" to the Countess of Hertford in 1728, says that as "this Poem grew up under your Encouragement, it has therefore a natural Claim to your Patronage" (*The Seasons*, 300).

[37] Even though Dryden lost his Laureateship, he could make "claims" on his old patron Dorset (*Lives of the Poets*, 1, 384).

[38] "Just praise is only a debt" (*Rambler* 155). J. E. Adams notes that, as an "acknowledgement of a moral debt," such praise "deserves no economic return." See "The Economics of Authorship," 475.

bounty" (*Lives of the Poets*, vol. 1, p. 408). Johnson's language even hints that the writer in this respect has powers – and responsibilities – far greater and more solemn than those of a king or patron: he must make "the last terrestrial rewards."

JOHNSON AND DRYDEN

Given Johnson's understanding of the function of praise, and of the system of dependence under which a writer in his age works, it is surprising that he does not seem more sympathetic to the plight of a figure like Dryden. Johnson takes the occasion of the "Life of Dryden" to make extended observations on the attempts by a poet to make a living in that earlier age before "the nation had yet learned to be liberal" (*Lives of the Poets*, vol. 1, p. 386). Although Johnson confesses partiality for Dryden (perhaps because – as has been noticed – he sensed an affinity with him), he seems to apportion more blame to the poet than to the age or to the poet's various paymasters – king, patrons, and booksellers. On three separate occasions Johnson deplores, in strong language, the "strain of flattery" which "disgraces" Dryden's genius. Almost every one of Dryden's twenty-eight plays has a dedication "written with such elegance and luxuriance of praise as neither haughtiness nor avarice could be imagined able to resist. But he seems to have made flattery too cheap" (p. 366). And finally in the long discussion of Dryden's character, Johnson presents the full indictment:

His works afford too many examples of dissolute licentiousness and abject adulation ... Such degradation of the dignity of genius ... cannot be contemplated but with grief and indignation ... In the meanness and servility of hyperbolical adulation, I know not whether, since the days in which the Roman emperors were deified, he has ever been equalled, except by Afra Behn in an address to Eleanor Gwyn ... Of this kind of meanness he never seems to decline the practice, or lament the necessity. (pp. 398–400)

In trying to account for the severity of these judgments, it is worth noting first that Johnson's admiration (and affection) for Dryden is not in doubt. He characteristically wants to hold his literary heroes up to the highest standard. Second, it is clear that Johnson had little admiration for the licentious court of Charles II – however much he thought the king himself a fine gentleman and a "man of parts" who "rewarded merit" (*Life of Johnson*, vol. 1, p. 442; vol. 11, pp. 41, 341).

As a moralist for whom "merit" and "honor" were ethical terms, Johnson may not have fully appreciated the importance of "honor," status, and reputation in a court-based culture or the panegyrist's traditional role of holding up idealized images. Nor, with his rigorous view of the writer's moral responsibility to confer praise justly, would he have had sympathy with the idea of panegyrical praise as a test of rhetorical skill. Johnson seems to sense that Dryden looks on "the task of praise" as an opportunity to perform and continuously to invent new ways of praising, and seems "more delighted with the fertility of his invention than mortified by the prostitution of his judgement" (*Lives of the Poets*, vol. 1, p. 400). What strikes Johnson is that Dryden's fund of flattery seems inexhaustible: "As many odoriferous bodies are observed to diffuse perfumes from year to year without sensible diminution of bulk or weight, he appears never to have impoverished his mint of flattery by his expences, however lavish" (p. 399). By means of his own metaphysical conceit ("odoriferous bodies" yoked by violence with a "mint"), Johnson displays *his* power, and turns Dryden's defect into the virtue of comprehensiveness and unfailing fertility:

He had all forms of excellence, intellectual and moral, combined in his mind, with endless variation; and when he had scattered on the hero of the day the golden shower of wit and virtue, he had ready for him, whom he wished to court on the morrow, new wit and virtue with another stamp. (p. 399)

Johnson may have come to blame but has stayed to praise. The dedicator's "meanness" disappears in royal bounty (the poet as coiner) or even Olympian profusion (a Zeus-like poet, sending golden showers).

In the end, however, Johnson stands on principle – his own principles – and judges Dryden by the central standards that, in 1780, he imposes on himself and on all writers. The flattery of the Duchess of York "disgraces genius" because "it is an attempt to mingle earth and heaven, by praising human excellence in the language of religion" (p. 359).[39] It can be no surprise that the critic offended by Milton, who in *Lycidas* "mingled the most awful and sacred truths" with "trifling fictions," will be offended by a poet who assured the Duchess of York that "Your Person is so admirable, that

---

[39] Cf. *Rambler* 104: "the terms peculiar to the praise and worship of the Supreme Being, have been applied to wretches whom it was the reproach of humanity to number among men" (*Works*, IV, 193).

it can scarce receive addition, when it shall be glorify'd."[40] To praise
in this fashion is not simply to go too far, but to set a limit on God
himself. Elsewhere, Dryden's failing is not that he dedicates his
works, but that he weakens the legitimate force of dedication to
inspire or to restrain. By dedicating so many works to so many
different patrons, he dilutes the poet's power and ironically (for a
poet always complaining of his poverty) lowers its value or "price."
"That praise is worth nothing of which the price is known" (p. 366).
There are two different charges here. First, that praise "becomes
cheap as it becomes vulgar" (*Rambler* 136). It "owes its value only to
its scarcity." Second, that such vulgar praise, when needed to cover
one's nastiness, can always be bought for a known price. In the end,
the danger of "hyperbolical adulation" is not so much that the praise
is excessive as that it is indiscriminate. To look on the great with
respect is appropriate, but to "look on grandeur with undistin-
guishing reverence" is to abandon all responsibility. The poet's
obligation is to distribute honor more carefully, and to keep sharp
"the distinction of good and evil" (*Rambler* 136).[41] To do any less is
"abuse of superlative abilities" (*Lives of the Poets*, vol. 1, p. 398), and
for one who never forgot the Parable of the Talents, such abuse is a
grave error for which the writer must be answerable.

PATRONAGE AS MORAL OCCASION

As the solemn reminder of the poet's responsibilities suggests,
Johnson is ultimately concerned with the patronage system not as an
economic or political arrangement, but as an occasion for moral
reflection. And although he is sometimes exercised by the insolence,
pretension, or cruelty of the patron, Johnson as moralist focuses
primarily on the writer. Although he sometimes honors the fortitude
and the patience in adversity of the long-suffering dependent,
Johnson more commonly assumes a stance of ironic detachment, and
writes with most force about writers foolishly proud of their own
"independence."

One of Johnson's recurrent moral themes, whether he is writing
about writers or not, is the gap between what we fondly long for (or

---

40 Dedication to *The State of Innocence*, in *Works*, xii, 84. Cf. "the Majesty of your Mind deters
    [the beholders] from too bold approaches; and turns their Admiration into Religion."
41 Cf. *Rambler* 104 on "the crime of obliterating the distinction between good and evil"
    (*Works*, iv, 194).

even expect), and what we are likely to find. Examples abound in the
Lives of the Poets, but Gay may stand as representative. It became
commonplace in the eighteenth century to complain that Gay never
got the recognition he deserved, but Johnson will have none of it. His
emphasis lies on Gay's financial windfalls, the "want of oeconomy"
(vol. II, p. 280) that left him unable to manage his money or his
career, and on the care given him by his friends. And yet for all this
"recompense" and "tenderness," Gay remains unhappy, always
longing for more. Johnson represents him "as a man easily incited to
hope, and deeply depressed when his hopes were disappointed"
(p. 272). His position as secretary to the Earl of Clarendon in 1713
gives him "hopes of kindness from every party" (p. 270), but they are
disappointed when the queen dies the next year. He is "simple
enough" (p. 272) to imagine that the success of his play, *The What d'ye
Call It*, "would raise the fortune of its author." Johnson finds the
expectation "simple" (that is, naive and silly) and the reaction
excessive (Gay melodramatically "sunk into dejection"). One of the
dangers of hope and expectation, as Johnson often says in the
Rambler, is that it prevents you from attending to the present. Gay
was given shares in the South Sea Company, and, as they rose in
value, he "dreamed of dignity and splendor." He refused advice to
take his profit, or even to buy an annuity, which, the poet Fenton
urged, would at least "make you sure of a clean shirt and a shoulder
of mutton every day." When the bubble burst he lost everything, and
Gay again "sunk under the calamity" (p. 274).

But he is rescued by his friends, and his health is restored. Still he
dreams of preferment and convinces himself that he is about to be
rewarded. Instead of blaming the capriciousness of patrons, Johnson
implies that the hopeful poet is only fooling himself. Gay "thought
himself in favour," and when promised a reward, he "doubtless
magnified [it] with all the wild expectations of indigence and vanity"
(p. 274). When the Princess of Wales (to whom he had been
presented) becomes queen in 1727, Gay (in his own mind, at least)
"was to be great and happy." When offered the minor court post of
Gentleman Usher to the queen's little daughter – and Johnson
doesn't suggest that the childlike Gay, "play-fellow" of the wits
(p. 268), was qualified for much more – he is again disappointed.
Pope make much of this incident, and implicitly sees it as a failure of
the patronage system. Johnson demurs: Gay, he said, "*thought himself
insulted*" (p. 274) – the locution is one of Johnson's favorite means to

distinguish between a reasonable and a self-pleasing conclusion. And Johnson doesn't think we need to waste much sympathy for "poor Gay." "All the pain which he suffered from neglect or, as he perhaps termed it, the ingratitude of the court, may be supposed to have been driven away by the unexampled success of *The Beggar's Opera*" (p. 275). The play, which Johnson calls a "lucky *Opera*" – so much for Gay's misfortunes – of course (in the famous witticism) made Gay rich.

Johnson's account of Gay's final years continues to challenge the myth of the neglected poet with suggestions that Gay was self-deluded and in the end self-destructive. His play *Polly*, a continuation of *The Beggar's Opera*, is banned, and Gay feels "forced" (p. 279) to publish it by subscription – which proves very successful: "*what he called* oppression ended in profit." Gay is then taken into the house-hold of the Duke of Queensberry – "yet another recompense for this supposed hardship" (p. 280) – and treated less as a retainer than as an incompetent. Since Gay couldn't seem to manage his own money, Queensbury in effect became his trustee, and doled out Gay's money to him as an allowance. But his disappointment and discontent persist, and ultimately (so Johnson implies) lead to his death:

> It is *supposed* that the discountenance of the Court sunk deep into his heart, and gave him more discontent than the applauses or tenderness of his friends could overpower. He soon fell into his old distemper, an habitual colick, and languished, though with many intervals of ease and cheerful-ness, till a violent fit at last seized him, and hurried him to the grave. (pp. 280–81)

Refusing to sentimentalize, Johnson makes Gay a valetudinarian who in effect brings his end on himself. Refusing to accept Pope's image of "blameless" and "neglected Genius" ("Epistle to Dr. Arbuthnot," lines 256–60), Johnson blames Gay's unrealistic expec-tations and suggests that, as with many of the cases in the *Rambler*, Gay's unhappiness is his own fault. At the end of his own life, when it was suggested to Johnson by Boswell that it was unjust that he had "not [been] called to some great office, nor had attained to great wealth," Johnson became aroused and – in terms that recall the "Life of Gay" – refused to blame "the world": "All the complaints which are made of the world are unjust. I never knew a man of merit neglected: it was generally by his own fault that he failed of success." Johnson then went on to reject the old complaints about patrons: "When patronage was limited, an authour expected to find a

Maecenas, and complained if he did not find one. Why should he complain? This Maecenas has others as good as he, or others who have got the start of him" (*Life of Johnson*, vol. IV, p. 172).

The disappointed hopes for patronage, then, provide Johnson, in the "Life of Gay" and elsewhere, rich opportunities for acerbic observations about the folly of hope. But even when poets find that ease and prosperity which Gay sought all his life, Johnson finds in their situation an opportunity to reflect on the fleeting nature of all temporal happiness. Repeatedly in the *Lives* poets have their hopes fulfilled, but do not enjoy them long. Thomson, comfortable in a place found him by Lyttelton, "was now at ease, but was not long to enjoy it; for, by taking cold on the water between London and Kew, he caught a disorder, which, with some careless exasperation, ended in a fever that put an end to his life" (*Lives of the Poets*, vol. III, p. 294). Halifax in 1714 wins one honor after another and attains the pinnacle of success: "At the queen's death he was appointed one of the regents; and at the accession of George the First was made earl of Halifax, knight of the garter, and first commissioner of the treasury." The end follows quickly: "More was not to be had, and this he kept but a little while, for on the 19th of May, 1715, he died of an inflammation of the lungs" (vol. II, pp. 45–46). Parnell, recommended by friends, gets a prebend in 1713 and then in 1716 a vicarage worth £400 a year. "But his prosperity did not last long. His end, whatever was its cause, was now approaching. He enjoyed his preferment little more than a year" (vol. II, p. 51). The pattern is so common in the *Lives* – an aspect of what Paul Fussell called "the irony of literary careers"[42] – that the reader almost comes to expect that an account of preferment and worldly success will lead quickly to a laconic report of the poet's death. Ambrose Philips, after the death of his patron, purchases (at favorable terms) an annuity of £400, and "now certainly hoped to pass some years of life in plenty and tranquillity; but his hope deceived him: he was struck with a palsy [less than a year later], and died" (vol. III, p. 323). Gilbert West is at last "sufficiently rich, but wealth came too late to be long enjoyed; nor could it secure him from the calamities of life" (vol. III, p. 331). In 1757 Dyer published *The Fleece*, "his greatest poetical work," but "He did not indeed long survive that publication, nor long enjoy the increase of his preferments, for in 1758 he died" (vol. III, p. 345).

[42] *Samuel Johnson and the Life of Writing*, 246–78.

Even when poets have long and successful literary careers and attain "independence" from patrons, Johnson finds in their lives matter for moral reflection. What surprises us, given Johnson's own proud independence, is that instead of celebrating those few writers who managed to become independent of patronage, Johnson finds them merely proud. Swift, it will be recalled, comes in for sharp attack:

> Much has been said of the equality and independence which he preserved in his conversation with the Ministers, of the frankness of his remonstrances, and the familiarity of his friendship ... No man, however, can pay a more servile tribute to the Great, than by suffering his liberty in their presence to aggrandize him in his own esteem. (vol. III, p. 21)

To understand Johnson's charge we can recall the principle of subordination, which he himself invokes at this juncture: "between different ranks of the community there is necessarily some distance." In other contexts Johnson does not always insist that "distance" be maintained between writers and their patrons. Dryden, for example, is not blamed for his "familiarity with the great" (vol. I, p. 398). But in the case of Swift, Johnson suggests that any writer who prides himself on his familiarity with his patron is fooling himself.

> He who is called by his superior to pass the interval may properly accept the invitation ... He who knows himself necessary may set, while, that necessity lasts, a high value upon himself, as, in a lower condition, a servant eminently skilful may be saucy; but he is saucy only because he is servile. (vol. III, pp. 21–22)

Swift had been praised by his friends and admirers for neglecting, on principle, "those ceremonies which custom has established as the barriers between one order of society and another" (p. 61). Such freedom – Johnson calls it a "transgression of regularity" – Swift considered "greatness of soul." But Johnson, noting Swift's haughty manner, finds no "magnanimity": "petulance and obtrusion[43] are rarely produced by magnanimity, nor have often any nobler cause than the pride of importance and the malice of inferiority" (III, 22). And by accepting a place at his patron's table by "courtesy," Swift in fact suffered a loss of rank and dignity: "He that encroaches on another's dignity puts himself in his power: he is either repelled with helpless indignity, or endured by clemency and condescension" (p. 61). The history of Swift's unsuccessful attempts

---

[43]   Thrusting oneself "into any place or state by force or imposture" (*Dictionary*).

to win preferment, as Johnson makes clear (and as Swift himself seemed to realize), shows that Johnson's analysis, harsh and painful as it is, may only be too accurate.[44]

"Independence" is for Johnson a kind of delusion, and for that reason all the more ridiculous when it becomes the basis for pride. Gay thinks that by leaving his job with a silk-mercer to join the household of the Duchess of Monmouth, he will escape "the restraint or servility of his occupation." Johnson concedes that he gained "leisure" for writing, "but he certainly advanced little in the boast of independence" (vol. II, p. 268). Gray, in his quarrel with Walpole (the son of an earl), was one of those "men, whose consciousness of their own merit sets them above the compliances of servility," and "are apt enough in their association with superiors to watch their own dignity with troublesome and punctilious jealousy, and in the fervour of independence to exact that attention which they refuse to pay."[45] Johnson concedes Walpole's superiority of rank and finds that Gray, in the "fervour of independence," insists too much on his own "dignity."

Even Pope, the great example in the century of a poet who managed to free himself from the shackles of patronage, does not escape Johnson's judging eye. Many perhaps now read the "Life of Pope" expecting to find Johnson celebrating the poet's freedom from patronage and his financial success. And to some extent, Johnson does, implicitly contrasting Pope with Dryden, his great example of a poet unfortunately trapped in an economy of flattery. Pope "never set genius to sale" (vol. III, p. 205). Having made his fortune while still a young man by the Homer translations, he was free to please only himself: "His independence secured him from drudging at a task, and labouring upon a barren topick: he never exchanged praise for money, nor opened a shop of condolence or congratulation ... When he could produce nothing new, he was at liberty to be silent" (p. 219). But instead of singling out Pope as the forerunner of the modern independent writer, Johnson treats him as an exception to the rule, luckily exempt from the conditions under which writers typically have to labor.

His "independence" in fact is a kind of pride. When the relationship with Halifax is broken off, Pope "fed his own pride with the dignity of independence" (Johnson is perhaps thinking of Pope's

---

[44] See above pp. 109–110.　　[45] *Lives of the Poets*, III, 422.

Bufo – "*Fed* with soft Dedication all day long"[46]). As I noted earlier, Johnson quotes Pope's cold and withholding letter to Halifax, and rather than seeing it as the appropriate way for a poet to retain his dignity before a lord, a forerunner of his own firm letter to Chesterfield forty years later, sees only "frigid gratitude." Not that Pope didn't assign a high value to rank and to his close association with men of high birth. Indeed, Johnson presses Pope hard for parading his acquaintance with lords: "Next to the pleasure of contemplating his possessions seems to be that of enumerating the men of high rank with whom he was acquainted, and whose notice he loudly proclaims not to have been obtained by any practices of meanness or servility [which Dryden fell into]; a boast which was never denied to be true, and to which very few poets have ever aspired" (pp. 204–05). Hobnobbing with the great is presented not as the natural goal of every writer but an odd and unusual aspiration. Although Pope pretends to think little of mere high birth, he is not to be believed: "his scorn of the Great is repeated too often to be real: no man thinks much of that which he despises" (p. 211). Even his keeping free of the court comes under Johnson's suspicion: "As he happened to live in two reigns when the Court paid little attention to poetry he nursed in his mind a foolish disesteem of Kings, and proclaims that 'he never sees Courts.' Yet a little regard shewn him by the Prince of Wales melted his obduracy" (pp. 209–10). In the end what looks at first like dignified independence comes to look to Johnson like pride in "his own importance" (p. 211), a failure to comprehend or acknowledge the claims of the larger human world, and (encouraged by Swift) a kind of solipsistic self-regard:

In the letters both of Swift and Pope there appears such narrowness of mind as makes them insensible of any excellence that has not some affinity with their own, and confines their esteem and approbation to so small a number, that whoever should form his opinion of the age from their representation would suppose them to have lived amidst ignorance and barbarity, unable to find among their contemporaries either virtue or intelligence, and persecuted by those that could not understand them. (p. 212)

The independent poet, like his own dunces, finally sees all in self.

In the light of such probing analysis on Johnson's part, we are compelled to conclude that he was no enemy of private patronage. The system of patronage, reflecting the hierarchical order of society, was in Johnson's view by and large successful in providing support to

---

[46]   *Ibid.*, 217. Cf. "Epistle to Dr. Arbuthnot," line 233.

writers. Granted, the system was subject to abuse by both parties. Fawning dedicators are no less corrupt than praise-gulping patrons. But the presence of abuse does not argue that the system itself is flawed. Always ready to challenge a tired cliché, Johnson doubted that genius was in the eighteenth century often neglected.[47] He ultimately turns the force of his critique on the vain expectations and vaunted independence of poets. The former is an evasion of responsibility and present duty; like Gay, such a poet is in effect a child. The latter at once degrades a writer from his proper rank (as in the case of Swift) and denies his place in a wide social network in which all are properly dependent on each other (as in the case of Pope). But turning his attention to a moral critique may be seen as Johnson's own evasion of – or incomplete understanding of – patronage as an *economic* exchange, an arrangement that, in a society still deeply conscious of rank, provides economic value to both parties.

Johnson was perhaps more critical of private patronage in his early years, when he was writing the *Life of Savage* (1744), the *Rambler* (1749–50), and the letter to Chesterfield (1755). But there are clear lines of continuity and even similarities in phrasing between the treatment of patronage in the *Rambler* and in the *Lives of the Poets*. As often in Johnson, apparent inconsistency turns out to be difference in emphasis. Cynics may suggest that in his later years a pensioner was not likely to attack the patronage system, and sentimentalists may suggest that he "mellowed." But it seems plausible that as Johnson reflected in his last years on "independence" – a state that many of his literary colleagues (Churchill, Gibbon, Hume) aimed at or celebrated – and on the plight of most writers of his day, who exchanged one kind of dependency for another, he may have concluded (as did contemporaries like Goldsmith) that the patronage system was no bad way to encourage and sustain genius. Not that he nostalgically hoped to bring it back (here he parts company with Goldsmith). Johnson senses that his own times are more beneficial to writers, if only because the booksellers are more "liberal." But approval of the literary marketplace emerging in his own day does not lead Johnson, like some later commentators, to hunt out and celebrate every instance in literary history in which patrons can be cast as villains and writers as victims or heroes.

---

[47] See *Rambler*, 59, 77, 136, and 166 on the "established customs of complaining" of the "neglect of learning."

CHAPTER 10

The persistence of patronage

It is a commonplace in studies of literary patronage to report that the patronage system sharply declined – or even died – sometime around 1755, when Johnson wrote his famous letter to Chesterfield. As early as 1832 Carlyle declared that

> At the time of Johnson's appearance on the field, Literature ... was in the very act of passing from the protection of Patrons into that of the Public; no longer to supply its necessities by laudatory Dedications to the Great, but by judicious Bargains with the Booksellers.

In Carlyle's theatrical imagination, Johnson's letter was "that far-famed Blast of Doom, proclaiming into the ear of Lord Chesterfield, and, through him, of the listening world, that patronage should be no more!"[1]

Subsequent writers on the literary system of the eighteenth century typically repeated, in more moderate terms, Carlyle's thesis, not failing to see in Johnson's 1755 letter to Chesterfield the symbolic end of an era, but conceding that a new era had not yet dawned. Macaulay was insistent. He declared that when Johnson arrived in London "the age of patronage had passed away. The age of general curiosity and intelligence had not arrived ... At the time Johnson commenced his literary career, a writer had little to hope from the patronage of powerful individuals. The patronage of the public did not yet furnish the means of comfortable subsistence."[2] Forster in *The Life and Times of Oliver Goldsmith* (1877) obviously has Macaulay's idea of a kind of limbo or interregnum in mind when he declares

---

[1]   Review of J. W. Croker's 1831 edition of Boswell's *Life of Johnson*, in *Fraser's Magazine*, 5 (May 1832), 396–98.

[2]   A review of Croker's Boswell, in *The Edinburgh Review* (Sept. 1831), 1–38, repr. in Macaulay's *Critical and Historical Essays*, 6 vols. (1900), 11, 338, 340. He repeated the claim in his 1856 *Britannica* essay on Johnson: "Literature had ceased to flourish under the patronage of the great, and had not yet begun to flourish under the patronage of the public" (reprinted in Macaulay, *Selected Writings*).

summarily that "the patron was gone, and the public had not come."[3] Beljame's story of the rise of the "independent man of letters" ends in 1744 with the death of Pope, who is said to have pointed the way toward the author as proud professional. In Pope's time both political and private patronage are alleged to have ceased: "The tradition of literary patronage had been broken," Beljame says, echoing Macaulay: the author's "only hope was to ... write for the publishers. But the publishing business was still in its infancy."[4] Collins' *Authorship in the Days of Johnson* asserts that patronage declined "from about 1750" (p. 189), acknowledges some "belated examples" of patronage after 1750, but finds them "very occasional exceptions to the average prospects of a writer" (p. 201).

And the cliché has persisted to the present day. James Saunders, whose theme in the words of his title is the establishment of *The Profession of English Letters*, finds Johnson the first "true professional" (p. 145), and uncritically quotes as confirmation Goldsmith's "boast" that writers "have now no other patrons than the public" (p. 119). In his *Age of Patronage* (1971), Foss (reverting to Macaulay's formula) reports that by the end of Pope's life "the old patronage of the king, the court and the lords had fallen away; the new patron, the problematic public, was waiting to take over."[5] In a 1985 essay Johnson's letter is still "the generally accepted (and highly over-simplified) symbol of the decline of patronage."[6] Alvin Kernan supplemented the thesis by seeing in Johnson's meeting with George III in the King's Library in 1763 (just a few years later than the letter to Chesterfield) the symbolic moment of transition from a court-dominated culture, in which authors deferred to and were dependent upon patrons, to a world of print culture, in which the author was an independent professional.[7]

I have already suggested that Johnson's letter is not so much evidence of the end of the era of the patron, as of an injured but proud author's sense that a patron had failed to observe the system's norms. My argument in this chapter is that reports of the decline and

---

[3]   *Oliver Goldsmith*, 1, 89. Forster cites Macaulay, and quotes extensively (1, 190–92) from the account of "the encouragement of learning" in Goldsmith's *Enquiry into the State of Polite Learning in Europe.*

[4]   *Men of Letters*, 344.

[5]   *The Age of Patronage*, 207.

[6]   Robert Folkenflik, "Patronage and the Poet Hero," 367.

[7]   *Printing Technology, Letters & Samuel Johnson.* Mark Rose approvingly quotes Kernan's remark that Johnson's letter was the "Magna Carta of the modern author" (*Authors and Owners*, 4).

death of patronage c. 1750 are not only highly derivative, but considerably exaggerated, and that a careful review of the available evidence shows that (1) the claims for decline are based on relatively unreliable testimony; (2) explanations for the alleged decline are confused and inconsistent; (3) the patronage system was still very much in place in the latter half of the eighteenth century, and provided support of one kind or another to virtually every writer of stature in the period; and (4) although it did not "decline," patronage took some new forms, and what most characterizes the latter half of the eighteenth century is not the supplanting of patron by bookseller but the contestation of still-powerful patronal authority by the bookseller as well as by all the other participants in the literary system.

THE DECLINE OF PATRONAGE?

The "decline" of literary patronage in the later eighteenth century was not actually invented by nineteenth-century literary historians. Macaulay and his followers almost wholly base their claims about such a "decline" on the writings of contemporary witnesses – they routinely cite the same passages and incidents in the lives and work of Johnson and Goldsmith. In fact, claims of the decline of patronage are commonplace in the eighteenth century, a cliché of authorship. As Goldsmith remarked, "There is nothing authors are more apt to lament, than want of encouragement from the age"[8] – and Goldsmith appears to have meant not only his own age, but any age. There is another reason to treat contemporary claims of neglect with some skepticism: most of the testimony comes from eighteenth-century writers who in one way or another have an ax to grind.

One of the earliest laments comes from James Ralph, whose *Case of Authors by Profession* appeared in 1758. Ralph complained that "the Times ... were favorable to *Prior, Addison*, &c ... because the Link of Patronage which held the Great and Learned together, was then in full Force ... We of the present Day ... having nothing but Phantoms before our Eyes; are only the Dupes of our own Delusions" (p. 72). But it must be remembered that Ralph's *Case of Authors*, as its title implies, is an advocacy document. And as its modern editor notes, it was written in polemical response to an attack on the

---

[8] *Enquiry into the Present State of Polite Learning in Europe*, ch. 10, in *Collected Works*, I, 307. Hume wrote to Smollett in 1768 of "the indifference of ministers towards literature, which has been long, and indeed always, the case in England" (*Letters of David Hume*, II, 186).

mercenary motives of modern writers in John Brown's accusatory *Estimate of the Manners and Principles of the Times* (1757). Anyone who looks into Ralph's work, furthermore, will see that its mode of proceeding is not sober exposition but spirited satire. As for its claims that modern writers have been cut off from patronage, Ralph had had long experience as a paid writer for various political factions, and in 1758 had been enjoying for some five years a pension of £300 a year from the ministry.[9]

One year after Ralph's *Case of Authors* appeared, Goldsmith, in his *Enquiry into the State of Polite Learning* (1759), reported that "our writers of rising merit are generally neglected" by the traditional patrons of literature. But Goldsmith's words, cited later as documentary evidence, were, in the words of a contemporary reviewer, "little else than the trite commonplace remarks and observations, that have been, for some years past, repeatedly echoed from Writer to Writer, throughout every country where Letters, or the Sciences, have been cultivated."[10] Writers have in effect *always* complained about negligent patrons.[11] Furthermore, Goldsmith was not a disinterested witness. He was writing as an impecunious journalist, feeling neglected, seeking support, and aiming for fame and independence. Perhaps to increase his chances of gaining a hearing (and to head off charges of partiality), he presents himself in the anonymous *Enquiry* as a gentleman with wide knowledge of the world speaking freely to other gentlemen of taste and learning. But contemporary reviewers saw through the pose, and guessed that the author was probably a "Literary Understrapper" who "affects to be thought to stand in the rank of Patrons," and "arrogates to himself, a place among those by whom authors are starved."[12] The *Enquiry* did not strike the *Critical Review* as a "scrupulous enquiry" into the real state of polite learning.[13]

Other contemporary testimony should be treated with equal skepticism. Fielding's recurrent complaint that England is a country "where there is no public provision for men of genius"[14] is only

[9] It has been shown that Ralph's *Case of Authors* influenced later writers. See R. W. Kenny, "Ralph's *Case of Authors;*" 104–13.

[10] *Monthly Review*, 21 (November 1759), 382.

[11] For Renaissance complaints about the stinginess of patrons, see Arthur Marotti, "Patronage, Poetry, and Print," 45n.

[12] *Monthly Review*, 21 (Nov. 1759), 389; *Gentleman's Magazine*, 29 (April 1759), 170.

[13] *Critical Review*, 7 (April 1759), 372.

[14] Quoted in Forster, I, 91. Cf. Fielding's equally overstated complaint that "there is no one

narrowly true – pensions were not handed out to all men of genius, as English writers imagined they were in the France of Louis XIV. (This did not prevent Fielding, who appealed to Walpole for patronage, from enjoying private support from a number of sources.) When Johnson declared that "we have done with patronage" he was not speaking on oath. Given to bold claims in conversation, Johnson knew perfectly well that he was not speaking the literal truth. He wrote more than twenty dedications for other writers, and was at that time drawing a pension from the king. When Gibbon records that he "cannot boast of the friendship or favour of princes" and notes that "the patronage of English literature has long since been devolved on our booksellers" (Bonnard, *Memoirs of My Life*, p. 188 [full details given in footnote 75]), he perhaps writes literal truth – for he had no *pension* from the king, but writes disingenuously: Gibbon had been a placeman of Lord North and a frequent beneficiary of Lord Sheffield's largesse.

Other claims that patronage had "devolved on our booksellers" are questionable on other grounds. Smollett, for example, writing of the year 1758, declares that "no Maecenas appeared among the ministers, and not the least ray of patronage glimmered from the throne. The protection, countenance, and gratification, secured in other countries by the institution of academies, and the liberality of princes, the ingenious in England derived from the generosity of the public, endued with taste and sensibility, eager for improvement, and proud of patronizing extraordinary merit."[15] But his glowing report, presented as "history," needs to be read in the context of his own campaign as editor of the *Critical Review* to promote an academy in England and to raise the level of public "taste and sensibility."[16] Smollett's covert purposes, in other words, would tend to make him emphasize the importance of public taste and the decline of the authority (and the "encouragement") of traditional patrons.[17] He

Patron of true Genius, nor the least Encouragement left for it in the Kingdom," quoted in Battestin, *Henry Fielding*, 389.

15　*Continuation of the Complete History of England*, 11, 412.

16　Compare his report on the year 1760: "genius ... though neglected by the great, flourished under the culture of a public which had pretensions to taste, and piqued itself on encouraging literary merit" (*ibid.*, IV, 125–26). "Never was pursuit after knowledge so universal, or literary merit more regarded, than at this juncture by the body of the British nation; but it was honoured by no attention from the throne, and little indulgence did it reap from the liberality of particular patrons" (p. 128).

17　In another context in 1770 Smollett noted that the ministry took a great interest in writers: "One good Writer was of more importance to the Government than twenty placemen in

may also have wanted to make George III – the current monarch – look good by contrast to his immediate predecessor, George II. Smollett's silence in the *History* about the role of booksellers, whom he elsewhere called "contemptible Reptiles,"[18] suggests that his version of "history" is carefully edited.

Another partisan witness to the mid-century decline of patronage is William Warburton. Once, he declares in his *Letter from an Author to a Member of Parliament*, "Men in public Stations thought it the Duty of their Office to encourage Letters," but *"Letters are now left, like Virtue*, to be their own Reward."[19] But Warburton's claim is subordinated to his larger rhetorical end. The purpose of his *Letter* is to defend authorial copyright, and it serves that purpose for him to minimize the "slender ... Pittance" (p. 3) that his fellow authors now enjoy from patrons, so that the legal protection of an author's literary property will seem all the more important. By the same token Warburton paints a picture of a golden age of patronage, in part to explain why until recently *"Authors* had the less Occasion to be anxious about Literary Property" (p. 2).

A different kind of evidence that needs to be read with equal caution is mid-century satire on patrons, as in Samuel Foote's stage comedies, *The Author* (1757) and *The Patron* (1764). Collins cites ridicule in the latter of a foolish patron, Sir Thomas Lofty, who laps up flattery but "has neither genius to create, judgement to distinguish, nor generosity to reward," and a dismissive remark in the former to the effect that the word *patron* "has lost its use" (cited in Collins, *Authorship in the Days of Johnson*, pp. 194–96). Collins goes on to cite other examples of contemporary ridicule in the writings of Smollett and Churchill in the 1750s and 1760s. But it is important to note that such remarks occur in works of *satire* – where ridicule is a generic requirement, and where the author (or his dramatic character) have license to exaggerate. Second, it should be remembered that ridicule of foolish patrons was long conventional in Augustan England, and can be found in the poems and prefaces of Pope, Dryden, Rochester,

---

the House of Commons." See *The Whiteford Papers*, ed. W. A. S. Hewins (Oxford, 1898), 149, quoted in Robert Rea, *The English Press in Politics*, 4.

[18] In a private letter of that year to Richardson. See *The Letters of Tobias Smollett*, 92. Cf. the "tyrant" booksellers in ch. 94 of *Peregrine Pickle* (1751). By contrast, the author of the almost exactly contemporary "The Distresses of an Hired Writer," (April 1761), 198–200, regards the same scene with alarm as a "fatal revolution whereby ... booksellers, instead of the great, became the patrons and paymasters of men of genius."

[19] *A Letter From an Author to a Member of Parliament Concerning Literary Property* (London, 1747), 2.

and others, when the patronage system was said to be at its height. Finally, it does not follow from an attack on a foolish patron that the entire system of patronage has been called into question, or declared to have degenerated.

The thesis that patronage disappeared after 1750 has also been sustained by what was until relatively recently the dominant historiographical view of the period, the so-called "Whig interpretation of history." According to such readings of eighteenth-century England, the central theme of the age is the steady and inevitable march toward political freedom and modernity, as England was transformed from a court-centered culture to an increasingly middle-class world centered on the marketplace, on the increasing power of trade and manufacturing, and on the expansion of the voting franchise. It is no accident that Macaulay, looking back on the bad old days of Charles II from the vantage of post-Reform Bill England, could deplore in equal terms the political dominance of "Stuart absolutism" and the cultural dominance of the aristocracy, conditions which in his view led Dryden to fawning servility on his noble and royal patrons. Nineteenth-century "Whig" interpretations of the eighteenth century seize on signs of change to proclaim the breakdown of an old decadent order and the rise of the new.

Even though the "Whig" interpretation of history was challenged by twentieth-century historians, one of the central tenets of that interpretation has survived today, especially among Marxists – that the story of the eighteenth century is a story of progress, of liberation, of innovation, of the appearance of the modern, of social, economic, intellectual, and cultural change. Literary students who read the work of E. P. Thompson or Roy Porter thus find contextual corroboration of conventional claims about the decline of the system of patronage – an institution that had been one of the hallmarks of the traditional order. But the neo-Whig interpretation has been sharply challenged on the same grounds as the old – that it overestimates change, minimizes essential continuity, and antedates the end of the traditional socio-political order based, as John Cannon observes, on the "great network of patronage that ran through all society."[20]

---

[20] John Cannon, *Samuel Johnson*, 174. Artistic patronage, he says, was "but one subdivision of that network". Curiously, Cannon goes on to assert (in passing) that while the "economic, social, and political power" of the aristocracy "remained intact," the system of aristocratic literary patronage "broke down almost completely during Johnson's lifetime" (p. 181). I hope to persuade Cannon to take a closer look at literary patronage.

In the revised edition of his *English Society in the Eighteenth Century* (1990), Porter concedes

INFLUENCE AND INDEPENDENCE

Claims for the decline of patronage after 1750 should then be regarded with some skepticism on the grounds that they are often commonplaces, echoed from one writer to another, or the reports of interested witnesses and partisan historians. The claims are also suspect on internal grounds. When pressed hard, they seem strikingly inconsistent and vague. Consider Goldsmith's mutually contradictory claims that patronage declines (1) because writers don't need it any more (in the literary marketplace, they are said to be "certain of living without dependence" – *Collected Works*, vol. II, p. 499); (2) because patrons have failed (either by neglecting authors of genius, or providing "ill directed encouragement" vol. I, p. 288] to the undeserving); or (3) because writers themselves have abused the system by soliciting too many subscriptions (vol. II, p. 310). Indeed, Goldsmith's several observations on the condition of authors mark him as radically ambivalent or radically undecided: on the one hand he laments the disappearance of the golden days of patronage (vol. I, p. 311) and the arrival of an era of writing for money, and on the other he can "bravely assert the dignity of [authorial] independence" (vol. II, p. 345).

In his account of the conditions of authorship in the days of Johnson, Collins follows Goldsmith uncritically, even to the extent of replicating his inconsistency. His primary argument is that patronage declined because writers could now support themselves: "Apart from any other considerations, this was a state of things sufficient in itself to put an end to patronage" (*Authorship in the Days of Johnson*, p. 191).[21] (Writers are in Collins' account both congratulated for their self-sufficiency and censured for their avarice.) His secondary argument, inconsistent with the first, is to declare that the aristocracy failed to appreciate literature, or to deplore the "preponderance of the decadent and unworthy patrons of the day" (p. 189). Finally, "contemptible writers" (p. 193) give patronage a bad name with their servile flattery. Quite apart from its inconsistency, and its uncritical reliance on Goldsmith, Collins' narrative is strongly ideological

some of the power of the neo-Tory argument, and finds the traditional ruling order remarkably resilient and durable, the lower orders loyal and law-abiding. See pp. 104ff, 121, 289, 299–300, 343–44. In his preface he grants that Georgian England was still an "'old order,' dominated by title, land, and church" (p. xiii).

21 "Competence was within the reach of a hard-working writer" (p. 210).

(independence is simply good and dependence is bad, even dishonorable) and his ending is virtually predetermined. He sets out to retell the old story of the rise of the independent professional writer – the sequel to his first book is entitled *The Profession of Letters*[22] – and he seems determined to show that patronage had correspondingly disappeared. Even Carlyle's account of Johnson's historic letter to Chesterfield betrays – beneath its ardor – some confusion about cause and sequence: did Johnson's trumpet blast announce the forthcoming end of patronage, or was patronage already "passing" from the scene? Was Johnson's letter a prophecy or a retrospective *finis*?

A more adequate account of the system of patronage will need to guard against the deficiencies of Goldsmith, Collins, and others. It will also need to be more careful and precise with some key terms, such as *depend, independence, influence, support*. It is commonplace for writers on patronage to say that in the latter half of the century authors received "less support" from patrons, came to "depend" less on them, were correspondingly more "independent," and thus that the patron's "influence" on literature declined. In order for such claims to carry real authority, they need to be based not on a few statements by and anecdotes about well-known writers but on a systematic survey of writers and patrons. And they need to be substantiated by quantitative evidence about the number of patrons active in the period, the number of writers supported, and the various kinds and amounts of support. This means looking beyond the Civil List and the Secret Service funds – we have known since the 1930s about writers receiving such royal or ministerial support[23] – to the biographical records and household accounts of scores of writers and private patrons. Even then, much evidence remains relatively inaccessible in unpublished papers in public records offices in London and county towns, as well as in many provincial archives.

But quantitative evidence, even if it were complete, tells only part of the story. "Dependence" and "influence" are not easily quantified. At a time when a writer might receive many different forms of income – copy money from a bookseller, fees for journalistic services, payments from subscribers, an author's "third night" at the play-

---

22 *The Profession of Letters: A Study of the Relation of Author to Patron, Publisher, and Public, 1780–1832.*

23 From Sir Lewis Namier (*The Structure of Politics at the Accession of George III*, first published in 1929) and Laurence Hanson (*Government and the Press, 1695–1763*, published in 1936).

house, outright gifts, assistance paid directly to printers, salary from a sinecure or from an appointment in church or government secured through the efforts of a patron,[24] or an annual pension, it is very difficult to estimate by simple quantitative measurement a writer's "dependence" on a patron who provided an office, or an annuity, a gift, or merely an introduction, recommendation, or invitation. Even if we could conclude that – say – only 10 percent of an author's income was directly attributable to patronage, we could not confidently say that such an author did not feel significantly grateful and therefore dependent.[25] Quite apart from a writer's particular circumstances, cultural habits of deference, along with an awareness that great men could influence events in politics, the church, the universities, and the marketplace, could dispose writers to feel some dependency.

"Influence" is another slippery term. It is sometimes used to refer to patronal influence on authors – on their literary practice, their published political sentiments, or their material circumstances. It is also used to refer to patrons' influence on readers – on their opinions about literary merit, or their bookbuying habits. "As both Collins and Korshin make clear," William Epstein says,

hierarchical patronage gradually lost its influence on literature not because it ceased to support authorship ... but because the size of the reading public and the number of authors or potential authors increased dramatically. There were simply too many authors to support and too large and diverse a readership to influence.[26]

Even granting the point that the number of authors and readers increased, while for most of the century the number of peers remained almost constant,[27] it does not follow that overall patronal influence is correspondingly decreased. There are a number of questionable assumptions buried in Epstein's conclusion: that patronage derived primarily from the crown and the peerage, that the number of patrons and the total amount of patronage remained

---

24 "Public offices" and "church livings" are considered forms of "patronage" for writers by the author of *Letters concerning the Present State of England* (1772), 327, 331–32.

25 *Pace* Paul Korshin, who notes that the "key to dependency in the patron-client relationship is always the size of the benefaction" ("Types of Eighteenth-Century Literary Patronage," 461n).

26 "Patronizing the Biographical Subject: Johnson's Savage and Pastoral Power," in *Johnson After Two Hundred Years*, ed. Paul Korshin (Philadelphia: University of Pennsylvania, 1986), 144.

27 According to Cannon (*Aristocratic Century*, 15) the peerage totalled 173 in 1700 and 189 in 1780.

fixed, that the influence of patronage corresponds to the number of patrons and the amount of patronage, and that the situation can be analyzed like a problem in physics, in which (to use Goldsmith's terms) "streams of liberality" when "diffused" must become "proportionably shallow."[28] But all of these assumptions remain unproven. Patronal influence on the nation's "readership," while very important, is very difficult to measure. Thus we should be hesitant to declare that the influence of patronage *increased* between 1780 and 1800 (when the peerage increased from 189 to 267) *or decreased* (because a larger peerage allegedly had less "social cohesion" and therefore less reason to compete among itself for patronal preeminence).[29]

Patronal "influence" on authors, likewise, is not (except in a few cases) easily quantified. As Clifford observed, it is difficult to document authorial gratitude.[30] If a writer is paid by the ministry to produce pamphlets in defense of current policy, then it is safe to assume that he will do what he is told, and there is evidence to suggest that in some cases ministers took an active hand in sketching the argument that the paid writer would then flesh out. The same applies to those writers paid by opposition leaders to write *against* the ministry, as in the contentious 1760s.[31] Even writers like Johnson who considered their pensions to be rewards probably felt some general obligation.[32] Whether writers allegedly pensioned into silence were influenced is of course difficult to prove, for it is in the interest of the participants to suppress or destroy the evidence.[33]

As for authorial "independence" – writers in the latter part of the century are commonly said to be "independent" (or, with lexical laxity, "*increasingly* independent") of patrons – it is important to be cautious in drawing conclusions from contemporary witnesses or in constructing any large argument. "Independence" is a matter of great concern to writers of the period – Goldsmith, Churchill,

---

[28] Goldsmith, *Collected Works*, I, 310.

[29] As Cannon suggests (*Samuel Johnson*, 181).

[30] *Dictionary Johnson*, 277.

[31] Robert Rea, *The English Press in Politics*; John Brewer, *Party Ideology and Popular Politics*.

[32] See above, pp. 65–67. Suggesting not that Johnson "wrote the later political pamphlets because he had been pensioned," Cannon doubts "whether he would have written them had he not been" (*Samuel Johnson*, 71).

[33] The practice of silencing writers seems to have continued past mid-century. Horace Walpole thought that Henry Fox, Lord Holland, after falling out with his private chaplain, the writer Philip Francis, sent him £500 "to silence that wretch" (*Memoirs of the Reign of King George II*, II, 36).

Johnson, Hume, and Gibbon all celebrate it – but we should regard all declarations of authorial independence as representations of authorial desire rather than achievement. Thus when Goldsmith declares that in the present day an author may now "bravely assert the dignity of independence" (*Collected Works*, vol. II, p. 345), his very language is political rather than economic, a hopeful manifesto from an aspiring writer. Even in Johnson's case, a declaration of literary independence ("No man ... who ever lived by literature, has lived more independently than I" – *Life of Johnson*, vol. I, p. 443) is self-enhancing rewriting of personal history, uttered one year to the day after Johnson wrote to Bute to thank him for the king's pension.[34] Many writers who prospered at the hands of the booksellers had in effect not really become "independent" but had exchanged one form of dependency for another, as Goldsmith himself wryly noted, when he has an author ironically remark that he "effectually keeps his liberty" by never stirring out of his garret (*Collected Works*, vol. II, p. 133). Of the writers of the day only those who were or had become, as we now say, independently wealthy, were in any real sense independent: Boswell (who was born to wealth and position), and in their later careers Hume and Gibbon (and even they, as I will show, were recipients of patronage in their youth).

Finally, "independence" can be little more than a manufactured rhetorical illusion, to suit the needs of the patron. For example, in the early 1760s Bute waged an active campaign to influence public opinion through the press, and in effect commissioned numerous pamphlets in support of his policies. But he was aware that such pamphlets often aroused suspicion, and risked being dismissed as paid propaganda. The support of an "independent" writer was more valuable – perhaps Johnson was considered valuable for this reason. When reliable pensioner John Campbell produced a resoundingly pro-ministry pamphlet in 1762, Bute wrote to him with editorial suggestions: "the turn of the pamphlet, as well as the title carrys too much of the air of coming from Government itself. A few alterations would correct this, & by that means stamp the writer with more independency."[35]

---

[34] Cf. his later remark to Boswell that "You may be prudently attached to great men, and yet independent" (*Life of Johnson*, II, 10).

[35] Letter from Bute to Campbell, quoted in Brewer, *Party Ideology and Popular Politics*, 225.

WRITERS AND PATRONS

The case that patronage declined sharply after 1750, then, is a weak one on several internal grounds. It remains now to consider evidence that the system in fact persisted in healthy fashion to the end of the century and beyond. One way of demonstrating that the system of literary patronage was still in place after mid-century is to set against laments about the decline of patronage the equally high hopes that, with the accession of George III, patronage would increase. I have already shown that Bute was an active literary patron both before and after 1760.[36] The dedication of Charlotte Lennox's translation of *The Greek Theatre of Father Brumoy* to the future king in 1759, on the eve of his accession to the throne, ardently declares that "the encouragement which your Royal Highness has given to the endeavours of genius, has already kindled new ardors of emulation, and brightened the prospects of the learned and the studious, who consider the birth of your Royal Highness as the birth of science, and promise to themselves and to posterity, that from this day shall be reckoned a more illustrious period of letters and of patronage" (Hazen, *Johnson's Prefaces and Dedications*, p. 94). And after he became king, some contemporaries thought that the promise was fulfilled. The author of the *Letter concerning the State of England* (1772), in a review of "The Present State of Patronage among the Great; Men of Letters, Artists, &c. their Rewards," claimed that George III "has given more rewards to merit than half a score of his predecessors" (p. 321).[37]

Another way of demonstrating the persistence of patronage after 1750 is to note in brief survey fashion that virtually every writer of any significant reputation took part in the system in one way or another, as recipients of support from private patrons or from the ministry. Among the poets, for example, Mark Akenside enjoyed a pension of £300 per annum from Jeremiah Dyson, Secretary to the Treasury and Cofferer to the Household.[38] In his short "Life" of John Dyer, Johnson repeatedly emphasized the personal agency of Dyer's several patrons in securing church livings for him. In 1741 his

---

[36] See above, pp. 61–69.

[37] The anonymous author seems to be pro-ministry but not a mere propagandist: he is not an admirer of Johnson, and is concerned that recent creations of new peers have disturbed "the balance of government in favor of the Crown" (pp. 18–21).

[38] Johnson, *Lives of the Poets*, III, 414–15. Dyson also helped Akenside secure his appointment as Physician to the new queen in 1761. See Dyce's *Life of Collins*, in *Poetical Works*, lxiii. Dyce says Akenside's pension was probably more than £300 (p. xliii).

"first patron, Mr. Harper, gave him ... Calthorp in Leicestershire, of eighty pounds a year ... In 1751, Sir John Heathcote gave him Coningsby, of one hundred and forty pounds a year; and in 1755 the Chancellor [Lord Hardwicke] added Kirkby, of one hundred and ten" (*Lives of the Poets*, vol. III, p. 344).[39] Gray was given the position of Professor of Modern History at Cambridge in 1768 by the Prime Minister, the Duke of Grafton, at the "King's commands."[40] In addition, he received what amounted to "patronage" from his friends Walpole, who published his poems at the Strawberry Hill Press, and Mason, who helped procure an offer of the Laureateship from the Lord Chamberlain, the Duke of Devonshire – which Gray saw fit to refuse.[41] Shenstone dedicated his "Choice of Hercules" (1740) to Lord Lyttelton, his neighbor at Hagley, and was in line for a pension from Bute in 1763, but died before it could be offered.[42]

Smart dedicated his *Poems on Several Occasions* (1752) to the Earl of Middlesex (one of Charlotte Lennox's patrons), and signed up over 700 subscribers. Although he failed to attract the substantial support he sought and later was imprisoned for debt, he did receive "something handsome" from the Earl of Northumberland in return for an "Ode" to his lordship.[43] In the 1760s Smart wrote dedications to two members of the Delaval family who provided him "great and frequent favour" over the years.[44] James Beattie won a pension of £200 a year for his *Essay on Truth* (1773), which attracted the attention

---

[39] Dyer's key patron seems to have been Philip Yorke, son of the Lord Chancellor. The younger Yorke, having met Dyer in 1750, made him chaplain to his wife, and later acted as intermediary with his father and with Heathcote for the livings of Coningsby and Kirkby. See "Advertisement" to *Poems by John Dyer* and Williams, *Poet, Painter, and Parson*, 122–25. See above, pp. 59–60.

[40] Gray himself emphasized that the position was in the king's gift: "it is the best thing the Crown has to bestow (on a layman) here" (*Correspondence*, IV, 127). He was apparently recommended for the position by his friend Richard Stonehewer, secretary to Grafton. See Johnson, *Lives of the Poets*, III, 428.

[41] See *ibid.*, 444, and Gray, *Correspondence*, II, 543–44.

[42] Johnson, *Lives of the Poets*, III, 350, 352–55. Shenstone had provided his *Poems upon Various Occasions* (1737) with a dedication (Johnson, *Lives of the Poets*, III, 349–50n). Johnson views the trustee of Shenstone's maternal grandfather's estate (to which he was heir) as a functional patron: " ... Mr. Dolman, to whose care he was indebted for his ease and leisure" (p. 350).

[43] For Smart's efforts to win the earl's patronage, see Charles Ryskamp, "Christopher Smart and the Earl of Northumberland," 320–32.

[44] See *The Annotated Letters of Christopher Smart*, 79–83, 102–05. Smart's last work, *Hymns for the Amusement of Children* (1771) was dedicated to Prince Frederick, second son of George III. For a censorious account of Smart's "sycophancy" toward patrons and public heroes, see Moira Dearnley, *The Poetry of Christopher Smart*, 31–37.

of the king.[45] Bute was interested in James Macpherson's Ossian poems and "bore the expenses of the publication of *Fingal* and *Temora*," and then found places for Macpherson in the province of West Florida (Collins, *Authorship in the Days of Johnson*, p. 206). Macpherson went on to receive a pension of £600 a year to "supervise the newspapers," and to serve as "a most laborious and able writer in favour of Government."[46] Lesser poets, including Gilbert West and David Mallet, enjoyed both pensions and places in the 1750s and 60s.[47] The career of William Julius Mickle, the translator of Camoens (1776), was marked, in the words of one recent critic, by his "obsessive reliance on patronage": he was "always in search of a patron" but he "hated being patronized."[48] And as I've previously noted, a number of poets from peasant or laboring class background, from Stephen Duck to Mary Leapor and Ann Yearsley, came to the attention of patrons who promoted their publication and managed their careers and money.[49]

Of the few major poets at mid-century who apparently enjoyed no patronage, Collins had fairly substantial private means,[50] but before inheriting property at his mother's death addressed a hopeful "Epistle" to Sir Thomas Hanmer, aspired to an Oxford fellowship, and tried (unsuccessfully) to get the Duke of Richmond to appoint him to a church living.[51] It is not clear whether the subsequent dedication to Lyttelton of his "Ode Occasioned by the Death of Mr Thomson" or his unpublished "Lines Addressed to James Harris" (in which the addressee is praised as "gentlest patron") yielded any fruit.

Goldsmith turned down several offers of governmental positions.[52] He dedicated *The Traveller* to his brother (a poor churchman), and

---

[45]   See Dyce, *Memoirs of Beattie*, xlv; Forster, *Goldsmith*, II, 391.

[46]   See Walpole, *Correspondence*, XXVIII, 431; XXIX, 167; Collins, *Authorship in the Days of Johnson*, 201; Rea, *The English Press*, 133.

[47]   Johnson, *Lives of the Poets*, III, 328–31, 405–08.

[48]   Frank Brady, *Mickle, Boswell, Garrick, and the Siege of Marseilles*, 253. The subscription list for Mickle's *Lusiad* has nearly 600 names. For Mickle's appeals to Lyttelton, see Mary Rose Davis, *The Good Lord Lyttelton*, 296–99.

[49]   See above, pp. 43–44, 191–203.

[50]   He inherited property from his mother and from an uncle, and enjoyed an allowance (and later an inheritance of £2,000) from another uncle. See Mary Margaret Stewart, "William Collins, Samuel Johnson, and the Use of Biographical Details," 471–82.

[51]   P. L. Carver, *The Life of a Poet*, 35–36.

[52]   Forster reports that the Earl of Northumberland in his capacity as Lord-Lieutenant of Ireland offered a position in Ireland (*Goldsmith*, I, 379–81), and notes that Goldsmith also refused an invitation to write for the government, (I, 434; II, 71), but accepted hospitality from Robert Nugent, Viscount Clare (I, 380, II, 227–28). He is said to have asked Bute for support to travel to Asia but Forster found no evidence (*Goldsmith*, I, 291).

The Deserted Village to his friend Reynolds. Given Goldsmith's attitude toward patronage which varied from proud defiance of a would-be professional writer, to sad nostalgia for the golden days of Pope and Swift, to hopes for a pension,[53] it is difficult to conclude much from Goldsmith's career about the decline of the patronage system, and misleading to think of him as typical.[54]

In the latter part of the century poets continued to find private support of one kind or other. Few writers were more cossetted than Cowper in the rural refuge provided for him by Mrs. Unwin.[55] Through the efforts of William Hayley, a pension of £300 a year was granted to Cowper in 1794. His *Tirocinium* (1784) was dedicated to Mrs. Unwin's son, his translation of the *Odyssey* to the Dowager Countess Spencer, and his *Iliad* to his noble kinsman Earl Cowper. The subscription edition was promoted by his family and friends; Cowper thought the list "an illustrious catalogue in respect of rank and title."[56] It was a profitable catalog too, with 700 subscribers.

Crabbe clearly assumed that a writer should and would be the beneficiary of aristocratic patronage. And that assumption was eventually borne out. He made approaches to men of rank, including Lords North, Shelburne,[57] and Thurlow (whom Cowper was simultaneously addressing).[58] He found his first real patron in Edmund Burke, who provided several of the traditional benefits, including extended hospitality at Beaconsfield and introductions to both book-

---

53   On unsuccessful attempts by Goldsmith's friends to secure a pension, see *ibid.*, 11, 387, 391, 392.

54   Hawkins thought Goldsmith was a fool for looking a gift horse in the mouth: "Thus ... did this idiot in the affairs of the world trifle with his fortunes, and put back the hand that was held out to assist him!" (*ibid.*, 1. 380). Goldsmith's refusal was at least in part based on principle. Cf. *Citizen of the World* 106, in which he worries about finding out "the secret of flattering the worthless, and yet of preserving a safe conscience" (*Collected Works*, 11, 414).

55   Cowper's career in patronage might have begun much earlier. In 1763 he was offered the Clerkship of the Journals in the House of Lords by his uncle, Ashley Cowper, Clerk of the Parliaments, but collapsed under the prospect of a hearing to establish his credentials. For details, see James King, *William Cowper*, 44–45.

56   *Letters and Prose Writings*, 111, 418. Cowper addressed a poem ("The Valediction") to Thurlow, whom he had known at the Inns of Court. He sent a copy of his 1782 *Poems* (containing a poem "On the Promotion of Edward Thurlow") to the Lord Chancellor (see *Letters and Prose Writings*, 11, 28). Thurlow had literary interests and literary friends. He translated Terence in his youth and critiqued Cowper's *Homer* in the 1790s.

57   See Crabbe's "To the Right Honourable the Earl of Shelburne" (1780). Shelburne was an admirer of Johnson and – in the 1790s – patron of Priestly, Bentham, and Richard Price.

58   Later he dedicated *The Newspaper* (1785) to Thurlow: "It is, my Lord, the province of superior rank, in general, to bestow this kind of patronage." Thurlow initially refused, but then responded to his appeal with £100 (*Complete Poetical Works*, 1, 673).

seller (Dodsley) and minister (Thurlow).[59] With Burke's help, he became domestic chaplain to the Duke of Rutland (son of Savage's old patron) by the age of twenty-eight, and was over the next thirty years (through his patron's influence) appointed to several church livings.[60] Crabbe's *Village* (1783) contains an elegy for the death of his patron's brother, Lord Robert Manners, and his *Tales*, published thirty years later in 1812, were dedicated to the Dowager Duchess.[61] Crabbe's son thought that Tale v, "The Patron," in *Tales of the Hall* was based on Crabbe's service as chaplain and "literary dependent" in Rutland's family. But if Crabbe at first found them "painful circumstances" (*Life of Crabbe*, p. 99) he became so acculturated to the patronage system that he eventually showed what his son called "aristocratic and Tory" leanings, and succeeded in "raising himself by his talents into a higher walk of society": "In appearance, manners, and disposition, he was entirely the gentleman ... Perhaps it may be said, that [in his last years] no one so humbly born and bred, ever retained so few traces of his origin" (pp. 150, 205). Crabbe served as loyal family retainer, backing the duke's candidate at election, and writing some twenty-three poems for his patroness's album.[62] If Crabbe's career were given as much prominence in the standard literary histories as Goldsmith's, the picture of literary patronage in the latter half of the eighteenth century would be quite different.[63]

The career of Robert Burns provides equally clear evidence that patronage was not dead in the 1780s and 90s. He successfully published his Kilmarnock *Poems* (1786) by subscription, dedicating one poem in the volume ("The Cotter's Saturday Night") to one local gentleman who secured 145 subscribers, and another ("A Dedication to G– H– Esq.") to a local solicitor (and his landlord) who signed up forty more. Some recent critics have suggested that Burns' "ritualized flattery" masks "naked ambition" or even con-

---

[59] See *The Life of George Crabbe*, 79–82, 85, 87, 89, 98.

[60] *Ibid.*, 107, 119, 183.

[61] *The Borough* (1810) was dedicated to the fifth duke, and *Tales of the Hall* (1819) to his wife. *Poems* (1807) was dedicated to Lord Holland.

[62] Only one of the poems was published in Crabbe's lifetime. They are collected as "Poems in Honour of the Family and Friends of the Dukes of Rutland, 1784–1827" in *Complete Poetical Works*, 111, 327–65. On Crabbe's electoral support, see 111, 411.

[63] Collins, who concluded that patronage was dead and unneeded by 1780, must say that Crabbe was "distinctly old-fashioned in the way in which the hope of a patron [hopes, it should be added, that were fully met] seems to have been firmly at the back of his mind" (*Profession of Letters*, 116).

tempt of the world of patronage,[64] but an unprejudiced reading of Burns' poems suggests that while he refuses to grovel, he finds it perfectly appropriate for the poet to ask forthrightly for benevolence from "the great," and for the patron to "bestow" it. His poem "To Robert Graham of Fintry Esquire, with a Request for an Excise Division" (1788) somewhat facetiously presents the poet as a grass-hopper ("unmindful of tomorrow") and a "woodbine" in need of a sturdy prop. Striking a delicate balance between presumption and pathos, Burns in effect compliments the patron's taste for witty banter, and deftly claims to distinguish his own plain speaking from the "shameless front" of poetic beggars. I'd rather starve than stoop, he says, but "I trust, meantime, my boon is in thy gift." A place in the excise was in fact granted the next year. In his later "Lament for James, Earl of Glencairn" (1791) Burns (who lived out Chatterton's fantasy) casts himself as an old "Bard" lamenting the death of "his Lord." Glencairn is "my noble master," "my benefactor," "my last, best, only friend."[65] And in verses sent with a copy of the "Lament" to one of Glencairn's gentleman friends – an implicit appeal that the poet not live unfriended – Burns does not hold back from calling his old "benefactor" a *patron*: "The *Friend* thou valued'st, I, the *Patron*, lov'd" (*Poems and Songs*, no. 334A).

Dramatists who participated in the patronage system included – in addition to John Home[66] – Hugh Kelly, who wrote in behalf of the government in the *Public Ledger*, and was later pensioned by Lord North (Collins, *Authorship in the Days of Johnson*, p. 201); and Arthur Murphy, who took time out from a career as playwright and biographer to edit the pro-Bute *Auditor* in 1762–63, and (for his reward) to serve as Commissioner of Bankrupts (p. 200). He was pensioned in 1803.[67] Richard Sheridan, as theatre manager for thirty years, was in a position to provide support rather than receive it. But he did not dispense altogether with the traditional gestures of

---

64   Robert Folkenflik has argued that "one can assert one's independence at the very moment of giving thanks for patronage" ("Patronage and the Poet Hero," 367). Peter Murphy's account is ambiguous. On the one hand Burns "accepts the hierarchy of patronage" (p. 7), and on the other "He found the obsequious posture oppressive, as any person would, but I think that the structure itself was perfectly congenial to him" (*Poetry as an Occupation and an Art in Britain*, 59).

65   Dreaming of a world in which the Bard would find protection from the Lord, Chatterton invented a patron for his "Rowley" in the medieval mayor of Bristol, William Canynges. Burns found such lords still living in Ayrshire.

66   See above, pp. 61–62.

67   Collins, *The Profession of Letters*, 122.

compliment to literary patrons. *The School for Scandal* (1777) was privately dedicated to Frances Anne Crewe, in a verse address that advertises the names of two titled ladies (the Marchioness of Granby and the Duchess of Devonshire). The printed edition of *The Critic* (performed 1779) was dedicated in 1781 to Mrs. Crewe's mother. And as member of parliament for thirty years, he was part of the system of political rather than literary patronage. For supporting Rockingham, he was rewarded with places in the foreign office and the treasury.[68]

In part because the novel was not an established literary form with an official pedigree and not yet a form on which men of taste might be expected to exercise their judgment, novels were somewhat less likely than poems to be fitted out with dedications. But novelists of the mid- and late-eighteenth century were nonetheless participants in and beneficiaries of the patronage system. Fielding, whose writing career extended from the 1720s into the 1750s, had support from a sequence of patrons, including Lady Mary Wortley Montagu, Dodington, Chesterfield, Ralph Allen (dedicatee of *Amelia* in 1751), Lord Lyttelton (dedicatee of *Tom Jones*), the Duke of Bedford, and Lord Chancellor Hardwicke.[69] As a clergyman Sterne was named to various livings through the good offices of various patrons, including the Archbishop of York, the Dean of York Cathedral (to whom he dedicated a published sermon in 1747), and Lord Fauconberg.[70] Sterne dedicated *Tristram Shandy*, volumes I–II (beginning with the second edition) in 1760 to William Pitt, then serving as Secretary of State (volume IX was also dedicated to him in 1767). Charlotte Lennox, as I have noted, was the recipient of patronage for several decades, from the 1740s into the 1760s. The subscription edition of Fanny Burney's *Camilla* (1796) was promoted by influential friends at court, and cleared for the author more than £2,000. Of the novelists who were not recipients of patronage, Richardson was a self-made printer, Beckford the fabulously wealthy heir of the Lord Mayor, and Godwin a radical whose opinions had in effect excluded him from support of all but a few.

Of other prose writers Johnson is of course the best known

---

[68] Under-Secretary of State for Foreign Affairs in 1782 and Secretary to the Treasury in 1783. In 1788 he served as confidential advisor to the Prince of Wales.

[69] The subscription list of his *Miscellanies* (1743) has 427 names.

[70] Sterne had provided some "literary services" to the Archbishop. See Arthur Cash, *Laurence Sterne: The Earlier Years*, 66, 114, 216, 257, and *The Later Years*, 28–29.

example of a writer of reputation who enjoyed patronage in the latter half of the eighteenth century. In addition to the 1762 pension, Johnson at the end of his life received an offer from the Lord Chancellor, Lord Thurlow, to provide up to £600 a year.[71] Some of Johnson's contemporaries also enjoyed significant state support. Hume served in a string of diplomatic positions – in his autobiographical sketch he carefully and proudly names each of the aristocratic patrons who offered him a place – and later as Under-Secretary of State for Scotland. When he resigned the place in 1768 his pension was doubled. Smollett was paid by Bute to edit the pro-ministry *Briton* in 1762–63. He was offered the "Place" of Consul at Nice (which he declined) and may have been offered a pension.[72] Burke served as secretary to the Marquis of Rockingham. The historian William Robertson, after being appointed Principal of the University of Edinburgh,[73] was named a Chaplain in Ordinary to the king, and in 1764 appointed Historiographer-Royal for Scotland at £200 a year (Collins, *Authorship in the Days of Johnson*, p. 203). Hugh Blair had a pension of £200 a year granted in 1780. Sheridan's father, Thomas, whose reputation was made on his *Lectures on Elocution* (1762), was one of those pensioned by Bute. Thomas Birch, editor of the *General Dictionary* (1738–41) and of editions of Milton, Bacon, Spenser, and Raleigh, served as a source of London political news for his patron Philip Yorke, Earl of Hardwicke, in the 1760s. Soame Jenyns, now known as the author of the *Free Inquiry into the Nature and Origin of Evil* savaged by Johnson, was a member of parliament for forty years, Lord of Trade and Plantations for twenty-five years, and the recipient of a pension from Secret Service funds (for his contributions as a political writer) in the 1750s. Philip Francis, admired by Johnson for his translation of Horace, was admired by politicians for his literary usefulness; he served as private chaplain to Henry Fox, Lord Holland, and later wrote in defense of the Bute and Grenville ministries in the 1760s, at a pension of £600 – and later £900 – per year. Horace Walpole, a gentleman writer with his own fortune, was

---

[71] Thurlow offered to take over Johnson's pension of £300 and in return allow Johnson to draw on him "to the amount of five or six hundred pounds" – presumably per annum. For details, see Boswell, *Life of Johnson*, IV, 350, and Johnson's *Letters*, IV, 398–400. Thurlow had been asked to arrange to have Johnson's pension doubled; when the king refused, Thurlow offered his own funds.

[72] He made several unsuccessful appeals to Pitt, Bute, and Shelburne to obtain a consulship in a warmer climate. See the *Letters of Tobias Smollett*, 110–11.

[73] See above, pp. 64–65.

at the same time a member of parliament from 1741 to 1768, and the beneficiary of his father's influence. He held several sinecures for fifty-nine years.[74]

The example of Gibbon shows that even gentleman-writers who boasted of their "independence" took part in political controversy and were grateful recipients of public and private patronage. As early as 1761, in his first literary public appearance, Gibbon dedicated his *Essai sur l'étude de la littérature* to his father. But he carefully sent presentation copies to the Duke of Richmond, the Marquis of Caernarvon (son of the Duke of Chandos), the Earls of Lichfield, Waldegrave, Egremont, Shelburne, Bute, Hardwicke, Bath, Granville, and Chesterfield. Later Gibbon sheepishly claimed that the copies were sent "by my father's direction," and upon the advice of David Mallet (at that time a pensionary of Bute).[75] Whether or not Gibbon's self-protective testimony is to be believed, it is clear that by his action he was signaling to established literary patrons and to ministers that he was a man of useful talents. In July 1779 Gibbon was appointed one of the "Lords Commissioners of Trade and Plantations" at a salary of more than £700 a year.[76] Like Johnson before him, he was then asked by high administration representatives (acting on the request of the Chancellor and Secretary of State) to review official papers concerning Britain's treatment of France under the terms of the 1763 Peace of Paris. He produced a *Mémoire Justicatif* in defense of British action.[77] In 1781 Lord North found a seat for him in Parliament,[78] and after a change of ministry cost Gibbon his place on the Board of Trade promised "a secure seat at the board of customs or excise ... on the first vacancy" (Bonnard, *Memoirs of My Life*, 165).[79] In 1783 Gibbon wrote Loughborough acknowledging "obligation of duty and gratitude which I owe to his Majesty's

---

[74]   Usher of the Exchequer, Clerk of the Estreats, and Comptroller of the Pipe. Even Boswell had something of a patron in the Earl of Lonsdale. Lonsdale arranged to have Boswell elected to two legal offices in Carlisle. Boswell hoped that Lonsdale, who controlled a number of boroughs, would make him an MP. See Frank Brady, *James Boswell, The Later Years*, 344, 364, 406–08.

[75]   See Bonnard's edition of Gibbon's *Memoirs of My Life*, 102.

[76]   For the assistance of a "powerful friend" (the Attorney General, Alexander Wedderburne, Lord Loughborough) in securing the place, see the *Letters of Edward Gibbon*, 11, 219.

[77]   *Miscellaneous Works*, v, 1–34. On the circumstances leading to Gibbon's *Mémoire*, see J. E. Norton, *A Bibliography of the Works of Gibbon*, 22–33.

[78]   *Letters*, 11, 250.

[79]   Patricia Craddock observes that despite his inherited and earned income, Gibbon (burdened with debt) couldn't afford to live in London "as a Member of Parliament and society": the placeman's salary helped (*Edward Gibbon*, 121).

Government" and offering his services in negotiating the Peace of Paris.[80] After North's resignation (which closed off further government patronage) Gibbon was a regular guest at North's London house.[81] In 1788 Gibbon expressed his gratitude in the preface to volume IV of his *Decline and Fall*: "Were I ambitious of any other Patron than the Public, I would inscribe this work to ... Lord North." The tribute is a dedication in everything but name: the author offers gracious compliments to a man who has been generous – and who is in a position to continue to be so – and yet retains his proud sense of "independence."[82]

SUBSCRIPTION AND PATRONAGE

Another measure of the persistence of patronage through the century is the evidence about subscription lists gathered by Robinson and Wallis.[83] Subscription has rightly been described as a kind of democratized patronage, whereby a large number of patrons may, for a relatively small outlay, find their names listed among the subscribers.[84] While evidence is still being collected, it has already been shown that the number of books published by subscription remained fairly constant during the period 1720–80 at about 250 per decade. Claims that the subscription system was abused by undeserving writers, and that, in consequence, patrons withheld their support,[85] are disputed by such figures, particularly when one takes into account what happens after 1760: rather than declining, the

---

[80] *Letters*, II, 358.

[81] And also at Sheffield Place (home of John Holroyd, later Lord Sheffield), where Gibbon kept part of his library. See *Memoirs of My Life*, 180, 181, 187.

[82] Craddock notes that *Decline and Fall* "only just paid for its own expenses, the much-loved library" (*Edward Gibbon*, 131).

[83] See "Book Subscription Lists," 255–86; *Book Subscription Lists: A Revised Guide*, together with four "Supplements" (1976, 1977, 1980, 1981), and the *CheckList of Eighteenth-Century Books Containing Lists of Subscribers*, eds. R. C. Alston, F. J. G. Robinson, and C. Wadham.

[84] Subscribers were considered as "patrons" as early as 1772. See the *Letters concerning the Present State of England*: "the public in general may be called the patron, when authors make their appeal either in printing by subscription, or publishing on their own account" (327). See also the *Monthly Review*, ser. 2. vol. 18 (1795), where subscribers are said to provide "patronage" (p. 229).

[85] Complaints about excessive use of the subscription system in England are found as early as 1725: "the Publick have been wearied out with repeated Subscriptions to Persons, who ... have no Right to them" (from *The Weekly Journal or Saturday's Post*, March 20, 1725, quoted in Clayton Atto, "The Society for the Encouragement of Learning," 263). Cf. Goldsmith's *Enquiry* (1759), in his *Collected Works*, I, 310, and the *Letter concerning the Present State of England* (1772), 329, along with Jean Bernard Le Blanc, *Letter on the English and French Nations* (1747), cited in Goldsmith, *Collected Works*, I, 310n..

number of books published per decade by subscription *increases* sharply, to an average of almost 300, and then to 420 during the 1780s and 498 during the 1790s.[86]

One scholar who has analyzed the subscription lists up to 1750 observes that "the extent to which [they] were dominated by the peerage is remarkable."[87] While it may be true that subscription lists later in the century contain a smaller proportion of peers, it does not follow that the system of patronage had declined. Nor does it follow that subscription lists had been so transformed as to become merely a bookseller's marketing device. Indeed, one might argue that, although patronage had become more diffused than earlier in the century, *more* patrons were active in the system than ever before. This may indicate that patronage was increasingly felt to be the responsibility not just of the nobility, but of merchants, professionals, and manufacturers too. As Robinson and Wallis suggest, there was "social cachet to be gained from vicarious association with the more noble supporters."[88] It was perhaps not so much that the social center of gravity (and cultural authority) was shifting downward, but that members of an increasingly wealthy and self-confident middle class were aping the manners of their betters and aspiring to move up.

If most of the major writers of the latter part of the eighteenth century took part in the patronage system in one way or another, then it is clear that patronage was by no means dying at mid-century and "dead" by 1780. But the presence of a dedication does not in itself signify that the system of patronage was intact. The dedication, it might be argued, was by 1750 a mere formality, signifying no more than (say) a fine leather binding. Nor does a mere listing of writers and patrons, in the absence of a complete study of writers' total incomes, show that writers derived more than a trivial proportion of their support from various forms of patronage. Some work on literary earnings has been done,[89] and with the increased attention

---

[86] Robinson and Wallis, *Book Subscription Lists: A Revised Guide. Fourth Supplement* (July 1981), 25.

[87] W. A. Speck, "Politicians, Peers, and Publication by Subscription," 65.

[88] *Book Subscription Lists. A Revised Guide*, iii. It was common for subscribers to be listed by rank within each letter: "the nobility and the gentry precede the clergy, and the tradesmen conclude the entry, normally with the book trade in the rear" (vi). Engaged in promoting a subscription, Lennox thought many of her acquaintance would be "proud of standing in the same list with the Queen." See *The Letters of Samuel Johnson*, 11, 202.

[89] J. D. Fleeman, "The Revenue of a Writer: Johnson's Literary Earnings," 211–30, supplemented by Thomas Kaminski, *The Early Career of Samuel Johnson*. See also Judith P. Stanton, "Charlotte Smith's 'Literary Business'," 375–401.

in recent years to the idea of the "professional writer," biographers are beginning to pay more attention to details of payments from booksellers for copy and from editors for journalistic services, as well as salaries and inheritances. We will in the future probably recover more evidence about the year-to-year financial circumstances of writers, and the percentage of authorial incomes deriving from patronage. Such evidence will probably show that, over time, most writers derived less and less from patronage, and more and more from booksellers. But I would argue that to focus exclusively on quantitative data is to misrepresent the cultural importance of patronage as an institution. Quite apart from the size and number of governmental pensions and direct payments from private patrons to writers, the writers of the late eighteenth century were not considered, either by themselves or by the culture at large, as completely independent operators, free agents in the literary marketplace. Rather they were seen as still implicated in a traditional economy and a hierarchically organized society, in which it was felt appropriate that writers have a place.

RESPONSIBILITY AND AUTHORITY

Even in the late eighteenth century the notion survives that somehow authors ought to be supported by "the nation." Such a notion is behind Burke's lament, in the *Annual Register* for 1759, that the nation, "which admires [Johnson's] works, and profits by them" – Burke is probably thinking of the *Dictionary*, published just four years earlier – "has done nothing for the author" – that is, has not provided him a pension.[90] And it lies behind the language of a dedication of a new edition of Shakespeare's plays in 1768 by Edward Capell to the Prime Minister, the Duke of Grafton. Shakespeare's works, he says, are "part of the kingdom's riches." Letters confer on the country a kind of "estate in fame ... the worth and value of which or sinks or raises her in the opinion of foreign nations." Shakespeare is thus "an object of national concern" to a statesman like Grafton, who by patronizing a literary project will be "a benefactor to his country and somewhat entitl'd to her good will."[91] To be sure, Capell's language is calculated for his audience, and its sincerity might be questioned. But the very presence of such language in the printed dedication –

[90] *Annual Register*, 2 (1759), 479.
[91] *Mr. William Shakespeare, his Comedies, Histories, and Tragedies*, 1, A3.

which Grafton accepted – indicates that such sentiments were still considered at least conventionally true and appropriately rehearsed in public.[92]

A clearer sign of the perceived responsibility of the great to protect the nation's writers is found in Henry Mackenzie's favorable review of Burns' Kilmarnock *Poems* (1786). "To repair the wrongs of suffering or neglected merit; to call forth genius from the obscurity in which it had pined indignant and place it where it may profit or delight the world; these are exertions which give to wealth an enviable superiority, to greatness and to patronage a laudable pride."[93] Writing at a time when new men were making great fortunes from trade and industry – he deplored the "sudden accumulation of wealth in vulgar hands" – Mackenzie in effect encouraged families of "noble and illustrious ancestry" to retain their traditional place in society by discharging their duty toward the maintenance of culture.[94] As if to hedge against the failure of the nobility, he also took care to instruct the newly rich on the conduct proper to men of wealth and high office. In an essay in *The Mirror* in 1780 Mackenzie observed that "he who attains elevation of place or extent of fortune, increases not only the pleasures he has to enjoy, but the duties he has to perform." Acknowledging that "in a commercial country" wealth confers "the dignity of title or of birth," his essay in effect offers advice to the newly rich on the difficult "art of a *patron*."[95]

The persistence of old attitudes is also implied – if somewhat paradoxically – by the flourishing in the late eighteenth century of the "calamities of authors" tradition, associated especially with Isaac

---

92　The lawyers, like Lord Camden, who argued in 1774 against perpetual copyright, declaring that "Men of Genius" wrote not for "Gain" but for "Glory," seem to assume that an author's material needs will be somehow taken care of – though it should be noted that they do not go on to argue explicitly that the nation (or the peerage) has a responsibility to provide for them. For details, see Rose, *Authors and Owners*, esp. 92–112.

93　See the unsigned essay in *The Lounger*, 97 (Dec. 9, 1786), repr. in *Robert Burns: The Critical Heritage*, ed. Donald Low, 71. MacKenzie's implicit appeal to patrons is prompted by his discovery that Burns felt the need to seek "shelter and support" in the West Indies. By calling forth Burns from obscurity, MacKenzie consciously acts as a kind of "patron" himself.

94　Mackenzie's up-to-date language presents the patron as sentimental rescuer, bringing forth the flowers otherwise fated to blush unseen in the desert air.

95　Difficult because patrons are often "bunglers" who "make enemies by offices of friendship, and purchase a lampoon at the price of a panegyric," especially (so it seems) if the patrons are "possessors of suddenly-acquired fortunes." See *The Mirror*, No. 91 (March 21, 1780), 361–63.

D'Israeli.[96] Stories about neglected authors were of course not new. Laments about the world's indifference to the poverty of Cowley, Butler, Oldham, and others are common in the late seventeenth century. But such laments are louder at the end of the eighteenth century. And they imply that the nation *should* have supported its writers. As D'Israeli puts it, "whenever great authors obtain their due rights, the calamities of literature will be greatly diminished" (*Miscellanies*, 1840, p. 51). His biographical anecdotes are laced with complaints against the "insolence," "penuriousness," and "stinginess" of "hard-hearted patrons" (pp. 59, 62). D'Israeli is writing at a time when the literary market is sometimes said to be fully in place, and when authors could now support themselves with dignity. But that was not D'Israeli's view. As he saw it, it was the booksellers who thrived while authors continue to starve. It was not until the middle of the nineteenth century that it was widely assumed that writers could – and should – support themselves by their own literary labors.[97]

If it was still assumed that authors somehow deserved to be supported by a grateful nation, it was also assumed that if a patron class continued to have responsibility for supporting literature, they also retained a kind of authority over it. People of wealth and literary education (of the sort associated with at least nominal residence at university) were still assumed to hold literary opinions to which it was proper to defer. For Hume, such deference sustains literary standards. "Men of delicate taste" – and for Hume's contemporaries this especially means men of birth and education – "are easily to be distinguished in society, by the soundness of their understanding and the superiority of their faculties above the rest of mankind." It is right, in Hume's view, that such men set the "standard of taste."[98] Many men of birth and wealth of course had no literary sensibility at all, but they still retained their authority. Goldsmith comments in the *Citizen of the World* on the "authority" of the rich, and on the way in

---

[96] D'Israeli began publishing his *Curiosities of Literature* in 1791. His *Calamities of Authors* was first published in 1812 and often reprinted. John Nichols' *Literary Anecdotes of the Eighteenth Century*, with much information about the financial circumstances of writers, began appearing in 1812.

[97] Macaulay's *History* (1849) of the Restoration period is informed with the idea that the system of patronage was degrading to both parties. It might be noted that Macaulay himself was financially comfortable – in large part because his civil service job in India in the 1830s brought him £10,000 a year. See John Clive, *Macaulay: The Shaping of the Historian*, 233, 475.

[98] "Of the Standard of Taste," in *Essays Moral, Political, and Literary*, 243.

which public opinion is ultimately shaped – at two or three removes – by a "great man" who commends a book with an idle remark. English readers – unfortunately, in Goldsmith's view – are still "sway'd in their opinions, by men who often from their very education, are incompetent judges."[99] The "great" may in fact be incompetent, but they still wield cultural authority.

THE LANGUAGE OF DEDICATIONS

Another kind of evidence that patrons retained cultural authority is the very language of dedications. It might be objected that such language is merely conventional compliment, or that an author who writes a dedication is not to be considered as upon oath. But if the author is Samuel Johnson, we might take seriously the assumptions about patronal authority found in the words in which the late-eighteenth-century dedicator addresses a patron. Although Johnson dedicated none of his works to patrons, and signed his own name to no formal dedication, he wrote some two dozen dedications for other writers from the 1750s to the 1780s.[100] In writing dedications for others, Boswell reports, "he considered himself as by no means speaking his own sentiments" (*Life of Johnson*, vol. II, p. 2), but he knew what was appropriate to say in composing a dedication, knew what another self-respecting writer could sign, and what a patron would be pleased to receive.

Johnson's dedications follow established convention in complimenting the patron's "benevolence" or "beneficence,"[101] "greatness" of mind,[102] "protection," "encouragement," and "paternal care" of literature.[103] Like many an author before him, Johnson also acknowledges that the patrons he addresses are the arbiters of taste. The "Judgment" of the Earl of Middlesex, he makes Charlotte Lennox say, has "long given a Standard to the National Taste."[104]

99 *Citizen of the World*, No. 57 (July 9, 1760), in *Collected Works*, II, 236–37. Goldsmith goes on to note that a book written by a "nobleman" will "pass for perfection without farther examination ... title being alone equivalent to taste, imagination, and genius" (p. 237).
100 They are conveniently collected in Hazen, *Johnson's Prefaces and Dedications*.
101 See the 1760 dedication to the Italian ambassador of Baretti's *Dictionary of the English and Italian Languages* (Hazen, *Johnson's Prefaces and Dedications*, 8) and the 1766 dedication to the king of George Adams' *Treatise on the Globes* (*ibid.*, 4).
102 Dedication of Adams, *Treatise on the Globes* (*ibid.*, 3) and the 1785 dedication to the king of Charles Burney's *Account of the Commemoration of Handel* (*ibid.*, 32).
103 See *ibid.*, 4, 40, 62.
104 Dedication of *The Female Quixote* in 1752 to Charles Sackville, Earl of Middlesex and later

The Earl of Orrery is the "Judge whom *Pliny* himself would have wished for his Assessor to hear a literary Cause" (Hazen, *Dedications*, p. 109). He even reflects the traditional idea that the patron who encourages and rewards a work is somehow the "owner" of it. In writing Percy's dedication of the *Reliques of English Poetry* (1765) to the Countess of Northumberland (descendant of a line of Northumberlands and Percys – who had both inspired and encouraged the writers of the old heroic songs) Johnson tells her that "those songs which the bounty of your ancestors rewarded, now return to your Ladyship by a kind of hereditary right" (Hazen, *Dedications*, p. 168).[105]

What is distinctive about Johnson's dedications is perhaps his repeated observations on the patron's "condescension" in taking notice of a writer's works – Johnson uses the term in at least seven of his dedications.[106] The term is a revealing one. In the *Dictionary* Johnson defines it as "voluntary submission to equality with inferiours." It is, Johnson makes clear, a "happy quality," and a kind of "courtesy."[107] In the context of patronage, "condescension" affirms a social order of hierarchy and subordination, in which the patron stands higher than the author but, in ideal circumstances, descends to a kind of "equality." Such happy condescension, furthermore, has the effect of *raising* the author and his book. Burney's *Account of the Commemoration of Handel* is "dignified by the patronage of our Sovereign" (Hazen, *Dedications*, p. 33). William Payne's 1772 *Elements of Trigonometry* will be fortunate in obtaining "the sanction of your Lordship's approbation" (Hazen, *Dedications*, p. 154).[108]

The other distinctive term in Johnson's dedicatory language is

second Duke of Dorset. In 1732 he had been the dedicatee of the *Collection of Pieces in Verse and Prose which have been published in occasion of the Dunciad*, with a dedication signed by Richard Savage, and probably written by Pope. Middlesex was the grandson of the poet and patron Charles Sackville, Earl of Middlesex and later Earl of Dorset (1638–1706). Walpole said of the younger Sackville: "he possessed the hereditary talent of his family; and though a poet of no eminence, had a genteel style in his verses that spoke the man of quality" (quoted in *DNB*).

[105] Cf. Capell's dedication of his *Shakespeare* to Grafton, whose grandfather had "honour'd me early with his patronage … This little present, and the person who tender it" are "a minute part of your inheritance, descending to you from Him" (1, A3v).

[106] Hazen, *Johnson's Prefaces and Dedications*, 3, 29, 32, 62, 66, 101, 154. Hazen remarks that the word is Johnson's "favorite phrase" (p. 61).

[107] Although the word was beginning to acquire its modern meaning in the eighteenth century, Johnson still uses it in its positive sense.

[108] Compare the dedication of Burney's *Handel*, in which the king is praised for giving "Your sanction to musical emulation" (Hazen, *Johnson's Prefaces and Dedications*, 32).

"benefits" – the favors received by the *beneficiary* from the *benefactor*.[109] As I have argued, this is a traditional Senecan term used to describe the freely offered gift from superior to inferior that serves to bind society in harmonious union. The term is found not only in the late seventeenth and early eighteenth century – when patronage is said to be at its height – but is commonly found in Johnson's writings, and serves as evidence that older habits of thinking about patronage survive.[110] The world, he has George Adams write to the king, may "receive benefits or suffer evils, as Your influence is extended or withdrawn" (Hazen, *Dedications*, p. 4). Johnson knows not "what greater benefit [the Earl of Shaftesbury] can confer on [his] country, than that of preserving worthy names from oblivion, by joining them with [his] own" (Hazen, *Dedications*, p. 23).

The term appears not only in Johnson's ghost-written dedications, but in letters of thanks to those patrons who had offered him support. In responding to Bute's grant of the 1762 pension, Johnson reports that he will "endeavour to give your Lordship the only recompense, which generosity desires, the gratification of finding that your benefits are not improperly bestowed."[111] And in responding to Thurlow's offer of financial support in 1784, Johnson declines graciously: "From your Lordship's kindness, I have received a benefit which only Men like You can bestow."[112] Each letter acknowledges a hierarchical difference between the patron who freely "bestows" and the author who evens the score by gratefully acknowledging an "obligation."[113] It is not surprising to discover that in the letter to Chesterfield Johnson hopes that "it is no very cynical asperity not to confess obligation where no *benefit* [emphasis added] has been received."[114]

---

109   In the *Dictionary* a "benefactor" is "he that confers a benefit." A "benefaction" is "the benefit conferred." A "benefit," derived as Johnson knows from *beneficium*, is simply a "favour" or a "kindness." But Johnson's own use of the term makes clear that a "benefit" is typically conferred from a superior to an inferior.

110   Cf. *Rambler* 166: "Benefits which are received as gifts from wealth, are exacted as debts from indigence." Johnson broods on the proper relationship between "the distressed and necessitous" and "those who [flatter] themselves with their own dignity," that is, between author and patron.

111   July 20, 1762, in *Letters of Samuel Johnson*, I, 208.

112   *Ibid.*, IV, 400.

113   Contrast Junius on "benefits," emphasizing not hierarchy but equality: "The first foundation of friendship is not the power of conferring benefits, but the equality with which they are received and *may* be returned" (Letter 35, in *Letters of Junius*, 174). In *Rambler* 166 Johnson discusses the pleasure of reciprocal kindness, and the unfortunate condition of the poor man who has "no power to confer benefits."

114   *Letters of Samuel Johnson*, I, 64–65.

Was Johnson merely offering the expected deference, complying with the convention in accepting the polite fiction that an author is properly subordinate to a lordly patron? Probably not, when we recall Johnson's opinions about the importance of *writing* his real and decided opinion (regardless of what he might freely say in conversation about the flattery and falsehood of dedicators) and the value of subordination in society. His deference to patronal authority is furthermore reflected in the larger culture, in which, as Linda Colley has argued, deference to one's betters persisted well into the nineteenth century. The persistence of the old hierarchical order is often assumed by and reflected in the fiction writers of the day. The world of Fanny Burney's *Evelina* (1778) is presided over by (and the heroine rewarded with) Lord Orville, a man of "noble mind" and "exalted benevolence" (Letter 80). Lady Catherine de Bourgh's haughty consciousness of deference owed to her superior rank serves as a foil to Darcy's quiet generosity as landlord, master, and patron. And at the end of *Mansfield Park* (1814) Fanny Price, who has moved into the parsonage at Mansfield with Edmund Bertram, finds everything "perfect ... within the view and patronage of Mansfield Park."

PATRONAGE CONTESTED

The system of patronage was very much intact at the end of the century, but this is not to say that the institution was not undergoing change. Some changes have already been noted: the increase in the number of patrons (including subscribers) meant that patronage was less concentrated in the hands of a few "universal" patrons like Dorset and Halifax, and was more diffused over ranks and occupations. And as more and more books were published outside of London, or by provincial writers, more patrons were recruited from county towns and villages, like the Northampton subscribers to Mary Leapor's poems.

Another difference is that new institutions arose to take over some of the traditional functions of patronage. The Society for the Encouragement of Learning was one such institution, founded in 1735 "to supply the want of a regular and public encouragement of learning."[115] In an attempt to win support for Johnson's *Irene* in 1741, his friend Cave wrote to Thomas Birch, a member of the Society,

[115] For an account of the Society, see Atto, "The Society for the Encouragement of Learning," 263–88.

asking for their assistance.[116] Another is the Society for the Encouragement of Arts, Commerce, and Manufacturers in Great Britain – commonly called the Society of Arts. Organized in 1754, it had 700 members by 1758 and 2100 members, including Johnson, within a decade.[117] The Society's subscribers included many drawn from the traditional ranks of patronage – titled nobility and government ministers – but almost half the members came from the middle ranks.[118] By offering "premiums" in six categories (one of which was "polite arts") and organizing artistic exhibitions, the Society sought to "render Great Britain the school of instruction as it is already the centre of traffic to the greatest part of the known world" (Colley, *Britons*, p. 91).[119] The Society of Artists, founded in 1759, mounted an annual exhibition to bring the work of painters and other artists to the attention of "Judges & Patrons of Merit," and published a catalog, for which Johnson probably contributed a preface in 1762.[120] Similar societies sprang up throughout the country. Subscription libraries and local "book societies" frequently appear in eighteenth-century subscription lists.[121] Crabbe was an honorary member of the Cambridge Book Society in 1809.[122] Perhaps the best known literary "premium" in the eighteenth century was the Seatonian Prize, established annually at Cambridge University beginning in 1751 by the will of the Reverend Thomas Seaton of Kislingbury. The £10 prize added modestly to Smart's annual income and significantly to his reputation and prestige – he was a five-time winner during the years 1750 to 1756.[123]

Other forms of collective support were less formal. The well-

---

[116] See Boswell, *Life of Johnson*, I, 152–53.

[117] See James Clifford, "Johnson and the Society of Artists," 333–48.

[118] See Linda Colley, quoting from D. G. C. Allan's London University dissertation, *Britons*, 94. A member boasted in 1758, with some exaggeration, that the Society had enrolled "all the Ministers of State and most of the chief nobility." Allan, "The Society of Arts and Government, 1754–1800," 443.

[119] "Premiums" (from two to five guineas) for "literary essays" were also offered in the inaugural number of the Edinburgh *Bee* in 1791. As early as 1759 Goldsmith worried that "Premiums . . . for literary excellence" were "misapplied" (*Collected Works*, I, 309).

[120] See James Clifford, "Johnson and the Society of Artists," 345–47.

[121] See Robinson and Wallis, *Book Subscription Lists: A Revised Guide*, xiii.

[122] *The Life of George Crabbe*, 167–68. Crabbe allowed "The Borough" to be read at a meeting of the Literary Fund "for the benefit of distressed authors" (p. 168).

[123] Parodying Seaton's will, which gave "my Kislingbury Estate" to Cambridge, Smart referred to his Seatonian prize poems as his "Kislingbury estates" (*Annotated Letters of Christopher Smart*, 53). But the prize (after publication expenses) only amounted to about £10 (see Arthur Sherbo, *Christopher Smart*, 279). Still, Smart expressed his thanks in a poem "On Gratitude, to the Memory of Mr. Seaton."

known "salons" of the Bluestockings (Elizabeth Montagu, Hannah More, Mrs. Boscawen, and Mrs. Vesey), a feature of the latter half of the eighteenth century, served to generate interest and support for writers, especially women writers, in whom they took an interest, including Ann Yearsley, Anna Williams, and Elizabeth Carter. Perhaps equally important were the informal literary "circles" that focused on an established writer. Successful writers, including Dryden, Swift, and Pope, had long made use of their influence with patrons and booksellers to provide occasional assistance to up-and-coming or merely needy authors. (Johnson followed their example.) But the literary "circle," involving a network of authors, editors, and printers meeting regularly, is more characteristic of the mid- and late-century. Richardson's "circle" functioned as a kind of patron, as in the case of Mary Leapor, stimulating interest, collecting subscriptions, writing proposals, etc.[124]

By encouraging the arts, literary circles and patriotic societies were in effect assuming some of the responsibility for promoting British culture that had traditionally belonged to the peers and ministers. As I have suggested, the aristocracy and government were still encouraged to exercise their traditional function, and to a considerable extent did so. But an *implicit* challenge to the cultural authority of the aristocracy was being made, and such a challenge is perhaps the most significant feature of the patronage system in the latter half of the eighteenth century.

Because it is important not to overstate the adversarial nature of the challenge, or to imply any open cultural war, "challenge" may be too strong a word for the tensions and strains in the culture as it slowly but inexorably moved from one economy to another, from a world governed by hierarchy and deference to one governed by competition in an open marketplace. The transition to the new economy may have been slower than "Whiggish" historians have suggested, and in any case the changeover was not complete by 1800. New forms, attitudes, and institutions did not suddenly replace old; despite contemporary claims, patrons did not massively withdraw from the scene; nor were they simply supplanted by the bookseller; they co-existed, jostling for primacy, and for authority.[125]

---

[124] Richardson's efforts to assist women writers attracted praise from John Duncombe's *Feminiad* (1754).

[125] John Brewer observes that "increasingly, the aristocracy constituted the top end of a large market rather than the market *tout court*. They could no longer exercise such complete

There is some evidence, it must be granted, that private patrons may have reduced their role, and cut back the amount of support they once provided. The Duke of Chandos, for example, after subscribing regularly in the 1720s to proposals presented to him by a variety of aspirants, determined about 1732 to retrench, and to limit his subscriptions to projects proposed by his "friends" (i.e, those with whom he had an established political connection).[126] It is possible that in his eyes the "value" of writing had fallen because of the laws of supply and demand, or because a reputation for literary judgment may have counted for less in the great world,[127] but it is more likely that he was trying to control his expenses as his family fortune began to collapse. (Chandos suffered major losses in the South Sea Bubble and in other failed investments. Having continued to spend heavily on elections, he "impair'd his estate," and died in debt in 1744.)[128] Thus, little can be deduced from such withdrawals from patronage.[129]

The *Monthly Review* in 1759 conceded that patrons may have refused appeals, but defended them against the charge that they had abandoned literature or that good poets went without patrons. It is more frequently found, so claimed the *Monthly*, that "the Patrons of Literature and the Polite Arts have been disgusted at the dissolute manners of their professors, than that these arts have really wanted patronage." Patrons in such conditions cannot offer support "without appearing to protect bad men, and promoting the interests of those who would repay their benevolence by insolence and ingratitude."[130] Other patrons may have concluded that a reputation for "magnificence" did not have the same value it once had, now that the Palladian building boom had scattered country houses throughout England, and vast piles such as Walpole's Houghton Hall

control or command through their purchasing power and patronage" ("Commercialization and Politics," in *The Birth of a Consumer Society*, eds. McKendrick, Brewer, and Plumb, 197–98). My point is that the aristocracy continued to constitute "the top end" and continued to exercise *some* control.

126   Chandos "made it a rule never to subscribe for new books unless the authors were his friends" (Baker and Baker, *James Brydges*, 69).
127   In 1757 James Ralph thought that the "credit and Value of Authorship" – note the economic terms – had been "sunk" (*Case of Authors*, 40–41).
128   Namier, *The Structure of Politics*, 255, quoting a letter from Chandos's grandson, and Cannon, *Aristocratic Century*, 127, quoting Chandos' twentieth-century biographers, Baker and Baker.
129   Goldsmith satirically speculated that "the great" found it too difficult to develop a taste for poetry – "to read poetry requires thought, and the English nobility were not fond of thinking" – so they took up first music and then painting, "because in this they might indulge a happy vacancy and yet still have pretensions to delicacy and taste as before" (*Collected Works*, 11, 148).
130   *Monthly Review*, 21 (November 1759), 389.

were attracting criticism for their vulgarity and "false Magnificence."[131] There were always other ways in which rich landowners
could spend their money, whether in "improving" their own estates
– making them more economically efficient, improving agricultural
yields and rent rolls, or in modernizing an old house and landscaping
the park – or investing in new commercial and industrial ventures.
An increased attention to "estate-management," to amassing investment capital rather than spending,[132] may have dampened aristocratic enthusiasm for patronage of the arts.[133] It has even been
argued that under a new political economy the man of letters was
defined as non-productive, and expenditures on the arts a waste of
time and money.[134]

For those who retained literary tastes, a more crowded literary
world, with more authors, more booksellers, more books, and more
readers, might have meant that a patron could not easily achieve
eminence in the eyes of writers and other patrons. An increasingly
democratized literary world might mean that it was increasingly
difficult to determine which writers were likely to confer the kind of
honor and fame that a patron seeks. A contributor to *The Bee* in 1791
argued that as the number of authors increased, patrons were
unwilling to devote the effort required to "attempt a discrimination"
between those who deserved support and those who did not. They
"took refuge in indiscriminate rejection."[135] Other potential
patrons, like the younger Pitt, may have assumed that with a thriving
marketplace authors no longer needed support from patrons, and
should be expected to support themselves.[136]

---

[131] See above, pp. 38–39.

[132] Cf. Adam Smith: "That portion of his revenue which a rich man annually spends, is in
most cases consumed by idle guests and menial servants, who leave nothing behind them
in return for their consumption. That portion which he annually saves, as for the sake of
the profit it is immediately employed as a capital, is consumed ... by a different set of
people, by labourers, manufacturers, and artificers, who re-produce with a profit the value
of their annual consumption." *The Wealth of Nations*, 321.

[133] See J. R. Wordie, *Estate Management in Eighteenth-Century England*, and R. A. C. Parker, *Coke of Norfolk*.

[134] Cf. Adam Smith: "The labour of some of the most respectable orders in society ... does
not fix or realize itself in any ... vendible commodity, which endures after that labour is
past, and for which an equal quantity of labour could afterwards be procured ... In the
same class must be ranked ... churchmen, lawyers, physicians, men of letters of all kinds"
(*The Wealth of Nations*, 315). For discussion of this passage, see Zeynep Tenger and Paul
Trolander, "Genius Versus Capital," 181–83.

[135] See the series of papers "On the History of Authors by Profession," by "A. D.," in *The Bee*,
3 (1791). I quote from the second paper in the series, p. 15.

[136] Tenger and Trolander note that for Adam Smith writers don't need any further

But such arguments for the appearance of a new cultural "economy" in which patronage of literature played a less prominent role – while they may eventually be shown to be valid – are difficult to substantiate. And as I have suggested, other evidence is available to show that patrons in large numbers, and from all ranks, continued to enlist as subscribers and to accept formal dedications. Even if patrons did not in significant numbers *withdraw* from the literary world, however, their status within it had changed by the closing decades of the eighteenth century. Such challenges to patronal authority, as I have argued, can be found as early as the writings of Dryden, Swift, and Pope, who in one way or another proudly resisted the power of patronage and symbolically asserted their own countervailing power and authority. The "cultural economy" of literary patronage, even at its height, involved cases in which one participant, whether author, patron, or bookseller, attempted to manipulate the system to his advantage. Some booksellers tried to buy copy cheap and sell dear.[137] Some patrons, like Robert Harley (or Halifax, or Chesterfield, or the Earl of Northumberland), seem to have attempted to acquire a reputation for beneficence without actually laying out much money or political capital.[138] And possibly apocryphal anecdotes about patrons refusing dedications that lacked sufficient compliment, or of writing an author's dedication for him, suggest that some patrons insisted overmuch on their traditional authority to correct an author's work.[139] What is new after about 1750 is that such contestation becomes general. All the participants in

encouragement than the "liberty" to write "for their own interest." See *Wealth of Nations*, 748, and Tenger and Trolander, "Genius versus Capital," 183.

[137] Dryden complained that all English booksellers were mercenary, "more devoted to their own Gain, than the publick honour." See his "Life of Lucian" (publ. 1711, pp. 55–56, quoted in Winn, *John Dryden*, 481). Such complaints seem to increase after 1750. "The Rules of Trade," observed James Ralph, "oblige [the booksellers] to buy as cheap and sell as dear as possible" (*Case of Authors*, 21). As a result, lamented Goldsmith, "it is the interest of the one to allow as little for writing, and of the other to write as much as possible" (*Collected Works*, 1, 316).

[138] See Swift's repeated complaints about Harley's failure to find him a place in the English church, and Johnson's remark that Harley "lamented" that Pope's genius "should be wasted upon a work not original [i.e., the Homer translations]; but proposed no means by which he might live without it" (*Lives of the Poets*, 111, 110). Of Northumberland, the *DNB* notes that "although his expenditure was unexampled in his time, he was not generous, but passed for being so owing to his judicious manner of bestowing favors."

[139] One of Peter Motteux's patrons was said to be unsatisfied with a dedication, and to have written one for Motteux to sign. Horace Walpole allegedy rejected a dedication because he did not like the terms. See Wheatley, *The Dedications of Books to Patrons and Friends*, 34–36, 37.

the literary system – authors, readers, critics, booksellers, and patrons – advance claims for their own literary authority. Each party in effect resists or contests the authority of every other party.[140] With respect to the system of literary patronage, the patron's traditional authority is in effect being contested on every side.

The authority of the patron is contested by theorists like Pope who in effect argued that the best judges – those with the best taste – were not necessarily the best born.[141] Other theorists – especially at mid-century – by emphasizing the importance of originality and of "genius" in effect shifted emphasis from the writer as humble craftsman, executing a plan, to writer as noble inventor. That this shift of emphasis implied a challenge to patronal authority is suggested by Young's *Conjectures on Original Composition* (1759), where original writers are said to be qualified for the "noble title of an author."[142]

Patronal authority is challenged by critics who advocate the establishment of a literary "academy" to set proper standards, and (*faute de mieux*) settle for raising the status of the professional critic or the critical reviewer as the culture's best judge of literary merit.[143] Smollett championed the old idea of an academy and campaigned to raise the critical standards of his readers at the *Critical Review*.[144] Although he may have been somewhat quixotic in his aspirations (Smollett later had to concede that he had largely failed), he was not alone. Goldsmith seconded Smollett's attempt to displace the cultural authority of the merely rich or "great," or of those self-appointed critics who think it "proper to be a judge of genius," and invest themselves "with full power and authority over every caitiff who aims at their instruction or entertainment." His *Citizen of the*

---

[140] On authorial resistance to booksellers, see Betty Rizzo, "The English Author–Bookseller Dialogue," 353–74. Her figures show that such dialogues were most common in the third quarter of the eighteenth century, for which she lists fifteen examples.

[141] On assertions by professional critics of their own authority, see Zeynep Tenger and Paul Trolander, "'Impartial Critick' or 'Muse's Handmaid'."

[142] *Conjectures*, 57. On the 18th-century "discourse of genius," see Tenger and Trolander, "Genius Versus Capital."

[143] For attempts by critics like Dennis and Gildon to claim the authority to fix rules and set critical standards, see Tenger and Trolander, who consider that aristocratic patronage had declined by the early eighteenth century, and emphasize that critics were in effect challenging the authority of the booksellers and the poets themselves ("'Impartial Critick' or Muse's Handmaid'"). But in my view aristocratic patrons still held considerable cultural authority, and the challenge of the professional critics was just as much directed at the patrons as at the booksellers.

[144] See James Basker, *Tobias Smollett*.

World No. 57, a mirror of British manners and matters, and a means of suggesting that they might be otherwise ordered, reports on the "manner of criticising in China," where "the learned are assembled in a body to judge of every new publication." Such learned bodies were not assembled in England in Goldsmith's lifetime, and some observers thought that they never would be, since they ran counter to the English spirit of "the liberty of the subject" to make his own judgments. (An authoritative academy of the sort found in France, it was argued, was no less tyrannical than an absolute monarch.) But the *Critical Review* and the *Monthly Review* did make an effort to "judge of every new publication," if only by commenting briefly in the regular "Monthly Catalogue."[145] That the reviewers acquired considerable power and authority is suggested by Fanny Burney's dedication of *Evelina* in 1777 not to a titled nobleman but "To the Authors of the Monthly and Critical Reviews." Although her tone is facetious and mock-respectful of "those who publicly profess themselves Inspectors of all literary performances," she nonetheless acknowledges the power of the "magistrates of the press, and Censors for the public."

The economic domination of the patrons was challenged by the booksellers who, as they became collectively richer and organized into "congers", controlled a larger share of the resources invested in authors. The cultural authority of the patron was challenged too by the booksellers, the "Masters of all the Avenues to every Market" (Ralph, *Case of Authors*, p. 60), who increasingly determined what gets published, and (by commissioning collections and anthologies) what writers become part of the nascent "canon" of "English Poets."[146] And it is implicitly challenged by the courts, who in their successive rulings on literary copyright, establish more firmly that the originator and the owner of a literary work – until such time as he sells his rights to it – is the author. Even the *language* of the copyright law and the debate over its meaning suggests that the *function* of the patron was being appropriated by the law itself, which, in the 1709 statute,

---

[145] Goldsmith wrote twenty-three of the seventy-one brief notices in the Monthly Catalogue of the *Monthly Review* for May 1757, together with two longer reviews. In one such notice he notes, for example, that "To direct our taste [traditionally the patron's role], and conduct the Poet up to perfection, has ever been the true Critic's province." See Goldsmith's *Collected Works*, I, 10, and Richard Taylor's *Goldsmith as Journalist*.

[146] See Thomas Bonnell, "Bookselling and Canon-Making," 53–69, and Linda Zionkowski, "Territorial Disputes in the Republic of Letters," 3–22.

provided for the "Encouragement of Learning" and for the "protection" of authors.[147]

One of the clearest indications that patrons were in effect engaged in a contest for authority with other participants in the literary system is the Johnson–Chesterfield incident. Like Dryden before him, Johnson in the 1747 *Plan of a Dictionary* both acknowledges the patron's authority and insists on his own privileges. As Chesterfield's "delegate," Johnson hopes to gain "authority" and "power." But he does not expect to defer to his lordship in all matters, or to serve merely as his spokesman. As he writes to Chesterfield in the *Plan*, in a nice balance of deference and self-assertion, the earl has "commissioned me to declare my own opinion." And he concludes his proposal on the same note: "This, my Lord, is *my* idea of an English dictionary" (emphasis added).[148] In appropriating the patron's authority, Johnson walks a fine line separating servility from impudence. But Chesterfield, as I have suggested earlier, also insisted in the essays in *The World* on his prerogative as "voter" who surrendered his "rights and privileges" only for a limited "term." And even when he was rebuffed by Johnson's haughty letter, Chesterfield continued to behave in lordly – Johnson would have said "insolent" – fashion. He never backed off from his claim that standards are to be set by "people of fashion and letters," by "those who have learning, and are at the same time in the polite world."[149] Far from showing displeasure, he displayed Johnson's letter on a table for his visitors to see. This is arguably not affected indifference (as Boswell thought) or insolence, but a determination to behave as if he in fact *were* Johnson's patron. He acted the role of critic (pointing out to Dodsley "the severest passages, and observed how well they were expressed"[150]), and virtually of sponsor. By writing the famous letter Johnson challenges Chesterfield's "authority."[151] By displaying the letter Chesterfield tries to reclaim it.

The same contestation of patronal authority can be found in Johnson's dedications. I have already suggested that they show how

---

[147] For an account of the debate, see Mark Rose, *Authors and Owners*.

[148] *The Plan of a Dictionary of the English Language*, D3v, [D4v]. Cf. "I have been since determined by your Lordship's opinion to interpose my own judgment" ([D3v]).

[149] Letter No. 887, in *Letters*, III, 695. See J. H. Neumann, "Chesterfield and the Standard of Usage," 463–75.

[150] *Life of Johnson*, I, 265.

[151] Even at the level of style. Carey McIntosh has remarked on Johnson's command of the conventions of "courtly" language. Johnson "confronts" Chesterfield, he says, "as an equal." See his *Common and Courtly Language*, 145.

the system of patronage was in place, and how traditional patronal authority was still being recognized by dedicating authors. But Johnson's dedications, while they do not reject the old idea that the patron has responsibility for and a kind of authority over literature, in effect imply that the patron must now *share* that authority with the author. Thus, in the dedications which Johnson wrote, the author approaches the patron with head high.[152] Rather than throwing himself at the feet of his patron, he "can boldly solicit the patronage of Your Majesty" (Hazen, *Dedications*, p. 3), and claim the "privilege" to "approach the High and the Illustrious" (p. 65). An author such as Metastasio, he says, has a "natural right to the notice of the Great" (p. 68). An author can properly plead his own "qualifications" (p. 8), as well as the earnestness of his intentions – the author in Johnson's dedications commonly "mean[s] well" (p. 102); he has "endeavoured at extensive and general usefulness" (p. 40).[153] Unlike earlier dedicators, who self-deprecatingly and disingenuously present their works as the product of an idle hour, Johnson insists on the author's "long Labour, and diligent Enquiry" (p. 76). The author can also vouch for the significance of the subject. A work is "not only interesting but important" (p. 115). Johnson's tone is sometimes almost didactic, as if his purpose is to point out why the "science of musical sounds" deserves study (p. 29), or why the works of Roger Ascham deserve to be reprinted (p. 23). The "usefulness" of trigonometry "to the commerce of mankind" is "so apparent that it is not unworthy the attention of persons in the most elevated stations" (p. 154).[154] The patron may be judge of the "justness" of Metastasio's "civil reflections," but the author himself, as judge, can say with confidence that "nothing but what appeared worthy to engage the most exalted mind, should have been presented to You" (p. 68). Johnson commonly distributes equal emphasis to the patron's merits and the author's useful labors. And he commonly implies, or even declares, that the author's own knowledge and powers of judgment make him the patron's virtual equal. In the dedication of Robert James'

---

[152] Robert Anderson in 1806 commented on Johnson's style of "dignified remonstrance" (in Hazen, *Johnson's Prefaces and Dedications*, 117).

[153] For other claims by the ghost-writing Johnson of authorial "usefulness," see *ibid.*, 3, 73, 154.

[154] In dedicating Payne's *Introduction to Geometry* to the Duke of York, Johnson claims that "an address to such a patron admits no recommendation of the science" – since the patron is already well versed in it. But in fact Johnson's brief dedication is precisely that: a "recommendation of the science."

Medicinal Dictionary to the famous Dr. Richard Mead Johnson makes James compliment Mead's "Reputation for superior Skill in those Sciences which I have endeavoured to explain and facilitate." But the expositor is confident of his own "superior Skill," and is not intimidated by the authority of the great physician. At Johnson's prompting, James now makes "public Appeal" to Mead's "Judgment," to show the world that "I fear His Censure least, whose Knowledge is most extensive" (p. 73).[155]

The authority of the patron, then, was being contested on every side – by theorists, critics, booksellers, judges on the bench, and authors themselves. But such challenges did not mean that the patronage system had been overthrown. In fact, they suggest precisely the opposite, for what has already been overthrown does not need to be challenged. Patronal authority, like many other cultural forms from the *ancien régime,* showed remarkable resilience in English literary culture throughout the eighteenth century. Indeed, though the nineteenth century would see the maturation of a literary marketplace, culture retained old habits. Wordsworth and Coleridge, it has been noted, enjoyed some of the traditional benefits of patronage.[156] And even George Eliot's *Middlemarch,* on the eve of the Reform Bill, is recognizably still a world of patrons and dependents.[157]

---

[155] It is possible that Johnson may have felt more free to adopt a tone of "dignified remonstrance" because he was not writing in his own name. But his attitude in the dedications toward men of rank – a mixture of deference and firm self-respect – is not unlike his conversational comments, as reported in Boswell, about the mental qualities of several men of rank with whom he was acquainted. See *Life of Johnson,* IV, 179, 327 (Thurlow), IV, 174 (Shelburne), IV, 332–33 (Chesterfield), II, 40–41 (King George III).

[156] See Johnson, *Lives of the Poets,* III, 305n.

[157] The patronage system, a central element of pre-Reform Britain, is at last breaking down, in part because it is unsatisfying both to patrons (Mr. Brooke, Dorothea, Bulstrode) and to dependents (Ladislaw, Lydgate).

CHAPTER II

Conclusion

In his essay on eighteenth-century literary patronage twenty years ago, Paul Korshin raised some fundamental questions about "the social utility and psychology" of patronage: "Is the patronage system ... beneficial to the literary climate in a given century? Does the psychology of the patron–client association damage or advance the creative arts?" ("Types of Eighteenth-Century Literary Patronage," p. 453). Although he does not attempt to provide full answers, he suggests that the system of patronage, often charged with failure, was in fact "surprisingly workable," and that although it "benefited relatively few writers," it "survived because it was necessary" (p. 473). It may now be possible to provide more of an answer to Korshin's questions. A complete assessment of the "utility" and "effectiveness" of the patronage system would probably require more knowledge than is now available – about the individual economic circumstances of most writers (not just the well-studied few) and about the precise size and nature of benefactions. But it should be possible to offer some critical assessment of the traditional charges against the system of patronage.

The charge that merit sometimes went unrewarded cannot be wholly rebutted – as the case of Charlotte Lennox shows, though she did not go without patronage altogether. But the number of such cases is probably smaller than we have been told. The loud complaints of Richard Savage and Edward Young seem, upon examination, to be without solid foundation. The charge that patrons abandoned the traditional "responsibilities" that accompanied their privileged place in the world has also been overstated. Various forms of patronage – particularly job-related patronage in church, state, or private house-hold – continued to flow throughout the century. Perhaps it is true to say that it "benefited relatively few writers" – relative, that is, to the total number of aspirants. But the system supported more writers than most students of the period realize. As I have noted, virtually every writer in the current canon, both major and minor, received some kind of patronage.[1] It is probably true to say that the patronage system as a whole looks capricious: it did not clearly distinguish between the first-rate and the third-rate writers. For every Samuel Johnson who received a pension, there is a Thomas Sheridan who in our minds (and in Johnson's) did not deserve the same reward. But the distribution of rewards was at least as rational as any other reward system before or since. By and large, and despite contemporary complaints, reward tended to follow merit (although rewards were often late in coming.) There were of course exceptions, political hacks like Arnall who were paid enormous sums, and writers of real distinction like Goldsmith and Smart who struggled, during part of their careers, without much compensation or recognition.[2] (But many of those discussed as hacks were serious writers, Goldsmith's career in patronage is atypical, and Smart had more support than most students realize.) The literary marketplace, either in the eighteenth century or in the twentieth, is no better, and is probably a lot worse, at distinguishing writers of merit from those who happen to appeal to popular taste. Indeed, some contemporaries in the eighteenth century believed that the intervention of patrons would help distinguish between the worthy and the undeserving. Dryden in 1693 urged his patron Mulgrave that "some Lord Chamberlain should be appointed, some Critick of Authority shou'd be set before the door, to keep out a Crowd of little Poets" (*Works*, vol. v, p. 275). In 1772 the author of the *Letters concerning the State of England* imagined that a reward system based wholly on patrons would serve to direct support only to writers of merit and would therefore reduce the number of bad books (p. 328).

Another standard complaint is that patronage is a form of enslavement, rendering a writer gallingly dependent on the whims (and the opinions) of those who happen to be wealthy or highborn. But there is abundant evidence that eighteenth-century writers found that when they turned to the emerging marketplace for support they had

[1]   One contemporary argued that a "system of patronage" which provides only a few pensions serves to "keep up the emulation of the whole body of writers" (*Letters concerning the State of England* [1772], 322).

[2]   It was not uncommon for contemporaries to point to other neglected genius – in Collins and Savage, for example (see Goldsmith, *Collected Works*, I, 315). But Johnson attributes their poverty to their *own* neglect.

simply exchanged one set of chains for another. Goldsmith, Ralph, Lennox, and others at mid-century felt enslaved to the booksellers, or to the whims of the tyrannical public, who were no more enlightened in their opinions or standards than the patrons.[3] And did patrons in effect limit what a writer could say? Under patronage, said Johnson, a writer "must say what pleases his patron" (*Life of Johnson*, vol. v, p. 59). Perhaps in individual cases a writer was constrained from expressing his or her full mind, but if we regard the system as a whole then it must be conceded that controversial writers – like Savage, or Wilkes, or Burns, or Junius – were not silenced by their indebtedness. For every Bute who funded a stable of pro-ministerial writers in the 1760s there was an Earl Temple, who fed an increasingly vocal opposition.

With respect to literary experimentation or novelty, did the inherently conservative patronage system tend to prefer the safe and the familiar? It might be suspected that patronage tended to maintain the economic "value" of poetry, which (though an established and prestigious genre) was said to find less favor than prose with the booksellers.[4] If it did so, the burden of proof is on the champions of the booksellers to show that they were any bolder, any more likely to welcome the new and untried.

Contemporaries also suggested that patronage acted not to *discover* and *nourish* talented writers, but simply to reward those who had already succeeded in gaining attention. This in effect is Johnson's complaint against Chesterfield. Ralph charged that in order to gain ministerial support, a writer needs already to have reached an audience: "The Voluntier [author] ... must be in Possession of the Public, before he can hope for such Connections and Confidence" (*Case of Authors*, p. 30).[5] But the author of the *Letters concerning the State of England* thought that "more than has been apparent" could be

---

3   Although the young and ambitious Burke complained that "genius" in England was not "patronized by any of the nobility," he was by no means eager to rely on "the capricious patronage of the public" (quoted in Forster, *Goldsmith*, 1, 89).

4   Richard Cumberland complained that "publishers hate poetry" (*Memoirs*, 1, 353); Goldsmith wondered at "how any man could be so dull as to write poetry at present, since prose itself would hardly pay" (*Collected Works*, 1, 131). The *British Magazine*, 2 (April 1761), 199, notes that works of politics sell better than poetry. According to Dodsley in 1747, "so very few Poems sell, that it is very hazardous purchasing almost any thing" (quoted in *The Poems of Gray, Collins, and Goldsmith*, ed. Roger Lonsdale, 409).

5   The same charge was made against booksellers. In 1765 Langhorne called Millar "a favourer of genius, *when once it has made its way to fame*" (quoted in Lonsdale, *ibid.*, 409). But Ralph Griffiths strongly denied the charge and defended Millar's practice (*ibid.*, 409).

attributed to the "encouragement" provided to unknown writers by a patron's money, "for profit may have been the instigation to performances which have ended in fame" (pp. 320–21). And to judge by the large number of obscure writers who received the support of a subscription edition, patronage did not simply go to established authors. Indeed, patronage would seem to have provided a means of support for many writers – women, peasant poets, regional authors – who would not otherwise have had a hearing.[6] It is very likely that poets like Mary Leapor, Ann Yearsley, and Robert Woodhouse would have wasted their sweetness on the desert air if they had not been adopted by patrons.

For their part, patrons were well served by the system. If Halifax, Dorset, and Chandos are still remembered today, it is largely in their capacity as patrons of the liberal arts.[7] It seems clear that the patronage system served the interests of the elites of the day, and tended to confirm traditional patterns of deference. Those patrons who took on milkmaid and shoemaker poets as clients were probably attempting to keep their clients in "their place." Some observers today will thus find patronage socially and politically regressive and therefore deplorable. But they would have to concede that the system also made it possible for commoners with money and literary interests – from Bubb Dodington to Ralph Allen – to win honor and reputation as patrons of the arts. And as patronage broadened, the system enabled many from the middle ranks – merchants, professionals, booksellers – to appear on subscription lists with their "betters."

As for the writers themselves, did their social status suffer under patronage? Collins and other celebrants of the literary marketplace and the professional writer thought patronage "unbecoming the dignity of the profession of letters" (*Authorship in the Days of Johnson*, p. 212), but they must confront and explain away the complaints of writers like Goldsmith who lament that a writer *for the market* is "a thing little superior to the fellow who works at the press" – where "fellow" expresses contempt but suspects kinship.[8] With authors

6 The Robinson-Wallis Book Subscription Lists show thirty-nine authors whose works were published by subscription in the British Isles at some place other than London during the period 1700–1800. But the real total is probably higher. The authors of the 1983 *CheckList* note that the ESTC as of December 1982 showed that the real total of books published by subscription in the century is probably 10,000.

7 Chandos' modern biographers subtitle their biography "Patron of the Liberal Arts."

8 *Enquiry*, ch. 10, in *Collected Works*, I, 316.

flooding the streets, Goldsmith complains of loss of status. It is not just that each writer's individual share of the pie is smaller, but that the author is now lumped with mere "mechanics" and "tradesmen." (The anonymous *Enquiry*, in which Goldsmith's complaints appear, is allegedly written by a young "man of taste.")[9]

Finally, it has been suggested somewhat paradoxically that the patronage system is not beneficial to literature because it tended to make those writers it rewarded too comfortable. Collins argued that "the security it gave was liable unconsciously to relax the efforts of a writer, and so to deprive the world" (*Authorship in the Days of Johnson*, p. 211). Collins was as usual probably depending on Goldsmith, who passed on the "old observation" that "authors, like running horses, should be fed but not fattened ... [W]e should reward them with a little money and a great deal of praise, still keeping their avarice subservient to their ambition."[10] Unfortunately, he continues, patronage is not well distributed in England. Talent sometimes receives too much reward, "so that a life begun in studious labour, is often continued in luxurious indolence" (Goldsmith, *Collected Works*, vol. I, p. 309).[11] There were no doubt examples of bright young men whose early promise was extinguished by a comfortable college fellowship or church living. And it has even been noted that Johnson wrote a good deal less after he received his pension than before.[12] But, with the late *Lives of the Poets* in mind, it is difficult to name a writer of accomplishment whose literary efforts were significantly relaxed by patronage. In any case, it was very rare for a pensioned writer to receive more than £300 a year. Even in eighteenth-century terms, that is comfort but not luxury.

Most of the charges against the patronage system, then, can be rebutted with evidence that, if it doesn't dismiss the charge, at least

9   *Ibid.* Goldsmith takes the position that the subscription system, once restricted to young gentlemen of merit, is now open to those with neither birth nor merit.

10   Goldsmith may have found the observation in Du Bos's *Critical Reflections on Poetry and Painting*, where it is presented as a witticism of Charles IX. Cf. Smart's irony: "the poorer a man is kept, the more he'll endeavour to merit the publick favour ... Those therefore that encourage learning least are in fact the greatest *Maecenas's*" ("A New System of Castle-Building," in *The Student*, II [1750], 381). I owe the reference to Betty Rizzo.

11   Cf. Gibbon's version of the dangers of financial comfort: "in circumstances more indigent or more wealthy, I should never have accomplished the task, or acquired the fame, of an historian ... my industry might have been relaxed in the labour and luxury of a superfluous fortune. Few works of merit and importance have been executed either in a garret or a palace" (*Memoirs of My Life*, 53).

12   See, for example, James W. Saunders: "After the pension, there was an immediate relaxing of Johnson's industry" (*The Profession of English Letters*, 144).

requires some careful reformulation. Another way to approach the problem of assessment is to inquire whether literature in the fully established marketplace of the nineteenth century or the mass-culture of the twentieth century is in fact healthier than under a system of court patronage, as in the Renaissance, and the mixed system of patronage and market that prevailed in the eighteenth century. The answer is probably "in some ways yes, in some ways no."[13] But one important factor should not be underestimated – what Goldsmith and Ralph called the "link" of patronage which "held the Great and the Learned Together."[14] Patronage was one means – the schools and universities were another – for bringing together representatives of the worlds of genius and power, if only in controlled and limited ways, for conversation and "familiarity." These occasions even provided opportunities for the "Man of Wit" (in Steele's terms) to prove himself a "Man of Business,"[15] and for not a few writers – Dryden, Addison, Swift, Pope, Prior, Fielding, Hume, Johnson, Gibbon – to participate integrally in the public and political life of the nation. If, as has been increasingly observed in recent years, marginalization has been the fate of high culture since the end of the eighteenth century, it is in part the end of the patronage system that has contributed to this result. As authors became independent of patronage, they were less likely to be received at court or at the tables of ministers and magnates, or to be found at the sites of organized political opposition. And a good thing too, many would say, that artists no longer have to defer to the political and economic masters of the state. But for the transformation of literature into a specialized and increasingly "professional" art, the culture has paid a price.

In a book which argues that the patronage system, though it persisted, was nonetheless *resisted*, it is appropriate to ask what difference authorial resistance in fact made? Did it manage to alter the system, to weaken it? Did it serve to elevate the image of authorship or the status of writers? Did it produce greater rewards? It is very hazardous to generalize on the basis of a relatively small sample, and difficult to establish a cause–effect relationship in

---

13 In the late nineteenth century Forster deplored the effects of the marketplace, and called for parliament to grant "its thanks, its peerages, and its pensions" to men of letters (*Goldsmith*, II, 437).

14 Ralph, *Case of Authors*, 72. Cf. Goldsmith: "the link between patronage and learning" (*Collected Works*, I, 310).

15 Dedication of vol. 4 of *The Tatler* to Halifax.

literary history between the acts of individual agents and large-scale socio-economic change. Dryden managed to secure support from a wide range of patrons, even after his loss of royal patronage in 1688. Though we can probably conclude that his contract with Tonson to translate Virgil helped (as Johnson later said of Millar) "raise the price of literature," it cannot be demonstrated that he actually increased the support he himself received from patrons by proclaiming his right to it. On the other hand, it seems reasonable to suppose that by declaring his own rights, dignity, and independence, he derived some personal satisfaction from what may have only been symbolic resistance, and may well have provided Pope with some hints for the claims that a writer might make for protection and encouragement. Swift, Savage, and Young all thought they were mistreated and undervalued by the patronage system. But despite their resistance they were in fact comparatively well rewarded. And Swift, like Dryden, probably taught Pope how to "use" his social betters to personal advantage. Savage willfully offended his patrons, biting the hand that fed him, but he nonetheless discovered a way to manipulate the system successfully. By contrast, Charlotte Lennox, who also offended, was apparently punished for it. Pope remains the central figure, and the writer whose calculated resistance to and manipulation of the patronage system clearly led to his own benefit.

Pope's resistance also had some longer-term effects. He became the very model of the "independent" writer for mid-century biographers, and (together with Johnson) the model for nineteenth-century literary historians of the "professional" writer. Ironically, it was precisely these historians, as I have argued, who spread misconceptions about the death of patronage at the hands of Pope and Johnson. It now seems clear that cultural institutions like patronage are more enduring than Forster and Beljame once thought, and that the acts of the heroes of literary history have more measurable effect on later writers than on the multifarious world of patrons, booksellers, and readers. But the *collective* resistance to or contestation of the authority of the patron over many decades – by authors, booksellers, theorists, and critics – seems indeed (together with other purely economic factors) to have led to the decline of the legitimacy of the patronage system.

Bibliography

PRIMARY WORKS

Aristotle, *Nicomachean Ethics*, in *Introduction to Aristotle*, ed. Richard McKeon (New York: Random House, 1947).

Behn, Aphra, *Works*, vol. 1, ed. Janet Todd (Columbus: Ohio State University Press, 1992).

Boswell Papers, Beinecke Library, Yale University.

Boswell, James, *The Life of Samuel Johnson*, ed. G. B. Hill, rev. L. F. Powell, 6 vols. (Oxford: Clarendon, 1934–50).

The Correspondence and Other Papers of James Boswell Relating to the Making of the "Life of Johnson", ed. Marshall Waingrow (New York: McGraw-Hill, 1969).

Burney, Frances, *Diary and Letters*, ed. Charlotte Barrett, preface and notes by Austin Dobson, 6 vols. (London: Macmillan, 1904–05).

Burke, Edmund, *Party, Parliament, and the American Crisis, 1766–1774*, vol. 11 of *The Writings and Speeches of Edmund Burke*, eds. Paul Langford and William Todd (Oxford: Clarendon, 1981).

Burns, Robert, *Poems and Songs*, ed. James Kinsley (Oxford: Oxford University Press, 1969).

Bute, John Stuart, Lord, "Register of Correspondence," British Library, Add. MSS 5720, 36796.

Caldwell Papers (Glasgow, 1854).

Capell, Edward, ed., *Mr. William Shakespeare, his Comedies, Histories, and Tragedies*, 10 vols. (London, 1768).

The Case of Patronage Stated (Edinburgh, 1782).

The Cause Between Patronage and Popular Election (Edinburgh, 1769).

Chatham Papers, Public Records Office (London), 30/8.

Chesterfield, Philip Dormer Earl of, *Characters* (1778, 1845), facs. ed., intro. Alan McKenzie (Los Angeles: Clark Library, 1990).

Letters, ed. Bonamy Dobrée, 6 vols. (London: Eyre & Spottiswoode, 1932).

Churchill, Charles, *Poetical Works*, ed. Douglas Grant (Oxford: Clarendon, 1956).

Cobb, Samuel, *Poetae Britannica* (London, 1700).

Congreve, William, *Complete Plays*, ed. Herbert Davis (Chicago: University of Chicago Press, 1967).

Works, 5th ed. (London, 1752).

Considerations on the Right of Patronage (Edinburgh, 1766).

Cowper, William, *Letters and Prose Writings*, eds. James King and Charles Ryskamp, 5 vols. (Oxford: Clarendon, 1979–86).

Crabbe, George, *The Complete Poetical Works*, eds. Norma Dalrymple-Champneys and Arthur Pollard, 3 vols. (Oxford: Clarendon, 1988).

Crabbe, George (the younger), *The Life of George Crabbe, By his Son*, intro. E. Blunden (London: Cresset, 1947).

"Z. C.," *A Discourse of Patronage* (1675).

Dennis, John, *Critical Works*, ed. E. N. Hooker. 2 vols. (Baltimore: Johns Hopkins University Press, 1939).

Dodington, George Bubb, *The Political Journals of George Bubb Dodington*, eds. John Carswell and Lewis Dralle (Oxford: Clarendon, 1965).

Dodsley, Robert, *The Correspondence of Robert Dodsley, 1733–1764*, ed. James E. Tierney (Cambridge: Cambridge University Press, 1988).

Douglas, John, *Seasonable Hints From an Honest Man on the Present Important Crisis of a New Reign and a New Parliament* (London, 1761).

Du Bos, Abbé, *Critical Reflections on Poetry and Painting*, 3 vols., tr. Thomas Nugent (London, 1748).

Duck, Stephen, *Poems on Several Occasions*, 2nd ed. (London, 1737).

Dryden, John, *Letters of John Dryden*, ed. Charles Ward (Durham: Duke University Press, 1942).

The Poems of John Dryden, ed. James Kinsley, 4 vols. (Oxford: Clarendon, 1958).

Works, eds. E. N. Hooker et al., 17 vols. to date (Los Angeles: University of California Press, 1961–).

Works, ed. Sir Walter Scott, rev. George Saintsbury, 18 vols. (Edinburgh: Paterson, 1882–93).

Dyer, John, *Poems* (London, 1761).

Fielding, Henry, *Complete Works*, ed. W. E. Henley, 16 vols. (London: Heinemann, 1903).

Enquiry into the Causes of the Late Increase of Robbers (London, 1751).

The Jacobite's Journal and Related Writings, ed. W. B. Coley (Middletown: Wesleyan University Press, 1985).

Joseph Andrews and Shamela, ed. Martin Battestin (Boston: Houghton Mifflin, 1967).

Miscellanies: Volume One, ed. H. K. Miller (Middletown: Wesleyan University Press, 1972).

New Essays by Henry Fielding, ed. Martin Battestin (Charlottesville: University of Virginia Press, 1989).

Works, ed. James P. Browne, 11 vols. (London, 1902–03).

Garth, Sir Thomas, *The Dispensary*, 6th ed. (London, 1706).

Gibbon, Edward, *Letters*, ed. J. E. Norton, 3 vols. (London: Cassell, 1956).

Memoirs of My Life, ed. Georges Bonnard (London: Thomas Nelson, 1966).

Miscellaneous Works, 5 vols. (London, 1814).

Goldsmith, Oliver, *Collected Works*, ed. Arthur Friedman, 5 vols. (Oxford: Clarendon, 1966).

Gordon, Thomas, *A Dedication to a Great Man Concerning Dedications* (London, 1718).

Gray, Thomas, *Correspondence*, eds. Paget Toynbee and Leonard Whibley, 3 vols. (Oxford: Clarendon, 1935).

Halifax, Charles Montague Earl of, *Poetical Works of the Right Honorable Charles Late Earl of Halifax*, 2nd ed. (London, 1716).

Hardwicke Papers, British Library, Add. MSS 35350, 35396–35401.

Hazen, Allen, *Samuel Johnson's Prefaces & Dedications* (New Haven: Yale University Press, 1937).

Hill, Aaron, *Works*, 2nd ed. (London, 1754).

Hobbes, Thomas, *Leviathan*, in *English Works*, ed. Sir William Molesworth, 11 vols. (London, 1839).

Hume, David, *Essays Moral, Political, and Literary*, ed. Eugene Miller (Indianapolis: Liberty Classics, rev., 1987).

Letters, ed. J. Y. T. Greig, 2 vols. (Oxford: Clarendon, 1932, 1969).

Jenkinson, Charles, *The Jenkinson Papers, 1760–1766*, ed. Ninetta S. Jucker (New York: Macmillan, 1949).

Johnson, Samuel, *A Dictionary of the English Language*, 4th ed., 2 vols. (London, 1773).

Letters of Samuel Johnson, ed. Bruce Redford, 5 vols. (Princeton: Princeton University Press, 1992–94).

Life of Savage, ed. Clarence Tracy (Oxford: Clarendon, 1971).

Lives of the English Poets, ed. G. B. Hill, 3 vols. (Oxford: Clarendon, 1905).

The Plan of a Dictionary of the English Language (London, 1747).

Works, 12 vols. (London, 1810).

Works, 16 vols. to date (New Haven: Yale University Press, 1958–).

"Junius," *Letters of Junius* (Edinburgh, 1793).

Leapor, Mary, *Poems upon Several Occasions*, 2 vols. (London, 1748, 1751).

Lennox, Charlotte, *The Female Quixote*, ed. M. Dalziel (Oxford: Oxford University Press, 1970).

The Lady's Museum (London, 1760, 1761).

The Life of Harriot Stuart (London, 1751).

Poems on Several Occasions. Written by a Young Lady (London, 1747).

Letters concerning the Present State of England (London, 1772).

Letters by Several Eminent Persons Deceased. Including the Correspondence of John Hughes, Esq., 3 vols. (London, 1772).

Lucian, *Lucian*, 8 vols., tr. A. M. Harmon (London: Heinemann, 1969).

Lynch, Francis, *The Independent Patriot* (London, 1737).

Machiavelli, Niccolo, *The Prince*, tr. Luigi Ricci (New York: New American Library, 1952).

Memoirs of the Life of John Lord Somers (London, 1716).
Memoirs of Wool, 2 vols., 2nd ed. (London, 1756–57).
Milton, John, *Complete Poems and Selected Prose*, ed. Merritt Hughes (New York: Odyssey, 1957).
Mitchell, Joseph, *The Sine-cure* (London, 1725).
　The Equivalent (London, 1725).
　The Promotion, and the Alternative (London, 1726).
　A Familiar Epistle to the Right Honourable Sir Robert Walpole (London, 1735).
Montagu, Lady Mary Wortley, *Complete Letters*, ed. Robert Halsband, 3 vols. (Oxford: Clarendon, 1965–67).
The Nature of Patronage (1735).
Oldham, John, *Poems*, ed. Harold Brooks, with Raman Selden (Oxford: Clarendon, 1987).
"On the History of Authors by Profession," by "A. D.," *The Bee*, vol. 1 (1791), pp. 62–64; vol. 3 (1791), pp. 13–15, 52–54, 87–89.
"The Patron or a Portraiture of Patronage and Dependency," British Library Add. MS 12523.
Patronage Anatomized and Detected (Glasgow, 1782).
Percy, Thomas, *Reliques of English Poetry* (London, 1765).
Pope, Alexander, *The Twickenham Edition of the Poems of Alexander Pope*, eds. John Butt et al., 11 vols. (London: Methuen, 1938–68).
　The Correspondence of Alexander Pope, ed. George Sherburn, 5 vols. (Oxford: Clarendon, 1955).
　The Prose Works of Alexander Pope: The Earlier Works, 1711–1720, ed. Norman Ault (Oxford: Blackwell, 1936).
　The Prose Works of Alexander Pope, Vol. II, The Major Works, 1725–1744, ed. Rosemary Cowler (Hamden: Archon, 1986).
　Works, eds. Whitwell Elwin and J. W. Courthope, 10 vols. (London: John Murray, 1871–89).
Ralph, James, *The Case of Authors by Profession or Trade* (London, 1758), facs. ed., intro. Philip Stevick (Gainesville: Scholars' Facsimiles and Reprints, 1966).
The Right of Patronages Considered, and Some of the Antient and Modern Arguments for the Exercise of that Right in Presenting to Churches, Surveyed (Edinburgh, 1731).
Rowe, Nicholas, *The Fair Penitent*, ed. Malcolm Goldstein (Lincoln: University of Nebraska Press, 1969).
Savage, Richard, *Love in a Veil* (London, 1718).
　Poetical Works, ed. Clarence Tracy (Cambridge: Cambridge University Press, 1962).
Seneca, *De Beneficiis*, in *Moral Essays*, 3 vols., tr. John W. Basore (London, Heinemann, 1935).
Shadwell, Thomas, *The Virtuoso*, eds. M. H. Nicolson and D. S. Rodes (Lincoln: University of Nebraska Press, 1966).
Shaftesbury, Anthony Ashley Cooper, Earl of, *Characteristicks*, 3 vols. (London, 1749).

Smart, Christopher, *The Annotated Letters of Christopher Smart*, eds. Betty Rizzo and Robert Mahony (Carbondale: Southern Illinois University Press, 1991).

Smith, Adam, *An Inquiry into the Nature and Causes of the Wealth of Nations*, ed. Edwin Cannan (New York: Modern Library, 1937).

Smollett, Tobias, *Continuation of the Complete History of England* (London, 1760). *Letters of Tobias Smollett*, ed. Lewis M. Knapp (Oxford: Clarendon, 1970).

Somerville, Thomas, *My Own Life and Times, 1741–1814* (Edinburgh, 1841).

Steele, Sir Richard, *The Spectator*, vol. 1 (London, 1712).

The Story of the Tragedy of Agis, with Observations on the Play, the Performances, and their Reception (London, 1758).

Swift, Jonathan, *Jonathan Swift: The Complete Poems*, ed. Pat Rogers (New Haven: Yale University Press, 1988).

Correspondence, ed. Harold Williams, 5 vols. (Oxford: Clarendon, 1963).

Journal to Stella, ed. Harold Williams, 2 vols. (Oxford: Blackwell, 1974).

Poems, ed. Harold Williams, 3 vols., 2nd ed. (Oxford: Clarendon, 1958).

Prose Works, ed. Herbert Davis, 14 vols. (Oxford: Blackwell, 1939–68).

A Tale of a Tub, eds. A. C. Guthkelch and D. N. Smith, 2nd ed. (Oxford: Clarendon, 1958).

The Tatler, ed. D. F. Bond, 3 vols. (Oxford: Clarendon, 1987).

Thomson, James, *Liberty, The Castle of Indolence, and Other Poems*, ed. James Sambrook (Oxford: Clarendon, 1986).

The Seasons, ed. James Sambrook (Oxford: Clarendon, 1981).

Voltaire, *Letters concerning the English Nation* ed. Nicholas Cronk (New York: Oxford University Press, 1994).

Walpole, Horace, *Correspondence*, eds. W. S. Lewis et al., 48 vols. in 49 (New Haven: Yale University Press, 1937–83).

Memoirs of the Reign of King George II, ed. Lord Holland, 2nd ed., rev. (London: Colburn, 1846, repr. AMS, 1970).

Memoirs of the Reign of King George III, ed. Sir Denis Le Marchant, 4 vols. (London: Bentley, 1845).

A Catalogue of Royal and Noble Authors of England, Scotland, and Ireland, ed. Thomas Park, 4 vols. (London, 1806).

[Warburton, William,] *A Letter From an Author to a Member of Parliament Concerning Literary Property* (London, 1747).

[Yorke, Philip], *Athenian Letters; or the Epistolary Correspondence of an Agent of the King of Persia, residing at Athens during the Peloponnesian War*, 4 vols. (London, 1741).

Yorke, Philip C., *Life and Correspondence of Philip Yorke, Earl of Hardwicke, Lord High Chancellor of Great Britain* (Cambridge, 1913).

Young, Edward, *Complete Works*, ed. James Nichols, 2 vols. (London, 1854, repr. Hildesheim: Olms, 1968).

Conjectures on Original Composition (1759), in Miriam W. Steinke, *Edward Young's "Conjectures on Original Composition" in England and Germany* (New York: Stechert, 1917), 41–73.

Correspondence, ed. Henry Pettit (Oxford: Clarendon, 1971).
Night Thoughts, ed. Stephen Cornford (Cambridge: Cambridge University Press, 1989).
Poetical Works, ed. John Mitford, 2 vols. (London, 1844, repr. Westport, CT: Greenwood, 1970).

SECONDARY WORKS

Adams, James E., "The Economics of Authorship: Imagination and Trade in Johnson's *Dryden*," *SEL*, 30 (1990), 467–86.

Adams, Robert M., "In Search of Baron Somers," in *Culture and Politics from Puritanism to the Enlightenment*, ed. Perez Zagorin (Berkeley: University of California Press, 1980), 165–202.

Allan, D. G. C., "The Society of Arts and Government, 1754–1800: Public Encouragement of Arts, Manufactures, and Commerce in Eighteenth-Century England," *ECS*, 7 (1973–74), 434–52.

Alston, R. C., Robinson, F. J. G., and Wadham, C., *A Check-List of 18th-Century Books Containing Lists of Subscribers* (Newcastle: Avero, 1983).

Arendt, Hannah, *Between Past and Future: Eight Exercises in Political Thought* (New York: Viking, 1961).

Atto, Clayton, "The Society for the Encouragement of Learning," *The Library*, 4th ser., 19 (1938), 263–88.

Ayre, William, *Memoirs of Alexander Pope*, 2 vols. (London, 1745), facs. repr. as vols. XX–XXI of *Popeiana* (New York: Garland, 1974).

Baker, C. H. C., and Baker, M. I., *The Life and Circumstances of James Brydges, First Duke of Chandos, Patron of the Liberal Arts* (Oxford: Clarendon, 1949).

Barrell, John, *English Literature in History, 1730–1780: An Equal Wide Survey* (New York: St. Martin's, 1983).

Basker, James, *Tobias Smollett: Critic and Journalist* (Newark: University of Delaware Press, 1988).

Bate, Walter Jackson, *Samuel Johnson* (New York: Harcourt Brace Jovanovich, 1975).

Battestin, Martin, with Battestin, Ruthe, *Henry Fielding: A Life* (London: Routledge, 1989).

Belanger, Terry, "Publishers and Writers in Eighteenth-Century England," in *Books and Their Readers in Eighteenth-Century England*, ed. Isabel Rivers (Leicester: Leicester University Press, 1982), 5–25.

"From Bookseller to Publisher: Changes in the London Book Trade, 1750–1850," in *Book Selling and Book Buying: Aspects of the 19th Century British and American Book Trade*, ed. R. G. Landon (Chicago: American Library Assn., 1978), 7–16.

Beljame, Alexandre, *Men of Letters and the English Public in the Eighteenth Century, 1660–1744, Dryden, Addison, Pope*, tr. E. O. Lorimer, ed. Bonamy Dobrée (London: Kegan Paul, 1948).

Biographica Britannica, 6 vols. (London, 1747–66).

Biographica Dramatica, 3 vols. (London: Longman et al, 1812).

Bonnell, Thomas, "Bookselling and Canon-Making: The Trade Rivalry over the English Poets, 1776–1783," *Studies in Eighteenth-Century Culture*, 19 (1989), 53–69.

Boulton, James T., ed., *Johnson: The Critical Heritage* (New York: Barnes and Noble, 1971).

Bourdieu, Pierre, *Outline of a Theory of Practice*, tr. Richard Nice (Cambridge: Cambridge University Press, 1977).

Brady, Frank, *James Boswell, The Later Years, 1769–1795* (New York: McGraw-Hill, 1984).

  Mickle, Boswell, Garrick, and the Siege of Marseilles, Transactions of the Connecticut Academy of Arts and Sciences (North Haven: Archon, 1986).

Braudy, Leo, *The Frenzy of Renown: Fame and its History* (New York: Oxford University Press, 1986).

Brewer, John, *Party Ideology and Popular Politics at the Accession of George III* (Cambridge: Cambridge University Press, 1976).

  The Sinews of Power: War, Money, and the English State, 1688–1783 (New York: Knopf, 1989).

Brewster, Dorothy, *Aaron Hill: Poet, Dramatist, Projector* (New York: Columbia University Press, 1913).

Brown, Cedric, ed., *Patronage, Politics, and Literary Traditions in England, 1558–1658* (Detroit: Wayne State University Press, 1991).

Brown, Mary Elizabeth, *Dedications: An Anthology of the Form Used from the Earliest Days of Book-Making to the Present Time* (New York: Putnam, 1913).

Burkolter, Verena, *The Patronage System: Theoretical Remarks* (Basel: Social Strategies Publishers Co-operative Society, 1976).

Bywaters, David, *Dryden in Revolutionary England* (Berkeley: University of California Press, 1991).

Cannon, John, *Aristocratic Century: The Peerage of Eighteenth-Century England* (Cambridge: Cambridge University Press, 1984).

  Samuel Johnson and the Politics of Hanoverian England (Oxford: Clarendon, 1994).

Carlyle, Thomas, [review of Croker's ed. of Boswell's *Life of Johnson*], *Fraser's Magazine*, 5 (1832), 379–413.

Carré, Jacques, "Burlington's Literary Patronage," *British Journal for Eighteenth-Century Studies*, 5 (1982), 21–32.

Carswell, John, *The Old Cause: Three Biographical Studies in Whiggism* (London: Cresset, 1954).

Carver, P. L., *The Life of a Poet: A Biographical Sketch of William Collins* (London: Sidgwick & Jackson, 1967).

Cash, Arthur, *Laurence Sterne: The Early and Middle Years* (London: Methuen, 1975).

  Laurence Sterne: The Later Years (London: Methuen, 1986).

Cater, Jeremy, "The Making of Principal Robertson in 1762: Politics at the

University of Edinburgh in the Second Half of the Eighteenth Century," *Scottish Historical Review*, 49 (1970), 60–84.

Clark, J. C. D., *English Society, 1688–1832: Ideology, Social Structure, and Political Practice During the Ancien Régime* (Cambridge: Cambridge University Press, 1985).

  Samuel Johnson: Literature, Religion, and English Cultural Politics from the Restoration to Romanticism (Cambridge: Cambridge University Press, 1994).

Clark, Jane, "The Mysterious Mr. Buck: Patronage and Politics, 1688–1745," *Apollo* (May 1989), 317–22.

Clement, Frances, "Lansdowne, Pope, and the Unity of *Windsor-Forest*," *MLQ*, 33 (1972), 44–53.

Clifford, James, *Dictionary Johnson: Samuel Johnson's Middle Years* (New York: McGraw-Hill, 1979).

  "Johnson and the Society of Artists," in *The Augustan Milieu*, eds. H. K. Miller, Eric Rothstein, and G. S. Rousseau (Oxford: Clarendon, 1970), 263–88.

  "Problems of Johnson's Middle Years – the 1762 Pension," in *Studies in the Eighteenth Century*, iii, eds. R. F. Brissenden and J. C. Eade (Toronto: University of Toronto Press, 1973), 1–19.

  Young Sam Johnson (New York: McGraw-Hill, 1955).

Clive, John, *Macaulay: The Shaping of the Historian* (New York: Knopf, 1973).

Colley, Linda, *Britons: Forging the Nation 1707–1837* (New Haven: Yale University Press, 1992).

Collins, A. S., *Authorship in the Days of Johnson* (New York: Dutton, 1929).

  The Profession of Letters: A Study of the Relation of Author to Patron, Publisher, and Public, 1780–1832 (New York: Dutton, 1929).

Cotterill, Anne, "The Politics and Aesthetics of Digression: Dryden's *Discourse Concerning the Original and Progress of Satire*," *SP*, 91 (1994), 464–95.

Craddock, Patricia, *Edward Gibbon, Luminous Historian 1772–1794* (Baltimore: Johns Hopkins University Press, 1988).

Cumberland, Richard, *Memoirs*, 2 vols. (London, 1807).

Davis, Mary Rose, *The Good Lord Lyttelton: A Study in Eighteenth-Century Politics and Culture* (Bethlehem: Times Publishing Co., 1939).

Dearnley, Moira, *The Poetry of Christopher Smart* (London: Routledge & Kegan Paul, 1968).

Delany, Patrick, *Observations upon Lord Orrery's Remarks on the Life and Writings of Dr. Jonathan Swift* (London, 1754; repr. New York: Garland, 1974).

Dickinson, H. T., *Liberty and Property: Political Ideology in Eighteenth-Century Britain* (New York: Holmes and Meier, 1977).

D'Israeli, Isaac, *Calamities of Authors*, 2 vols. (London, 1812).

  An Essay on the Manner and Genius of the Literary Character, 3rd ed. (London, 1793).

  Miscellanies (London, 1840).

"The Distresses of an Hired Writer," *British Magazine*, 2 (1761), 198–200.

Doody, Margaret, "Swift Among the Women," *Yearbook of English Studies*, 18 (1988), 68–92.

Dussinger, John, "Dr. Johnson's Solemn Responses to Beneficence," in *Domestick Privacies: Samuel Johnson and the Art of Biography*, ed. David Wheeler (Lexington: University of Kentucky Press, 1987).

Dyce, Alexander, *Poetical Works of James Beattie* (London: Pickering, 1831). *Poetical Works of William Collins* (London: Pickering, 1827, 1835).

Ehrenpreis, Irvin, *Swift: The Man, His Works, and the Age*, 3 vols. (Cambridge: Harvard University Press, 1962–83).

Eisenstadt, S. N., and Roniger, L., "Patron-Client Relations as Model of Structuring Social Exchange," in *Comparative Studies in Society and History*, 22 (1980), 42–77.

eds., *Patrons, Clients, and Friends* (Cambridge: Cambridge University Press, 1984).

Eliot, George, *Essays*, ed. Thomas Pinney (London: Routledge and Kegan Paul, 1963).

Epstein, William, "Patronizing the Biographical Subject: Johnson's Savage and Pastoral Power," in *Johnson After Two Hundred Years*, ed. Paul Korshin (Philadelphia: University of Pennsylvania Press, 1986), 141–57.

Evans, Robert C., *Ben Jonson and the Poetics of Patronage* (Lewisburg: Bucknell University Press, 1989).

Fabricant, Carole, "The Literature of Domestic Tourism and the Public Consumption of Private Property," in *The New Eighteenth Century*, eds. Felicity Nussbaum and Laura Brown (New York: Methuen, 1987), 254–75.

Feather, John, "The Book Trade in Politics: The Making of the Copyright Act of 1710," *Publishing History*, 8 (1980), 19–44.

"The Commerce of Letters: The Study of the Eighteenth-Century Book Trade," *Eighteenth-Century Studies*, 17 (1984), 405–24.

"The English Book Trade and the Law, 1695–1799," *Publishing History*, 12 (1982), 51–75.

Ferguson, Moira, "Resistance and Power in the Life and Writings of Ann Yearsley," *The Eighteenth Century: Theory and Interpretation*, 27 (1986), 247–68.

Fleeman, J. D., "The Revenue of a Writer: Johnson's Literary Earnings," *Studies in the Book Trade in Honour of Graham Pollard* (Oxford: Bibliographical Society Publications, 1975).

Folkenflik, Robert, "Patronage and the Poet-Hero," *Huntington Library Quarterly*, 48 (1985), 363–79.

Forster, Harold, *Edward Young: The Poet of the Night Thoughts, 1683–1765* (Alburgh: Erskine Press, 1986).

Forster, John, *The Life and Times of Oliver Goldsmith*, 2 vols., 6th ed. (London: Bickers and Son, 1877).

Foss, Michael, *The Age of Patronage: The Arts in England, 1660–1750* (Ithaca: Cornell University Press, 1971).

Foxon, David, *Alexander Pope and the Early Eighteenth-Century Book Trade*, ed. James McLaverty (Oxford: Clarendon, 1991).

Fussell, Paul, *Samuel Johnson and the Life of Writing* (New York: Harcourt, Brace, Jovanovich, 1971).

Gardiner, Anne Barbeau, "Dryden's Patrons," in *The Age of William III and Mary II: Power, Politics, and Patronage, 1688–1702*, eds. Robert P. Maccubbin and Martha Hamilton-Phillips (Williamsburg: College of William and Mary, 1989), 326–32.

Garrison, James, *Dryden and the Tradition of Panegyric* (Berkeley: University of California Press, 1975).

Gellner, Ernest, and Waterbury, John, eds., *Patrons and Clients in Mediterranean Societies* (London: Duckworth, 1977).

Gerrard, Christine, *The Patriot Opposition to Walpole: Politics, Poetry, and National Myth, 1725–1742* (Oxford: Clarendon, 1994).

Greene, Graham, *Lord Rochester's Monkey* (London: Bodley Head, 1974).

Greene, Richard, *Mary Leapor: A Study in Eighteenth-Century Women's Poetry* (Oxford: Clarendon, 1993).

Griffin, Dustin, *Alexander Pope: The Poet in the Poems* (Princeton: Princeton University Press, 1978).

"The Beginnings of Modern Authorship: Milton and Dryden," *Milton Quarterly*, 24:1 (1990), 1–7.

"Johnson's *Lives of the Poets* and the Patronage System," *The Age of Johnson*, 5 (1992), 1–33.

Regaining Paradise: Milton and the Eighteenth Century (Cambridge: Cambridge University Press, 1986).

"Swift and Patronage," *Studies in Eighteenth-Century Culture*, 21 (1991), 197–205.

Griffith, R. H., *Alexander Pope: A Bibliography*, 2 vols. (Austin: University of Texas Press, 1922–27).

Grundy, Isobel, "Samuel Johnson as Patron of Women," *The Age of Johnson*, 1 (1987), 59–77.

Gundersheimer, Werner, *Ferrara: The Style of a Renaissance Despotism* (Princeton: Princeton University Press, 1973).

Hammond, Paul, *John Dryden: A Literary Life* (New York: St. Martin's, 1991).

Hanson, Laurence, *Government and the Press, 1695–1763* (London: Oxford University Press, 1936).

Haskell, Francis, *Patrons and Painters: A Study in the Relations between Italian Art and Society in the Age of the Baroque* (New Haven: Yale University Press, rev. ed., 1980).

Hawkins, Sir John, *Life of Samuel Johnson* (London, 1787).

Hodgart, Matthew, "The Subscription List for Pope's *Iliad*, 1715," in *The Dress of Words*, ed. R. B. White, Jr. (Lawrence: University of Kansas Libraries, 1978), 25–34.

Holladay, Gae, and Brack, O. M., Jr., "Johnson as Patron," in *Greene*

Centennial Studies, eds. Paul Korshin and Robert Allen (Charlottesville: University of Virginia Press, 1984), 172–99.

Hornbeck, Katherine, "New Light on Mrs. Montagu," in *The Age of Johnson*, ed. F. W. Hilles (New Haven: Yale University Press, 1949), 349–61.

Horne, Thomas, "Politics in a Corrupt Society: William Arnall's Defense of Robert Walpole," *Journal of the History of Ideas*, 41 (1980), 601–14.

Hume, Robert, "Securing a Repertory: Plays on the London Stage, 1660–1665," in *Poetry and Drama, 1570–1700*, eds. Antony Coleman, Antony Hammond, and Arthur Johnston (London: Methuen, 1981), 156–72.

"Texts Within Contexts: Notes Toward a Historical Method," *Philological Quarterly*, 71 (1992), 69–100.

Hurd, Richard, *Moral and Political Dialogues* (London, 1759).

Hyde, Lewis, *The Gift: Imagination and the Erotic Life of Property* (New York: Random House, 1983).

Isles, Duncan, "The Lennox Collection," *Harvard Library Bulletin*, 18 (1970), 317–44, and 19 (1971), 36–60, 165–86, 416–35.

Jaffe, Nora, *The Poet Swift* (Hanover, NH: University Press of New England, 1977).

Kaminski, Thomas, *The Early Career of Samuel Johnson* (New York: Oxford University Press, 1987).

Kenny, R. W., "Ralph's *Case of Authors*: Its Influence on Goldsmith and Isaac D'Israeli," *PMLA*, 52 (1937), 104–13.

Kernan, Alvin, *Printing Technology, Letters, and Samuel Johnson* (Princeton: Princeton University Press, 1987).

Kettering, Sharon, *Patrons, Brokers, and Clients in Seventeenth-Century France* (New York: Oxford, 1986).

King, James, *William Cowper* (Durham: Duke University Press, 1986).

Kinsley, James, and Kinsley, Helen, eds., *Dryden: The Critical Heritage* (New York: Barnes and Noble, 1971).

Korshin, Paul, "The Johnson-Chesterfield Relationship: A New Hypothesis," *PMLA*, 85 (1970), 247–59.

"Johnson and Literary Patronage: A Comment on Jacob Leed's Article," *Studies in Burke and his Time*, 12 (1970–71), 1804– 11.

"Types of Eighteenth-Century Literary Patronage," *Eighteenth-Century Studies*, 7 (1974), 453–73.

Landry, Donna, *The Muses of Resistance: Laboring-Class Women's Poetry in Britain, 1739–1796* (Cambridge: Cambridge University Press, 1990).

"The Resignation of Mary Collier: Some Problems in Feminist Literary History," in *The New Eighteenth Century*, eds. Felicity Nussbaum and Laura Brown (New York: Methuen, 1987), 99–120.

Le Blanc, Jean Bernard, *Letter on the English and French Nations* (London, 1747).

Leed, Jacob, "Johnson and Chesterfield: 1746–47," *Studies in Burke and his Time*, 11 (1970), 1677–1690.

"Johnson, Chesterfield, and Patronage: A Response to Paul Korshin," *Studies in Burke and his Time*, 13 (1971–72), 2011– 15.

"Patronage in *The Rambler*," *Studies in Burke and his Time*, 14 (1972–73), 5–21.

Lees-Milne, James, *Earls of Creation: Five Great Patrons of Eighteenth-Century Art* (London: Century Hutchinson, 1962).

Leranbaum, Miriam, *Alexander Pope's Opus Magnum, 1729–1744* (Oxford: Clarendon, 1977).

Life of Mr. Richard Savage (London, 1727, repr. Los Angeles: Clark Library, 1988).

Lonsdale, Roger, ed., *Poems of Gray, Collins, and Goldsmith* (London: Longmans, 1969).

Lovat-Fraser, J. A., *John Stuart, Earl of Bute* (Cambridge: Cambridge University Press, 1912).

Low, Donald, ed., *Robert Burns: The Critical Heritage* (London: Routledge, 1974).

Lytle, G. F., and Orgel, S., eds., *Patronage in the Renaissance* (Princeton: Princeton University Press, 1981).

Macaulay, Thomas Babington, *Critical and Historical Essays*, ed. F. C. Montague, 3 vols. (London: Methuen, 1903).

Selected Writings, eds. John Clive and Thomas Pinney (Chicago: University of Chicago Press, 1972).

Mack, Maynard, *Alexander Pope: A Life* (New York: Norton, 1985).

Mackenzie, Henry, [essay on "the art of a patron"], *The Mirror*, 91 (1780), 361–63.

Marotti, Arthur, "Patronage, Poetry, and Print," in *Patronage, Politics, and Literary Traditions in England 1558–1658*, ed. Cedric Brown (Detroit: Wayne State University Press, 1991).

Marshall, David, "Writing Masters and 'Masculine Exercises' in *The Female Quixote*," *Eighteenth-Century Fiction*, 5 (1993), 105–35.

McCaulay, George Campbell, *James Thomson* (London: Macmillan, 1908).

McFadden, George, *Dryden the Public Writer, 1660–1685* (Princeton: Princeton University Press, 1978).

McIntosh, Carey, *Common and Courtly Language: The Stylistics of Social Class in 18th-Century English Literature* (Philadelphia: University of Pennsylvania Press, 1986).

McKelvey, James L., "William Robertson and Lord Bute," *Studies in Scottish Literature*, 6 (1969), 238–47.

McKendrick, Neil (with John Brewer and J. H. Plumb), ed., *The Birth of a Consumer Society: The Commercialization of 18th-Century England* (London: Europa, 1982).

"Memoirs of Mrs. Lenox," *Edinburgh Weekly Magazine*, 58 (1783), 33–36.

Murphy, Peter, *Poetry as an Occupation and an Art in Britain, 1760–1830* (Cambridge: Cambridge University Press, 1993).

Namier, Sir Lewis, *The Structure of Politics at the Accession of George III* (London: Macmillan, 1929, 2nd ed., 1963).

Neumann, J. H., "Chesterfield and the Standard of Usage," *MLQ*, 7 (1946), 463–75.

Nichols, John, *Literary Anecdotes of the Eighteenth Century*, 8 vols. (London, 1812–14).

Nokes, David, *Jonathan Swift: Hypocrite Reversed* (Oxford: Oxford University Press, 1985).

Norton, J. E., *A Bibliography of the Works of Edward Gibbon* (Oxford: Clarendon, 1940).

Oldmixon, John, *History of England* (London, 1735).

Orrery, John Boyle, Earl of, *Remarks on the Life and Writings of Dr. Jonathan Swift* (London, 1752).

Owen, J. B., "Political Patronage in Eighteenth-Century England," in *The Triumph of Culture: Eighteenth-Century Perspectives*, eds. Paul Fritz and David Williams (Toronto: Hakkert, 1972).

The Rise of the Pelhams (London: Methuen, 1957).

Parker, R. A. C., *Coke of Norfolk: A Financial and Agricultural Study, 1707–1842* (Oxford: Clarendon, 1975).

Payne, Deborah, "'And Poets Shall by Patron-Princes Live': Aphra Behn and Patronage," in *Curtain Calls: British and American Women and the Theatre, 1660–1820*, eds. M. A. Schofield and C. Macheski (Athens: Ohio University Press, 1991), 105–19.

Peck, Linda Levy, *Court Patronage and Corruption in Early Stuart England* (Boston: Unwin Hyman, 1990).

Plumb, J. H., "The Commercialization of Leisure in Eighteenth-Century England," in *The Commercialization of Eighteenth-Century England: The Birth of a Consumer Society*, eds. Neil McKendrick, John Brewer, and J. H. Plumb (Bloomington: Indiana University Press, 1982), 265–85.

The Commercialization of Leisure in Eighteenth-Century England (Reading: University of Reading, 1973).

The Growth of Political Stability in England, 1675–1725 (London: Macmillan, 1967).

Porter, Roy, *English Society in the Eighteenth Century* (London: Penguin, rev. ed. 1990).

Price, Uvedale, *Essays on the Picturesque*, 2 vols. (London, 1794–98).

Pyle, Edmund, *Memoirs of a Royal Chaplain, 1729–1763*, ed. Albert Hartshorne (London: Bodley Head, 1905).

Radcliffe, David Hill, "Genre and Social Order in Country House Poems of the 18th Century: Four Views of Percy Lodge," *SEL*, 30 (1990), 445–65.

Rea, Robert, *The English Press in Politics, 1760–1774* (Lincoln: University of Nebraska Press, 1963).

Reade, A. L., *Johnsonian Gleanings*, 11 vols. (London: Francis, 1909–52).

Rizzo, Betty, "Christopher Smart, The 'C. S.' Poems, and Molly Leapor's Epitaph," *The Library*, ser. 6/5 (1983), 21–31.

"The English Author–Bookseller Dialogue," *The Age of Johnson*, 2 (1989), 353–74.

"Mary Leapor: An Anxiety for Influence," *The Age of Johnson*, 4 (1991), 313–43.

"The Patron as Poet Maker: The Politics of Benefaction," *Studies in Eighteenth-Century Culture*, 20 (1990), 241–66.

Roberts, David, *The Ladies: Female Patronage of Restoration Drama, 1660–1700* (Oxford: Clarendon, 1989).

Robinson, F. J. G., and Wallis, P. J., "Book Subscription Lists," *The Library*, 5th ser., 29 (1974), 255–86.

Book Subscription Lists: A Revised Guide (Newcastle: Hill, 1975), and "Supplements" (1976, 1977, 1980, 1981).

Rogers, Deborah, "The Commercialization of 18th-Century English Literature," *Clio*, 18:2 (1989), 171–78.

Rogers, Pat, "Book Dedications in Britain 1700–1799: a Preliminary Survey," *British Journal of Eighteenth-Century Studies*, 16 (1993), 213–33.

Rose, Mark, *Authors and Owners: The Invention of Copyright* (Cambridge: Harvard University Press, 1993).

Ruffhead, Owen, *Life of Alexander Pope* (London, 1769, repr. Hildesheim: Olm, 1968).

Ryskamp, Charles, "Christopher Smart and the Earl of Northumberland," in *The Augustan Milieu*, eds. H. N. Miller, Eric Rothstein, and G. S. Rousseau (Oxford: Clarendon, 1970), 320–32.

Sachse, William, *Lord Somers: A Political Portrait* (Manchester: Manchester University Press, 1975).

Saunders, James, *The Profession of English Letters* (London: Routledge and Kegan Paul, 1964).

Schakel, Peter, *The Poetry of Jonathan Swift* (Madison: University of Wisconsin Press, 1978).

Seary, Peter, *Lewis Theobald and the Editing of Shakespeare* (Oxford: Clarendon, 1990).

Séjourné, Philippe, *The Mystery of Charlotte Lennox: First Novelist of Colonial America (1727? – 1804)* (Aix: Ophrys, 1967).

Sher, Richard, "The Favourite of the Favourite: John Home, Bute, and the Politics of Patriotic Poetry," in *Lord Bute: Essays in Re-interpretation*, ed. K. W. Schweizer (Leicester: Leicester University Press, 1988), 196–205.

Sherbo, Arthur, *Christopher Smart: Scholar of the University* (Lansing: Michigan State University Press, 1967).

"Some Observations on Johnson's Prefaces and Dedications," in *English Writers of the Eighteenth Century*, ed. John Middendorf (New York: Columbia University Press, 1971), 122–42.

Small, Miriam, *Charlotte Ramsay Lennox* (New Haven: Yale University Press, 1935).

Speck, W. A., "Politicians, Peers, and Publication by Subscription 1700–1750," in *Books and Their Readers in the Eighteenth Century*, ed. Isabel Rivers (Leicester: Leicester University Press, 1982), 47–68.

Spence, Joseph, *Observations, Anecdotes, and Characters of Books and Men*, ed. James Osborn, 2 vols. (Oxford: Clarendon, 1966).

Stanton, Judith, "Charlotte Smith's 'Literary Business': Income, Patronage, and Indigence," *The Age of Johnson*, 1 (1987), 375–401.

Stewart, Dugald, *Collected Works*, ed. Sir William Hamilton, 11 vols. (Edinburgh: Constable, 1854–77).

Stewart, Mary Margaret, "William Collins, Samuel Johnson, and the Use of Biographical Details," *SEL*, 28 (1988), 471–82.

Stone, George Winchester, *The London Stage, 1747–1776* (Carbondale: Southern Illinois University Press, 1968).

Summerson, Sir John, "The Classical Country House in 18th-Century England," *Journal of the Royal Society of Arts*, 107 (1958–59), 539–87.

Taylor, Richard, *Goldsmith as Journalist* (Rutherford: Fairleigh Dickinson University Press, 1993).

Tenger, Zeynep, and Trolander, Paul, "Genius versus Capital: Eighteenth-Century Theories of Genius and Adam Smith's *Wealth of Nations*," *MLQ*, 55 (1994), 169–89.

" 'Impartial Critick' or 'Muse's Handmaid': The Politics of Critical Practice in the Early Eighteenth Century," *Essays in Literature*, 21 (1994), 26–42.

Thomas, Claudia, *Alexander Pope and his Eighteenth-Century Women Readers* (Carbondale: Southern Illinois University Press, 1994).

Thompson, E. P., "Eighteenth-Century English Society: Class Struggle without Class?" *Social History*, 3 (1978), 133–65.

Tracy, Clarence, *The Artificial Bastard: A Biography of Richard Savage* (Toronto: University of Toronto Press, 1953).

Turner, Cheryl, *Living by the Pen: Women Writers in the 18th Century* (London: Routledge, 1992).

Unwin, Rayner, *The Rural Muse: Studies in the Peasant Poetry of England* (London: Allen and Unwin, 1954).

Vertue, George, *The Notebooks of George Vertue, The Walpole Society 1933–34*, vol. XXII (Oxford: The Walpole Society, 1934).

Vieth, David, "Irony in Dryden's Ode to Anne Killigrew," *SP*, 63 (1965), 91–100.

"Irony in Dryden's Verses to Sir Robert Howard," *EiC*, 22 (1972), 239–43.

Waith, Eugene, "The Voice of Mr. Bayes," *SEL*, 3 (1963), 335–43.

Wallace, John, "John Dryden's Plays and the Conception of a Heroic Society," in *Culture and Politics from Puritanism to the Enlightenment*, ed. Perez Zagorin (Berkeley: University of California Press, 1980), 113–34.

Warton, Joseph, *Essay on the Genius and Writings of Pope*, 3rd ed. (London, 1772).

Wasserman, Earl, *Pope's Epistle to Bathurst: A Critical Reading with an Edition of the Manuscripts* (Baltimore: Johns Hopkins University Press, 1960).

Weinbrot, Howard, *Britannia's Issue: The Rise of British Literature from Dryden to Ossian* (Cambridge: Cambridge University Press, 1993).

Wheatley, Henry, *The Dedications of Books to Patron and Friend* (London: Stock, 1887).

Whistler, Laurence, *Sir John Vanbrugh, Architect and Dramatist* (London: Cobden-Sanderson, 1938).

Williams, Franklin B., Jr., *Index of Dedications and Commendatory Verses in English Books Before 1641* (London: Bibliographical Society, 1962).

Williams, Harold, "Swift's Early Biographers," in *Pope and His Contemporaries*, eds. James Clifford and Louis Landa (Oxford: Clarendon, 1949), 114–28.

Williams, Ralph, *Poet, Painter, and Parson: The Life of John Dyer* (New York: Bookman, 1956).

Winn, James, *John Dryden and His World* (New Haven: Yale University Press, 1987).

"The Laureateship," in *The Age of William III and Mary II*, eds. Robert Maccubbin and Martha Hamilton-Phillips (Williamsburg: College of William and Mary, 1989), 319–25.

Wordie, J. R., *Estate Management in Eighteenth-Century England: The Building of the Leveson-Gower Fortune* (London: Royal Historical Society, 1982).

Zionkowski, Linda, "Territorial Disputes in the Republic of Letters: Canon Formation and the Literary Profession," *Eighteenth Century*, 31 (1990), 3–22.

Zwicker, Steven, *Politics and Language in Dryden's Poetry: The Arts of Disguise* (Princeton: Princeton University Press, 1984).

Index

To keep the index from being overcharged, I have tried to restrict citations to substantive occurrences of the item in the text. Aristocrats are cited under their titles, and cross listed under family name, except for those (e.g., Walpole, Dodington) commonly known by family name.